Value Investing

"James Montier combines a profound understanding of behaviorial finance with a fierce adherence to the tried and tested principles of value-investing. He is always readable, thought-provoking and, above all, correct."

Edward Chancellor, author of *Devil Take the Hindmost: A history of financial speculation*

"James' latest effort is a must read. It combines great academic and practitioner approaches written in a humorous and entertaining style. It has practical real world examples that don't require advanced mathematics to comprehend. I advise everyone to read and study this wonderful book. All of my students now have Value Investing: Tools and Techniques for Intelligent Investment to add to their required reading."

Mark Cooper, Partner at Omega Advisors & Adjunct Professor at Columbia Business School

"A preponderance of evidence shows that successful long-term investing requires a strong value orientation and a proper temperament, virtues commonly blunted by behavioural and incentive-based biases. Montier, a leading light in value investing and behavioural finance, shows you what's wrong with standard investment Read thinking and offers important insight into how to improve your process. Value Investing, live its lessons, and prosper."

Michael J. Mauboussin, Chief Investment Strategist at Legg Mason Capital Management, and author of *Think Twice: Harnessing the Power of Counterintuition*

James Montier is a member of GMO's asset allocation team. Prior to that he was global strategist for Société Générale and Dresdner Kleinwort. He has been the top rated strategist in the annual extel survey for most of the last decade. He is also the author of three other books – Behavioural Finance (2000, Wiley), Behavioural Investing (2007, Wiley) and The Little Book of Behavioral Investing (Forthcoming, Wiley). James is a regular speaker at both academic and practitioner conferences, and is regarded as the leading authority on applying behavioural finance to investment. He is a visiting fellow at the University of Durham and a fellow of the Royal Society of Arts. He has been described as a maverick, an iconoclast, an enfant terrible by the press.

Value Investing

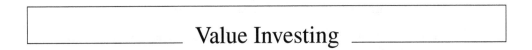

Tools and Techniques for Intelligent Investment

James Montier

A John Wiley and Sons, Ltd., Publication

Registered office
John Wiley & Sons Ltd, The Atrium, Southern Gate, Chichester, West Sussex, PO19 8SQ, United Kingdom

For details of our global editorial offices, for customer services and for information about how to apply for permission to reuse the copyright material in this book please see our website at www.wiley.com.

Library of Congress Cataloging-in-Publication Data

Montier, James.
  Value investing : tools and techniques for intelligent investment / James Montier.
    p. cm.
  Includes bibliographical references and index.
  ISBN 978-0-470-68359-0
1. Value investing.   2. Investment analysis.   3. Corporations–Valuation.   I. Title.
  HG4521.M7866   2009
  332.6–dc22

                                                      2009027977

ISBN 978-0-470-68359-0

A catalogue record for this book is available from the British Library.

Typeset in 10/12pt Times by Aptara Inc., New Delhi, India

To Wendy
With all my love

Contents

Preface

Part I: Why everything you learned in business school is wrong

In fairness I should have entitled Part I 'Why Everything you Learned in Business School is Wrong (unless you went to Columbia)'. Equally well I could have used the title 'Six Impossible Things Before Breakfast'.

The seductive elegance of classical finance theory is powerful, yet value investing requires that we reject both the precepts of modern portfolio theory (MPT) and almost all of its tools and techniques. The existence of MPT wouldn't bother me nearly as much as it does, if real-world investors didn't take its conclusions into investment practice. Sadly, all too often this is exactly what happens. Unfortunately, the prescriptions of MPT end up thwarting the investor. They lead us astray from the things on which we really should be concentrating.

Milton Freidman argued that a model shouldn't be judged by its assumptions but rather by the accuracy of its predictions. The chapters in Part I attempt to demonstrate that the basic edicts of MPT are empirically flawed. The capital asset pricing model (CAPM), so beloved of MPT, leads investors to try to separate alpha and beta, rather than concentrate upon maximum after tax total real return (the true object of investment). The concept that risk can be measured by price fluctuations leads investors to focus upon tracking error and excessive diversification, rather than the risk of permanent loss of capital. The prevalent use of discounted cash flow models leads the unwary down the road of spurious accuracy, without any awareness of the extreme sensitivity of their models. As Third Avenue Management put it: DCF is like the Hubble telescope, if you move it an inch you end up studying a different galaxy. Thus, following MPT actually hinders rather than helps the investor.

Part II: The behavioural foundations of value investing

MPT holds that all returns must be a function of the risk entailed. Thus, the believers in this approach argue that the outperformance of value stocks over time must be a function of their inherent riskiness. I've always thought that this was a classic example of tautological thinking. The chapters in Part II attempt to demonstrate an alternative perspective – that the source of the value outperformance is a function of behavioural and institutional biases that prevent many investors from behaving sensibly.

We will cover the most dangerous (and one of the most common) errors that investors make – overpaying for the hope of growth (or capitalizing hope if you prefer). The chapters in Part II also try to provide you with the tools to enable you to start thinking differently about the way you invest. Value investing is the one form of investing that puts risk management at the very heart of the approach. However, you will have to rethink the notion of risk. You will learn to think of risk as a permanent loss of capital, not random fluctuations. You will also learn to understand the trinity of sources that compose this risk: valuation, earnings and balance sheets.

In Part II we will also try to introduce you to ways of overriding the emotional distractions that will bedevil the pursuit of a value approach. As Ben Graham said: 'The investor's chief problem – and even his worst enemy – is likely to be himself.'

Part III: The philosophy of value investing

The chapters in Part III set out the core principles involved in following a value approach. The first chapter lays out the 10 tenets of my approach to value investing, and details the elements you will need to be able to display if you intend to follow the value approach:

- Tenet I: Value, value, value
- Tenet II: Be contrarian
- Tenet III: Be patient
- Tenet IV: Be unconstrained
- Tenet V: Don't forecast
- Tenet VI: Cycles matter
- Tenet VII: History matters
- Tenet VIII: Be sceptical
- Tenet IX: Be top-down and bottom-up
- Tenet X: Treat your clients as you would treat yourself

The remaining chapters explore some of the issues in more depth, such as the need for patience, and the need to think independently. One of the most important chapters in Part III concerns the role of process versus outcomes. As we have no control over outcomes, the only thing we can control is the process. The best way to achieve good outcomes is to have a sensible investment process as this maximizes the chances of success. As Ben Graham said: 'I recall . . . the emphasis that the bridge experts place on playing a hand right rather than playing it successfully. Because, as you know, if you play it right you are going to make money and if you play it wrong you lose money – in the long run.'

Part IV: The empirical evidence

Nassim Taleb talks about the need for empirical scepticism. This, in effect, is a desire to check your beliefs against the evidence. The two chapters in Part IV provide a very brief look at the evidence on value investing. The first looks at the proposition that an unconstrained global approach to value investing can create returns. The second considers a deep value technique, much loved by Ben Graham, and shows that it still works today (a direct response to those who argue that Graham's approach is outdated or outmoded). I could have included additional chapters in Part IV, but many excellent surveys on the evidence supporting value investing are easily available to the interested reader. The ultimate proof of the value approach is that almost all (if not all) of the world's most successful investors take a value approach. As Warren Buffett opined:

I would like you to imagine a national coin-flipping contest. Let's assume we get 225 million Americans up tomorrow morning and we ask them all to wager a dollar. They go out in the morning at sunrise, and they all call the flip of a coin. If they call correctly, they win a dollar from those who called wrong. Each day the losers drop out, and on the subsequent day the stakes build as all previous winnings are put on the line. After ten flips on ten mornings, there will be approximately 220,000 people in the United States who have correctly called ten flips in a row. They each will have won a little over $1,000.

Now this group will probably start getting a little puffed up about this, human nature being what it is. They may try to be modest, but at cocktail parties they will occasionally admit to attractive members of the opposite sex what their technique is, and what marvellous insights they bring to the field of flipping.

Assuming that the winners are getting the appropriate rewards from the losers, in another ten days we will have 215 people who have successfully called their coin flips 20 times in a row and who, by this exercise, each have turned one dollar into a little over $1 million. $225 million would have been lost, $225 million would have been won.

By then, this group will really lose their heads. They will probably write books on 'How I Turned a Dollar into a Million in Twenty Days Working Thirty Seconds a Morning.' Worse yet, they'll probably start jetting around the country attending seminars on efficient coin-flipping and tackling skeptical professors with, 'If it can't be done, why are there 215 of us?'

By then some business school professor will probably be rude enough to bring up the fact that if 225 million orangutans had engaged in a similar exercise, the results would be much the same – 215 egotistical orangutans with 20 straight winning flips.

I would argue, however, that there are some important differences in the examples I am going to present. For one thing, if (a) you had taken 225 million orangutans distributed roughly as the US population is, if (b) 215 winners were left after 20 days, and if (c) you found that 40 came from a particular zoo in Omaha, you would be pretty sure you were on to something. So you would probably go out and ask the zookeeper about what he's feeding them, whether they had special exercises, what books they read, and who knows what else. That is, if you found any really extraordinary concentrations of success, you might want to see if you could identify concentrations of unusual characteristics that might be causal factors.

Scientific inquiry naturally follows such a pattern. If you were trying to analyse possible causes of a rare type of cancer – with, say, 1,500 cases a year in the United States – and you found that 400 of them occurred in some little mining town in Montana, you would get very interested in the water there, or the occupation of those afflicted, or other variables. You know it's not random chance that 400 come from a small area. You would not necessarily know the causal factors, but you would know where to search.

I submit to you that there are ways of defining an origin other than geography. In addition to geographical origins, there can be what I call an intellectual origin. I think you will find that a disproportionate number of successful coin-flippers in the investment world came from a very small intellectual village that could be called Graham-and-Doddsville. A concentration of winners that simply cannot be explained by chance can be traced to this particular intellectual village.

Part V: The 'Dark Side' of value investing: Short selling

The recent market woes have led to the all-too-predictable backlash against short sellers. Indeed this pattern seems to have existed since time immemorial. As stated in *the New York Times*:

In the days when square-rigged galleons plied the spice route to the East, the Dutch outlawed a band of rebels that they feared might plunder their new-found riches.

The troublemakers were neither Barbary pirates nor Spanish spies — they were certain traders on the stock exchange in Amsterdam. Their offence: shorting the shares of the Dutch East India Company, purportedly the first company in the world to issue stock.

Short sellers, who sell assets like stocks in the hope that the price will fall, have been reviled ever since. England banned them for much of the 18th and 19th centuries. Napoleon deemed them enemies of the state. And Germany's last Kaiser enlisted them to attack American markets (or so some Americans feared).

Jenny Anderson, New Yark Times, 30 April 2008

However, far from being the Sith lords, the short sellers I have met are among the most fundamental-oriented analysts I have come across. These guys, by and large, really take their analysis seriously (and so they should since their downside is effectively unlimited). So the continued backlash against short sellers as rumour mongers and conspirators simply leaves me shaking my head in bewilderment. I can only assume that the people making these claims are either policy-makers pandering to shorted companies, or shorted companies themselves. Rather than being seen as some malignant force within the markets, in my experience short sellers are closer to accounting police – a job that the SEC at one time considered its remit.

This viewpoint was confirmed by an insightful study by Owen Lamont (2003) (then at Chicago University). He wrote a paper in 2003 examining the battles between short sellers and the companies they shorted. He examined such battles between 1977 and 2002 in the USA. He focused on situations where the companies being shorted protested their innocence by suggesting that they were the subject of a bear raid, or a conspiracy, or alleged that the short sellers were lying. He also explored firms that requested investigation by the authorities into the shorts, urged the stockholders not to lend shares out, or even set up repurchase plans (presumably to create a short squeeze). If I may paraphrase the immortal words of the Bard: 'Methinks he doth protest too much'!

Lehman provides a classic example. As the *Wall Street Journal* noted:

'What were they thinking? Lehman Brothers documents released Monday showed that in June, when the investment bank was negotiating to raise about $5 billion from the Korea Development Bank, senior Lehman executive David Goldfarb emailed Lehman Chief Executive Richard Fuld with a suggestion. The firm should 'aggressively' go into the stock market and use $2 billion of the proceeds to buy back stock, thereby 'hurting Einhorn bad!!'. He was referring to hedge fund short seller David Einhorn, a critic of Lehman. Mr. Fuld, who was testifying before Congress Monday, wrote back in agreement. Lehman didn't get the money and filed for bankruptcy protection instead.'

David Einhorn's response to such matters is a lovely line: 'I'm not critical because I am short, I am short because I am critical.'

The results Lamont uncovered in his study show the useful role played by short sellers. Figure 1 shows the average cumulative return to the shorted stock. In the 12 months after the battle started, the average stock underperformed the market by 24%. In the three years after the battle started, these stocks underperformed the market by 42% cumulatively! The shorts were right – too often it was the companies that were lying and conspiring to defraud investors, not the reverse!

The chapters in Part V section explore how to hunt for potential short opportunities, or if you never want to short, they provide you with some thoughts about the characteristics of stocks in which you don't what to be invested.

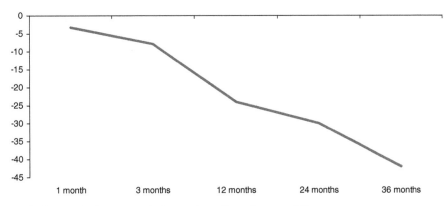

Figure 1   Lamont's shorts: cumulative market-adjusted returns (%)
Source: Lamont (2003). SG Equity research

Part VI: Real-time value investing

The proof of the pudding is always in the eating. The chapters in Part VI provide real-time analysis of the market's behaviour over one of the most turbulent periods in investing history. They are a case study in the power of value approach. If following a value-oriented approach works in such a market, it stands in good stead for the future. The topics covered here include: how to think about the risk of value traps; how to think about financial stocks from a deep value perspective; the role of cheap sources of insurance; why you need to act when markets are cheap and not be overcome by emotional paralysis; and the case against government bonds.

I hope this book provides you with a framework for thinking about how to invest, and show that such an approach pays dividends for an investor with the ability to think and act differently from the herd. As ever, only you can be the ultimate arbiter of my success. I would welcome your comments and feedback. I can be reached at james.montier@gmail.com.

Foreword

Books about investing, like this one by James Montier, are written, bought and read because they promise to make the reader riches. Sometimes the promise is explicit as in Joel Greenblatt's outstanding book *You Too Can Be a Stock Market Genius*. More often it is unstated but implied. In all cases, the promise has to come to terms with the single most important brute fact about investing. Only in Lake Wobegon, Minnesota (the mythical town created by the American humorist Garrison Keillor where all the children are above average) can all investors outperform the market. The average return of all investors must mathematically be equal, before management fees and trading costs, to the average return on all investment assets. This is not a statement of the once dominant, but increasingly widely discredited, academic assumptions that markets are efficient; that no individual can expect, except by luck, to outperform the collective wisdom of all other investors which is embodied in market prices. Some individual investors, most notably Warren Buffett, do earn above average returns by wide margins in many years. But what is inescapable is that these above average returns for some investors must always be offset by below average returns for others.

Another way to say this is that every time a reader of this book buys an asset, thinking that it will produce relatively high returns in the future, another investor is selling that asset thinking that it will produce relatively low returns in the future. One of them is always wrong. Any sound investment process must, therefore, begin by answering the question of why, more often than not, it places the user on the right side of the exchange. This is an investment imperative that is recognized to some extent. For example, the investment management course at Harvard Business School has for many years been built around the question, 'what is my edge?'. Unfortunately putting things in these terms poses too easy a challenge. Everyone is prone to think they have an edge. Eighty percent or more of James Montier's students expect to finish in the top half of his classes. Thirty percent of these will not. They are, by the way, relatively modest. When I carried out these surveys in class, typically ninety percent or more of my students expected to finish in the top-half of the class (but then I am undoubtedly an easier grader than James). Ninety-five percent or more of surveyed people typically think they have a better sense of humor than average. Almost by definition, investment managers, who are well-compensated and morally self-aware, must think they have some edge. Even amateurs who invest for themselves must expect to be compensated for their time and effort by out-performing a passive market index investment. Any 'edge' must stand-up to rigorous scrutiny and at least half of them will fail.

However, in another sense, the 'what-is-my-edge' question is too demanding. There are well-documented investment approaches that have been recognized for at least 75 years which, carefully followed, will enable any investor to outperform the market by a significant margin on average over many years. These approaches – falling generally under the name of Value Investing – are properly the subject of this excellent book.

The justification for repackaging these truths (in novel and entertaining form) is primarily that they are followed systematically by only a small minority of investors; a fraction that has been growing, if at all, only slowly over time. Also the effective application of value principles is an evolving discipline that has lead to both improved understanding of the factors involved and better ways of deploying them in practice. This book makes significant contribution to both areas.

The fundamental 'edge' that has enabled value investors consistently to outperform market returns by three percent or more is rooted in the psychology of individual investment behavior. Three factors are paramount. First, many investors have always been prone to reach for dramatic large returns whatever the cost to them on an average basis. Lotteries have succeeded in every society we know of and they have always been lousy investments. The investment equivalents of lotteries are growth stocks – the Microsofts, Intels, Ciscos and other less successful internet era stocks that promised instant wealth. Montier demonstrates once again how portfolios of such stocks have systematically underperformed the market both in the US, other developed countries, and more recently, in emerging markets. The corollary of this search for growth and glamour is the undervaluation of boring, low growth, obscure and hitherto disappointing investments. A second factor, loss aversion, reinforces this bias. Investors, like individuals in everyday life, irrationally shy away from ugly, threatening situations that are likely to lead to losses, but also in some instances to outsized gains. Subjects in psychological studies offered risky alternatives to stated sure gains embrace the sure gains. When offered the same alternatives, stated as sure losses (from higher starting points), they embrace the risks, being driven to do so by the prospect of 'losses'. In investing this means that ugly stocks with poor performance in threatened industries or circumstances are sold without consideration of whether there is any compensating upside potential. They tend, therefore, to be oversold and as Montier again demonstrates, portfolios of such stocks outperform the market as a whole in all countries and all extended time periods. A third basic human tendency reinforces these first two. Investors, like all human beings have difficulty dealing with uncertainty and do so badly. At the simplest level, they accept irrationally low returns for certain outcomes (even when the uncertainty is negligibly small) in both experiments and actual markets. More damagingly, they suppress uncertainty in a variety of ways. They extrapolate past trends with unwarranted confidence. They tend to treat attractive stocks as if they are attractive for sure. They treat unattractive stocks as if they are certain to fail. Reality is, of course, messier than this, as James Montier, thoroughly demonstrates. High fliers come down to earth in large numbers and death-bed recoveries are shockingly frequent. The result is to reinforce both the overvaluation of glamour stocks and the undervaluation of problematic ones. Value investors who eschew the former and embrace the latter must overcome all these deeply embedded psychological tendencies. It is not surprising, therefore, that they are a small, if well-off, minority.

Institutional forces reinforce these basic human tendencies. It is always more comfortable in the herd than outside. Institutions naturally tend to concentrate in the same overvalued kinds of stocks as individuals. This bias is reinforced by institutional incentives. Investment companies that perform at or near the level of their peers, because of investor inertia, usually do not suffer big losses of assets under management even if their long run performance is poor. If a fund manager underperforms significantly the consequences are more dire. Simple risk mitigation, therefore, drives institutional money managers to mirror the portfolios of their competitors. Institutions must also market themselves which they do most effectively by telling stories about investments which hide underlying uncertainties, by emphasizing blockbuster winners, and by demonstrating their avoidance of potentially unattractive situations (known as window dressing). In doing this, they both reproduce individual investor biases and reinforce them.

In addition, institutions have a preference for selling reassuring methods that involve considerable mathematical complexity but are of dubious value in practice. They develop elaborate point forecasts of future variables as evidence of their statistical, economic and industry expertise. They build complex quantitative models, rooted in often out-dated academic orthodoxies, like the CAPM, to establish their mastery of risk management and of the latest investing technology. They offer complex derivative strategies of impenetrable mathematical intricacy. What they ignore are well-established historical regularities, basic qualitative economic principles and the reality of irreducible uncertainty. James Montier is particularly good about the shortcomings of these approaches and the opportunities they create for other investors.

The achievement of above average returns is not the sole measure of investment performance. Risk matters too and it is in the area of risk mitigation that this book is perhaps most valuable. Economies produce aggregate levels of risk that, like aggregate average returns, must be borne by investors as a whole. But, in contrast to average returns, poor investment strategies can actually create risk. The obvious example of this is gambling, whether in casinos or derivatives markets, which adds an element of uncertainty (and downside) to private wealth holdings that proper behavior could simply eliminate. Sadly most investors engage in behaviors that tend to increase rather than reduce risks. Perhaps the second most important fact about investing in practice is that for the typical investment fund average returns are six hundred basis points above returns that are weighted by the size of the fund (i.e. the return in a year when assets are \$2 billion counts twice as heavily as the return for a year when assets are \$1 billion). In part, this represents the negative effect on agility and choice of greater fund size. But it is also means that investors move into and out of funds at exactly the wrong times. And, these movements themselves amplify risks. Disciplined behavior that is not driven by the fashions of the moment is, as Montier shows, central to any useful risk mitigation strategy.

Diversification is equally important. Whether defined as variance or permanent impairment of capital, a diversified portfolio will have less downside than a concentrated one. Most of the events that lead to permanent impairment of the earnings capacity of investments are specific to particular firms, industries or countries – a drug kills patients, the newspaper business dies or a Marxist government seizes control of Venezuela. In a portfolio of five or fewer stocks, such an event will lead to painful losses. In a portfolio of fifty or more stocks the effect will be negligible.

This does not mean full diversification, since that involves buying the market as a whole and surrendering the benefits of a value strategy. But investors must be sufficiently diversified – holding at least 15 securities across a range of industries and countries – to obtain most of the risk reduction benefits that diversification provides. If, in addition to discipline and diversification, investors avoid overpaying for the glamour stocks of the moment, then permanent losses will arise only from permanently negative macroeconomic developments. As Montier shows these are rare. Even, in Japan through the 1990s, disciplined value approaches produced diversified portfolios with systematically positive overall returns. Negative macro-development – like the Great Depression – did produce near-permanent losses. But, while these cannot be anticipated with any degree of precision – especially with regard to timing – they do seem to be preceded by extended periods in which most investors forget that such risks exist. Under such circumstances, there are strategies of portfolio construction – defensive stocks, short-term government notes, cash and gold – and purchases of assets with valuable insurance properties, usually derivatives which tend to be cheap when investors overall perceive little macro risk and they are probably most valuable, that can protect against a significant part of downside losses. Montier, who is heavily risk focused, does an outstanding job of identifying these strategies.

Taken as a whole, therefore, this book has four compelling things that recommend it to all investors. First, it lays out the principles of smart investment practices in a systematic and compelling way. Second it supports these prescriptions with a vast amount of relevant historical and experimental data. Third, it demonstrates clearly how to apply them to current investing challenges. And finally, while entertaining, it is repetitive. This final aspect may not seem much of a recommendation, but in fact it is one of the most important aspects of the book. I find that unless I say things to my students at least four times, most of them miss the point. Whether this is because the value approach to investing is so unnatural to most human beings or because they pay attention less than half the time, I do not know. But, in either case, repetition is essential to effectively conveying a value discipline and, in this book, James Montier does it as well as I have ever seen.

Bruce Greenwald

Part I

Why Everything You Learned in Business School is Wrong

1

Six Impossible Things before Breakfast, or, How EMH has Damaged our Industry*

The efficient markets hypothesis (EMH) is the financial equivalent of Monty Python's Dead Parrot. No matter how much you point out that it is dead, the believers just respond that it is simply resting! I wouldn't really care if EMH was just some academic artefact, but as Keynes noted, 'practical men are usually the slaves of some defunct economist'. The EMH has left us with a litany of bad ideas, from CAPM to benchmarking, and risk management to shareholder value. The worst of its legacy is the terrible advice it offers on how to outperform – essentially be a better forecaster than everyone else. It is surely time to consign both the EMH and its offshoots to the dustbin of history.

- Academic theories have a very high degree of path dependence. Once a theory has been accepted it seems to take forever to dislodge it. As Max Planck said, 'Science advances one funeral at a time'. The EMH debate takes on almost religious tones on occasions. At one conference, Gene Fama yelled 'God knows markets are efficient!' This sounds like a prime example of belief bias to me (a tendency to judge by faith rather than by evidence).

- The EMH bothers me less as an academic concept (albeit an irrelevant one) than it does as a source of hindrance to sensible investing. EMH has left us with a long list of bad ideas that have influenced our industry. For instance, the capital asset pricing model (CAPM) leads to the separation of alpha and beta, which ends up distracting from the real aim of investment – 'Maximum real total returns after tax' as Sir John Templeton put it.

- This approach has also given rise to the obsession with benchmarking, and indeed a new species, Homo Ovinus – whose only concern is where it stands relative to the rest of the crowd, the living embodiment of Keynes' edict, 'That it is better for reputation to fail conventionally, than succeed unconventionally'.

- The EMH also lies at the heart of risk management, option pricing theory, and the dividend and capital structure irrelevance theorems of Modigliani and Miller, and the concept of shareholder value, all of which have inflicted serious damage upon investors. However, the most insidious aspects of the EMH are the advice it offers as to the sources of outperformance. The first is inside information, which is, of course, illegal. The second, is that to outperform you need to forecast the future better than everyone else. This has sent the investment industry on a wild goose chase for decades.

- The prima facie case against EMH is the existence of bubbles. The investment firm, GMO defines a bubble as at least a two-standard-deviation move from (real) trend. Under EMH, a two-standard-deviation event should occur roughly every 44 years. However, GMO found some 30 plus bubbles since 1925 – that is slightly more than one every three years!
- The supporters of EMH fall back on what they call their 'Nuclear Bomb', the failure of active management to outperform the index. However, this is to confuse the absence of evidence with the evidence of absence. Additionally, recent research shows that career risk minimization is the defining characteristic of institutional investment. They don't even try to outperform!

What follows is the text of a speech to be delivered at the CFA UK conference on 'Whatever happened to EMH?', dedicated to Peter Bernstein. Peter will be fondly remembered and sadly missed by all who work in investment. Although he and I often ended up on opposite sides of the debates, he was a true gentleman and always a pleasure to discuss ideas with. I am sure Peter would have disagreed with some, much and perhaps all of my speech, but I'm equally sure he would have enjoyed the discussion.

THE DEAD PARROT OF FINANCE

Given that this is the UK division of the CFA I am sure that The Monty Python Dead Parrot Sketch will be familiar to all of you. The EMH is the financial equivalent of the Dead Parrot (Figure 1.1). I feel like the John Cleese character (an exceedingly annoyed customer who recently purchased a parrot) returning to the petshop to berate the owner:

> E's passed on! This parrot is no more! He has ceased to be! 'E's expired and gone to meet 'is maker. 'E's a stiff! Bereft of life, 'e rests in peace! If you hadn't nailed 'im to the perch 'e'd be pushing up the daisies! 'Is metabolic processes are now 'istory! 'E's off the twig! 'E's kicked the bucket, 'e's shuffled off 'is mortal coil, run down the curtain and joined the bleedin' choir invisible!! This is an ex-parrot!!

The shopkeeper (picture Gene Fama if you will) keeps insisting that the parrot is simply resting. Incidentally, the Dead Parrot Sketch takes on even more meaning when you recall Stephen Ross's words that 'All it takes to turn a parrot into a learned financial economist is just one word – arbitrage'.

The EMH supporters have strong similarities with the Jesuit astronomers of the 17th century who desperately wanted to maintain the assumption that the Sun revolved around the Earth. The reason for this desire to protect the maintained hypothesis was simple. If the Sun didn't revolve around the Earth, then the Bible's tale of Joshua asking God to make the Sun stand still in the sky was a lie. A bible that lies even once can't be the inerrant foundation for faith!

The efficient market hypothesis (EMH) has done massive amounts of damage to our industry. But before I explore some errors embedded within the approach and the havoc they have wreaked, I would like to say a few words on why the EMH exists at all.

Academic theories are notoriously subject to path dependence (or hysteresis, if you prefer). Once a theory has been adopted it takes an enormous amount of effort to dislocate it. As Max Planck said, 'Science advances one funeral at a time.'

Figure 1.1 The dead parrot of finance!
Source: SG Global Strategy.

The EMH has been around in one form or another since the Middle Ages (the earliest debate I can find is between St Thomas Aquinas and other monks on the 'just' price to charge for corn, with St Thomas arguing that the 'just' price was the market price). Just imagine we had all grown up in a parallel universe. David Hirschleifer did exactly that: welcome to his world of the Deficient Markets Hypothesis.

> A school of sociologists at the University of Chicago is proposing the Deficient Markets Hypothesis – that prices inaccurately reflect all information. A brilliant Stanford psychologist, call him Bill Blunte, invents the Deranged Anticipation and Perception Model (DAPM), in which proxies for market misevaluation are used to predict security returns. Imagine the euphoria when researchers discovered that these mispricing proxies (such as book/market, earnings/price and past returns), and mood indicators (such as amount of sunlight) turned out to be strong predictors of future returns. At this point, it would seem that the Deficient Markets Hypothesis was the best-confirmed theory in social science.
>
> To be sure, dissatisfied practitioners would have complained that it is harder to actually make money than the ivory tower theorists claim. One can even imagine some academic heretics documenting rapid short-term stock market responses to news arrival in event studies, and arguing that security return predictability results from rational premia for bearing risk. Would the old guard surrender easily? Not when they could appeal to intertemporal versions of the DAPM, in which mispricing is only corrected slowly. In such a setting, short window event studies cannot uncover the market's inefficient response to new information. More generally, given the strong theoretical underpinnings of market inefficiency, the rebels would have an uphill fight.

In finance we seem to have a chronic love affair with elegant theories. Our faculties for critical thinking seem to have been overcome by the seductive power of mathematical beauty. A long long time ago, when I was a young and impressionable lad starting out in my study of economics, I too was enthralled by the bewitching beauty and power of the EMH/rational expectations approach (akin to the Dark Side in Star Wars). However, in practice we should always remember that there are no points for elegance!

My own disillusionment with EMH and the ultra rational *Homo Economicus* that it rests upon came in my third year of university. I sat on the oversight committee for my degree course as a student representative. At the university I attended it was possible to elect to graduate with a specialism in Business Economics, if you took a prescribed set of courses. The courses necessary to attain this degree were spread over two years. It wasn't possible to do all the courses in one year, so students needed to stagger their electives. Yet at the beginning of the third year I was horrified to find students coming to me to complain that they hadn't realized this! These young economists had failed to solve the simplest two-period optimization problem I can imagine! What hope for the rest of the world? Perhaps I am living evidence that finance is like smoking. Ex-smokers always seem to provide the most ardent opposition to anyone lighting up. Perhaps the same thing is true in finance!

THE QUEEN OF HEARTS AND IMPOSSIBLE BELIEFS

I'm quite sure the Queen of Hearts would have made an excellent EMH economist.

> Alice laughed: 'There's no use trying,' she said; 'one can't believe impossible things.'
>
> I daresay you haven't had much practice,' said the Queen. 'When I was younger, I always did it for half an hour a day. Why, sometimes I've believed as many as six impossible things before breakfast.
>
> Lewis Carroll, *Alice in Wonderland*.

Earlier I alluded to a startling lack of critical thinking in finance. This lack of 'logic' isn't specific to finance; in general we, as a species, suffer belief bias. This a tendency to evaluate the validity of an argument on the basis of whether or not one agrees with the conclusion, rather than on whether or not it follows logically from the premise. Consider these four syllogisms:

1. No police dogs are vicious
   Some highly trained dogs are vicious
   Therefore some highly trained dogs are not police dogs.

2. No nutritional things are inexpensive.
   Some vitamin pills are inexpensive.
   Therefore, some vitamin pills are not nutritional.

3. No addictive things are inexpensive
   Some cigarettes are inexpensive
   Therefore, some addictive things are not cigarettes.

4. No millionaires are hard workers
   Some rich people are hard workers
   Therefore, some millionaires are not rich people.

These four syllogisms provide us with a mixture of validity and believability. Table 1.1 separates out the problems along these two dimensions. This enables us to assess which criteria people use in reaching their decisions.

As Figure 1.2 reveals, it is the believability not the validity of the concept that seems to drive behaviour. When validity and believability coincide, then 90% of subjects reach the correct conclusion. However, when the puzzle is invalid but believable, some 66% still accepted the conclusion as true. When the puzzle is valid but unbelievable only around 60% of subjects accepted the conclusion as true. Thus we have a tendency to judge things by their believability rather than their validity – which is clear evidence that logic goes out of the window when beliefs are strong.

All this talk about beliefs makes EMH sound like a religion. Indeed, it has some overlap with religion in that belief appears to be based on faith rather than proof. Debating the subject can also give rise to the equivalent of religious fanaticism. In his book '*The New Finance: The Case Against Efficient Markets*', Robert Haugen (long regarded as a heretic by many in finance) recalls a conference he was speaking at where he listed various inefficiencies. Gene Fama was in the audience and at one point yelled; 'You're a criminal . . . God knows markets are efficient.'

Table 1.1 Validity and belief

		Belief	
		Believable	Unbelievable
Logic	**Valid**	Dogs (VB)	Vitamins (VU)
	Invalid	Cigarettes (IB)	Millionaires (IU)

Source: SG Equity Strategy.

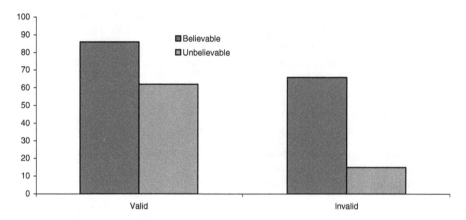

Figure 1.2 Percentage accepting conclusion as true
Source: Evans *et al*. (1983).

SLAVES OF SOME DEFUNCT ECONOMIST

To be honest I wouldn't really care if EMH was just some academic artefact. The real damage unleashed by the EMH stems from the fact that, as Keynes long ago noted, 'practical men. . . are usually the slaves of some defunct economist.'

So let's turn to the investment legacy with which the EMH has burdened us: first off is the capital asset pricing model (CAPM). I've criticized the CAPM elsewhere (see Chapter 2), so I won't dwell on the flaws here, but suffice it to say that my view remains that CAPM is CRAP (completely redundant asset pricing).

The aspects of CAPM that we do need to address here briefly are those that hinder the investment process – one of the most pronounced of which is the obsession with performance measurement. The separation of alpha and beta is at best an irrelevance and at worst a serious distraction from the true nature of investment. Sir John Templeton said it best when he observed that 'the aim of investment is maximum real returns after tax'. Yet instead of focusing on this target, we have spawned one industry that does nothing other than pigeon-hole investors into categories.

As the late, great Bob Kirby opined, 'Performance measurement is one of those basically good ideas that somehow got totally out of control. In many cases, the intense application of performance measurement techniques has actually served to impede the purpose it is supposed to serve.'

The obsession with benchmarking also gives rise to one of the biggest sources of bias in our industry – career risk. For a benchmarked investor, risk is measured as tracking error. This gives rise to Homo Ovinus (Figure 1.3) – a species who is concerned purely with where he stands relative to the rest of the crowd. (For those who aren't up in time to listen to Farming Today, Ovine is the proper name for sheep.) This species is the living embodiment of Keynes' edict that 'it is better for reputation to fail conventionally than to succeed unconventionally'. More on this poor creature a little later.

While on the subject of benchmarking we can't leave without observing that EMH and CAPM also give rise to market indexing. Only in an efficient market is a market cap-weighted

Figure 1.3   Homo Ovinus
Source: Worth1000.com.

index the 'best' index. If markets aren't efficient then cap weighting leads us to overweight the most expensive stocks and underweight the cheapest stocks!

Before we leave risk behind, we should also note the way in which fans of EMH protect themselves against evidence that anomalies such as value and momentum exist. In a wonderfully tautological move, they argue that only risk factors can generate returns in an efficient market, so these factors must clearly be risk factors!

Those of us working in the behavioural camp argue that behavioural and institutional biases are the root causes of the outperformance of the various anomalies. I have even written papers showing that value isn't riskier than growth on any definition that the EMH fans might choose to use (see Chapter 6).

For instance, if we take the simplest definition of risk used by the EMH fans (the standard deviation of returns), then Figure 1.4 shows an immediate issue for EMH. The return on value stocks is higher than the return on growth stocks, but the so-called 'risk' of value stocks is lower than the risk of growth stocks – in complete contradiction to the EMH viewpoint.

This overt focus on risk has again given rise to what is in my view yet another largely redundant industry – risk management. The tools and techniques are deeply flawed. The use of measures such as VaR give rise to the illusion of safety. All too often they use trailing inputs calculated over short periods of time, and forget that their model inputs are effectively endogenous. The 'risk' input, such as correlation and volatility are a function of a market which functions more like poker than roulette (i.e. the behaviour of the other players matters).

Risk shouldn't be defined as standard deviation (or volatility). I have never met a long-only investor who gives a damn about upside volatility. Risk is an altogether more complex topic – I have argued that a trinity of risk sums up the aspects that investors should be looking at. Valuation risk, business or earnings risk, and balance sheet risk (see Chapter 11).

Of course, under CAPM the proper measure of risk is beta. However, as Ben Graham pointed out, beta measures price variability, not risk. Beta is probably most often used by analysts in

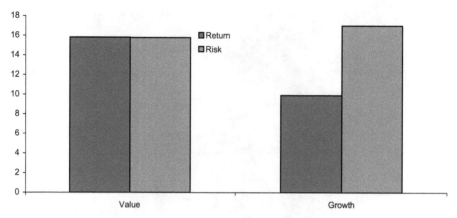

Figure 1.4 Risk and return for value and growth stocks (USA, 1950–2008, %)
Source: SG Equity Research.

their calculations of the cost of capital, and indeed by CFOs in similar calculations. However, even here beta is unhelpful. Far from the theoretical upward-sloping relationship between risk and return, the evidence (including that collected by Fama and French) shows no relationship, and even arguably an inverse one from the model prediction.

This, of course, ignores the difficulties and vagaries of actually calculating beta. Do you use, daily, weekly or monthly data, and over what time period? The answers to these questions are non-trivial in their impact upon the analysts calculations. In a very recent paper, Fernandez and Bermejo showed that the best approach might simply be to assume that beta equals 1.0 for all stocks. (Another reminder that there are no points for elegance in this world!)

The EMH has also given us the Modigliani and Miller propositions on dividend irrelevance, and capital structure irrelevance. These concepts have both been used by unscrupulous practitioners to further their own causes. For instance, those in favour of repurchases over dividends, or even those in favour of retained earnings over distributed earnings, have effectively relied upon the M&M propositions to argue that shareholders should be indifferent to the way in which they receive their return (ignoring the inconvenient evidence that firms tend to waste their retained earnings, and that repurchases are far more transitory in nature than dividends).

Similarly, the M&M capital structure irrelevance proposition has encouraged corporate financiers and corporates themselves to gear up on debt. After all, according to this theory investors shouldn't care whether 'investment' is financed by retained earnings, equity issuance or debt issuance.

The EMH also gave rise to another fallacious distraction of our world – shareholder value. Ironically this started out as a movement to stop the focus on short-term earnings. Under EMH, the price of a company is, of course, just the net present value of all future cash flows. So focusing on maximizing the share price was exactly the same thing as maximizing future profitability. Unfortunately in a myopic world this all breaks down, and we end up with a quest to maximize short-term earnings!

But perhaps the most insidious aspect of the EMH is the way in which it has influenced the behaviour of active managers in their pursuit of adding value. This might sound odd, but bear with me while I try to explain what might, upon cursory inspection, sound like an oxymoron.

All but the most diehard of EMH fans admit that there is a role for active management. After all, who else would keep the market efficient – a point first made by Grossman and Stigliz in their classic paper, 'The impossibility of the informational efficient market'. The extreme diehards probably wouldn't even tolerate this, but their arguments don't withstand the *reductio ad absurdum* that if the market were efficient, prices would of course be correct, and thus volumes should be equal to zero.

The EMH is pretty clear that active managers can add value via one of two routes. First there is inside information – which we will ignore today because it is generally illegal in most markets. Second, they could outperform if they could see the future more accurately than everyone else.

The EMH also teaches us that opportunities will be fleeting as someone will surely try to arbitrage them away. This, of course, is akin to the age old joke about the economist and his friend walking along the street. The friend points out a $100 bill lying on the pavement. The economist says, 'It isn't really there because if it were someone would have already picked it up.'

Sadly these simple edicts are no joking matter as they are probably the most damaging aspects of the EMH legacy. Thus the EMH urges investors to try to forecast the future. In my opinion this is one of the biggest wastes of time, yet one that is nearly universal in our industry (Figure 1.5). About 80–90% of the investment processes that I come across revolve around forecasting. Yet there isn't a scrap of evidence to suggest that we can actually see the future at all (Figures 1.6 and 1.7).

The EMH's insistence on the fleeting nature of opportunities combined with the career risk that bedevils Homo Ovinus has led to an overt focus on the short-term. This is typified by Figure 1.8 which shows the average holding period for a stock on the New York Stock Exchange. It is now just six months!

The undue focus upon benchmark and relative performance also leads Homo Ovinus to engage in Keynes' beauty contest. As Keynes wrote:

> Professional investment may be likened to those newspaper competitions in which the competitors have to pick out the six prettiest faces from a hundred photographs, the price being awarded to the competitor whose choice most nearly corresponds to the average preference of the competitors as

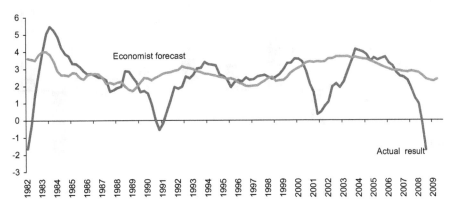

Figure 1.5 Economists are useless at forecasting – US GDP (%, 4q mav)
Source: SG Global Strategy.

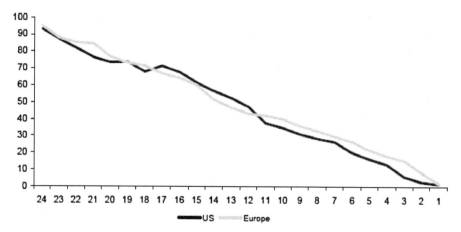

Figure 1.6 Forecast error over time: US and European markets 2001–2006 (%)
Source: SG Global Strategy.

a whole; so that each competitor has to pick, not those faces which he himself finds prettiest, but those which he thinks likeliest to catch the fancy of the other competitors, all of whom are looking at the problem from the same point of view. It is not a case of choosing those which, to the best of one's judgment, are really prettiest, nor even those which average opinion genuinely thinks the prettiest. We have reached the third degree where we devote our intelligences to anticipating what average opinion expects the average opinion to be. And there are some, I believe, who practice the fourth, fifth and higher degrees.

This game can be easily replicated by asking people to pick a number between 0 and 100, and telling them that the winner will be the person who picks the number closest to two-thirds of the average number picked. Figure 1.9 shows the results from the largest incidence of the game that I have played – in fact the third largest game ever played, and the only one played purely among professional investors.

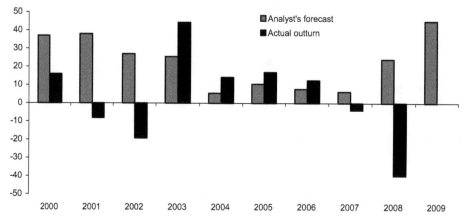

Figure 1.7 Analyst expected returns (via target prices) and actual returns (USA, %)
Source: SG Global Strategy.

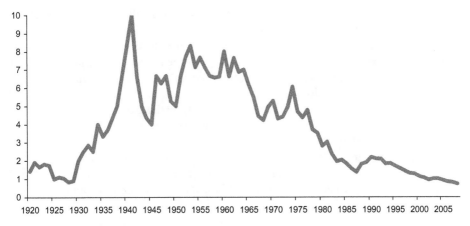

Figure 1.8   Average holding period for a stock on the NYSE (years)
Source: SG Global Strategy research.

The highest possible correct answer is 67. To go for 67 you have to believe that every other muppet in the known universe has just gone for 100. The fact we got a whole raft of responses above 67 is more than slightly alarming.

You can see spikes which represent various levels of thinking. The spike at 50 are what we (somewhat rudely) call level zero thinkers. They are the investment equivalent of Homer Simpson, 0, 100, duh 50! Not a vast amount of cognitive effort expended here!

There is a spike at 33 – of those who expect everyone else in the world to be Homer. There's a spike at 22, again those who obviously think everyone else is at 33. As you can see there is also a spike at zero. Here we find all the economists, game theorists and mathematicians of the world. They are the only people trained to solve these problems backwards. And indeed

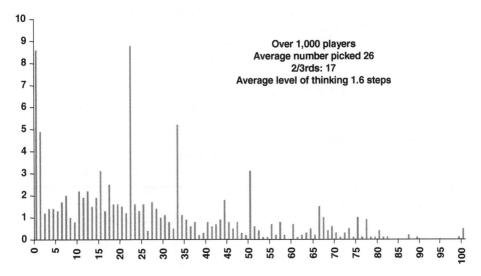

Figure 1.9   Frequency of choices in beauty contest game (%)
Source: SG Global Strategy.

the only stable Nash equilibrium is zero (two-thirds of zero is still zero). However, it is only the 'correct' answer when everyone chooses zero.

The final noticeable spike is at 1. These are economists who have (mistakenly...) been invited to one dinner party (economists only ever get invited to one dinner party). They have gone out into the world and realized that the rest of the world doesn't think like them. So they try to estimate the scale of irrationality. However, they end up suffering the curse of knowledge (once you know the true answer, you tend to anchor to it). In this game, which is fairly typical, the average number picked was 26, giving a two-thirds average of 17. Just three people out of more than 1,000 picked the number 17.

I play this game to try to illustrate just how hard it is to be just one step ahead of everyone else – to get in before everyone else, and get out before everyone else. Yet despite this fact, this seems to be exactly what a large number of investors spend their time doing.

PRIMA FACIE CASE AGAINST EMH: FOREVER BLOWING BUBBLES

Let me now turn to the prima facie case against the EMH. Oddly enough it is one that doesn't attract much attention in academia. As Larry Summers pointed out in his wonderful parody of financial economics, 'Traditional finance is more concerned with checking that two 8oz bottles of ketchup is close to the price of one 16oz bottle, than in understanding the price of the 16oz bottle.'

The first stock exchange was founded in 1602. The first equity bubble occurred just 118 years later – the South Sea bubble. Since then we have encountered bubbles with an alarming regularity. My friends at GMO define a bubble as a (real) price movement that is at least two-standard-deviations from trend. Now a two-standard-deviation event should occur roughly every 44 years. Yet since 1925, GMO have found a staggering 30 plus bubbles. That is equivalent to slightly more than one every three years!

In my own work I've examined the patterns that bubbles tend to follow. By looking at some of the major bubbles in history (including the South Sea Bubble, the railroad bubble of the 1840s, the Japanese bubble of the late 1980s, and the NASDAQ bubble[1]), I have been able to extract the following underlying pattern (Figure 1.10). Bubbles inflate over the course of around three years, with an almost parabolic explosion in prices towards the peak of the bubble. Then without exception they deflate. This bursting is generally slightly more rapid than the inflation, taking around two years.

While the details and technicalities of each episode are different, the underlying dynamics follow a very similar pattern. As Mark Twain put it, 'History doesn't repeat but it does rhyme'. Indeed the first well-documented analysis of the underlying patterns of bubbles that I can find is a paper by J.S. Mills in 1867. He lays out a framework that is very close to the Minsky/Kindleberger model that I have used for years to understand the inflation and deflation of bubbles. This makes it hard to understand why so many among the learned classes seem to believe that you can't identify a bubble before it bursts. To my mind the clear existence and ex-ante diagnosis of bubbles represent by far and away the most compelling evidence of the gross inefficiency of markets.

---

[1] Two economists have written a paper arguing that the NASDAQ bubble might not have been a bubble after all – only an academic with no experience of the real world could ever posit such a thing.

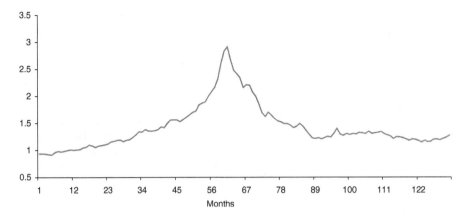

Figure 1.10   Our Bubble Index
Source: SG Global Strategy.

THE EMH 'NUCLEAR BOMB'

Now as a behaviouralist I am constantly telling people to beware of confirmatory bias – the habit of looking for information that agrees with you. So in an effort to avert the accusation that I am guilty of failing to allow for my own biases (something I've done before), I will now turn to the evidence that the EMH fans argue is the strongest defence of their belief – the simple fact that active management doesn't outperform. Mark Rubinstein describes this as the nuclear bomb of the EMH, and says that we behaviouralists have nothing in our arsenal to match it, our evidence of inefficiencies and irrationalities amounts to puny rifles.

However, I will argue that this viewpoint is flawed both theoretically and empirically. The logical error is a simple one. It is to confuse the absence of evidence with evidence of the absence. That is to say, if the EMH leads active investors to focus on the wrong sources of performance (i.e. forecasting), then it isn't any wonder that active management won't be able to outperform.

Empirically, the 'nuclear bomb' is also suspect. I want to present two pieces of evidence that highlight the suspect nature of the EMH claim. The first is work by Jonathan Lewellen of Dartmouth College.

In a recent paper, Lewellen looked at the aggregate holdings of US institutional investors over the period 1980–2007. He finds that essentially they hold the market portfolio. To some extent this isn't a surprise, as the share of institutional ownership has risen steadily over time from around 30% in 1980 to almost 70% at the end of 2007 (Figure 1.11). This confirms the zero sum game aspect of active management (or negative sum, after costs) and also the validity of Keynes' observation that it (the market) is professional investors trying to outsmart each other.

However, Lewellen also shows that, in aggregate, institutions don't try to outperform! He sorts stocks into quintiles based on a variety of characteristics and then compares the fraction of the institutional portfolio invested in each (relative to institutions' investment in all five quintiles) with the quintile's weight in the market portfolio (the quintile's market cap relative to the market cap of all five quintiles) – i.e. he measures the weight institutional investors place on a characteristic relative to the weight the market places on each trait.

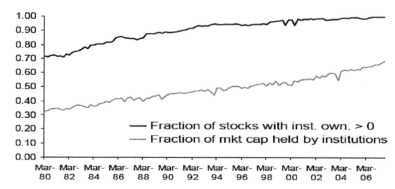

Figure 1.11   Institutional Ownership, USA 1980–2007 (%)
Source: Lewellen (2009).

Figure 1.12 shows the results for a sample of the characteristics that Lewellen used. With the exception of size, the aggregate institutional portfolio barely deviates from the market weights. So institutions aren't even really trying to tilt their portfolios towards the factors we know generate outperformance over the long term.

Lewellen concludes:

> Quite simply, institutions overall seem to do little more than hold the market portfolio, at least from the standpoint of their pre-cost and pre-fee returns. Their aggregate portfolio almost perfectly mimics the value-weighted index, with a market beta of 1.01 and an economically small, precisely estimated CAPM alpha of 0.08% quarterly. Institutions overall take essentially no bet on any of the most important stock characteristics known to predict returns, like book-to-market, momentum, or accruals. The implication is that, to the extent that institutions deviate from the market portfolio, they seem to bet primarily on idiosyncratic returns – bets that aren't particularly successful. Another implication is that institutions, in aggregate, don't exploit anomalies in the way they should if they rationally tried to maximize the (pre-cost) mean variance trade-off of their portfolios, either relative or absolute.

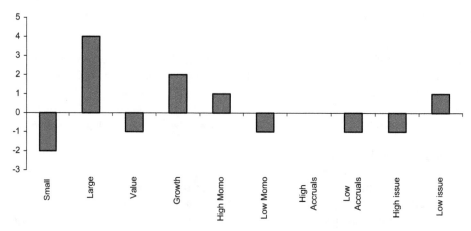

Figure 1.12   Institutional investors vs US market (weight differences)
Source: Lewellen (2009).

Put into our terms, institutions are more worried about career risk (losing your job) or business risk (losing funds under management) than they are about doing the right thing!

The second piece of evidence I'd like to bring to your attention is a paper by Randy Cohen, Christopher Polk and Bernhard Silli. They examined the 'best ideas' of US fund managers over the period 1991–2005. 'Best ideas' are measured as the biggest difference between the managers' holdings and the weights in the index.

The performance of these best ideas is impressive. Focusing on the top 25% of best ideas across the universe of active managers, Cohen *et al.* find that the average return is over 19% p.a. against a market return of 12% p.a. That is to say, the stocks in which the managers display most confidence outperformed the market by a significant degree.

The corollary to this is that the other stocks they hold are dragging down their performance. Hence it appears that the focus on relative performance – and the fear of underperformance against an arbitrary benchmark – is a key source of underperformance.

At an anecdotal level I have never quite recovered from discovering that a value manager at a large fund was made to operate with a 'completion portfolio'. This was a euphemism for an add-on to the manager's selected holdings that essentially made his fund behave much more like the index!

As Cohen *et al.* conclude, 'The poor overall performance of mutual fund managers in the past is not due to a lack of stock-picking ability, but rather to institutional factors that encourage them to over-diversify.' Thus, as Sir John Templeton said, 'It is impossible to produce a superior performance unless you do something different from the majority.'

The bottom line is that the EMH nuclear bomb is more of a party popper than a weapon of mass destruction. The EMH would have driven Sherlock Holmes to despair. As Holmes opined, 'It is a capital mistake to theorize before one has data. Insensibly one begins to twist facts to suit theories, instead of theories to suit facts.'

The EMH, as Shiller puts it, is 'one of the most remarkable errors in the history of economic thought'. EMH should be consigned to the dustbin of history. We need to stop teaching it, and brainwashing the innocent. Rob Arnott tells a lovely story of a speech he was giving to some 200 finance professors. He asked how many of them taught EMH – pretty much everyone's hand was up. Then he asked how many of them believed in it. Only two hands remained up!

A similar sentiment seems to have been expressed by the recent CFA UK survey which revealed that 67% of respondents thought that the market failed to behave rationally. When a journalist asked me what I thought of this, I simply said, 'About bloody time.' However, 76% said that behavioural finance wasn't yet sufficiently robust to replace modern portfolio theory (MPT) as the basis of investment thought. This is, of course, utter nonsense. Successful investors existed long before EMH and MPT. Indeed, the vast majority of successful long-term investors are value investors who reject most of the precepts of EMH and MPT.

Will we ever be successful at finally killing off the EMH? I am a pessimist. As Jeremy Grantham said when asked what investors would learn from this crisis: 'In the short term, a lot. In the medium term, a little. In the long term, nothing at all. That is the historical precedent.' Or, as JK Galbraith put it, markets are characterized by 'Extreme brevity of financial memory... There can be few fields of human endeavor in which history counts for so little as in the world of finance.'

2
CAPM is Crap*

The capital asset pricing model (CAPM) is insidious. It finds its way into all sorts of financial discussions. Every time you mention alpha and beta you are invoking the CAPM. Yet the model is empirically bogus. It doesn't work in any way, shape or form. Instead of obsessing about alpha, beta and tracking error it is high time we concentrated on generating total returns with acceptable levels of risks.

- There is an overwhelming amount of evidence that CAPM simply doesn't work. Beta is not a good description of risk. No wonder analysts have such trouble forecasting stock prices when they routinely use beta as a key input.
- CAPM woefully underpredicts the returns to low beta stocks and massively overestimates the returns to high beta stocks. Sadly our industry seems to have a bad habit of accepting a theory as a fact. This is at odds with a scientific approach which likes to test theoretical models by subjecting them to empirical evaluation.
- The CAPM fails because its assumptions are clearly at odds with reality. Two of the critical assumptions in particular stand out. Firstly, that we can all take any position we please (long or short) in any stock with absolutely no price impact. Secondly, that everybody uses Markowitz Optimization (MO) to assign portfolios. Even Harry Markowitz himself doesn't use MO! The CAPM is, in actual fact, Completely Redundant Asset Pricing (CRAP).
- Instead professional fund managers seemed obsessed with tracking error. To a tracking error focused investor the risk-free asset isn't an interest rate (as in CAPM) but rather the market itself. No wonder mutual fund cash levels seem to have undergone a structural decline – active management has become benchmark beta.
- An entire industry seems to have arisen dedicated to portable alpha. Yet if CAPM is bogus then the separation of alpha and beta is at best a distraction and, at worst, actually interfering with the true job of investors to generate returns. Our fixation with alpha and beta seems to stem from our desire to measure everything on ever-decreasing time scales. Instead of succumbing to this dark side of investment, we should refocus on delivering total (net) returns to investors at a level of acceptable risk.

*This article appeared in Global Equity Strategy on 16 January 2007. Copyright © 2007 by Dresdner Kleinwort, a Brand of Commerzbank AG. All rights reserved. The material discussed was accurate at the time of publication.

The capital asset pricing model (CAPM) is insidious. It creeps into almost every discussion on finance. For instance, every time you mention alpha and beta you are tacitly invoking the CAPM, because the very separation of alpha and beta stems from the CAPM model.

A BRIEF HISTORY OF TIME

Let's take a step back and examine a brief history of the origins of CAPM. It all started in the 1950s when Harry Markowitz was working on his PhD. Markowitz created a wonderful tool which allows investors to calculate the weights to give each stock (given expected return, expected risk, and the correlation) in order to achieve the portfolio with the greatest return for a given level of risk. Effectively investors using the Markowitz methods will have mean-variance efficient portfolios; that is to say, they will minimize the variance of portfolio return, given expected return, and maximize expected return given the variance.

Markowitz gave the world a powerful tool that is much used and loved by quants everywhere. However, from there on in, the finance academics proceeded down a slippery slope. Somewhere around the mid-1950s Modigliani and Miller came up with the idea of dividend and capital structure irrelevance. They assumed that markets were efficient (before the efficient market hypothesis was even invented), and argued that investors didn't care whether earnings were retained by the firm or distributed as income (this will be important later).

In the early 1960s the final two parts of the efficient markets school dawned to the unsuspecting world. The first of these was CAPM from Sharpe, Litner and Treynor. In the wonderful world of CAPM all investors use Markowitz Optimization. It then follows that a single factor will distinguish between stocks. This all-encompassing single factor is, of course, beta.

The second was the summation of all ideas, the birth of the efficient market hypothesis itself from Eugene Fama (another PhD thesis). I don't want to rant on about market efficiency as my views on this topic are well known.

CAPM IN PRACTICE

In general our industry seems to have a *bad habit of accepting theory as fact*. As an empirical sceptic my interest lies in whether CAPM works. The evidence from the offset has been appalling. Study after study found that beta wasn't a good measure of risk.

For instance, Figure 2.1 is taken from Fama and French's 2004 review of the CAPM. Each December from 1923 to 2003 they estimate a beta for every stock on the NYSE, AMEX and NASDAQ using 2–5 years of prior monthly returns. Ten portfolios are then formed, based on beta, and the returns are tracked over the next 12 months.

Figure 2.1 plots the average return for each decile against its average beta. The straight line shows the predictions from the CAPM. The model's predictions are clearly violated. *CAPM woefully underpredicts the returns to low beta stocks, and massively overestimates the returns to high beta stocks.* Over the long run there has been essentially no relationship between beta and return.

Of course, this suggests that investors might be well advised to consider a strategic tilt towards low beta and against high beta – a strategy first suggested by Fisher Black in 1993.

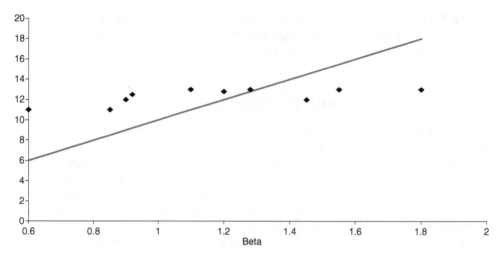

Figure 2.1 Portfolio returns by beta decile (1923–2003)
Source: Fama and French (2004). DrKW Macro research.

Nor is this simply another proxy for value. Table 2.1 (taken from some recent work by Vuolteenaho, 2006) shows that the beta arbitrage strategy holds across book to price (B/P) categories. For instance, within the growth universe (low B/P) there is an average 5% differential from being long low beta, and short high beta.

Within the value universe (high B/P), a long low beta, short high beta created an average difference of 8.3% p.a. over the sample. So growth investors and value investors can both exploit a strategic tilt against beta.

A 2006 paper from the ever-fascinating Jeremy Grantham of GMO reveals information on the largest 600 stocks in the USA: since 1963 those with the lowest beta have the highest return, and those with the highest beta have the lowest return – the complete inverse of the CAPM predictions. This is yet further evidence against the CAPM.

Nor is this purely a US problem. With the aid of Rui Antunes of our Quant team I tested the performance of beta with the European environment. Figure 2.3 shows that low beta on average has outperformed high beta! Yet another direct contradiction of the CAPM.

Another of CAPM's predictions states that the cap-weighted market index is efficient (in mean-variance terms). With everyone agreeing on the distributions of returns and all investors

Table 2.1 Jensen's alpha across beta and B/P categories (% p.a. 1927–2004)

	LowB/P	2	3	4	High B/P
High beta	−6.0	−3.0	−3.0	−3.0	−0.5
4	−3.0	−3.4	0.5	1.0	3.4
3	0.5	−0.2	−0.5	2.0	3.8
2	1.0	1.0	2.0	3.0	5.0
Low beta	−1.0	1.0	2.0	5.0	7.8

Source: Vuolteenaho (2006). Dresdner Kleinwort Macro research.

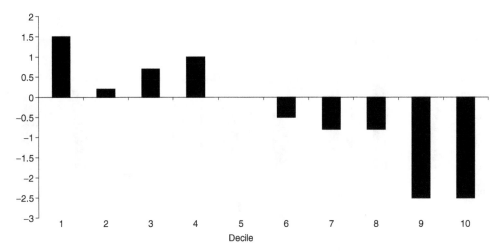

Figure 2.2 US portfolio relative returns by beta decile (1963–2006)
Source: Grantham (2006). DrKW Macro research.

seeing the same opportunities, they all end up holding the same portfolio, which by construction must be the value-weighted market portfolio.

There is a large amount of evidence to suggest that CAPM is also wrong in this regard. For instance, in a recent issue of the *Journal of Portfolio Management*, Clarke *et al.* (2006) showed that a minimum variance portfolio generated higher returns with lower risk than the market index.

Rob Arnott and his colleagues at Research Affiliates have shown that fundamentally weighted indices (based on earnings and dividends, for example) can generate higher return

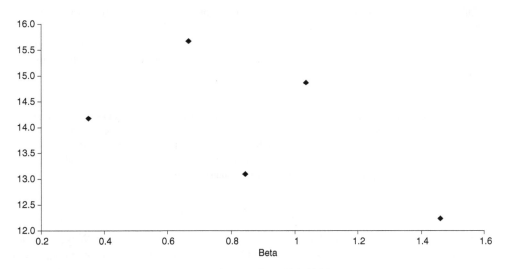

Figure 2.3 European portfolio returns by beta decile (1986–2006)
Source: DrKW Macro research.

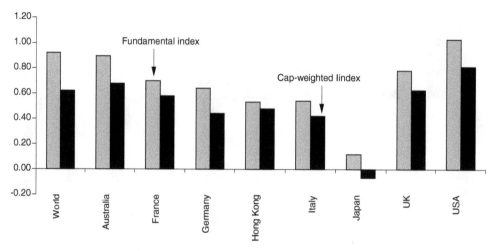

Figure 2.4   Risk-adjusted returns from selected Fundamental vs MSCI (1984–2004)
Source: Hsu and Campollo (2006). DrKW Macro research.

and lower risk than a cap-weighted index.[1] Remember that the fundamentally weighted index is still a passive index (in as much as it has a set of transparent rules which are implemented in a formulaic fashion).

Figure 2.4 shows the return per unit of risk on selected Fundamental Indices vs the MSCI benchmark. It clearly shows that the cap-weighted indices are not mean variance efficient. On average the Fundamental Indices shown outperformed MSCI cap-weighted equivalents by an average 278 bps p.a. between 1984 and 2004. They delivered this outperformance with lower risk than the MSCI equivalents, and the Fundamental Indices had a volatility that was on average 53 bps lower than the MSCI measure. Something is very wrong with the CAPM.

Of course, those who believe in CAPM (and it is a matter of blind faith, given the evidence) either argue that CAPM can't really be tested (thanks for a really useless theory guys) or that a more advanced version known as ICAPM (intertemporal) holds. Unfortunately the factors of the ICAPM are undefined, so once again we are left with a hollow theory. Neither of these CAPM defences is of much use to a practitioner.

Ben Graham once argued that

> Beta is a more or less useful measure of past price fluctuations of common stocks. What bothers me is that authorities now equate the beta idea with the concept of risk. Price variability, yes; risk no. Real investment risk is measured not by the percent that a stock may decline in price in relation to the general market in a given period, but by the danger of a loss of quality and earning power through economic changes or deterioration in management.

WHY DOES CAPM FAIL?

The evidence is clear: CAPM doesn't work. This now begs the question: Why? Like all good economists, when I was first taught the CAPM I was told to judge it by its empirical

---

[1] See, for example, Hsu and Campollo (2006).

success rather than its assumptions. However, given the evidence above, perhaps a glance at its assumptions might just be worth while:

1. No transaction costs (no commission, no bid–ask spread).
2. Investors can take any position (long or short) in any stock in any size without affecting the market price.
3. No taxes (so investors are indifferent between dividends and capital gains).
4. Investors are risk averse.
5. Investors share a common time horizon.
6. Investors view stocks only in mean-variance space (so they all use the Markowitz Optimization model).
7. Investors control risk through diversification.
8. All assets, including human capital, can be bought and sold freely in the market.
9. Investors can lend and borrow at the risk-free rate.

Most of these assumptions are clearly ludicrous. The key assumptions are numbers 2 and 6. The idea of transacting in any size without leaving a market footprint is a large institution's wet dream . . .but that is all it is – a dream.

The idea that everybody uses the Markowitz Optimization is also massively wide of the mark. Even its own creator Harry Markowitz,[2] when asked how he allocated assets, said 'My intention was to minimize my future regret. So I split my contributions 50–50 between bonds and equities.' George Aklerof (another Nobel prize winner) said he kept a significant proportion of his wealth in money market funds; his defence was refreshingly honest, 'I know it is utterly stupid.' So even the brightest of the bright don't seem to follow the requirements of CAPM.

Nor is it likely that a few 'rational' market participants can move the market towards the CAPM solution. The assumption that must be strictly true is that we *all* use Markowitz Optimization.

Additionally, institutional money managers don't think in terms of variance as a description of risk. Never yet have I met a long-only investor who cares about up-side standard deviation; this gets lumped into return.

Our industry is obsessed with tracking error as its measure of risk not the variance of returns. The two are very different beasts. Tracking error measures variability in the difference between the returns of fund managers' portfolios and the returns of the stock index. Low beta stocks and high beta stocks don't have any meaning when the investment set is drawn in terms of tracking error.

To tracking error obsessed investors the risk-free asset isn't an interest rate, but rather the market index. If you buy the market then you are guaranteed to have zero tracking error (perhaps a reason why mutual fund cash levels seem to have been in structural decline – Figure 2.5).

---

[2] It is worth noting that Harry Markowitz recently wrote an article in the *FAJ* observing that if one broke the unlimited borrowing assumption of CAPM then the conclusions of the model change drastically, the cap-weighted market is no longer the optimal portfolio and beta is no longer lineally related to return. See Markowitz (2005).

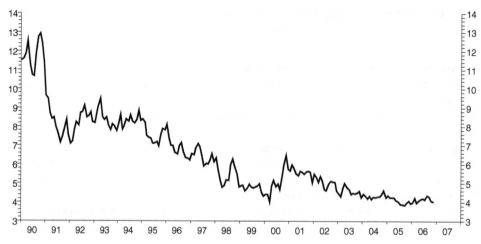

Figure 2.5 Cash levels of US mutual funds (% of total assets)
Source: DrKW Macro research.

CAPM TODAY AND IMPLICATIONS

Most universities still teach CAPM as the core asset pricing model (possibly teaching APT alongside). Fama and French (2004) wrote:

> The attraction of CAPM is that it offers powerful and intuitively pleasing predictions about how to measure risk and the relation between expected return and risk. *Unfortunately, the empirical record of the model is poor – poor enough to invalidate the way it is used in applications.*

Remember that this comes from the high priests of market efficiency.

Analysts regularly calculate betas as an input into their cost of capital analysis. Yet the evidence suggests that beta is a really, really bad measure of risk; no wonder analysts struggle to forecast share prices!

An entire industry appears to have arisen obsessed with alpha and beta. Portable alpha is one of the hot topics if the number of conferences being organized on the subject is any guide. Indeed Figure 2.6 shows the number of times portable alpha is mentioned in any 12 months. Even a cursory glance at the figure reveals an enormous growth in discussion on the subject.

However, every time you mention alpha or beta remember that this stems from CAPM. Without CAPM, alpha and beta have no meaning. Of course, you might choose to compare your performance against a cap-weighted arbitrary index if you really wish, but it has nothing to do with the business of investing.

The work from Rob Arnott mentioned above clearly shows the blurred line that exists between these concepts. The fact that Fundamental Indices outperform cap-weighted indices, yet are passive, shows how truly difficult it is to separate alpha from beta.

Portable alpha strategies may not make as much sense as their exponents would like to have us believe. For instance, let us assume that someone wants to make the alpha of a manager whose universe is the Russell 1000 and graft in onto the beta from the S&P 500. Given that these are both large-cap domestic indices, the overlap between the two could well

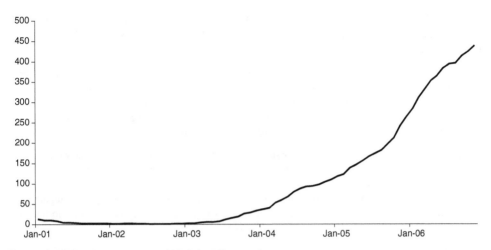

Figure 2.6 Word count on portable alpha (12m sum)
Source: DrKW Macro research.

be significant. The investor ends up being both potentially long and short exactly the same stock – a highly inefficient outcome as the cost of shorting is completely wasted.

Now the proponents of portable alpha will turn around and say that obviously the strategy works best when the alpha and the beta are uncorrelated, i.e. you are tacking a Japanese equity manager's alpha onto a S&P 500 beta. However, if the investor's are already long Japanese equities within their overall portfolio, they are likely to have Japanese beta, hence they end up suffering the same problem outlined above are both long and short the same thing. Only when the alpha is uncorrelated to all the elements of the existing portfolio can portable alpha strategies make any sense.

My colleague Sebastian Lancetti suggested another example to me. It is often argued that hedge funds are alpha engines; however, the so-called attack of the clones suggests that they are in large part beta betters. If their performance can be replicated with a six-factor model, as is claimed by the clone providers, then there isn't too much alpha here.

Alpha is also a somewhat ephemeral concept. A fund's alpha changes massively depending upon the benchmark it is being measured against. In a recent study, Chan *et al.* (2006) found that the alphas delivered on a variety of large cap growth funds ranged from 0.28% to 4.03%, depending upon the benchmark. For large cap value managers, the range was −0.64% to 1.09%.

The terms alpha and beta may be convenient shorthand for investors to express notions of value added by fund managers, and market volatility, but they run the risk of actually hampering the real job of investment – to generate total returns.

A simple check for all investors should be: 'Would I do this if this were my own money?' If the answer is 'No', then it shouldn't be done with a client's money. Would you care about the tracking error of your own portfolio? I suggest the answer is 'NO'. In a world without CAPM the concept of beta-adjusted return won't exist. In as much as this is a fairly standard measure of risk adjustment, it measures nothing at all, and potentially significantly distorts our view of performance.

Perhaps the obsession with alpha and beta comes from our desire to measure everything. This obsession with performance measurement isn't new. While researching another paper (on Keynes and Ben Graham) I came across a paper written by Bob Kirby (1976). In the 1970s Kirby was a leading fund manager at Capital group where he ran the Capital Guardian Fund. He opined:

> Performance measurement is one of those basically good ideas that somehow got totally out of control. In many, many cases, the intense application of performance measurement techniques has actually served to impede the purpose it is supposed to serve – namely, the achievement of a satisfactory rate of return on invested capital. Among the really negative side-effects of the performance measurement movement as it has evolved over the past ten years are:
>
> 1. It has fostered the notion that it is possible to evaluate a money management organization over a period of two or three years – whereas money management really takes at least five and probably ten years or more to appraise properly.
> 2. It has tried to quantify and formulize, in a manner acceptable to the almighty computer, a function that is only partially susceptible to quantitative evaluation and requires a substantial subjective appraisal to arrive at a meaningful conclusion.

It is reassuring to see that good ideas such as Kirby's can be as persistent as bad ideas such as the CAPM. Kirby also knew a thing or two about the pressures of performance. During 1973, Kirby refused to buy the rapidly growing high-multiple companies that were in vogue. One pension administrator said Capital Guardian was 'like an airline pilot in a power dive, hands frozen on the stick; the name of the game is to be where it's at'. Of course, had Kirby been 'where it's at' he would have destroyed his client's money.

Ben Graham was also disturbed by the focus on relative performance. At a conference one money manager stated: 'Relative performance is all that matters to me. If the market collapses and my funds collapse less that's okay with me. I've done my job.' Graham responded:

> That concerns me, doesn't it concern you?... I was shocked by what I heard at this meeting. I could not comprehend how the management of money by institutions had degenerated from the standpoint of sound investment to this rat race of trying to get the highest possible return in the shortest period of time. Those men gave me the impression of being prisoners to their own operations rather than controlling them...They are promising performance on the upside and the downside that is not practical to achieve.

So, in a world devoid of market index benchmarks, what should be we doing? The answer, I think, is to focus upon the total (net) return and acceptable risk. Keynes stated:

> The ideal policy . . .is Where it is earning a respectable rate of interest on its funds, while securing at the same time that its risk of really serious depreciation in capital value is at a minimum.

Sir John Templeton's first maxim was 'For all long-term investors, there is only one objective – maximum total real returns after taxes.' Clients should monitor the performance of fund managers relative to a stated required net rate of return and the level of variability of that return they are happy to accept.

3

Pseudoscience and Finance: The Tyranny of Numbers and the Fallacy of Safety*

In the world of modern finance, a love of numbers has replaced a desire for critical thinking. As long as something has a number attached to it, it is taken as gospel truth. Research shows that people are often fooled by the use of pseudoscience. Simply making things sound complex makes people believe them more! Risk managers, analysts and consultants are all guilty of using pseudoscience to promote an illusion of safety. We all need to be on our guard against the artificial deployment of meaningless numbers. Critical thinking and scepticism are the most unrated (and scarce) tools in our world.

- A recent study by Weisberg *et al.* revealed just how easily most of us are fooled by anything that sounds vaguely scientific. They put neuroscience language into a standard psychological explanation for a variety of biases. Some of these explanations were 'good' (genuine) and some were 'bad' (circular restatements of the bias itself). Both good and bad explanations were rated as much better when they contained the meaningless neuroscience information.
- Garner *et al.* have shown that people are easily distracted by 'seductive details'. After reading just a few paragraphs loaded with 'interesting' but irrelevant information, people simply can't recall the important stuff! Suddenly the world of analysts is starting to make some sense to me!
- Finance is loaded with pseudoscience and seductive details. For instance, risk management is clearly pseudoscience of the highest order. Numbers like Value at Risk (VaR) are used to create comfort, but actually just generate the illusion of safety. The presence of fat tails, endogenous correlations and risks of using trailing input all combine to render VaR impotent. It is no surprise that the mea maxima culpa from UBS cited overreliance on VaR as one of the core problems.
- Analysts are also guilty of using pseudoscience. They are providers of seductive details. Read most analysts' reports and they are full of 'interesting' but irrelevant information. The idea that forecasting earnings to two decimal places over the next five years is surely laughable. It has no merit. All the more so with the latest reporting season revealing the biggest overestimation of profits growth ever recorded!
- Performance measurement is another example of the reign of pseudoscience in finance. Weasel words such as alpha, beta and tracking error are used to promote confusion in this arena. Style drift, holding-based style analysis, and returns-based style analysis are all used

---

to make the industry sound important. But all are seriously flawed when it comes to the meaning behind the numbers.

- Simply because something can be quantified doesn't mean that it is sensible. There is no substitute for rigorous critical or sceptical thinking. Blind faith in numbers for numbers' sake is a path to ruin.

In the world of modern finance, a love of numbers has replaced a desire for critical thinking. This is a highly regrettable trend. Don't get me wrong, I am a big fan of using empirical evidence to ascertain the truth of many of the wild claims that seem to circulate in our industry (a process I have called Evidence Based Investing). However, all too often we seem to take pseudoscience as gospel truth, accepting anything with a number as a fact.

BLINDED BY PSEUDOSCIENCE

A recent study by Weisberg *et al.* (2008) revealed some intriguing findings about the way in which we can be blinded by pseudoscience and just how gullible we are when it comes to pseudoscientific explanations.

In their clever experiment, Weisberg *et al.* (2008) gave three groups of people (naïve students, students in neuroscience, and experts) a set of descriptions of psychological phenomena which varied along two dimensions: (i) the quality of the explanation and (ii) the use of neuroscience.

A sample discussing the curse of knowledge can be found in Table 3.1. In all cases the 'good' explanations were genuine explanations that had been given by researchers. The 'bad' explanations are simply circular restatements of the phenomenon, with no explanatory power at all.

For the 'with neuroscience' condition, information on an area of the brain known to be involved with the general sort of phenomena under discussion was inserted. However, because this was already known, it shouldn't have any impact upon the perceived validity of the explanation.

Participants were asked to rate the explanations of the phenomena, and told that in some cases they would be reading false explanations. They rated the explanations on a 7-point scale from −3 (very unsatisfactory explanation) to +3 (very satisfactory explanation).

Figures 3.1–3.3 show the results obtained across the three different groups. The novices (those without any training in psychology or neuroscience) did a pretty good job of telling good explanations from bad in the absence of neuroscience information (Figure 3.1). However,

Table 3.1   The curse of knowledge

	Good explanation	Bad explanation
Without neuroscience	The researchers claim that this 'curse' happens because subjects have trouble switching their point of view to consider what someone else might know, mistakenly projecting their own knowledge onto others	The researchers claim that this 'curse' happens because subjects make more mistakes when they have to judge the knowledge of others. People are much better at judging what they themselves know.
With neuroscience	Brain scans indicate that this 'curse' happens bacause of the frontal lobe brain circuitry, known to be involved in self-knowledge. Subjects have trouble switching their point of view to consider what someone else might know, mistakenly projecting their own knowledge onto others.	Brain scans indicate that this 'curse' happens because of the frontal lobe brain circuitry, known to be involved in self-knowledge. Subjects make more mistakes when they have to judge the knowledge of others. People are much better at judging what they themselves know.

Source: Weisberg *et al.* (2008).

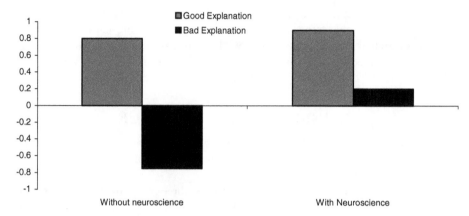

Figure 3.1   Novice rating of the quality of explanation
Source: Weisberg *et al.* (2008).

as soon as that was added, it markedly impaired their ability to tell good explanations from bad. In particular bad explanations with a neuroscience element were rated as much better than bad explanations without any neuroscience language.

The second group comprised the students taking courses in intermediate level cognitive neuroscience. These students should have learnt about the basic logic and construct of neuroscience experiments. However, Figure 3.2 shows that their responses weren't significantly different from the novice group. They seemed to place heavy weight on neuroscience input, downplaying the good explanation in its absence! Bad explanations were once again boosted by the presence of neuroscience information. It seems as if these students were only interested in the item they were studying.

The third and final group were 'experts' – characterized by advanced degrees in cognitive neuroscience or cognitive psychology. This group showed different behaviour to the previous two. As Figure 3.3 shows, this group discriminated between good and bad explanations in the absence of neuroscience. It also appears that when faced with needless information on

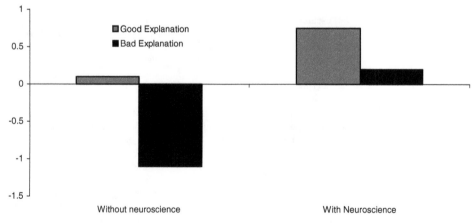

Figure 3.2   Student ratings of the quality of explanation
Source: Weisberg *et al.* (2008).

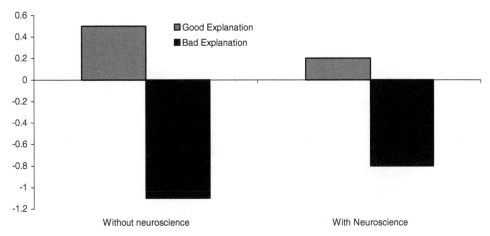

Figure 3.3   Expert ratings of the quality of explanation
Source: Weisberg *et al.* (2008).

neuroscience, this group marked down good explanations. Effectively they punished explanations that used pointless neuroscience. This finding also confirms that the neuroscience information itself had no value.

WATCHING TV IMPROVES YOUR MATHS ABILITY

Another example of this form of pseudoscientific blindness can be found in McCabe and Castel (2008). They had participants read three brief articles, each summarizing the results of fictitious brain-imaging studies. The articles made claims that were not necessitated by the data, giving participants some basis for scepticism in their ratings of the soundness of the argument.

One article argued that 'Watching TV is related to maths ability'. It concluded that because watching television and completing arithmetic problems both led to activation in the temporal lobe, watching television improved maths skills. This similarity in activation was depicted in a bar graph or brain image, or was only explained in the text. Each article was approximately 300 words long, presented on a single page, with the image embedded in the text.

After reading each article, participants were asked to rate if the scientific reasoning in the article made sense. Responses were made on a four-point scale, with response options including 'strongly disagree', 'disagree', 'agree', and 'strongly agree' (coded 1, 2, 3 or 4, respectively).

Figure 3.4 presents the ratings as a function of the image shown to participants. Yet again participants were fooled by the presence of the brain image. Studies that showed such a picture were rated as much more scientifically sound!

SEDUCTIVE DETAILS

In general, these findings fit into a larger body of work concerned with 'seductive details'. In a paper written in 1989, Ruth Garner and colleagues first noticed that people were often

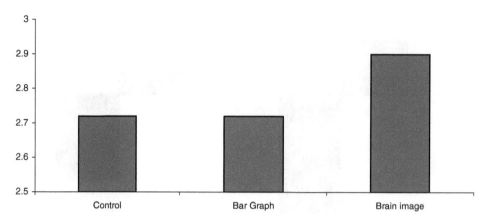

Figure 3.4   Rating of scientific reasoning (1 = low, 4 = high)
Source: McCabe and Castel (2007).

distracted by 'interesting' but 'uninformative' noise. In their test, people were given three paragraphs to read, such as:

> Some insects live alone, some live in big colonies. Wasps that live alone are called solitary wasps. The Mud Dauber Wasp is a solitary wasp. The Click beetle lives alone. When a Click beetle is on its back, it flips itself into the air, and lands right side up whilst making a clicking noise. Ants live in big colonies.

It is fairly obvious that the important information is the first sentence. The story about the Click beetle is interesting but not important. Some of the participants were given paragraphs with just the important information in them, other received paragraphs like the one above.

Having read the paragraphs, subjects were then asked to recall the important information contained within the text they had read. The ability to recall the important information was massively determined by whether the paragraph had contained seductive details or not. Of those reading the paragraphs that contained just the important facts, 93% could recall the important generalizations. Of those faced with paragraphs containing seductive details, only 43% could recall the important elements!

APPLICATIONS TO FINANCE

Risk Management

Over the years I have been a vocal critic of risk management (see Chapter 36 of *Behavioural Investing*, for example). It is a prime example of the way in which we can be blinded by numbers. It is comforting to be presented with a number that represents the Value at Risk (VaR), but it is also almost totally meaningless. The illusion of safety is created by false belief in the infallibility of numbers.

VaR is fundamentally flawed – after all it cuts off the very bit of the distribution that we are interested in: the tails! This is akin to buying a car with an airbag that is guaranteed to work unless you have a crash. It also ignores the fact that risk is endogenous, not exogenous, within many financial applications (again see Chapter 36 of *Behavioural Investing* for more on this and full analysis of the errors contained within the VaR approach). The entire risk management industry is an example of pseudoscience: people pretending to measure and quantify things that just can't be measured or quantified.

My favourite recent analysis of the failure of VaR came from a speech given by Dave Einhorn (2008):

> By ignoring the tails, Value at Risk creates an incentive to take excessive but remote risks. Consider an investment in a coin-flip. If you bet $100 on tails at even money, your VaR to a 99% threshold is $100, as you will lose that amount 50% of the time, which is obviously within the threshold. In this case the VaR will equal the maximum loss.
>
> Compare that to a bet where you offer 217 to 1 odds on $100 that heads won't come up seven times in a row. You will win more than 99.2% of the time, which exceeds the 99% threshold. As a result, your 99% VaR is zero even though you are exposed to a possible $21,700 loss. In other words, an investment bank wouldn't have to put up any capital to make this bet.

In the light of this analysis, it isn't a surprise that the recently published catalogue of errors that UBS confessed (*see UBS Shareholder Report on UBS's Write-Downs*) contained yet another mea culpa on the use of VaR:

> Time series reliance: The historical time series used to drive VaR and Stress are based on five years of data, whereby the data was sourced from a period of relatively positive growth. Regular work being performed during the relevant period focused on confirming the efficacy of existing scenarios based on broad-based economic developments and historical events. When updates to methodologies were presented to Group and IB Senior Management, hindsight suggests that these updates did not attribute adequate weight to the significant growth in the US housing market and especially the Subprime market. The Market Risk function did not develop scenarios that were based on more fundamental attributes of the US housing market.
>
> Lack of Housing Market Risk Factor Loss limits: In a similar vein, it appears that no attempt was made to develop an RFL structure that captured more meaningful attributes related to the US housing market generally, such as defaults, loan to value ratios or other similar attributes to statistically shock the existing portfolio.
>
> Overreliance on VaR and Stress: MRC relied on VaR and Stress numbers, even though delinquency rates were increasing and origination standards were falling in the US mortgage market. It continued to do so throughout the build-up of significant positions in Subprime assets that were only partially hedged. Presentations of MRC representatives to UBS's senior governance bodies did not provide adequate granularity of Subprime positions UBS held in its various businesses. No warnings were given to Group Senior Management about the limitations of the presented numbers or the need to look at the broader contextual framework and the findings were not challenged with perseverance.

The presence of fat tails, endogenous correlations and risks of trailing inputs have been known for years. Yet despite this people continue to use such methods, arguing that something is better than nothing. However, we must consider if some medicine is really better than no medicine, especially if the wrong treatment can kill you. This misplaced faith in pseudoscience has once again extracted a high price.

Analysts and their Addiction to Numbers

However, risk managers aren't alone in deploying pseudoscience. Analysts are guilty too. They are providers of seductive details. The idea that forecasting earnings to two decimal places over the next five years has any merit is surely laughable. Bear in mind that the 2000 or so analysts employed on the Street have recently displayed just how truly appalling they are at forecasting.

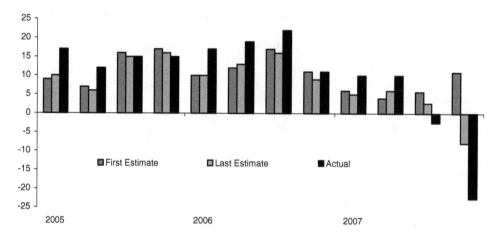

Figure 3.5 Who needs analysts? Recent performance of growth forecasts (USA)
Source: Bloomberg.

At the start of the third quarter of 2007, average estimates called for US earnings to increase by 5.7%. By the end of the quarter, analysts had cut by more than half to 2.7%. Companies ended up reporting a 2.5% drop in profits. Analysts were 8.2 percentage points too high!

Forecasts for the fourth quarter were even worse. Analysts predicted 10.9% growth before flipping the projection to a decline of 7.9%. S&P 500 companies reported that profit dropped 22.6%, resulting in an overestimation of profits growth by 33.5 percentage points, the biggest miss ever (Figure 3.5).

Not to worry, of course, as analysts say, everything will be alright by the second half of the year. They have pencilled in earnings declines of 11.3% and 3.5% in 2008's first and second quarters, but then a recovery occurs with a 13.9% rise in the third quarter and a jump to 54.5% in the fourth quarter!

Do clients really value this kind of useless noise? Surely not. But whenever one asks analysts why they persist in producing this kind of rubbish, the invariable response is that their clients want it. Could it be that the buy-side has fallen for the pseudoscience and its seductive details?

My conversations with buy-siders tend to suggest not. The fund managers I speak to generally ignore the meaningless noise generated by analysts in terms of their forecasts, preferring instead to focus on analysts who are doing something different. But perhaps I have a biased sample!

Indeed, as I was going to print I came across a study by Bryan Armstrong of Ashton Partners seeking to explore the importance of sell-side estimates for buy-side institutions. Of the 30 portfolio managers surveyed, every single one stated that consensus estimates (Figure 3.6) were important to their investment decision-making process! Now I'm really worried.

Performance Measurement as Pseudoscience

The final application of pseudoscience that I wish to vent about in this note is performance measurement. This is surely another example of too much faith being placed in one number (or a few numbers at best). Alpha, beta and tracking error are the weasel words used to promote pseudoscience in this arena (refer to Chapter 2 for an onslaught against CAPM).

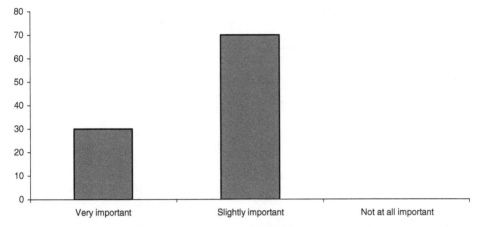

Figure 3.6   Percentage of portfolio managers saying consensus estimates were . . .
Source: Ashton Partners.

The use of such measures as tracking error for an active manager is akin to sending a boxer into the ring with instructions to make sure he is always within a point or two of his opponent, rather than with the aim of trying to win the bout.

Another aspect of the pseudoscience nature of performance measurement was bought home to me recently as I read an intriguing new paper by John Minahan (2009) on 'investment beliefs.' He describes the following situation:

> I was new to the industry. . .[a] manager came to my attention because she showed up in a holdings-based style analysis having migrated from value to growth, and this set off alarms regarding 'style discipline'. The manager had very good performance, and this happened during a period of time when growth was outperforming value, so on the surface it looked like the manager had broken her value discipline because growth was where the returns were.
>
> A closer examination of the portfolio revealed that the manager had very little turnover during this period, and that the stocks which were now plotting as growth had plotted as value when the manager bought them. All that had really happened was that the manager was correct with many of these stocks: earnings were up and prices even more, and stocks started plotting as growth stocks. She was able to explain the original investment thesis for any stock I asked about, and for those she still held, justify that the thesis was still intact. This led me to suspect that the style-box program I was using just wasn't subtle enough to accurately capture the manager's style, and that the style was in fact consistent through this period.
>
> When I discussed my concerns with the more senior consultant with whom I worked on this account, he dismissed my interpretation. He claimed that the style analyser was 'objective' whereas the manager's explanation was 'spin'. He told me that when I got a little more experience I will learn to be more sceptical of charming managers.

The senior consultant here is exceptionally guilty of blind faith in pseudoscience. Just because something is quantitative doesn't mean that it is infallible. Critical thought is still required. Minahan was most likely correct in his analysis. Indeed Fama and French (2007) have shown that much of the value premium comes from stocks that effectively migrate across 'style boundaries' (see Table 3.2).

Table 3.2   Migration across styles (USA 1927–2006)

	Portfolio	Minus	Same	Plus	Changed Size
Average Excess Returns					
Big Growth	−0.9	−12.0	0.8	15.6	−37.4
Big Neutral	1.2	−11.5	0.4	16.6	−31.1
Big Value	4.8	−36.3	3.2	16.9	−31.7
Average Transition Probability					
Big Growth		10.9	87.5	0.7	0.9
Big Neutral		8.6	75.1	15	1.2
Big Value		0.1	75.2	22.5	2.2
Average Contribution to Portfolio's Excess Returns					
Big Growth		−1.2	0.6	0.1	−0.4
Big Neutral		−0.9	0.3	2.2	−0.4
Big Value		0	2.3	3.3	−0.7

Source: Fama and French (2007).

CONCLUSIONS

As a fan of an empirical approach to finance it saddens me when I come across pseudoscience in finance. However, it is all too common. Blind faith in anything containing numbers is the curse of our industry. We need to seek to develop a more critical/sceptical mindset if we are to avoid stumbling into the seductive details of a pseudoscientific approach to our field.

Numbers don't constitute safety. Just because a risk manager tells you that the VaR is X, it doesn't mean a thing. Nor for that matter does an analyst saying that company Y is trading on a $Y \times 2010$ earnings, or a consultant saying that a fund manager was 3% alpha. All these need to be put in context. When critically appraised, all of these are likely to be classed as pseudoscience. The artificial deployment of meaningless numbers to generate the illusion of safety is something that we must all guard against.

4

The Dangers of Diversification and Evils of the Relative Performance Derby*

If religion has been the cause of most wars, then 'diversification' lies close to the heart of many financial disasters. All too often, too narrow a perspective is taken when thinking about diversification. Investors appear to forget that risk is endogenous (like poker) rather than exogenous (like roulette). In the equity world, diversification is often taken to the other extreme. The average US mutual fund holds anywhere between 100 and 160 stocks! The only explanation for so many holdings must be the obsession with the relative performance derby (where tracking error is all that matters). This is one of the key sources of poor performance.

- Much damage in the world of finance has been committed in the name of diversification. For instance, LTCM thought it was 'diversified' but all its positions were effectively 'convergence' trades. Modern risk management seems to have embedded similar flaws into its structure. All too often, the use of short histories of trailing data provides the illusion of safety.
- The most recent crisis once again has the fingerprints of naïve diversification all over it. No one appeared to give any thought to the unspoken risk that the USA might just witness a nationwide housing market downturn. Greenspan observed that real estate was 'especially ill-suited to develop into a bubble', blatantly ignoring the evidence provided by Japan and the UK.
- In the wonderful world of equities, diversification is taken to the other extreme. The average US mutual fund holds somewhere between 100 and 160 stocks. This is madness. Holding around 30–40 stocks will provide you with the vast majority of the benefits of diversification. Holding more stocks is simply a reflection of the relative performance derby, where the all-consuming concerns are tracking error and career risk.
- New research from Cohen *et al.* shows that the 'best ideas' (defined as the positions where the manager is most at odds with the index weight) actually generate significant returns (over 19% p.a. between 1991 and 2005) against a market return of 12% p.a. This suggests that the generally poor performance of active managers is a function of the focus on relative performance.
- Physics envy is rife in finance. The need to reduce everything to a number bedevils our industry. Much like risk, diversification can't be simply summed up into a number. There is no 'optimal' number of stocks to hold. Investors would be well advised to scrap their optimizers and instead aim for what Keynes described as 'a balanced position, i.e. a variety of risks in spite of individual holdings being large, and if possible opposed risk'.

ON THE DANGERS OF 'NARROW' DIVERSIFICATION

Much damage in the world of finance has been committed in the name of diversification. It is often lauded as the one free lunch available to investors. However, it is all too often abused. For instance, one of the issues that LTCM faced was that all its trades were effectively 'convergence' trades. While the positions were 'diversified' across geographies and markets, they had a common feature of convergence. Thus when the markets underwent a period of marked divergence, LTCM found its careful 'diversification' exposed as a pipedream.

In the past, I have often criticized Value at Risk for embedding similar errors in its structure. The low trailing correlations (i.e. a high potential for 'diversification,) used are sadly all too illusory. As the old saying goes, the only thing that goes up in a bear market is correlation. Yet despite such obvious flaws the 'modern approach to risk management' was hailed by the great and the good as representing a major breakthrough. Witness Bernanke's comments in 2006: 'The treatment of market risk and credit risk has become increasingly sophisticated. . . Banking organizations of all sizes have made substantial strides over the past two decades in their ability to measure and manage risks.'

In the most recent financial meltdown, diversification once again played a part. As Bruce Jacobs (2009) notes in an article in the *Financial Analysts Journal*: 'Although the agencies looked at diversification among borrowers within mortgage pools, they did not pay attention to diversification among mortgage originators and securitizers. The downgrades of subprime RMBSs in July 2007 turned out to be concentrated in the hands of only four issuers'.

'Narrow-framing' (our habit of not seeing through the way in which information is presented to us) also raised it head with respect to the very different default rates observed between corporate bonds of a certain grade and the equivalently graded ABS. As Table 4.1 shows on investment grade assets (above Baa), the ABS were 10 times more likely to witness a default that the equivalently rated corporate bonds – and this data ends in 2006. Imagine what this might look like now!

In addition, no one appeared to give any thought to the unspoken risk that the US might just witness a nationwide housing market downturn. Greenspan noted that real estate was 'especially ill-suited to develop into a bubble' – seemingly ignoring the evidence from Japan's experience in the late 1980s, and the UK's recurring property bubble issues. Instead he said that the US housing market was characterized by 'a little froth'!

A misunderstanding of the endogenous nature of correlations also helps to explain investors' love of commodities in the 2003–2007 period. I have previously described this as the myth of

Table 4.1 Five-year rolling default rates

Rating	Corporate Bond (82-06)	ABS (93-06)	ABS default rates/Corporate bond default rate
AAA	0.1	0.9	9
AA	0.2	6	30
A	0.5	5	10
Baa	2.1	20.8	10
Ba	11.3	48	4
B	27.7	58	2
Caa	50.9	82.8	2

Source: Moody's, SG Global Strategy.

exogenous risk. The near fatal mistake that investors seem to make repeatedly is to assume that market risk is like roulette. In roulette, the odds are fixed and the actions of other players are irrelevant to your decision. Sadly, our world is more like playing poker. In poker, of course, your decisions are influenced by the behaviour you witness around you.

Thus the low trailing correlations of commodities with other asset classes were used to justify 'diversification'. However, participants forgot that their actions had an influence on the nature of the correlation. Indeed, those implementing their commodity strategies via futures also forgot that their actions had an impact on the structure of the market, driving many commodities into contango, ensuring a negative roll return.

Time and again, the dangers of an overly narrow definition of diversification have been shown to play a role in financial market disasters. Investors need to think much more carefully about the roll diversification plays in their portfolios.

EQUITY PORTFOLIOS: THE OTHER EXTREME

In contrast to the above discussion, many equity investors appear to be obsessed with diversification. The average US mutual fund holds somewhere between 100 and 160 stocks! This seems like an exceptionally large number of stocks for an active manager to hold.

As Warren Buffet opined: 'Wide diversification is only required when investors do not understand what they are doing'. The idea that you need 160 stocks to diversify is simply ludicrous. Figure 4.1 shows that diversification benefits can largely be achieved with 30–40 stock portfolios. That is to say, you can have a return profile with roughly the same volatility as the overall equity market by holding around 30–40 stocks. In order to create this chart we have used US data for the last 20 years, and we are assuming equal weighting.

An alternative perspective is provided by showing the percentage of non-market risk that is eliminated as the number of stocks in the portfolio increases. This is shown in Figure 4.2. Holding two stocks eliminates around 42% of the risk of owning just one stock; this is reduced by 68% by holding four stocks; by 83% by holding eight stocks; by 91% by holding 16 stocks; and by 96% by holding 32 stocks.

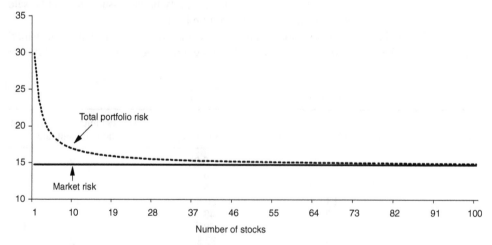

Figure 4.1 Diversification: total portfolio risk as a function of number of stocks held
Source: SG Global Strategy.

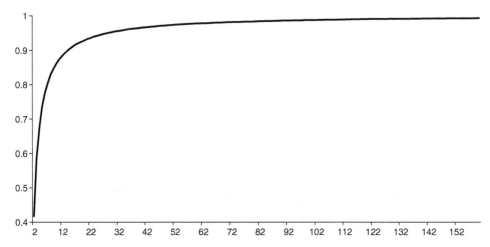

Figure 4.2 Percentage of non-market risk eliminated as a function of the number of stocks held
Source: SG Global Strategy.

Now, none of this is rocket science, so why does the average US mutual fund choose to hold nearly four times the number of stocks it needs to hold in order to meet diversification targets?

RELATIVE PERFORMANCE DERBY AS A SOURCE OF POOR PERFORMANCE!

The answer is, of course, that the average portfolio manager isn't concerned with total risk, but rather with risk measured relative to a performance benchmark (the index). This is a direct effect of what Seth Klarman so eloquently calls the 'short-term relative performance derby' that is fund management today.

Klarman describes most institutional investors 'like dogs chasing their own tails'. He continues: 'It is understandably difficult to maintain a long-term view when, faced with the penalties for poor short-term performance, the long-term view may well be from the unemployment line'. That said, he believes 'there is ample blame' for fund managers, consultants and end clients to share between them.

Klarman opines:

> There are no winners in the short-term, relative performance derby. Attempting to outperform the market in the short-term is futile... The effort only distracts a money manager from finding and acting on sound long-term opportunities... As a result, the clients experience mediocre performance... Only brokers benefit from the high level of activity.

Rather than worrying over absolute returns, the majority of professional investors while away their hours sweating over relative performance. To them, it isn't the total portfolio risk that matters, it is tracking error; and thus it is stock specific or idiosyncratic risk that matters most to such investors.

According to new research by Randy Cohen *et al.* (2009) the obsession with relative performance is one of the key sources of the generally poor performance of active managers. They examine the 'best ideas' of US managers over the period 1991–2005. 'Best Ideas' are

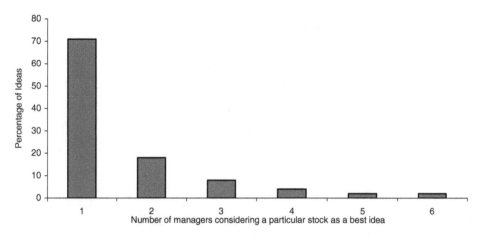

Figure 4.3   Overlap in best ideas (%)
Source: Cohen *et al.* (2009).

measured as the biggest difference between the managers' holdings and the weights in the index.

Interestingly, there isn't a massive degree of overlap between managers' best ideas. Cohen *et al.* find that 70% of best ideas do not overlap across managers. Less than 19% of best ideas are shared by two managers, and only 8% of best ideas overlap among three managers (Figure 4.3).

The performance of these best ideas is impressive. Focusing on the top 25% of best ideas across the universe of active managers, Cohen *et al.* find that average return is over 19% p.a. against a market return of 12% p.a.! That is to say, the stocks in which the managers display most confidence outperform the market by a significant degree. The corollary of this is that the other stocks they hold are dragging their performance down. Hence it appears that the focus on relative performance – and fear of underperformance against an arbitrary benchmark – is a key source of poor performance.

As Cohen *et al.* conclude, 'The poor overall performance of mutual fund managers in the past is not due to a lack of stock-picking ability, but rather to institutional factors that encourage them to overdiversify.' Or, as Sir John Templeton said, 'It is impossible to produce a superior performance unless you do something different from the majority.'

A (VERY SHORT) PRACTICAL GUIDE TO DIVERSIFICATION

Much like risk, diversification can't be simply summed up into a number. There is no 'optimal' number of stocks to hold. As Keynes opined:

> To suppose that safety-first consists in having a small gamble in a large number of different companies where I have no information to reach a good judgement, as compared to a substantial stake in a company where one's information is adequate, strikes me as a travesty of investment policy.

He also noted that one should aim for 'a balanced position, i.e. a variety of risks in spite of individual holdings being large, and if possible opposed risk.'

Gerald Loeb wrote the following on diversification in his ever insightful *The Battle for Investment Survival*:

> I think most accounts have entirely too much diversification of the wrong sort and not enough of the right sort. I can see no point at all in a distribution of so much per cent in oils, so much in motors, so much in rails etc.... This sort of thing might be necessary when capital reaches an unwieldy total, or it might be necessary where no intelligent supervision is likely. Otherwise, it is an admission of not knowing what to do and an effort to strike an average.

Loeb advised 'diversification between the position of varying companies in their business cycle or as between their shares in their market price cycle.'

As is often the case, Seth Klarman puts it best: speaking at the launch of the 6th edition of Graham and Dodd's *Security Analysis*, he opined:

> I think that when people make mistakes, it's often on both sides of diversification. And occasionally, new managers who aren't that experienced in the business will have a 20% position – or even two – in one portfolio. And those two positions might even be correlated – in the same industry – and represent the same exact kind of bet in two different names.
>
> Needless to say, that's absurdly concentrated – although it may not be if you have sufficient confidence and it's your own money. However, if you have clients, that's just not a good idea.
>
> On the other hand, I think 1% positions are too small to take advantage of what are usually relatively few great mispricings that you can find. When you find them, you need to step in and take advantage of them.

5

The Dangers of DCF*

Theoretically, discounted cash flow (DCF) is the correct way of valuing an asset. However, as Yogi Berra noted, 'In theory there is no difference between theory and practice. In practice there is.' The implementation of a DCF is riddled with problems. First off, we can't forecast, which kind of puts the kibosh on the whole exercise. Even if we choose to ignore this inconvenient truth, problems with the discount rate still make a mockery of the whole idea of DCF. No wonder DCF has such a poor reputation. The good news is that several alternatives exist. We explore three that avoid forecasting altogether!

- While the algebra of DCF is simple, neat and compelling, the implementation becomes a minefield of problems. The problems can be grouped into two categories: problems with estimating cash flows and problems with estimating discount rates.
- One of the recurring themes of my research is that we just can't forecast. There isn't a shred of evidence to suggest that we can. This, of course, doesn't stop everyone from trying. Last year, Rui Antunes of our quant team looked at the short-term forecasting ability of analysts. The results aren't kind to my brethren. The average 24-month forecast error is around 94%, the average 12-month forecast error is around 45%. My work on long-term forecasts is no kinder to the analysts: they are no better at forecasting long-term growth than they are short-term growth.
- Even if we ignore the inconvenient truth of our inability to forecast, we still get derailed by problems with the discount rate. The equity risk premium creates a headache, as no one seems to be able to agree what it is. Then we have all the fun and games over beta. Questions such as which time interval, which market, over what time period all have to be dealt with. And then you come up with a beta which unfortunately has no relationship with return at all (in direct contrast to classical theory).
- As if these problems weren't bad enough, they interact with each other when it comes to the terminal value calculation. In most DCFs this is the major contributor to the end value. If we assume a perpetual growth rate of 5% and a cost of capital of 9%, then the terminal multiple is $25\times$. However, if we are off by 1% on either or both of our inputs, then the terminal multiple can range from $16 \times$ to $50\times$!
- The good news is that we don't have to use DCF in this fashion. Alternatives do exist. For instance, using a reverse-engineered DCF avoids the need to forecast (and avoids anchoring on the current market price). Of course, the discount rate issues remain.

---

*This article appeared in Mind Matters on 9 September 2008. Copyright © 2008 by The Société Générale Group. All rights reserved. The material discussed was accurate at the time of publication.

- Ben Graham provided two methods for calculating intrinsic value. One based upon asset value, the other based upon earnings power (normalized earnings). Both of these methods can be implemented relatively easily and without the inherent problems of the DCF approach. Simpler, neater and more present-based (as opposed to forecast-based) methods are more likely to uncover opportunities with the markets. DCF should be consigned to the dustbin of theory, alongside the efficient markets hypothesis, and CAPM.

Ever since John Burr Williams wrote *The Theory of Investment Value*, we have known the correct way to value an asset is via the present value of its discounted cash flows. That is to say, an asset's value is nothing other than the sum of the cash flows that it can deliver (obviously discounted to reflect the impact of time). This is, of course, theoretically correct. However, as Yogi Berra opined, 'In theory there is no difference between theory and practice. In practice there is.'

When it comes to implementation, the DCF approach is riddled with problems. While the algebra of the DCF is simple and neat, when implemented, the DCF becomes a minefield of problems.

From my perspective, the problems with DCF-based valuations can be split into two groups: problems with estimating cash flows, and problems estimating the discount rates. Let's take each in turn.

Problems with Estimating Cash Flows

As regular readers will know, I believe that forecasting is a waste of time (see Chapter 9 of *Behavioural Investing* for the details). From the point of view of DCF, the forecasts are central. Most DCFs are based on relevant cash flows years into the future. However, there is no evidence that analysts are capable of forecasting either short-term or long-term growth.

Last year, Rui Antunes of our quant team investigated the scale of analysts' forecast errors over the short term. Rather than doing the analysis at the aggregate level, ever the pedant, Rui looked at the individual stock level.

Figure 5.1 shows the average scale of analysts' forecast errors over time. They start some two years before the actual reporting occurs, and trace out how the forecasts change as we head towards the announcements.

In the USA, the average 24-month forecast error is 93%, and the average 12-month forecast error is 47% over the period 2000–2006. Just in case you think this is merely the result of the

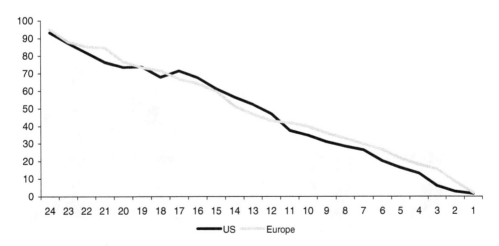

Figure 5.1   Forecast error over time: US and European markets 2001–2006
Source: SG Equity research.

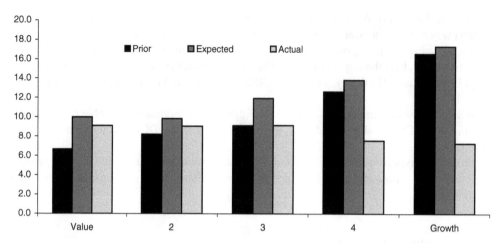

Figure 5.2   Growth: past, expected and actual (USA 1985–2007)
Source: SG Equity research.

recession in the early part of this decade, it isn't. Excluding those years makes essentially no difference at all.

The data for Europe is no less disconcerting. The average 24-month forecast error is 95%, and the average 12-month forecast error is 43%. Frankly, forecasts with this scale of error are totally worthless.

Long-term forecasts are no better. As I have shown many times before, analysts have no idea about long-term growth forecasts. As is shown in Figures 5.2 and 5.3, the inability to accurately assess growth is particularly pronounced where it is most important – in terms of the growth stocks.

In the USA, the portfolio of cheapest stocks on price to book (labelled 'value' in Figure 5.2) is expected to grow its earnings by around 10% p.a. according to the analysts. This is higher

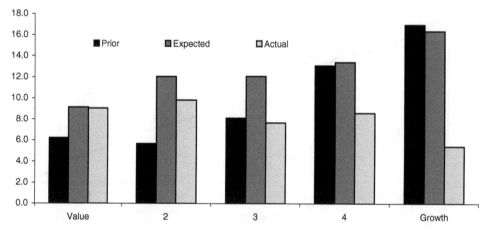

Figure 5.3   Growth: past, expected and actual (Europe 1985–2007)
Source: SG Equity research.

than the average growth rate of just 7% achieved in the prior five years. In terms of the actual growth that is delivered, these stocks generate an average of just over 9% – quite close to the analysts' forecasts.

At the other end of the spectrum we find a very different picture. Analysts expect growth stocks to generate around 17% p.a. (against a prior 16% p.a.). However, the actual delivered growth has been a meagre 7% p.a. on average!

The evidence for Europe looks very similar. Analysts expect the cheapest portfolio of stocks to grow earnings by around 9% p.a. over the long term. Once again, this is higher than the historically delivered growth of 6% on average in the prior five years. When it comes to how these value stocks actually perform in terms of earnings deliverance, they almost exactly match expectations, delivering around 9% p.a. over the long term.

Once again, the evidence at the other end of the spectrum is very different. Here analysts expect the growth stocks to deliver around 16% p.a. (close to the historical performance of 17% p.a.). In terms of the actual delivered growth, the most expensive stocks generate around 5% p.a. over the long term. So, regardless of market, it appears that analysts are most often wrong on the things they are most optimistic about!

As Bruce Greenwald observes in his wonderful book, *Value Investing: From Graham to Buffett and Beyond*, 'Profit margins and required investment levels, which are the foundations for cash flow estimates, are equally hard to project accurately into the far future.'

Problems with the Discount Rate

Not only is the estimation of the cash flows next to impossible, the estimation of the discount rate is also fraught with problems. The risk-free rate is the least controversial of the elements of the discount rate – most of us can agree that something like a long bond yield is quite a good approximation. However, thereafter everything goes to pot.

The equity risk premium is an arena of enormous disagreement. The text books generally use the ex post (after the fact) equity risk premium (ERP) which is substantially higher than any kind of measure of the ex ante ERP. Way back in 2001, Andy Lapthorne and I ran a survey of what our clients thought the ERP should be and, in general, a range of 3.5–4% was the outcome.

I've seen analysts use a nonsensical measure of the ERP – effectively an implied ERP. There is nothing wrong with using an implied ERP to evaluate the attraction of the overall market, but it makes no sense to then use this as an input into a stock valuation model, as you will end up with a circular outcome.

Even if everyone could agree on ERP, we need an estimate of beta (according to the classical approach). However, beta is bedevilled by issues. At least five issues have to be dealt with. Firstly, betas are inherently unstable. Fernandez (2004) calculated the betas of some 3,813 companies using 60-month returns each day from 1 December to 2 January. The median of the *maximum* betas recorded was three times greater than the median of the *minimum* betas recorded! Even when measured on an industry basis (rather than an individual stock basis) the maximum beta of an industry was nearly three times the minimum beta. Moves of 100 bps in beta value were not uncommon!

Second, betas depend significantly on the index used to calculate them against. Third, the beta also depends upon the time period used to derive the estimate, i.e. do we use 6 months, 52 weeks, or 36 months of back history. Fourth, the interval of return estimation also makes

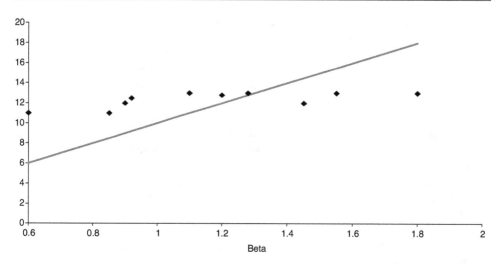

Figure 5.4   US portfolio returns by beta decile (1923–2003) % p.a.
Source: Fama and French (2004). SG Equity research.

a big difference to beta estimates. Betas based on daily returns are often very different from betas based on monthly, or quarterly data (Figure 5.4).

Finally, the biggest hurdle to using beta is the fact that it simply doesn't work. As I have shown before, far from the positive relationship predicted by theory, there is actually no (perhaps even an inverse) relationship between beta and returns (see Chapter 2 for more on the uselessness of CAPM).

INTERACTION PROBLEMS

The final problem from my perspective in the DCF calculations concerns the interaction of these previous two sets of problems. Almost every DCF is closed out with a terminal value calculation. This involves taking our 10-year forecasts and estimating a growth rate from year 10 to forever, then capitalizing this via a multiple.

Very small alterations in the underlying assumptions generate enormous differences in outcomes. If future perpetual growth is 5% and the future cost of capital is 9%, then the terminal value multiple is 25×. If the estimates are off by only 1% in either direction for either the cost of capital, the growth or both, the terminal value multiple can range from 50× to 16×. Given that the terminal value is often the biggest contribution to the DCF, these issues are non-negligible (Figure 5.5).

ALTERNATIVES

Sensitivity analysis is often presented as a solution to the problems inherent within the practical application of the DCF methodology. However, while this has the admirable benefit of making the uncertainty of the DCF transparent, it also has the potential to render the DCF useless, as the output from sensitivity analysis can easily justify any recommendation.

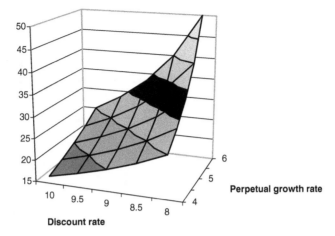

Figure 5.5 Terminal multiple in DCF as a function of the perpetual growth and discount rate
Source: SG Equity research.

Reverse-engineered DCF

So, if one can't use DCF, how should one think about valuation? Well, one solution that I have long favoured is the use of reverse-engineered DCFs. Instead of trying to estimate the growth 10 years into the future, this method takes the current share price and backs out what is currently implied. The resulting implied growth estimate can then be assessed either by an analyst or by comparing the estimate with an empirical distribution of the growth rates that have been achieved over time, such as is shown in Figures 5.6 and 5.7. This allows one to assess how likely or otherwise the implied growth rate actually is.

Of course, this model solves the problem of not being able to forecast the future, but it doesn't tackle the discount rate problems outlined above. We still need an estimate of cost of capital. My own approach to this is to set an ERP of around 4% and take a guess as to the

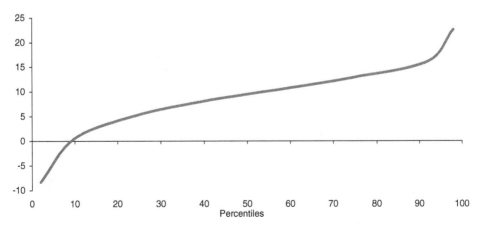

Figure 5.6 Distribution of growth in operating income before depreciation over 10 years (USA 1951–1998)
Source: Chan *et al.*, SG Equity research.

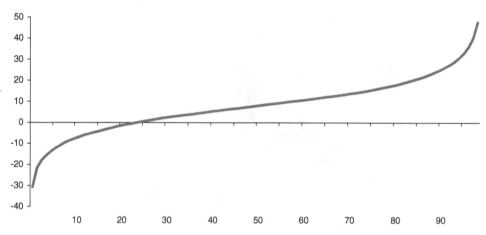

Figure 5.7 Distribution of growth in EBIT over 10 years (Europe 1990–2007)
Source: SG Equity research.

beta of the stock – which reflects my own arbitrary judgement of the fundamental risk of the business.

When I am teaching on behavioural bias, I often use the reverse-engineered DCF approach as an example of avoiding the common pitfall of anchoring in the context of valuation. All too often, I have seen analysts return from company meetings raving about the management and working themselves into a lather over the buying opportunity this stock represents. They then proceed to create a DCF that fulfils the requirements of a buy recommendation (i.e. 15% upside, say). They have effectively become anchored to the current price. When a reverse-engineered DCF is deployed this obsession with the current price is removed, as the discussion now takes place in terms of growth potential.

Asset Value

As ever in matters of investment, when confused it pays to return to the words of Ben Graham. He suggested two ways of approaching valuation. The first was asset based, and effectively represents a liquidation value for the firm. As Graham wrote, 'The first rule in calculating liquidating value is that the liabilities are real but the assets are of questionable value.' In order to reflect this, Graham suggested some rough rules of thumb for the value of assets (see Table 5.1).

Table 5.1 Percentage of liquidating value to book value

Type of assets	Normal range	Rough average
Current Assets:		
Cash assets (and marketable securities)	100	100
Receivables (less usual reserves)	79–90	80
Inventories (at lower of cost or market)	50–75	66 2/3
Fixed assets and Misc		
Real Estate, buildings, machinery, equipment, intangibles	1–50	15 (approx)

Source: Graham and Dodd (1934), *Security Analysis*.

Of course, if this is a strict fire sale, items such as intangibles have no worth at all. If, however, the business is being sold as a going concern, then intangibles have some value. Graham himself, obviously, preferred only working with current assets, and then deducting all liabilities to generate the famous net-nets of which he was so fond. Note the absence of forecasting in the asset value approach.

Earnings Power

The second method Graham favoured was what he called earnings power. He opined that 'What the investor chiefly wants to learn. . . is the indicated earnings power under the given set of conditions, i.e. what the company might be expected to earn year after year if the business conditions prevailing during the period were to continue unchanged'. He continued,

> It combines a statement of actual earnings, shown over a period of years, with a reasonable expectation that these will be approximated in the future, unless extraordinary conditions supervene. The record must over a number of years, first because a continued or repeated performance is always more impressive than a single occurrence, and secondly because the average of a fairly long period will tend to absorb and equalize the distorting influences of the business cycle.

Once earnings power has been computed it can either be capitalized at the cost of capital to give an estimate of value, or it can be compared to the price to generate a PE of sorts which Graham suggested should be no more than 'sixteen times' because that 'Is as high a price as can be paid in an investment purchase of a common stock. . . ten times earnings ratio is suitable for the typical case'.

Such an approach can be relatively easily operationalized. The method I use is to take an average EBIT margin over a reasonable time period (5 to 10 years), then multiply this by the average sales over the last 5 years, say. This gives me a normalized EBIT. Then I subtract interest payments and remove taxes to end up with an estimate of earnings power – all done without any of the messiness of forecasting!

These methods have been extended and refined by many over the years. For a full introduction to a value-oriented approach to asset valuation I can do no better than once again refer the reader to Bruce Greenwald's insightful book which details a modern take of these timeless approaches and extends them into the realm of franchise value as well.

So here we have at least three methods of valuing an equity, none of which requires us to leap through the same hoops as the DCF. While the DCF approach is the only theoretically correct approach to valuation, the assumptions and forecasts it requires for implementation remain a task beyond Hercules himself. Simpler, neater and more present (as opposed to forecast) based methods are far more likely to lead us to uncovering the opportunities within the markets, or at the very least stop us from falling victim to undue optimism.

6

Is Value Really Riskier than Growth?
Dream On*

Is value riskier than growth? This simple question lies at the heart of one the most contentious debates in modern finance. The zealots of market efficiency argue that the value premium must be the result of investors taking on fundamental risk. The behaviouralists argue that value outperforms because investors regularly make mistakes such as overpaying for growth. Looking at a wide variety of measures of risk we find that value stocks are no riskier (and often less risky) than growth stocks. The risk-based explanation of the value premium is as vapid and useless as the rest of the efficient markets hypothesis.

- As regular readers of my work will know I am a major advocate of a behavioural approach to markets. However, in an effort to practise what I preach and avoid confirmatory bias, I have decided to see if I can find any evidence of the value premium being driven by risk factors, as claimed by fans of the efficient market view of the world.
- At the most basic level, finance theorists equate risk with standard deviation. I believe this to be ludicrous. However, suspending my disbelief and using their measures I find that value stocks have generally had higher returns and lower risks than growth stocks. This is a direct violation of the basic tenet of classical finance that risk and return should be related.
- Not to be easily dissuaded from their faith in the efficient markets hypothesis (EMH), the believers then turn to beta, and say that value stocks must have a higher beta. Once again the evidence is contrary to their beliefs. In fact value stocks tend to have a lower beta than growth stocks. Another blow to the EMH.
- Ah, comes the response from the EMH camp, the risks associated with value stocks are only really apparent during periods of generally poor market conditions. When presented with the empirical evidence, this line of EMH defence crumbles as well. For instance, in the worst 10 months between 1950 and 2007, the stock market was down an average 13% p.m., value stocks were down around 12.5% p.m., and growth stocks were down almost 18% p.m.!
- Seemingly totally unwilling to throw in the towel, the EMH diehards then have to fall back on arguing that value stocks do worse in economic downturns. Once again this appears to be a dubious argument when confronted with the data. For instance, using the probability of a recession from the Wright model (based on the slope of the yield curve and level of short-term rates), when a recession is likely, the value premium (the outperformance of value over growth) is nearly 8% p.a. This is not vastly different from the 10% seen during times of expansion.

- Much as fans of the EMH would love us all to believe that value tends to outperform because it is riskier, there is virtually no evidence that this is actually the case. Over a wide range of measures, value appears to be no riskier (and often less risky) than growth. The risk-based explanations of the value premium are as hollow and as meaningless as the rest of EMH.

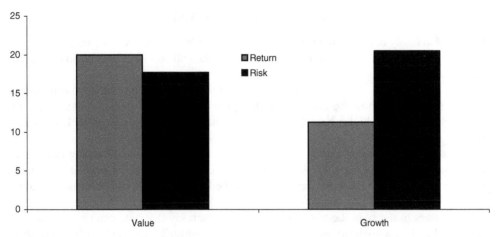

Figure 6.1   US value and growth returns and risk (% p.a. 1950–2007)
Source: SG Equity research.

Is value riskier than growth? This simple question lies at the heart of one of the most contentious debates in modern finance. The high priests of market efficiency argue that anything that outperforms over the long term must be a risk premium, because in their world risk and return are intimately related.

They tend to go strangely quiet when presented with evidence to show that risk and return aren't closely correlated (see Chapter 2). The alternative hypothesis is that the value premium is driven by the mistakes that investors make. As regular readers will know, I am an ardent proponent of this latter view.

However, in an effort to practise what I preach and avoid confirmatory bias I am going to examine the evidence for the efficient market hypothesis (EMH). That is to say, I am going to look to see if risk really does explain the outperformance of value over time.

RISK I: STANDARD DEVIATION

Let's start at the beginning. According to classical finance, the standard deviation is the appropriate measure of risk. Now this has always struck me as being clearly ludicrous. I've been doing this job for a long time now, and I've yet to meet a long-only fund manager who worries about upside surprise (see Chapter 37 of *Behavioural Investing* for more on this). However, suspending my disbelief over the sense of the measure, Figure 6.1 shows the return and risk of value and growth stocks.

For the purpose of this chapter I've used portfolios based on the cash flow to price in the USA[1]. The extreme most expensive 20% of the market has been labelled 'Growth', the cheapest 20% labelled 'Value'. As the figure shows, over the long term value stocks have enjoyed both higher returns and lower risk than growth stocks! Bad news for the EMH followers.

---

[1] The data I have used come via Ken French's website http://mba.tuck.dartmouth.edu/pages/faculty/ken.french/data_library.html.

RISK II: CAPM BETA AND CO.

Not to be so easily defeated, the EMH followers fall back on their favourite measure of risk: beta. After all if value has a higher beta than growth, then all is well in EMH land (well, kind of anyway).

Once again the evidence provides a challenge to the risk-based view of the value premium. Figures 6.2 and 6.3 show the 36-month rolling beta for value and growth. On average, the growth portfolio has a higher beta than the value portfolio. Not exactly what the EMH would predict.

To make the relationship crystal clear, Figure 6.3 shows the 36-month rolling beta on the long value/short growth portfolio. It is easy to see that on average the spread portfolio has a negative beta. Even on the rare occasions when the beta has been positive, it has remained minuscule (and statistically insignificant).

Never ones to throw in the towel, the EMH fans then say that beta can be time varying. Perhaps the risks associated with value stocks are only really apparent during periods of generally poor market conditions, they argue. According to this view, value stocks would be fundamentally riskier than growth stocks if (i) they underperform growth stocks in some states of the world, *and* if (ii) those states of the world are on average 'bad', during which the marginal utility of wealth is high. This would therefore make value stocks unattractive to risk-averse investors.

Figure 6.4 shows the upside and downside beta of value and growth. Contrary to the arguments above, the value beta is indistinguishable from the growth beta during down markets.

As a check, Table 6.1 shows the performance of value and growth stocks in various periods of market distress. In the 10 worst months (between 1950 and 2007) for the market as a whole, value did better than the market, and much better than growth stocks. This pattern holds as we include more and more negative months. So there is no evidence that value stocks are systematically more risky than growth stocks in periods of market problems. This is another blow to the EMH fans.

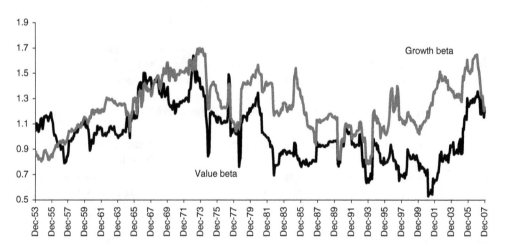

Figure 6.2   36-month rolling beta on US value and growth portfolios
Source: SG Equity research.

Figure 6.3   36-month rolling beta on US value minus growth
Source: SG Equity research.

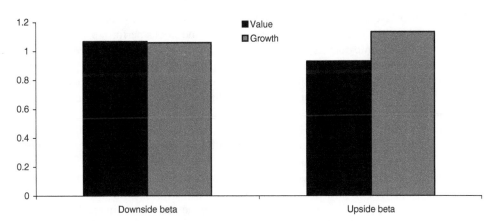

Figure 6.4   Upside and downside beta (USA, 1950–2007)
Source: SG Equity research.

Table 6.1   Average performance in periods of market distress (% p.m.)

	Mkt	Value	Glamour
Worst 10 months	−13.1	−12.5	−17.9
Worst 20 months	−10.9	−10.6	−14.2
Worst 30 months	−9.6	−8.9	−12.4
All negative months	−3.4	−2.2	−4.0

Source: SG Equity research.

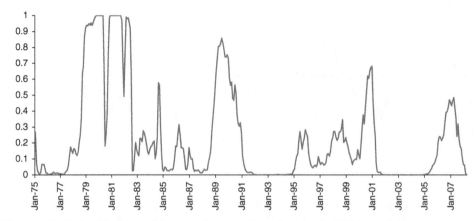

Figure 6.5   Probability of recession over the next 12 months from the Wright model
Source: SG Equity research.

RISK III: BUSINESS CYCLE RISK

With two of their favoured measures of risk falling dead by the roadside, those still marching to the beat of the EMH drum are forced to argue that value stocks perform particularly badly during times of economic distress, i.e. recessions.

So we now need ways of measuring recessions. Our first choice was the probability of recession as derived from the Wright model. This combines the slope of the yield curve and the level of fed funds to give an estimated probability of recession over the next 12 months (see Figure 6.5).

According to the 'value is risk' believers, value should do particularly badly in times of recession. However, as Table 6.2 shows, value still outperforms growth even in times of recession. The value portfolio has earned around 13% p.a. in recessions, and about 22% p.a. in expansions. The growth portfolio has earned 5% p.a. in recessions, and 17% p.a. in expansions, so value has outperformed growth by over 7.5% p.a. in expansions, and by nearly 10% p.a. in recessions. Therefore, there is no sign of value doing particularly badly in recessions here!

As a check we decided to look at the relationship between forecasts of GDP and value returns (Figure 6.6). This raises a slight problem as economists have never managed to forecast a recession! So we obviously can't use the actual forecast of a recession. Instead we have used two different approaches. The first is to look at the performance of value stocks when the GDP growth forecast is less than 2%. Table 6.3 shows the breakdown of returns when this approach is used.

Table 6.2   Does value underperform in recessions? (% p.m.) (1975–2007)

	Average probability of recession	Value	Growth	Spread
Recession (Prob >30%)	0.70	1.09	0.45	0.64
Expansion (Prob <30%)	0.08	2.22	1.42	0.81

Source: SG Equity research.

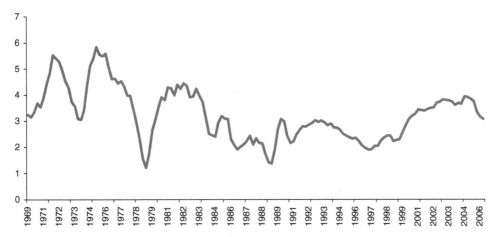

Figure 6.6   Consensus forecasts of US GDP growth 12 months ahead – never spotted a recession yet!
Source: SG Equity research.

Once again no evidence of value stock underperformance during tough economic conditions can be uncovered. Value stocks earn roughly the same regardless of forecasts. However, growth stocks do better than usual when low growth is forecast, but value stocks still outperform them!

Just in case you think there is something magical about the use of a 2% cut-off, Table 6.4 repeats the exercise but this time simply looking to see if the GDP forecast is above or below average (3.2% p.a.). Once again we can find no evidence suggesting that value underperforms during period of economic weakness. Regardless of the state of the economy, value stocks tend to outperform growth stocks.

Models from classical economics that justify the value premium as a result of business cycle risk are known as conditional CAPM models (i.e. the beta is conditional upon the state of the world). A simple test of these models can be formulated as follows:

$$\text{Value premium} = a + b \text{ Market return} + c \text{ (Market return} \times \text{ Variable of interest)}$$

The interaction term accounts for the extra return arising from the covariation of the value beta with the expected return on the market. Thus, comparing the alpha from the above with a standard CAPM alpha should reveal the amount of value premium that is generated by sensitivity to the economic cycle. Figure 6.7 shows the alpha calculated from a couple of such models. The first estimates the monthly alpha of the value premium from a standard CAPM regression (around 12% p.a.). The next two columns show the alpha after controlling for the Wright model and a recession dummy variable respectively. As can be clearly seen, the alpha

Table 6.3   Performance over the next 12 months (%)

	Mkt	Glamour	Value	Spread
GDP forecast <2	20.1	16.6	22.0	4.5
GDP forecast >2	17.0	10.9	22.5	10.9

Source: SG Equity research.

Table 6.4   Performance over the next 12 months (%)

	Mkt	Glamour	Value	Spread
GDP forecast below average	15.0	9.5	18.5	8.5
GDP forecast above average	20.1	14.1	27.2	12.2

Source: SG Equity research.

does not change. Effectively this tells us that the recession variables account for none of the value premium – confirming the previous analysis!

A recent paper by Petkova and Zhang (2005) claims to find that value stocks are indeed riskier than growth stocks. They use a conditional CAPM model with the state of the economy proxied by the default premium (credit spread), the term premium (the slope of the yield curve), the dividend yield and the short-term interest rate. They explain their choice of variables as 'standard from the time-series predictability literature'. This is tantamount to a confession of data mining; they selected their variables based on prior evidence of their predicted returns.

Cooper and Gubellini (2007) investigate the robustness of the Petkova and Zhang findings. They use a far wider range of conditioning variables, including many that are much better correlated with the business cycle than those used by Petkova and Zhang, such as industry production and leading indicators. Using some 2,047 possible specifications of conditioning variables they find that value is not riskier than growth in 90% of the cases! In other words, the findings of Petkova and Zhang appear to be the result of data mining, and represent nothing other than chance.

Much as fans of the EMH would love us all to believe that value tends to outperform because it is riskier, there is virtually no evidence that this is actually the case. Over a wide range of measures value appears to be no riskier (and often less risky) than growth. The risk-based explanations of the value premium are as hollow and as meaningless as the rest of EMH.

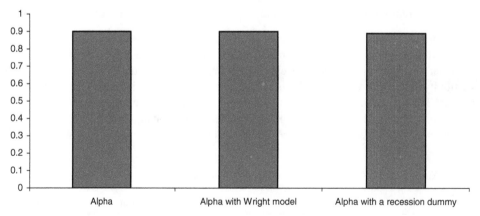

Figure 6.7   Alpha (% p.m.)
Source: SG Equity research.

7

Deflation, Depressions and Value[*]

One of the hallmarks of a post-bubble world is a greater degree of synchronization between the economic cycle and the stock market. For investors in the aggregate market this means that one can afford to sit back and wait for the cyclical lead indicators to turn. Does the same apply to value investing? The evidence from Japan suggests not. Following a simple long value/short glamour strategy allows one to be even 'lazier', and simply keep plodding away, ignoring any timing considerations. However, a very different outcome is shown during the Great Depression. During this period, nothing worked, you simply didn't want to be in equities!

- I have long argued that one of the key features of a post-bubble world is a tighter synchronization between the economic and equity cycles. This is powered by a change in the drivers of returns from multiple expansion (during the bubble years) to growth (in the post-bubble environment). Any failure of this growth means that investors de-rate equities as an asset class.
- The tighter synchronization of the economic and equity cycles means that investors in the overall market can afford to sit back and wait for the cyclical lead indicators to turn up to tell them when to return to the market. Does this also apply to value investors? In Ben Graham's terms, do we need to worry about *timing* as well as *pricing*? To assess this, I have looked at the experience of value during both the Japanese post-bubble world and the Great Depression.
- The Japanese experience suggests that value investors need not concern themselves with any form of market timing. Despite the pronounced cyclicality of the Japanese market, value strategies have plodded along nicely (a return of 3% p.a. vs a market return of −4% p.a.). An even more impressive performance is available to those who short. A long value/short glamour strategy has generated 12% p.a. in the post-bubble world!
- A very different picture is painted by the experience of the Great Depression. During this period, owning equities of any variety was a very poor idea. Value, growth and the market all did particularly poorly. The difference between the two episodes is the scale and depth of the events in question. In the Great Depression, the USA witnessed a 50% decline in industrial production from peak to trough. Consumer prices fell by almost 9% p.a. for three years. In contrast, for the last two decades, Japanese industrial production and inflation have been essentially flat.

---

[*]This article appeared in Mind Matters on 3 March 2009. Copyright © 2009 by The Société Générale Group. All rights reserved. The material discussed was accurate at the time of publication.

- Looking forward, at least three possible paths can be easily envisaged. The optimistic path (in which the stimulus plans work and the Fed manages to create inflation), the Japanese route (a protracted workout with low growth and low inflation), and the Great Depression II. In the first two outcomes, value should do well. In the third, holding any equity is likely to be a poor decision. Since I don't know which of these paths is more likely, I continue to believe that a slow steady deployment of capital into deep value opportunities in the face of market weakness is the most sensible option.

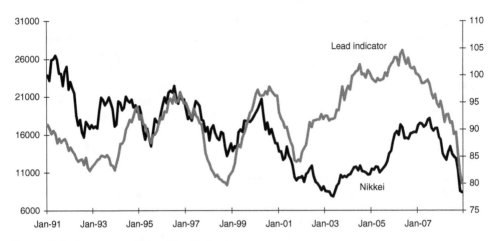

Figure 7.1   Japanese market and lead indicator
Source: SG Global Strategy.

I have long argued that one of the hallmarks of a post-bubble stock market is a greater degree of synchronization between the economic cycle and the stock market – witness the chart on Japan (Figure 7.1).

The reason for this increased synchronization is the role of the drivers of return. Effectively, your equity return can be split into contributions from three sources: the purchase price in terms of valuation, the growth of the underlying business, and any change in valuation multiples.

Figure 7.2 is one that I have used many times over the years. It performs a decomposition of US real returns into their component sources. Over the long term, very little of the investors' total real return has been driven by changes in multiple (only around 6%). However, in the long bull market this rose to 55%, and in the 1990s reached a staggering 75%!

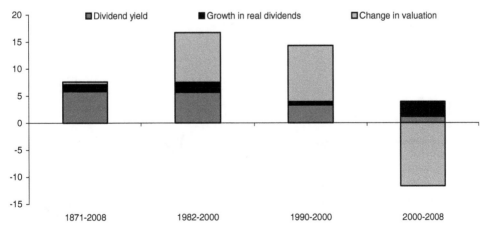

Figure 7.2   US total return decomposition
Source: SG Global strategy.

In the last decade a very different story has unfolded. Given the low starting dividend yield, investors were totally dependent on growth to generate their returns. Hence the market tends to sync up with economic growth that much more in a post-bubble world. Of course, when that growth disappears, investors force the multiples down to restore the valuation support.

Perhaps this allows investors the option of being lazy, and not having to get back into equities until evidence of a cyclical turn has occurred. This got me thinking: What does this all mean for value investing? Do value investors have to become more tactical in post-bubble environments?

Ben Graham noted

> Since common stocks, even of investment grade, are subject to recurrent and wide fluctuations in their prices, the intelligent investor should be interested in the possibilities of profiting from these pendulum swings. There are two possible ways by which he may try to do this: the way of *timing* and the way of *pricing*. By timing we mean the endeavour to anticipate the action of the stock market – to buy or hold when the future course is deemed to be upwards, to sell or refrain from buying when the course is downwards. By pricing we mean the endeavour to buy stocks when they are quoted below their fair value and to sell them when they rise above such value.

So, in Graham's terms, do value investors have to concern themselves more with timing (as well as pricing) in a post-bubble environment? In order to assess these questions I decided to investigate how value strategies performed in a couple of post-bubble experiences to see if they offer any guidance on the best way to invest from a value perspective.

VALUE AND JAPAN

The evidence suggests that while it may make sense to be lazy and wait for the turn from a market perspective, this isn't the case from a value perspective. Figures 7.3–7.5 tell the story. The first shows the returns to a buy and hold investor in Japan since their bubble burst. Not a pretty picture. The need to take a more tactical approach with respect to owning equities as an asset class is self-evident.

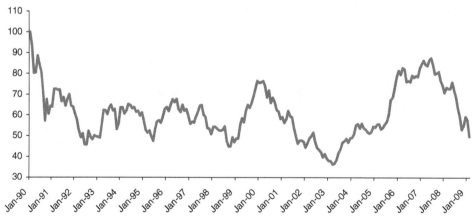

Figure 7.3 Buy and hold returns to Japanese equities ($ terms, 1990 = 100)
Source: SG Global Strategy.

Figure 7.4 Value vs the market (Japan, $ terms, 1990 = 100)
Source: SG Global Strategy.

However, Figure 7.4 adds in the returns to simply buying the cheapest stocks based on price to book (long only). Those following a value approach in Japan didn't even have to worry about trying to time the market: they could effectively be even lazier and just keep buying the cheap stocks. Such an approach has generated a return of 3% p.a. vs a market return of −4% p.a. (1990–2007).

For those with an ability to short, the returns were even more impressive. Figure 7.5 shows the advantage a long/short strategy can offer in this kind of world. The return achieved by following a long value/short glamour strategy in Japan's post-bubble world is an impressive 12% p.a. Thus the Japanese market's poor performance is largely a function of poorly performing 'glamour stocks.'

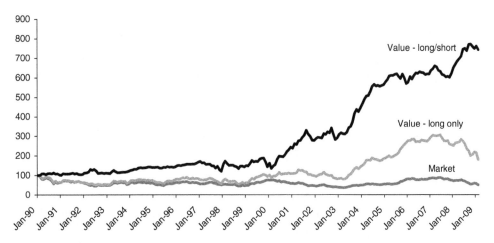

Figure 7.5 The advantage of the short side ($ terms, 1990 = 100)
Source: SG Global Strategy.

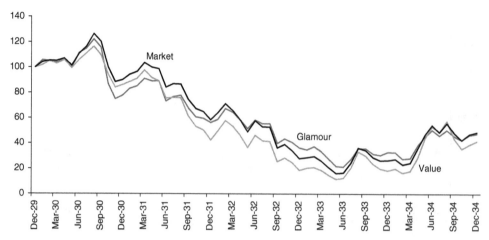

Figure 7.6 You don't want to hold equities into a depression! (USA, December 1929 = 100)
Source: Ken French, SG Global Strategy.

VALUE AND THE GREAT DEPRESSION

An alternative 'stress test' of the performance of value is to examine events during the Great Depression. I have used the data from Ken French's website to explore this issue. As Figure 7.6 shows, value wasn't a good strategy during the Great Depression, but neither was growth, or indeed the market overall. The bottom line is that in a world in which nominal GDP is halving you probably don't want to own equities (which doesn't seem much like rocket science to me).

This indiscriminate nature of equity performance during the Great Depression is confirmed by a recent study from Bridgewater Associates (2009). They note:

> While the earnings performance of individual companies and sectors varied widely, the dominant force on equity performance was the widening in risk premiums related to the financial deleveraging. With respect to earnings, the best 20 performing large companies sailed through the depression relatively unscathed. Their earnings were roughly flat from the peak in 1929 until the bottom in 1933. On the other hand, the earnings of the worst 20 performing large companies fell so much that the losses were nearly as big as the prior profits. Despite this radical difference in earnings performance, the prices of the best 20 and worst 20 earning companies fell by similar amounts, −80% for the best and −96% for the worst.

WHY THE DIFFERENCE BETWEEN THE GREAT DEPRESSION AND JAPAN?

The Great Depression was truly an economic Armageddon. The USA witnessed a 50% decline in industrial production from peak to trough, wholesale prices fell 10% p.a. for three years, and consumer prices fell by almost 9% p.a. for three years. Against this backdrop, it is not hard to see why one wouldn't want to own equities.

In contrast, in Japan the post-bubble environment has been much more moderate. Inflation has averaged somewhere close to zero since the bubble burst. Excluding the very recent implosion of Japanese industrial production (in the last three months), the series would have been essentially flat over the last two decades.

These two very different economic environments have very different implications for value investors. Value seems able to cope with the prolonged workout that characterized the Japanese experience. In contrast, in an environment like the Great Depression nothing really works very well.

Looking forward, at least three possible scenarios can easily be envisaged:

• The optimistic path – the stimulus package works, and the Fed manages to create inflation – good for value equities.
• The Japanese route – a protracted workout, with low growth and low inflation – good for value strategies, especially long/short strategies.
• The Great Depression II – economic and financial Armageddon descend upon us – not good for any equities.

I don't have got a clue which of these paths is most likely. Like any sane mortal I pray that it isn't the last. Perhaps we can take some succour from the fact that policymakers may have learned from some of the mistakes in the 1930s experience (such as raising rates to stay on the gold standard).

However, it is far from clear that the US authorities have learned the lessons from Japan. It appears as if policy is being made on the hoof (as one friend of mine put it, we are living in an adhocracy now!). As Adam Posen (a US economist who has carefully studied the Japanese experience) puts it:

> The guarantees that the US government has already extended to the banks in the last year, and the insufficient (though large) capital injections without government control or adequate conditionality also already given under Troubled Assets Relief Program (TARP), closely mimic those given by the Japanese government in the mid-1990s to keep their major banks open without having to recognize specific failures and losses. The result then, and the emerging result now, is that the banks' top management simply burns through that cash, socializing the losses for the taxpayer, grabbing any rare gains for management payouts or shareholder dividends, and the banks end up still undercapitalized. Pretending that distressed assets are worth more than they actually are today for regulatory purposes persuades no one besides the regulators, and just gives the banks more taxpayer money to spend down, and more time to impose a credit crunch.
>
> These kinds of half-measures to keep banks open rather than disciplined are precisely what the Japanese Ministry of Finance engaged in from the time when their bubble burst in 1992 through to 1998, and over that period the cost to the Japanese economy from bad lending quadrupled from 5 percent to over 20 percent of Japanese GDP. In addition, this 'convoy' system, as the Japanese officials called it, punished any better-capitalized and -managed banks that remained by making it difficult for them to distinguish themselves in the market; falsely pumping up the apparent viability of bad banks will do that. That in turn eroded the incentive of the better and more viable banks to engage in good lending behaviour versus self-preservation and angling for government protection.

However, if the Japanese experience is the right template for investors (or indeed if the stimulus package and Fed policy response work), then value investors have little to fear.

Ultimately, as Keynes said when asked about the future, 'We simply do not know.' I have no idea which of these paths is the more likely outcome. In the face of this ignorance, a slow steady deployment of capital into deep value opportunities each time Mr Market presents them seems like the most sensible path to me.

To me this represents a regret minimization approach – I end up with some exposure, and I'm dollar cost averaging down if this turns out to be the Great Depression II. Alternatively, if the stimulus works, or the USA follows the Japanese example, then as Jeremy Grantham says: 'If stocks look attractive and you don't buy them and they run away, you don't just look like an idiot, you are an idiot.'

Part II
The Behavioural Foundations of Value Investing

8

Learn to Love Your Dogs, or, Overpaying for the Hope of Growth (Again!)*

The promise of growth has a seductive allure, much like the siren's song. However, it rarely pays for investors to do what feels comfortable. For instance, star stocks (those with good historic and forecast growth) have underperformed dogs (poor past and forecast growth) by around 6% p.a.! While good stories are entertaining, they aren't a substitute for a proper investment process. Investors would do well to learn to love the dogs and shun the darlings. The market's current love affair with all things mining related may well prove to be yet another example of overpaying for the hope of growth.

- While the zealots of market efficiency would like us to believe that value outperforms because it is riskier than growth, those of us working in the behavioural field tend to think it stems from investors persistently overpaying for the hope of growth. Recently, we showed that the risk-based explanations for the value premium didn't stand up to scrutiny. The behavioural evidence looks much stronger (but I am biased!).
- If investors regularly overpay for the hope of growth, then we should see star stocks (those with past and forecast high growth) underperform dog stocks (those with low past and forecast growth). This is exactly the pattern found in the data. In general, dogs outperform stars by around 6% p.a. – not bad since we have ignored explicit valuation measures.
- It might seem unusual for me to be using analysts' expectations of long-term growth in my analysis. However, I often find that the growth implied from, say, a reverse-engineered DDM model is close to the analysts' long-term forecast. This isn't a huge shock since analysts often use their long-term growth forecasts to justify their target prices and hence recommendations. Strangely enough, target price and market price are often closely correlated, as analysts seem to be short-term momentum players.
- The habit of overpaying for growth is clearly demonstrated when valuation is included in the analysis. For instance, analysts expect value stocks to deliver around 9% p.a. over the long term (on average). The goods news for value investors is that they generally do deliver something close. However, the analysts expect growth stocks to deliver around 16% p.a. earnings growth over the long term. This doesn't compare well with the reality of around 5% p.a. delivered earnings growth! Disappointment doesn't sit well with expensive stocks.
- Perhaps the best current example of overpaying for the hope of growth is the mining sector. Despite earnings being massively above trend, analysts expect future earnings to continue

---

on an exponential path. A simple implied perpetuity growth rate model shows that mining would have to grow twice as fast as the economy forever more just to justify current prices! Investors and analysts clearly believe that 'This time is different.' Unfortunately those words have so far always been synonymous with overpaying for the hope of growth.

Table 8.1 Distribution of dogs and stars

	Low	Expected growth	High
Low	Dogs USA 7% Europe 5%		Old dogs, new tricks USA 4% Europe 6%
Past sales growth High	Fallen angels USA 1.5% Europe 7%		Stars USA 11% Europe 9%

Source: SG Global Strategy research.

Anyone who has sat through one of my presentations (poor souls) will have heard me ranting over the most persistent error I encounter, the willingness to overpay for the hope of growth. In this chapter, I wish to explore this error at the stock level, and provide yet another example of this error from the current market environment.

If you like, this chapter can be seen as my attempt to put the case for the behavioural explanation of value outperformance; as such it is the sister of Chapter 6 which showed that the risk-based explanations of the value premium were as vapid and meaningless as the rest of the efficient market hypothesis.

OF DOGS AND STARS

Let's start by examining the evidence that suggests that investors get too carried away with the hope of growth. Scott *et al.* (1999) suggested a simple taxonomy of stocks based around the interaction of the past and expected future growth rates, as shown below.

The four corners of Tables 8.1 and 8.2 provide the areas of interest to us. Stars are stocks that have both high historic growth (as measured by past five years' sales growth), and high forecast growth (as measured by analysts' long-term growth expectations from IBES). They tend to be the market darlings of the day.

Dogs are the diametric opposite of the stars. These stocks have low historic growth, and everyone has given up on them, hence they have low expected future growth as well. According

Table 8.2 Return performance (% p.a.) (USA 1985–2007, mkt = 13.4% p.a., Europe 1988–2007, mkt = 14.3% p.a.)

	Low	Expected growth	High
Low	Dogs USA 14.9% Europe 19.5%		Old dogs, new tricks USA 13.2% Europe 14.9%
Past sales growth High	Fallen angels USA 13.2% Europe 12.2%		Stars USA 9.9% Europe 12.4%

Source: SG Global Strategy research.

to the conventional wisdom, no one in their right mind would want to own stocks with dog-like characteristics.

While most stocks can be found along the diagonal from dogs to stars, the two extreme off-diagonal cells contain stocks that might be said to be either 'old dogs with new tricks' (that is, stocks with low past growth, but higher expected future growth), or 'fallen angels' (these are stocks with high past growth, but low expected growth). Table 8.1 gives the percentage of stocks that end up in the four cells of interest to us for the USA and Europe.

If investors regularly overpay for growth then we should see the stars underperform the market and the dogs. This is exactly what we do observe. Table 8.2 shows the annual performance of the various categories. Consistent with the idea that investors overpay for the hope of growth, the stars turn out to be disappointing relative to both the dogs and the overall market (underperforming by 6% and 3% respectively). This result is all the more impressive since it ignores explicit valuation considerations (obviously there is an implicit valuation).

ANALYST EXPECTATIONS AND IMPLIED GROWTH

One may well ask why someone who is an outspoken critic of analysts' ability to forecast would find anything of interest within their la-la land numbers. The answer lies in the fact that over the years I have found that analysts' long-term growth rate expectations come pretty close to the implied growth rates from a reverse-engineered dividend discount model (especially at extremes). For example, the analysts following RIMM are currently expecting long-term growth of around 33% p.a. Using my reverse-engineered DDM model, I find that the implied long-term growth is 35%. In contrast, those analysts covering Persimmon expect a long-term growth rate of −3% p.a. My reverse-engineered DDM shows that the market implies a −1% long-term growth rate.

As an aside, finding a stock with a negative long-term growth forecast is quite an achievement. A recent paper by Cusatis and Woolridge (2008) explored many facets of analysts' expected long-term growth. Particularly relevant to our discussion here is the reluctance of analysts to forecast negative long-term growth. Cusatis and Woolridge document that in their US sample (1984–2006) some 31% of firms end up with negative long-term earnings growth, yet analysts expect a mere 0.17% of firms to do so!

The close relationship between expected and implied growth rates doesn't particularly surprise me (nor I suspect many readers). I think this relationship stems from the fact that often analysts use their long-term growth forecasts to justify their target prices and hence recommendations. Strangely enough target price and market price are often closely correlated, as analysts seem to be short-term momentum players.[1]

As such the close relationship between long-term expected growth rates and implied growth rates is also likely to be relatively close.

Figure 8.1 illustrates this point using 200 randomly selected stocks in the S&P 500. I have used a simple three-stage DDM model (which I have used many times before) to generate a reverse-engineered estimate of implied long-term growth, and plotted it against the current analyst consensus for long-term growth. The tight correlation (greater than 0.6) between the two measures is obvious. Hence using analysts' long-term growth forecasts as a quick proxy for the implied growth rate from a stock appears to be justifiable.

---

[1] A viewpoint supported by Stickel (2007) and also by my work in Chapter 10 of *Behavioural Investing*.

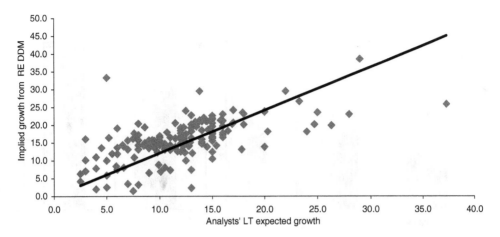

Figure 8.1 Analysis' long-term growth expectations vs implied growth from reverse-engineered DDM
Source: SG Global Strategy research.

BRINGING IN VALUATION

So far, we have dealt only with only implicit valuation considerations (i.e. those implied via growth). It is now time to make valuation an explicit component of our analysis. In order to do this we simply formed portfolios based around price to book.[2] The analysts' expected growth rate of earnings for each of the portfolios was calculated and compared with both the prior five years' growth, and the future five years' growth.

In the USA, the portfolio of cheapest stocks (labelled 'Value' in Figure 8.2) is expected to grow its earnings by around 10% p.a. according to the analysts. This is higher than the average growth rate of just under 7% achieved in the prior five years. In terms of the actual growth that is delivered, these stocks generated an average of just over 9% p.a. (not statistically different from the analysts' expectations).

However, stocks at the other end of the spectrum show a very different picture. Analysts expect growth stocks to generate around 17% p.a. (against a prior 16% p.a.). However, the actual delivered growth has been a meagre 7% p.a. on average! This is clear evidence that investors do indeed overpay for the hope of growth.

It is also noteworthy that there is a 0.98 correlation between past growth and forecast growth, and a −0.9 correlation between forecast growth and actual delivered future growth. As I have noted many times before, this strongly suggests that analysts tend to follow the representativeness heuristic (judging things by how they appear, rather than how likely they actually are) when coming up with long-term growth rates.

The evidence for Europe looks very similar (Figure 8.3). Analysts expect the cheapest portfolio of stocks to grow earnings by around 9% p.a. over the long term. Once again, this is higher than the historically delivered growth of 6% on average in the prior five years. When we see how these value stocks actually perform in terms of earnings deliverance, they almost match expectations, delivering around 9% p.a. over the long term.

---

[2] Results for other valuation criteria didn't alter the findings.

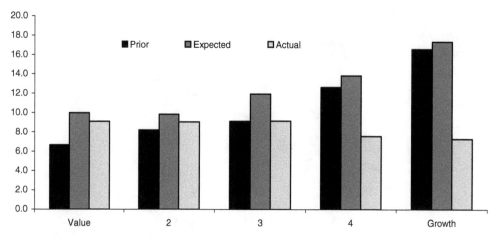

Figure 8.2   Growth: past, expected and actual (USA 1985–2007)
Source: SG Global Strategy research.

Once again, the evidence at the other end of the spectrum is very different. Here analysts expect the growth stocks to deliver around 16% p.a. (very close to the historical performance of 17% p.a.) However, the capitalist system (combined with the logic of mathematics) kicks in to ensure that this kind of growth remains a pipedream. In terms of actual delivered growth, the most expensive stocks generate around 5% p.a. over the long term.

Like their US brethren, the European analysts also have a strongly significant correlation between historical and forecast growth rates (0.88), but a negative correlation between forecast and out-turn (−0.77). Thus, as is usually the case, the stocks on which these analysts are most optimistic turn out to be the stocks on which they are most wrong!

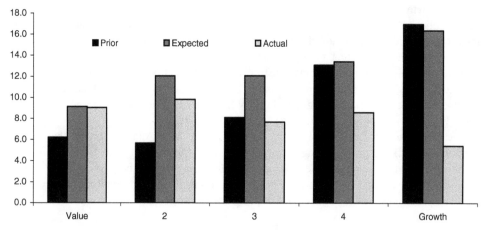

Figure 8.3   Growth: past, expected and actual (Europe 1985–2007)
Source: SG Global Strategy research.

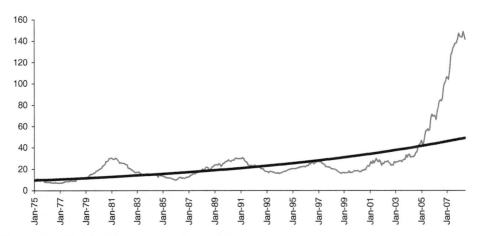

Figure 8.4 World mining sector earnings and trend
Source: SG Global Strategy research.

A CASE IN POINT: MINING

The best current example of investors overpaying for growth (in my opinion) is the mining sector. I have been advocating caution on this sector since February 2006, some 84% ago! Indeed the last time I wrote on mining I included the following: 'Of course, bubbles always last longer than everyone expects them to do.' This one has certainly lasted longer than I imagined! However, little has changed from my perspective to alter the conclusions I reached at that time, that mining is a prime example of investors overpaying for the hope of growth. Let's examine the evidence.

Figure 8.4 shows the world mining sector's earnings and a simple growth trend. Historically, the mining sector has seen earnings grow by around 5% p.a. over the long term. However, the thing that really stands out is the stratospheric level of earnings that we are currently seeing.

To make the situation even cleaer, Figure 8.5 shows the percentage deviation from trend. The last time we saw anything like this in terms of the scale of the deviation from trend was in

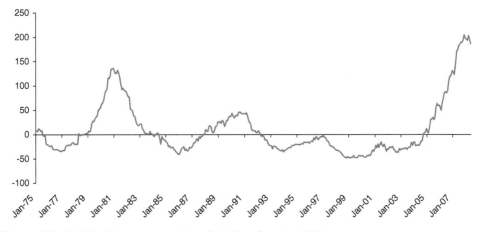

Figure 8.5 World mining sector earnings deviations from trend (%)
Source: SG Global Strategy research.

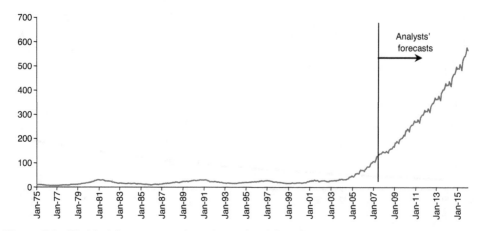

Figure 8.6   World mining sector earnings plus analysts' forecasts
Source: SG Global Strategy research.

the late 1970s/early 1980s. However, the current deviation is even greater, running at nearly 200% of trend earnings!

This is where the debate over the 'super cycle' seems to start to appear. Are earnings in the sector at a new, permanently high plateau (*à la* Irving Fisher in 1929), or are they set to return to something more like a normal level?

The analysts' answer is neither. Instead, earnings are expected to continue upon an exponential path. Figure 8.6 shows the growth forecasts from consensus analysts mapped onto the historical earnings series. According to IBES data, analysts are looking for around 27% growth in each of the next two years, followed by long-term growth of a mere 15% p.a.!

The fact that the Year 1 and Year 2 estimates are both so close in terms of growth is a concern. In general, mining analysts are a cautious bunch, generally predicting a return to trend in the underlying commodity prices. Hence their Year 2 estimates are often below their Year 1 estimates. The last time year two growth was higher than Year 1 growth was in the 2002/03 period when mining earnings were below trend. As Figure 8.7 shows, the current situation is unusual, and speaks to the analysts buying into 'This time is different.'

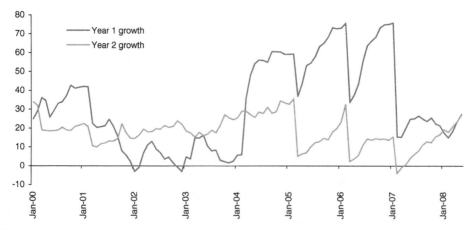

Figure 8.7   Year 1 and Year 2 consensus earnings growth estimates: Mining sector
Source: SG Global Strategy research.

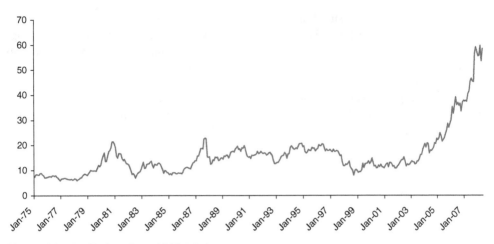

Figure 8.8 Cyclically adjusted P/E: Mining sector
Source: SG Global Strategy research.

As noted above, the analysts expect the mining sector to grow by 15% p.a. over the long-term. Using our three-stage reverse-engineered DDM model, the current price implies nearly 20% p.a. over the next 10 years – and that is just to justify the current market price, let alone provide any future returns. It looks as if the market is attempting to discount the entire future growth of China and others into the here and now.

A simple implied perpetuity growth rate calculation reveals that the mining sector is effectively pricing in almost 12% p.a. forever! Does this not strike anyone as slightly unrealistic? The mining sector seems unlikely to grow at twice the rate of the whole economy for ever!

From a valuation perspective, mining certainly looks to be priced as a growth asset. Using a cyclically adjusted P/E (based on the trend earnings data presented above) the mining sector (Figure 8.8) is trading on almost 60× against an average of 16×!

Figure 8.9 Mining sector Hussman P/E
Source: SG Global Strategy research.

The other valuation measure I have used in the past is the Hussman P/E, which compares today's price with the last peak in earnings. This is a way of measuring the trend in earnings, but is generally more robust for start and end point selection since we are measuring peak-to-peak earnings. This measure (Figure 8.9) shows that the mining sector is trading on over 19× against an average of 11×.

The backdrop of expensive valuations, combined with exceptionally high growth expectations, clearly suggests that investors are betting that 'This time is different.' Unfortunately those words have so far always been synonymous with overpaying for the hope of growth.

9

Placebos, Booze and Glamour Stocks[*]

Have you ever bought a (cheap) non-brand painkiller, and sworn that it didn't work as well as the (expensive) branded version? If so, your brain is probably playing tricks on you. We seem to have an in-built subconscious dislike of items that are at a discount. It is often said that in stock markets nobody likes a sale. Could a bias against cheapness be one of the causes of the value premium? The good news is that rational reflection seems to ameliorate this particular bias. The bad news is that staying rational while everyone else is losing their head is as hard as ever.

- It appears we are preprogrammed to equate price and quality. Now, in many contexts this may well be a useful heuristic. However, like most mental short cuts it can lead us far astray from rational decision making.
- For instance, which will work better: a painkiller that costs $2.50 per dose, or the same painkiller discounted and selling at just 10 cents? Rationally, they should have exactly the same effect (especially since both pills are nothing more than sugar pills). However, Dan Ariely and colleagues have found that people report the expensive version to be far more effective than the cheap version!
- If you prefer booze to pills, then consider the following. You are given some wine to taste and told it costs $10 a bottle, and then some more wine to taste and told it costs $90. The $90 wine was rated nearly twice as nice as the $10 wine. The only snag was that the wine was exactly the same in both cases. So we seem to display a bias against cheap goods.
- Could something similar be at work in the stock market? It is possible that investors tend to use the price = quality heuristic when considering stocks. It is often said that no one likes a sale in the stock market. Evidence from a new study by Statman *et al.* shows that the stocks that are most 'admired' tend to be those that have done well in both market and financial terms, and are relatively expensive. Those that are the most 'despised' tend to be poor past performers, and relatively cheap.
- Guess which wins out going forward? Strangely enough it is the most despised stocks that perform better in the future. Even after controlling for the market, size, style and momentum, the despised stocks still generate an alpha of around 2% p.a.
- What can be done to mitigate this bias against cheapness? The good news is that it appears that rational reflection can defeat the obsession with expense. So getting people to think carefully about the relationship between price and quality makes them more robust against this mental error. However, keeping a rational head on your shoulders when everyone else is losing theirs is likely to remain as hard as ever!

Have you ever bought a non-brand painkiller, taken it, and then thought it just wasn't as effective as the branded equivalent? If so the likelihood is that the brain is playing tricks on you. One of the everyday heuristics we seem to deploy is that price serves as a proxy for quality (much as confidence is used as a proxy for skill). Now, in many cases the price = quality heuristic works pretty well. For instance, buying an expensive pair of designer jeans will probably ensure a better fit and better quality workmanship than a pair bought at Walmart. However, this is not the case in every situation.

PAINKILLERS, PLACEBOS AND PRICE

Dan Ariely[1] and his colleagues have recently published a set of studies which cast some light upon the way we make decisions. The first study I wish to highlight was published in 2008 (Waber *et al.*, 2008) and concerns the impact of price upon the perceived effectiveness of painkillers.

Ariely *et al.* subjected participants to electric shocks (what is it about psychologists and the desire to shock people – literally) in order to trigger pain. At first the shocks were mild, producing a tingling sensation. As the experiment progressed so the intensity of the shock increased. The final shock was enough to set your heart racing, and force your eyes wide open.

Before the shocks are administered you read a short brochure on the painkiller (Veladone-Rx) you will be testing. The information states that 'Veladone is an exciting new medication in the opioid family', and that 'Clinical studies show that over 92% of patients receiving Veladone in double-blind controlled studies reported significant pain relief within only 10 minutes, and that the pain relief lasted up to eight hours'. The literature also stated the price of the new drug. Some people received a price of $2.50 for a single dose; others saw a brochure that showed a discounted price of just 10 cents per dose.

After the first set of shocks was completed, subjects were given a cup of water and a pill – which they were told was Veladone. In fact it was a sugar pill. Fifteen minutes after taking the pill, they were subjected to the set of shocks once again, and asked whether the painkiller was effective or not.

The results that Ariely *et al.* uncovered are shown in Figure 9.1. When the subjects were told that Veladone cost $2.50, some 85% of them reported that they felt less pain after taking the drug. In contrast, when they thought Veladone cost only 10 cents, only 61% said that the painkiller was effective.

So Ariely and colleagues clearly show a placebo effect, because the pills given were nothing other than sugar pills. However, they also show that the price had a distinct impact upon this placebo effect; the higher the price, the more subjects felt it had worked.

This work has some radical implications for health care, obviously. Modern science has long demonstrated strong support for the impact of placebo treatments. In some ways doctors have been exploiting placebo effects for years. For instance, often when you go to the doctor with a sore throat, he or she will give you antibiotics. However, somewhere around one-third of sore throats are caused by viruses – upon which antibiotics have absolutely no effect. Instead

---

[1] Dan has made a disproportionate number of appearances in my notes as he is one of the keenest observers of human nature I have come across. In addition, his research topics are always fascinating. He has recently written a book *Predictably Irrational*, which I suggest that everyone reads. It will certainly make my next reading list review. Personally I think *Predictably Irrational* will be the 'Freakanomics' of the behavioural psychological world.

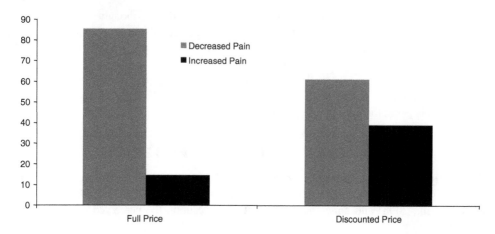

Figure 9.1   Percentage of subjects reporting...
Source: Waber *et al.* (2008).

we all end up taking too many antibiotics and help to create drug-resistant bacterial infections which threaten us all. Perhaps doctors should just prescribe an expensive sugar pill rather than antibiotics the next time they come across a viral infection.

DOES EXPENSIVE WINE TASTE BETTER?

The next example comes from a great study by Plassmann *et al.* (2008). They gave subjects five wines to taste, and asked them to rate each of the wines. All the wines were Cabernet Sauvignons. In fact, only three different wines were used in the experiment, as two wines were presented twice. In the first version of the experiment subjects were told the price of each wine. For example, Wine 2 was presented once as $90, and once as $10 (Table 9.1).

Figure 9.2 shows the scores the subjects awarded the wines based on a scale of 1 (didn't like at all) to 6 (really loved it). When faced with Wine 2 in the guise of a $10 bottle the average rating was around 2.4. However, when told the same bottle was a $90 bottle the average rating jumped to 4. In fact, the bottle retailed at $90!

A similar finding is true of Wine 1. So effectively price tends to an increase in perceived taste ratings of between 50 and 60%!

To ensure that it was the price that was driving the result, Plassmann *et al.* repeated the test, this time without the price disclosed. The results are shown in Figure 9.3. When the price was

Table 9.1   Which wine in which bottle?

Stated cost	Real wine
$5 wine	Wine 1
$10 wine	Wine 2
$35 wine	Wine 3
$45 wine	Wine 1
$90 wine	Wine 2

Source: Plassmann *et al.* (2008).

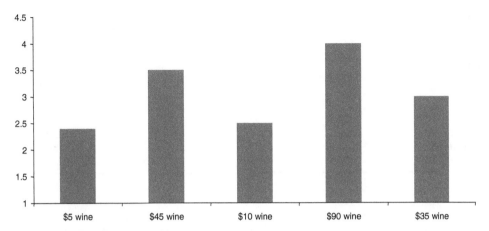

Figure 9.2 Average rating of the wine (1 = didn't like, 6 = really loved) with price information
Source: Plassmann *et al*. (2008).

absent the participants found that when presented with the same wine twice they rated the wine the same on each occasion.

The wines in the two charts are placed in comparable positions. This reveals that when told the wine was cheap (i.e. $5) people really marked the wine down, and when told a wine cost $90 they massively increased its ratings!

GLAMOUR STOCKS

Is it possible that something similar happens when people think about investing? It certainly seems plausible that investors might think that an expensive stock is a better option than a cheap stock as its expense might signal quality – just as people seem to think with painkillers and wine. Are stocks just another item that people dislike when they are on sale?

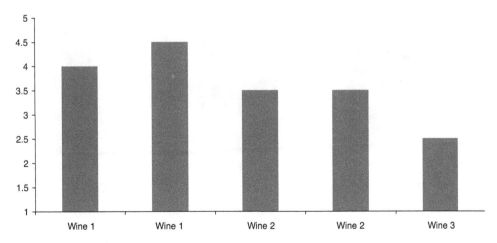

Figure 9.3 Average rating of wine (without price information)
Source: Plassmann *et al*. (2008).

Table 9.2   Characteristics of admired and despised companies

Characteristic	Admired companies	Despised companies
P/E	15.0	12.6
P/B	2.0	1.3
P/CF	9.7	7.3
Sales growth (last 2 years)	10.0%	3.5%
Earnings growth (last 2 years)	12.7%	5.2%
ROA	15.8%	12.5%
12M returns	21.5%	11.0%
36M returns	81.2%	38.4%

Source: Statman *et al*. (2008).

A new paper suggests that this may indeed be the case. Statman *et al*. (2008) examine the characteristics and performance of stocks rated as the most admired or despised in terms of their long-term investment value in the *Fortune* magazine's annual survey of companies. The period they study covers 1982–2006.

Table 9.2 below shows the key characteristics of the stocks in each of the portfolios. The stocks in the admired portfolio are certainly 'better' firms. They have an average sales growth of 10% p.a. over the last two years, compared with the 3.5% growth achieved by the despised stocks. They have done noticeably better over both the immediate past and the medium term (as measured by momentum). The admired stocks also tend to be more expensive, showing an average P/CF ratio of 9.7× vs 7.3× for the despised stocks.[2]

However, Statman *et al*. then monitor the performance of stocks over time, and Figure 9.4 shows the results they uncover. The despised stocks do significantly better than the admired stocks. This result holds even when returns are adjusted for market, size, style and momentum! For instance, with a four-year rebalancing, the despised stocks have a four–factor alpha of just over 2% p.a. and the admired stocks have a marginally negative alpha.

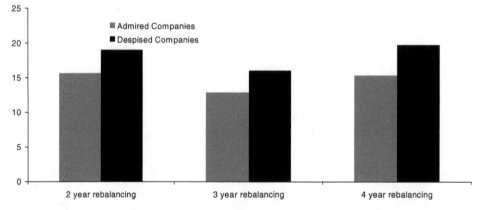

Figure 9.4   Performance of admired and despised stocks (% p.a.)
Source: Statman *et al*. (2008).

---

[2] A similar pattern can be found among analyst recommendations. See Chapter 10 of *Behavioural Investing* for more details

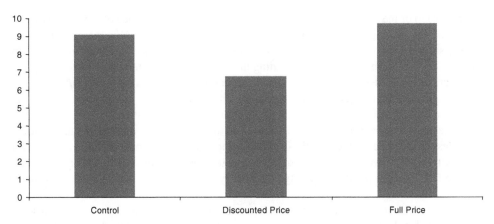

Figure 9.5 Number of puzzles solved
Source: Shiv *et al*. (2008).

BEATING THE BIAS

The good news is that it appears that cognitive reflection (that is, simply thinking about it) helps to counteract thia 'automatic' equating of price and quality. In order to illustrate this we turn to the work of Shi *et al*. (2005). They explore the impact of a 'mental energy' drink upon people's ability to solve anagrams. Before the drink was disturbed participants were told that they would be charged for the cost of the drink. Some were told they would pay the full price ($1.89), others were told the full price was normally $1.89, but the university had used a bulk order to reduce the cost to $0.89.

Figure 9.5 shows the results that Shiv *et al*. discovered. The control group just solved anagrams without the aid of the drink. However, note the marked deterioration in the performance of those who received a discounted drink! They solved around three less puzzles than the

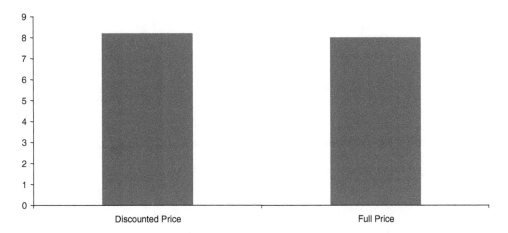

Figure 9.6 Number of puzzles solved
Source: Shiv *et al*. (2005).

control group or the full price group. So Shiv *et al.* find strong evidence of a negative placebo effect (the discounting hurt performance) but the full price drink didn't increase performance!

In a second experiment, Shiv *et al.* drew attention to the price–efficacy link by asking participants to rate the the drink after reading the following two statements. 'Given the price I was charged for SoBe (the name of the drink), I feel that SoBe is "very bad" (1)/"very good" (7) at improving mental performance'; and 'Given the price I was charged foe SoBe, I feel that SoBe is "very bad" (1)/"very good" (7) at improving concentration'.

The results are shown in Figure 9.6. There is no difference in the number of puzzles solved regardless of the price charged for the drink. So simply directing people to think about the link (or lack thereof) between price and quality seems to ameliorate the effect. This also suggests that the link between price and quality is generally a function of some sunconscious mental process.

Could it be that value investors have learned to override their 'natural' subconscious price = quality heuristic: After all, most value investors tend to spend a very long time analysing intrinsic value, effectively reflecting the use of rational tools rather than gut feelings.

10

Tears before Bedtime*

> **Whenever I write about value vs growth, I tend to classify growth as the polar opposite to value stocks. The growth managers always cry that this is an unfair definition. So in an effort to be even-handed, this chapter examines the evidence on growth investing without reference to valuation metrics. However, the results don't change. Growth investing is still likely to end in tears before bedtime.**

- We all have a habit of looking for information that agrees with us. So to try to confound this bias, we should seek out the information that would show we are wrong. Over the years, I have produced a number of papers showing that various measures of value tend to outperform. Whenever I do this work I tend to end up defining growth as the polar opposite of value stocks in terms of valuation. However, this may not be an altogether accurate definition of growth stocks.
- So how should we define growth? Perhaps the many books written on great companies might offer some suggestions. In *Built to Last*, Collins and Porras define 18 'visionary' firms – the *crème de la crème* of the corporate world. They also define a group of comparator companies (good companies in the same industries as the 'visionary' ones). Unfortunately, since the book was published the comparator companies have significantly outperformed the visionary firms!
- Perhaps, the *Fortune* survey of most admired companies will provide a better insight. Anginer *et al.* have recently tested portfolios of the most admired vs the most despised companies and found that the poor cousins outperform the stars by around 2.5% p.a. So there is little evidence that people are picking great stocks here either!
- The Anginer *et al.* study has parallels with some new research by Taylor and Butcher. They show that 'ugly' defendants are more likely to be found guilty and receive longer sentences than 'attractive' defendants in a mock case. Value stocks are the financial equivalent of 'ugly' defendants, while growth stocks are the 'attractive' stars of the day.
- The most logical place to look for growth is perhaps by utilizing the insights of thousands of financial analysts. In the past I have used their year-ahead forecasts to show that 'growth' doesn't pay. However, some growth managers argued that this was the wrong time horizon. So we now turn our attention to the five-year growth rate forecasts. Sadly, we find the stocks with the highest expected growth rates generate the lowest returns, and the stocks with the lowest forecast growth rates generate the highest returns!
- The reason for this appalling result is that analysts seem to put excessive weight on the firms' past growth performance when they form their forecasts. They fail to factor in the competitive erosion of abnormal profits that lies at the very heart of the capitalist

---

system. There is a wealth of data showing that profitability has strong mean-reverting properties. Return on assets tends to revert to the market average at around the 40% p.a. mark.

- So, despite explicitly excluding valuation-based measures of growth, the alternative definitions considered here continue to point to the sad conclusion that growth investing is all too likely to end in tears before bedtime for investors.

Much of the empirical work I do (always with the aid of our quant team) classifies stocks as either value or growth, depending upon their valuation. This is obviously a simple, if not perhaps simplistic, view of the world. Indeed, when I write anything extolling the wonders of value, some beleaguered growth manager will write to me saying that I am guilty of mis-defining growth.

BUILT TO LAST

In an effort to set the record straight I am looking at alternative definitions of growth. But where should I start? Inspired by Phil Rosenzweig's excellent book on the appalling content of most management books, *The Halo Effect*, I decided that the list of 'visionary' companies from Collins and Porras' book, *Built To Last: Successful Habits of Visionary Companies*, would make a suitable starting point.

The aim of Collins and Porras' book was to uncover the 'underlying, timeless, fundamental principles and patterns that might apply across eras'. They began by identifying some 200 leading companies across a wide range of industries. Then they whittled this group down to just 18 stocks – the *crème de la crème* of the corporate world, the financial equivalent of Crufts! Collins and Porras also selected a group of comparator companies, one from each of the industries in which the 'visionary' companies were active. These comparator companies weren't dogs; they were generally good performers, but just not great. For instance, Procter & Gamble was paired with Colgate–Palmolive, and so forth.

As Rosenzweig notes, Collins and Porras were not shy about stressing the amount of research that went into their selection.

> They read more than 100 books.... 3,000 articles.... All together, the material filled three 'shoulder-height storage cabinets, four bookshelves and twenty megabytes of computer storage'.

Of the 18 'visionary' companies that Collins and Porras selected, 14 are still going strong in their original form today (not bad for a study completed in 1990)! So built to last seems like an appropriate epitaph. However, were these companies good investments? The answer appears to be that they haven't exactly shone. Figure 10.1 shows the percentage of 'visionary' companies that have managed to exceed the total return on the S&P 500 over various time horizons. So 71% of them managed to outperform in the 10 years before the Collins and Porras study was completed (1980–1990). The average visionary company returned just over 21% in those 10 years, against 17.5% from the S&P 500.

However, going forward the picture was not so pretty. In the five years after the study was published only half of the companies managed to outperform the S&P 500. The average return from the 'visionaries' was 25% against 24% from the S&P 500. When we look over the period 1991–2007, the average return from the visionaries was 13%, against the S&P 500's 14%. In effect, on average, these stocks did no better than the S&P 500 (Figure 10.2).

The comparator companies did worse in the run-up to the study. With an average return of 12% versus the 17.5% from the S&P 500. However, after the study things for the comparisons began to improve. In the five years after the study, the comparison group turned in an average of 25% p.a. against 24% from the S&P 500. In the period 1991–2007, the comparator companies have delivered 14.6% p.a. against the S&P 500's 13.5%, and the visionaries 13%! Also noteworthy is the fact that a higher proportion of the comparator companies have actually delivered market beating returns.

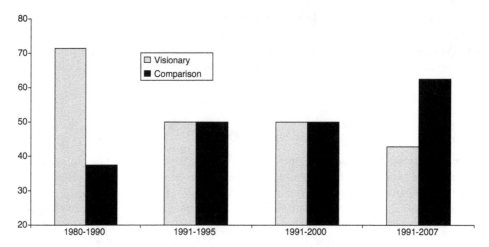

Figure 10.1   Percentage of 'visionary' and 'comparator' companies beating the S&P 500
Source: Dresdner Kleinwort Macro research.

The bottom line appears to be that the criteria used by Collins and Porras are of absolutely no use in picking winners when it comes to growth stocks. Those interested in a devastating critique covering much of the 'this is how to create a great company', should read Rosenzweig's excellent book.

ADMIRED OR DESPISED?

So where else can we turn for evidence on growth investing? A new paper by Anginer, Fisher and Statman (2007) looks at the returns to *Fortune's* most admired and despised companies. Since 1983, *Fortune* has published an annual survey of executives, directors and analysts who

Figure 10.2   The stock market performance of the visionary and comparator companies (1991=100)
Source: Dresdner Kleinwort Macro research.

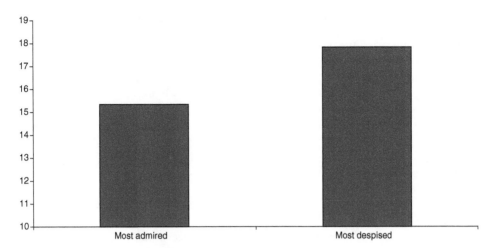

Figure 10.3 Percentage return of 'admired' and 'despised' Stocks (industry adjusted, % p.a. 1983–2006)
Source: Dresdner Kleinwort Macro research.

rate the 10 largest companies in their sector on eight attributes such as quality of management, HR skills, use of corporate assets, long-term investment value, etc.

Each year, portfolios are formed on the basis of the overall scores of the companies. Over the 23-year period, the mean annualized return for the despised portfolio was 17.5%, beating the admired portfolio by just under 2% p.a. When the returns are industry adjusted, the differential increases to 2.5% p.a (Figure 10.3).

Table 10.1 below shows average characteristics of stocks contained in the admired and despised portfolios. The stocks in the admired portfolio tended to be strong past performancers particularly on the 3–5 year time horizon. They also tend to be firms that are expensive judged on price to book (P/B) and price to cash flow (P/CF).

In contrast, those stocks in the despised portfolio tend to have relatively weak past long-term performance, and be what would generally be classified as value style characteristics (despite the fact that valuation was not an explicit criteria in the selection process).

Table 10.1 Characteristics of stocks

	Despised portfolio	Admired Portfolio
Returns in previous year	11.8	21.0
Returns in previous 3 years	35.8	80.3
Returns in the previous 5 years	81.4	176.3
P/B	1.3	2.1
P/E	15.2	16.7
P/CF	6.7	9.2
Sales growth	6.3	10.5

Source: Anginer *et al*. (2007).

DON'T BE AN UGLY DEFENDANT

So once again there is little evidence for growth investors here. Interestingly a recent psychology study may well relate to these findings. Taylor and Butcher (2007) gave 96 students identical accounts of an old lady being mugged. Each was shown a picture of the defendant. There were four possible photos, and each student was shown just one. Two of these photos were rated by an independent group as 'very attractive'; the other two were rated as 'homely' which appears to be a euphemism for butt ugly (a category I can speak on with some authority, being a leading member!)

The students were asked to assess the likely guilt of the defendant on a scale of 0–5. The attractive defendants scored an average of 2.3, the ugly defendants 4.4! A near doubling of the likely guilt score driven by looks alone! The students were also asked to recommend a jail sentence (up to a maximum of 10 months). The ugly defendants faced an average jail time of 7 months, the attractive defendants just 4 months (Figure 10.4).

Growth stocks are the attractive defendants of the finance world. It is easy to buy a stock like the most admired stocks from the *Fortune* list discussed above; however, thankfully the financial markets are slightly better than jurors at working out the end punishment!

ANALYSTS' VIEWS ON GROWTH

Let us turn to another possible source of hope for growth investors, the analysts' forecasts. In the past we have used Year 1 growth – but the growth managers cried 'unfair', arguing that one year ahead forecasts were simply too short term. So this time I've turned to the long-term earnings growth rate forecasts from analysts. These numbers are supposedly the analysts' views on the five-year outlook for earnings growth.

LaPorta (1996) showed that the stocks with the highest long-term earnings growth forecasts deliver the lowest returns! This work has recently been updated by Forsythe (2007). The results haven't changed. Using some 3,200 stocks from 1982–2006, those with the highest forecast

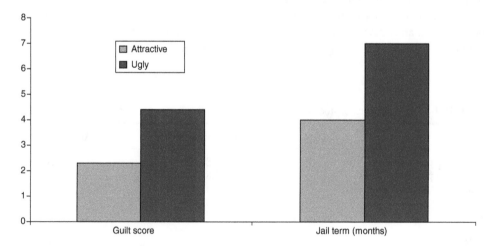

Figure 10.4   Don't be an ugly defendant
Source: Taylor and Butcher (2007).

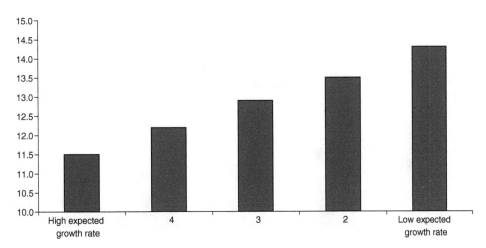

Figure 10.5 Returns based on forecast growth rates (% p.a 1982–2006, USA)
Source: Forsythe (2007).

growth rates ended up delivering 11.5% p.a. whereas the stocks with the lowest forecast growth delivered 14.5% p.a. (Figure 10.5).

With the able help (as ever) of Rui Antunes of the quant team, I decided to check the picture for MSCI World. The results are relatively similar to those for the USA. Figure 10.6 shows the risk-adjusted returns based around long-term forecast growth. The stocks with the highest long-term growth ended up with the lowest returns, whilst the stocks the lowest growth ended up with relatively high returns (Figure 10.6).

Why, therefore, are analysts' forecasts not very useful for producting long-term earnings growth? The answer, I think, is revealed in Figure 10.7. It shows the long-term earnings growth rate forecasts (middle bar) from analysts. I've also plotted the actual out-turn after five years (the third bar in each group). The results are bad news for analysts. There is statistically no

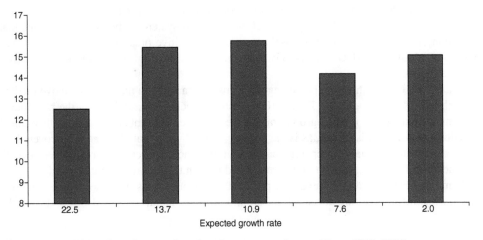

Figure 10.6 Risk-adjusted returns based on forecast growth rates (% p.a 1981–2006)
Source: Dresdner Kleinwort Macro research.

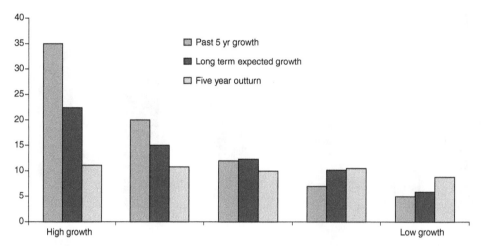

Figure 10.7 Long-term growth: historic, forecast and out-turn (1982–2005)
Source: Dresdner Kleinwort Macro research.

difference between the actual out-turns for those in the high-growth quintile and those in the low-growth quintile! Perhaps we should restore the ancient Scythians punishment for frivolous prophecies; they burnt to death any soothsayers whose predictions failed to come true![1]

However, the news just keeps getting worse. I've also plotted the growth rate in the five years before the analysts actually made their forecasts. Strangely enough the stocks with high expected growth had high historic growth, and those with low expected growth had low historic growth.

The analysts then appear to largely extrapolate past growth into the future. This probably stems from the psychological failure known as representativeness – a habit of judging things by how they appear rather than how likely they really are. So analysts look at fast-growing firms and conclude that they are genuine fast-growth companies, and vice versa for low-growth stocks. They ignore the base rate information; that is, the statistical likelihood of a given firm actually managing to maintain its competitive edge without any erosion.

This is a fatal error. At the very heart of the capitalist system is the belief that firms that earn abnormal profits will find themselves under competitive pressure and will tend to see their profitability eroded. Unsurprisingly, study after study has confirmed that this mechanism is alive and well.

Chan *et al.* (2003) show the percentage of firms that manage to maintain an above median growth rate as time goes past. Figure 10.8 illustrates their point, and shows the percentage of firms with an above median growth rate as we increase the number of years. A theoretical 'random' distribution is shown, as is the empirical distribution that Chan *et al.* uncovered. In general they are very hard to separate, but, if anything, the empirical distribution lies beneath the theoretical one, suggesting that the real world is even tougher than pure chance!

Fama and French (2000) found that profitability (measured as earnings found over total assets) was mean reverting at the rate of around 40% per annum. They also found 'that the

[1] http://www.greektexts.com/library/Herodotus/Melpomene/eng/101.html.

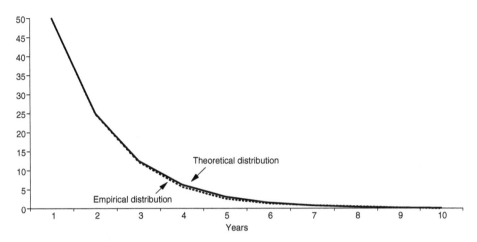

Figure 10.8   Percentage of firms with above median growth rates as a function of time
Source: Chan *et al.* (2003), Dresdner Kleinwort Macro research.

rate of mean reversion is higher when profitability is far from its mean, in either direction. The rate of mean reversion is also higher when profitability is below its mean.'

In their meta-analysis, Wiggins and Ruefli (2005) show that Fama and French's finding is fairly standard. Most studies seem to show mean reversion in profitability at around 30–50% per year. Wiggins and Ruefli argue that, if anything, the pace of erosion has been accelerating in recent years!

The final paper I wish to draw your attention to is by Michael Schill (2005). He has written a simply brilliant paper arguing that if you must forecast at least try to base it upon reason rather than fantasy (Hallelujah to that!)

Among the issues Schill explores is the mean-reverting nature of profitability. He takes all the public companies from 1994 to 2004 and sorts them into five groups, based around their current level of return on assets (ROA). Schill then follows what happens to the composition of these groups over the next three years. The results are shown in Figure 10.9. Those firms who start with the highest levels of profitability see that profitability decline over the next few years (hence the average rank of that quintile declines towards 3). At the other end of the spectrum, those firms in the lowest quintile of profitability see a recovery back towards average over three years.

Schill also reports a great experiment that sheds light onto the problem of forecasting that we discussed above. He gave 300 first-year MBA students a randomly assigned US-listed company and a year between 1980 and 2000. The students were asked to forecast sales growth (and operating margin) for their assigned company for the subsequent three years. The students were given the industry of their firm (but not the company's name), firm sales growth and operating margins for the past three years, historical and three-year forward industry average growth and margins, real GNP growth, inflation rates and interest rates.

The median values for the base-case forecast of expected sales growth (and the actual outturns) are shown in Figure 10.10. Strangely enough the student forecasters turned out to be enormously overoptimistic in their growth projections.

The students were also asked to provide a high-side and a low-side scenario. The high-side scenario was defined explicitly as the 80th percentile level; the low-side as the 20th percentile

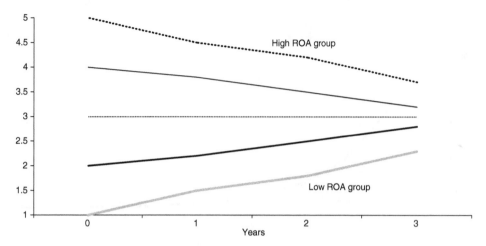

Figure 10.9   Average rank of ROA groups over time (USA, 1994–2004)
Source: Schill (2005), Dresdner Kleinwort Macro research.

level. Figure 10.11 plots the base case, and the high- and low-side scenarios, as well as the actual 80th and 20th percentile values. In Year 3 the high-side forecast was 4 percentage points (pp) above the base case, and the low-side forecast was 4 pp below the base case. The actual 80th percentile level was 8 pp above the base-case, and the actual 20th percentile level was 12 pp below the base-case. This represents a perfect example of overconfidence; the estimated variance was much lower than the actual variance. The students were simply far too confident in their forecasts!

In his forthcoming book, *Your Money and Your Brain*, Jason Zweig highlights some work by Scott Huettel of Duke University. Huettel *et al.* (2002) studied how the brain predicts repetition. They told people that a random sequence of squares and circles would be shown

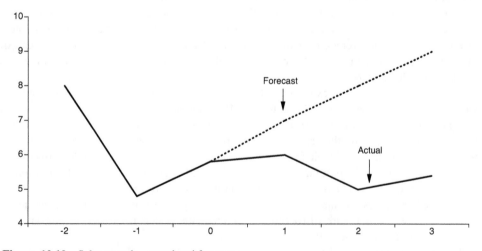

Figure 10.10   Sales growth – actual and forecasts
Source: Schill (2005).

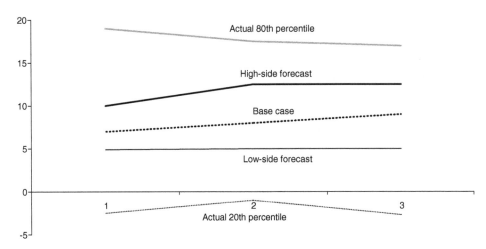

Figure 10.11   Sales growth – actual and forecasts variances
Source: Schill (2005).

to them. When people had only a single ■ or a single ● they didn't know what would come next in the sequence. However, if they saw ■■ then they expected another ■; after ●● they then expected another ●, despite the fact that the random nature of the sequences was fully disclosed!

It would appear, then, that our brains are hardwired to predict from the most minimal of patterns; even when people are told that the pattern is random, we just can't help ourselves!

CONCLUSIONS

The habit of looking for information that agrees with us (confirmatory bias) is one of the most common failures we see. In an effort to test our views on the importance of value, we should look for evidence that growth actually does better (i.e. the disconfirming evidence). Defining growth is a tricky business. However, on none of the measures covered here, could we find any evidence to refute the idea that growth investing is generally a path to disappointment. None of the measures we used was based on valuation, so our definitions of growth are more than simply the opposite of value. Even with this modification we found no evidence to suggest that 'growth' is a good option for investors to pursue.

While the siren stories attached to growth stocks are likely to keep drawing investors in, the most likely outcome remains disappointment. On the evidence presented here, growth investing remains a sure path to tears before bedtime for investors.

11

Clear and Present Danger: The Trinity of Risk*

Despite risk appearing to be one of finance's favourite four-letter words, it remains finance's most misunderstood concept. Risk isn't a number, it is a concept or a notion. From my perspective, risk equates to what Ben Graham called a 'permanent loss of capital'. Three primary (although interrelated) sources of such danger can be identified: valuation risk, business/earnings risk, and balance sheet/financial risk. Rather than running around obsessing on the pseudoscience of risk management, investors should concentrate on understanding the nature of this trinity of risks.

- Value investing is the only investment approach (of which I am aware) that truly puts risk management at the very heart of the process. Ben Graham was deeply critical of modern finance's obsession with standard deviation (and I'm sure he would have laughed out loud at VaR). He argued that investors should concentrate on the dangers of 'permanent loss of capital.'

- Graham went on to suggest at least three broad risks that could result in such a loss. We have termed these: valuation risk, business/earnings risk, and balance sheet/financial risk. Valuation risk is perhaps the most obvious of our trinity. Buying an asset that is expensive means that you are reliant upon all the good news being delivered (and then some). There is no margin of safety in such stocks.

- Some markets display more valuation risk than others. For instance, the UK market is trading on an 11× Graham and Dodd PE, and only 30% of stocks in the UK have G&D PEs >16×. In the USA, the G&D PE for the market is 16×, and some 52% of stocks are on G&D PEs >16×. However, valuation risk is far less concerning than a year or two ago.

- Business or earnings risk is considerably more worrying at the current juncture. As Graham said 'real risk is... the danger of a loss of quality and earnings power through economic changes or deterioration in management.' The markets certainly seem to be implying that business risk is high. The dividend swap markets are suggesting a near 50% decline in European dividends, a 40% decline in UK dividends, and a 21% decline in US dividends! The challenge to investors is to assess whether changes in earnings power are temporary or permanent. The former are, of course, opportunities, the latter are value traps.

---

*This article appeared in Mind Matters on 27 January 2009. Copyright © 2009 by The Société Générale Group. All rights reserved. The material discussed was accurate at the time of publication.

- Balance sheet/financing risk is the last of our triumvirate. As Graham noted: 'The purpose of balance sheet analysis is to detect . . . the presence of financial weakness that may detract from the investment merit of an issue.' In general, we have found that these risks get ignored by investors during the good times, but in a credit constrained environment they suddenly reappear on the agenda. We would suggest that rather than vascillating between neglect and obsession with respect to the balance sheet, a more even approach may well generate results.

Value investing is the only investment approach that puts risk management at the very heart of the process. The margin of safety is nothing if not a form of risk management against errors and bad luck.

Ben Graham warned that risk couldn't be measured in a neat easy way. He certainly didn't equate risk with standard deviation, and I'm sure he would have no time for VaR at all. Rather, Graham saw risk as the 'Permanent loss of capital.'

For several years I have argued that the permanent loss of capital can be split into three (interrelated) sets of risks: valuation risk, business/earnings risk, and balance sheet/ financing risk. Let's take each of these in turn and see how they apply to the current situation.

VALUATION RISK

As Graham wrote, 'The danger in . . . growth stock(s) [is that] for such favoured issues the market has a tendency to set prices that will not be adequately protected by a conservative projection of future earnings.' In other words, buying expensive stocks leaves you vulnerable to disappointment (as we saw in Chapter 8, see also Chapters 26 and 37 of *Behavioural Investing*).

Of course, given the way in which markets have declined over the last year, valuation risk has become less of an issue. That is not to say it is yet absent. As Figure 11.1 shows, the US equity market is currently just below 'fair value' – not yet at truly bargain basement prices. I have no idea whether this major recession will take us to truly bargain valuations, but serious bear markets have normally only ended when we are trading on 10×10-year moving average earnings. This is consistent with the S&P 500 at 500!

In late November, 2008, I was able to argue that the US market was trading on the cheap side of fair value. However, a 25% rally between late November and year end shows just how the short term can make a mockery of the long term on occasion.

Figure 11.1 S&P 500 Graham and Dodd PE
Source: SG Global Strategy research.

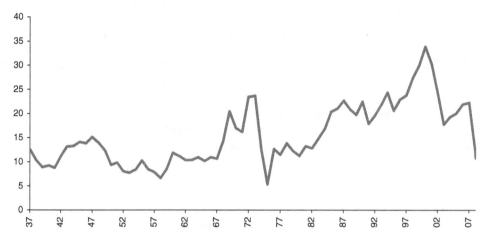

Figure 11.2 UK Graham and Dodd PE
Source: SG Global Strategy research.

Other markets continue to show more valuation support than the USA from a top-down perspective. For instance, both the UK and Europe are currently sitting on much more attractive multiples. As Figure 11.2 shows, the UK market is sitting on just under 11×.

This top-down valuation work is supported by looking at the percentage of stocks trading at Graham and Dodd PEs greater than 16×. You may well ask why 16×? The answer as ever lies in the writings of Graham who opined.

> We would suggest that about 16 times is as high a price as can be paid in an investment purchase of a common stock... Although this rule is of necessity arbitrary in its nature, it is not entirely so. Investment presupposes demonstrable value, and the typical common stock's value can be demonstrated only by means of an established, i.e. an average, earnings power. But it is difficult to see how average earnings of less than 6% upon the market price could ever be considered as vindicating that price.

Figure 11.3 shows the percentage of stocks (in the large cap universe) that are currently sitting on Graham and Dodd PEs of greater than 16×. In the USA, still over half the stocks find themselves in this position, better value can be found in the UK and Europe where only around one-third of stocks are still on G&D PE > 16×. Interestingly, it is in Japan where we find the highest percentage of stocks still trading on high PEs, some 57%!

Thus, despite market declines valuation risk is not yet absent from markets. We continue to drip-feed cash into deep value opportunities and sources of cheap insurance.

BUSINESS/EARNINGS RISK

The second source of risk from our perspective concerns business and earnings risk. As Graham put it.

> Real investment risk is measured not by the percent that a stock may decline in price in relation to the general market in a given period, but by the danger of a loss of quality and earnings power through economic changes or deterioration in management.

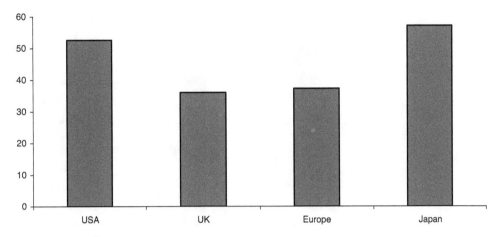

Figure 11.3   Percentage of stocks with G&D PEs > 16×
Source: SG Global Strategy research.

In an environment which is increasingly being acknowledged as the worst since the Great
Depression, a loss of 'earnings power through economic changes' must be a concern for
investors. Graham warned that markets were 'governed more by their current earnings than by
their long-term average. This fact accounts in good part for the wide fluctuations in common-
stock prices, which largely (though by no means invariably) parallel the changes in their
earnings between good years and bad.'
Graham went on.

> Obviously the stock market is quite irrational in thus varying its valuation of a company pro-
> portionately with the temporary changes in reported profits. A private business might easily earn
> twice as much in a boom year as in poor times, but its owner would never think of correspondingly
> marking up or down the value of his capital investment.

The challenge facing investors in this environment is to assess whether any changes in
earnings power are temporary or permanent. The former represent opportunities, the latter
value traps.

Keep an eye on the ratio of current EPS to average 10-year EPS. Stocks which look 'cheap'
based on current earnings, but not on average earnings, are the ones that investors should be
especially aware of, as they run a greater risk of being the sort of stock where the apparent
cheapness is removed by earnings falling rather than prices rising.

Figure 11.4 shows the percentage of stocks in the large cap universe that have current EPS
of at least twice 10-year average EPS. This serves as our proxy for earnings risk. In the USA,
only one-third of stocks find themselves in this situation (as befits the country first into this
crisis). The UK comes out as the worst on this measure, with 54% of stocks having current EPS
of at least twice 10-year average EPS. In Europe and Japan, 42% of stocks are in this position.
It appears to us that earnings and business risk are far more absent in these markets. The
good news is that, given the lower valuations mentioned above, this may already be partially
discounted.

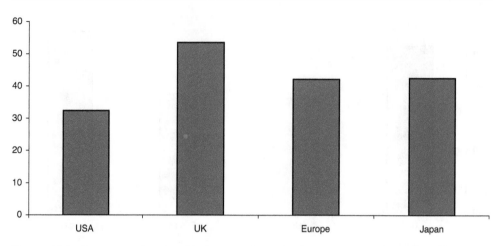

Figure 11.4 Percentage of stocks with current EPS > 2× 10-year average EPS
Source: SG Global Strategy research.

BALANCE SHEET/FINANCIAL RISK

The third of our unholy trinity of risks is balance sheet/financial risk. As Graham opines, 'The purpose of balance-sheet analysis is to detect . . . the presence of financial weakness that may detract from the investment merit of an issue.'

Investors tend to ignore balance sheet and financial risk at the height of booms. They get distracted by earnings, and how these cyclically high earnings cover interest payments. Only when earnings start to crumble do investors turn their attention back to the balance sheet. Similarly leverage is used to turn little profits into big profits during the good times, and many investors seem to forget that leverage works in reverse as well, effectively a big profit can rapidly become a loss during a downswing.

There are lots of ways of gauging balance sheet risk. Our colleagues in the quant team have long argued that the Merton Model and distance to default provide a useful measure of these dimensions. Being a simple and old-fashioned soul I turn to a measure that has served me well in the past during periods of balance sheet stress: good old Altman's Z.

Altman's Z score was designed in 1968 to predict bankruptcy using five simple ratios.

$$Z = 1.2X_1 + 1.4X_2 + 3.3X_3 + 0.6X_4 + 0.999X_5.$$

$X_1 =$ Working Capital/Total Assets. Measures liquid assets in relation to the size of the company.

$X_2 =$ Retained Earnings/Total Assets. Measures profitability that reflects the company's age and earning power.

$X_3 =$ Earnings Before Interest and Taxes/Total Assets. Measures operating efficiency apart from tax and leveraging factors. It recognizes operating earnings as being important to long-term viability.

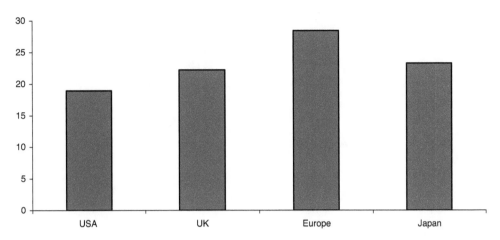

Figure 11.5 Percentage of stocks with Altman Z scored <1.8
Source: SG Global Strategy research.

$X_4 =$ Market Value of Equity/Book Value of Total Liabilities. Adds market dimension that
   can show up security price fluctuation as a possible red flag.
$X_5 =$ Sales/Total Assets. Standard measure for turnover.

A Z score below 1.8 is considered a good indication of future problems. While only a first
step, I have often found this measure useful for flagging up potentially troubling situations.
Figure 11.5 shows the percentage of large cap firms across countries which have Altman Z
scores below 1.8. The measure obviously won't work for financials or utilities so they have
been excluded from our sample.

Roughly speaking, we find very similar levels of balance sheet risk across countries. Somewhere between 20 and 25% of companies appear to have Z scores below 1.8, suggesting a
high probability of financial distress.

PUTTING IT ALL TOGETHER

These three elements (intertwined as they are) can all lead to a permanent loss of capital.
Ultimately, I would argue that risk is really a notion or a concept not a number. Indeed the use
of pseudoscience in risk management has long been a rant of mine.

12

Maximum Pessimism, Profit Warnings and the Heat of the Moment*

We are terrible at emotional time travel. In the cold light of day, we simply can't predict how we will behave in the heat of the moment. Sir John Templeton said 'The time of maximum pessimism is the best time to buy', however, buying when everyone else is despondently selling isn't the easiest thing to do. One potential solution to this problem is pre-commitment. While the removal of free-will tends to be greeted with horror, it is the easiest way of preventing the emotional hijacking of rational decisions. For example, Sir John, having done his analysis of intrinsic value in the cold light of day, would submit buy orders well below the market and simply wait for them to be filled.

- Psychologists have documented that we are very poor at predicting how we will feel in the future. For instance, when we are stuffed after a good meal, we can't imagine feeling hungry. Likewise, when starving we can't imagine feeling bloated. When we are in a cold, rational frame of mind we say we will behave in one fashion; when we are smack bang in the middle of a situation with our blood pumping, our previous plans are thrown out of the window.
- Let's imagine you are hired as a proofreader. You can set your own deadlines, hand everything in at the last moment, or go with a predetermined set of deadlines from the publishers. Most people go with handing everything in at the last moment: after all, they reason, they can do the work at their own pace and just hand it in at the end. However, those who work to preset deadlines were seen to find more errors and were far more punctual. The other two groups appear to have suffered procrastination writ large. This suggests that precommitment is a useful weapon in the arsenal against empathy gaps and procrastination.
- As highlighted above, Sir John Templeton used a form of precommitment when it came to buy orders at times of 'maximum pessimism.' By committing to buy a stock at his estimate of a good discount to intrinsic value (calculated at a time of peace and calm) Sir John was able to sit back and not get caught up in the panic of the moment.
- Profit warnings provide another example of the advantage of precommitment. If you are focused on the short term, when a stock 'profit warns,' you should sell it. Evidence clearly shows that stocks which warn continue to do poorly for around a year (often with further warnings). Hence you should sell at the profit warning. Of course, we don't; we procrastinate

and often end up doing nothing for a long time. A precommitment to sell after a profit warning would help to avoid this problem.

- By the time we do usually get around to selling, it is often the time we should be buying. The evidence suggests that buying a stock a year after a profit warning is generally a good idea. However, this may well seem like insanity after a year of poor performance, and investors losing faith left, right and centre. So a precommitment to buy a year after a profit warning might serve us well.

Why is it that when we are starving hungry we can never imagine feeling bloated, and yet after an enormous meal that leaves us feeling stuffed we can simply not contemplate wanting to eat again?

The simple answer is that we aren't good at predicting how we will feel in the future. In particular, we aren't good at estimating the influence that our emotions will have upon us when we are in the heat of the moment. When we are in a cold, rational frame of mind we say we will behave in one fashion; when we are smack bang in the middle of a situation with our blood pumping, our previous plans are thrown out of the window. This is an empathy gap, and empathy gaps matter.

EMPATHY GAPS

My all-time favourite example of an empathy gap comes from an experiment done by Dan Ariely and George Loewenstein (2006). They used a sample of 35 male undergraduates at the University of California to participate in an experiment for which the students would be paid $10.

Each participant was given a laptop and asked to rate how likely he was to find certain sexual stimuli attractive (to save the readers. blushes I have omitted the full list, but it contained acts such as being spanked and bondage). The subjects were asked to rate how much they would enjoy each act in the cold light of day. They then repeated the experiment in the privacy of their own homes while enjoying what might be delicately described as self-gratification.

Figure 12.1 shows the average attractiveness ratings in the two conditions. In the cold light of day the average rating was 35%. However, this rocketed to 52% when the men answered the questions in an aroused state. This is a 17 percentage point increase in the average rating. Across all the categories of question, the average increase in rating was over 70%!

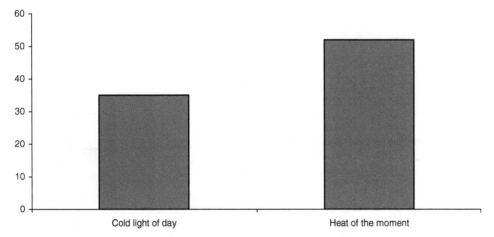

Figure 12.1   In the heat of the moment: the impact of arousal (%)
Source: SG Global Strategy research; Ariely and Loewenstein (2006).

PREVENTING EMPATHY GAPS AND THE PERILS OF PROCRASTINATION

Imagine you are hired as a proofreader for a set of essays each about 10 pages long. You can either set your own deadlines, hand everything in at the last moment, or go with a predetermined set of deadlines. Which would you choose?

Most people go with handing everything in at the last moment: after all, they reason, they can do the work at their pace and then hand it in whenever they like.

However, this ignores people's tendency to procrastinate. While we all start off with the best of intentions to space out the work evenly, inevitably other things arise, our best-laid plans are disrupted and we end up doing the work at the last minute (certainly this describes my experience with many students!).

Dan Ariely and Klaus Wertenbroch (see Ariely and Wertenbroch, 2002) decided to test out this idea. They recruited people to each of three situations outlined above (randomly selected for each one). The evidence they found is shown in Figure 12.2. Those who were told they had to follow the equally spaced deadlines found the most errors, and handed their work in with least delay. The group who chose their own set of deadlines found fewer errors and were nearly twice as late handing in their reports. However, the worst-performing group comprised those who were allowed to wait until the final deadline. This group found far fewer errors than the other two groups, and were nearly three times later in handing in their reports than those who worked to equally spaced deadlines (Figure 12.3).

These results suggest that precommitment is a useful weapon in our arsenal against empathy gaps and the procrastination to which we all seem prone. Let's turn to some examples in finance.

MAXIMUM PESSIMISM TRADES

Sir John Templeton was well known for saying, 'The time of maximum pessimism is the best time to buy, and the time of maximum optimism is the best time to sell.' Few would disagree with the sentiment. However, when 'everyone is busy despondently selling' it can be hard to stand against the tide and buy – this difficulty is the very definition of an empathy gap.

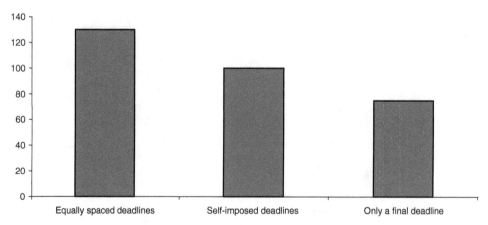

Figure 12.2   Number of errors found
Source: SG Global Strategy research; Ariely and Wertenbroch (2002).

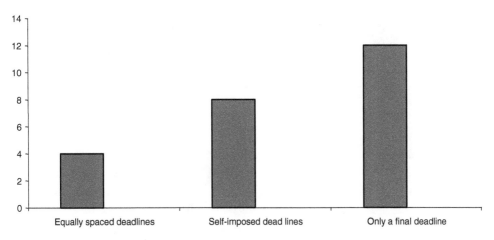

Figure 12.3   Delay in submission (days)
Source: SG Global Strategy research; Ariely and Wertenbroch (2002).

According to Sir John's great niece, in her book *Investing the Templeton Way*,

> There are clear psychological challenges to maintaining a clear head during a sharp sell off. One way Uncle John used to handle this was to make his buy decisions well before a sell off occurred. During his years managing the Templeton Funds, he always kept a 'wish list' of securities representing companies that he believed were well run but priced too high . . . he often had standing orders with his brokers to purchase those wish list stocks if for some reason the market sold off enough to drag their prices down to levels at which he considered them a bargain.

This is a prime example of precommitment in the face of a known empathy gap. By placing buy orders well below the market price, it becomes easy to buy when faced with despondent selling. The emotion has been removed form the situation.

PROFIT WARNINGS

Another example of the potential for precommitment to enhance performance comes in the form of profit warnings. For those with a short-term focus, profit warnings are a cause for concern. However, when they occur we find ourselves making excuses for the company. Perhaps calling the management in, who unsurprisingly reassure us that it was only inventory build or unexpected margin pressure but that everything will be alright next quarter. We walk away satisfied right up to the next profit warning! Procrastination at its very best.

Figure 12.4 shows the evidence for selling a stock after it has profit warned. Bulkley *et al.* (2004) examined some 455 UK profit warnings between 1997 and 1999. On the day the warning was announced the average stock dropped nearly 17%. However, notice thereafter that it continues to drift away. This argues in favour of an automatic rule of selling on profit warnings.

As noted above, we tend to hold onto our disappointments, and probably get round to selling them at just the wrong point. Figure 12.5 shows the evidence for being a contrarian. Around 12 months after a profit warnings (the point at which people are finally getting around to cutting their losses perhaps), things start to turn around. This also speaks to the tendency for

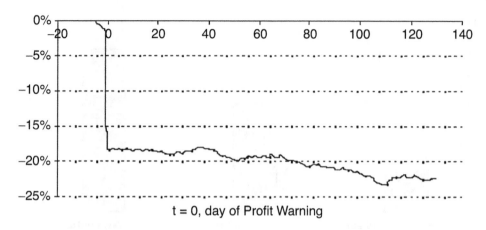

Figure 12.4   Average cumulated excess return
Source: Bulkley *et al.* (2004). SG Global Strategy research.

investors to extrapolate short-term problems for a firm into the indefinite future. From the perspective of a long-term investor, profit warnings are essentially just noise!

Here again a precommitment might help to remove the emotion. After a very poor 12 months of performance and the disappointment of a profit warning, few investors will be tempted to buy. However, the gains from doing so are obvious from Figure 12.5. Forcing yourself to buy 12 months after a profit warning could therefore be a useful tool.

LOCK-INS

The final financial application of precommitment that I wish to explore in this chapter is the use of lock-ins. One of the features of hedge funds that makes a great deal of sense is the lock-in. If you are running a long-term strategy, then persuading your clients to precommit their capital will restrict them to annoying phone calls when the fund hits a poor patch, rather

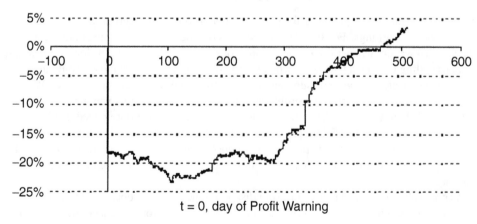

Figure 12.5   Average cumulated excess return
Source: Bulkley *et al.* (2004). SG Global Strategy research.

than outright redemptions. Lock-ins make a great deal of behavioural sense as a method of avoiding empathy gaps.

CONCLUSIONS

The bottom line is that we find it very hard to predict how we will behave when placed under pressure. The best way of avoiding empathy gaps is to do the work with a cool, rational head (well ahead of the time when you might experience the impact of emotion) and then precommit to that course of action. Hence, when the emotion strikes, the action is already set in motion and you can not interfere.

13
The Psychology of Bear Markets[*]

The mental barriers to effective decision-making in bear markets are as many and varied as those that plague rationality during bull markets. However, in bear markets the primary role of emotion is particularly pronounced as the resulting fear and shock short circuit more logical analysis. Experiments have shown that those that can't feel fear behave more rationally in the face of loss than those who can. Perhaps many of the extremes we experience during our moments of both euphoria and revulsion could be avoided if only we heed the words of King Solomon's advisers 'This too, shall pass'.

- It is a cliché that markets are driven by fear and greed. However, it is also disturbingly close to the truth. Having spent the best part of a decade exploring the psychology of bull markets, it makes a refreshing change to examine the drivers of bear market behaviour.
- Fear seems to lie at the heart of the psychology of bear markets. The bad news for us humans is that within the brain emotion appears to have primacy over cognitive functions. Our brains consist of two different (although interconnected) systems. One is a fast and dirty decision maker (the X-system), the other is more logical but slower (the C-system).
- The X-system's output is often unchecked (or at least checked only too late) by the C-system. For instance, if I were to place a glass box containing a snake on the table in front of you, and asked you to move as close as you could to the box, you would jump backward if the snake reared up – even if you aren't afraid of snakes. The reason for this is that the X-system 'recognized' a threat and forced the body to react, all of which was done before the C-system had a chance to point out the protection offered by the glass box. Effectively from an evolutionary standpoint a rapid response to fear carried a very low cost to a false positive, relative to the potentially fatal cost of a false negative.
- While such an approach may have kept us alive, it doesn't necessarily work in our favour when thinking about financial markets. In a fascinating experiment Shiv *et al.* show that when taking risk is rewarded over the long term, players who can't feel fear (due to a very specific form of brain damage) perform much better than the rest of us. Shiv *et al.* also show that the longer the game goes on, the worse people's performance becomes.
- The parallels of the Shiv *et al.* game with bear markets are (I hope) obvious. The evidence suggests that it is outright fear that drives people to ignore bargains when they are available in the market, if they have previously suffered a loss. The longer they find themselves in this position the worse their decision making appears to become.

---

[*]This article appeared in Mind Matters on 2 December 2008. Copyright © 2008 by The Société Générale Group. All rights reserved. The material discussed was accurate at the time of publication.

- Investors should consider the Buddhist approach to time. That is to say, the past is history and the future is a mystery, and so we must focus on the present. The decision to invest or not should be a function of the current situation (the value on offer) and not governed by prior experiences (or indeed our future hopes). Perhaps we would all do well to remember the sage words of King Solomon's advisers when charged to find an expression that would be 'true and appropriate in all times and situations', that 'This too, shall pass'.

After a decade of exploring the psychology of bull markets, it makes a refreshing change to able to think about the psychology that drives behaviour in bear markets. Of course, many of the same biases that lead us to extrapolate the good times at the peak lead us to do the same on the downside.

We seem to constantly fail to remember the wisdom of King Solomon (or rather his advisers). As Abraham Lincoln relayed the story,

> Solomon once charged his wise men to invent him a sentence, to be ever in view, which should be true and appropriate in all times and situations. They presented him with the words 'And this, too, shall pass away'. How much it expresses! How chastening in the hour of pride. How consoling in the depths of affliction:

If only we were capable of heeding these words!

Unfortunately, many of the biases we face seem to stem from the X-system (the automatic part of our brain's processing capabilities). As such they are outside of our conscious awareness and therefore can sometimes (indeed one could say, often) go unchecked by the more logical C-system.

FEAR AND BEAR MARKETS

Of particular note when considering bear markets is an insightful study by Shiv *et al.* (2005). They asked players to participate in the following game. At the start of the game you are given $20 and told the following – the game will last 20 rounds. At the start of each round you will be asked if you would like to invest. If you say yes then the cost will be $1. A fair coin will then be flipped. If it comes up heads you will receive $2.50 back, if it comes up tails then you will lose your $1.

Now there are two things we know about this game. Firstly, obviously it is optimal to invest in all rounds due to the asymmetric nature of the payoff (expected value is $1.25, giving a total expected value to the game of $25). In fact there is only a 13% chance that you end up with total earnings of less than $20 (i.e. the return you achieve if you don't invest at all and just keep the initial endowment). The second thing we know about this game is that the outcome in a prior round shouldn't impact your decision to invest in the next round – after all the coin has no memory.

Now cast your eye over Figure 13.1. It shows the percentage of time people chose to invest depending upon the outcome in the previous round. As you can see three groups of players were used in the experiment. The black bars (target patients) represent a very unusual group. They have a very specific form of brain damage;[1] effectively these individuals can no longer feel fear. The light grey bars (normals) are people like you and I (ostensibly without any brain damage). The dark grey bars (control patients) are those with brain damage in other parts of the brain not related to the processing of emotion (and fear).

It is the second group of three bars to which I wish to draw your attention. This is the percentage of time that players chose to invest after a round in which they had invested and lost. The first group of players – those who can't feel fear – behave quite optimally, investing around 85% of the time after they have suffered a loss. However, look at the other two groups. They display seriously suboptimal behaviour. In fact, so bad is the pain/fear of losing even $1

---

[1] Technically they have lesions on the orbitofrontal cortex, the amygdala or the right insular or somatosensory cortex – all areas associated with emotional processing in the X-system.

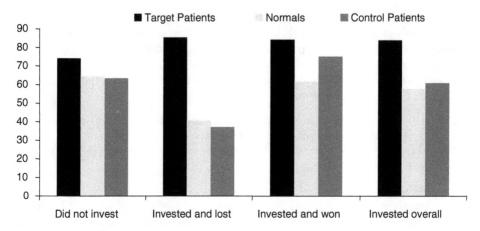

Figure 13.1 Percentage of decisions to invest as a function of outcome in the previous round
Source: Shiv *et al.* (2005).

that these groups invested less than 40% of the time after a round in which they had suffered a loss!

AS TIME GOES PAST

Equally (if not more disturbing) is the complete lack of learning that both 'normals' and 'patient controls' display over the course of the game. Figure 13.2 shows the overall percentage of time that the various groups of players chose to invest broken down into four groups of five games. Of course, if players were rational and learned from their experience then these lines would slope upwards from left to right (i.e. the longer the game went on, the more they would invest). Unfortunately, for both 'normals' and 'patient controls' the lines slope downwards

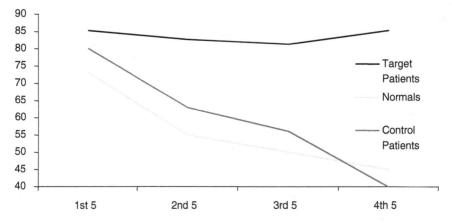

Figure 13.2 Percentage investing over time
Source: Shiv *et al.* (2005).

from left to right – that is to say, the longer the game went on, the less they decided to invest. They were getting worse at the game as time went past.

The parallels with bear markets are (I hope) obvious. The evidence above suggests that it is outright fear that drives people to ignore bargains when they are available in the market, if they have previously suffered a loss. The longer they find themselves in this position the worse their decision making appears to become.

Of course, this game is designed so that taking risk yields good results. If the game were reversed and taking risk ended in poor outcomes, the normals would outperform the players who can't feel fear. However, I would argue that the former is a better description of the current environment than the latter. When markets are cheap, the odds are good for high future returns. But, of course, markets are cheap because of all the bad news we are currently receiving.

THE IMPACT OF BRAIN DRAIN

The fact that time seems to drain the ability to think rationally fits with a lot of the work done looking at the psychology of self-control. Baumeister (2003) argues that self-control (effectively our ability to hold our emotions in check) is like a muscle – too much use leads to exhaustion. He concludes his survey of the field by highlighting the key findings of his research:

> When self-esteem is threatened, people become upset and lose their capacity to regulate themselves ... when self-regulation fails people may become increasingly self-defeating in various ways, such as taking immediate pleasures instead of delayed rewards. Self-regulation appears to depend on limited resources that operate like strength or energy, and so people can only regulate themselves to a limited extent.

People tend to display the ability for self-regulation in varying degrees. In the past I have administered a test known as the cognitive reflection test[2] (CRT) to measure how easy each of us finds it to override our X-system. The CRT is made up of three questions.

1. A bat and a ball together cost $1.10. The bat costs a dollar more than the ball. How much does the ball cost?
2. It takes 5 machines 5 minutes to make 5 widgets. How long will it take 100 machines to make 100 widgets?
3. In a lake there is a patch of lily pads. The patch doubles in size every day. If it takes 48 days for the patch to cover the entire lake, how long would it take for the patch to cover half the lake?

Each question has an obvious but unfortunately incorrect answer (the X-system response), and also a less obvious but nonetheless correct answer (the logical C-system solution). Because X-system is a 'satisfier' rather than a 'maximizer', it searches for solutions that look approximately correct. If left unchecked it provides these as the 'true' answers. If one engages in self-regulation, then the C-system is activated to check the output and override it where necessary.

I have given over 700 fund managers and analysts these three questions (among many others) over the years. Figure 13.3 shows the percentage of respondents by the number of

---

[2] This test was originally created by Shane Frederik of MIT.

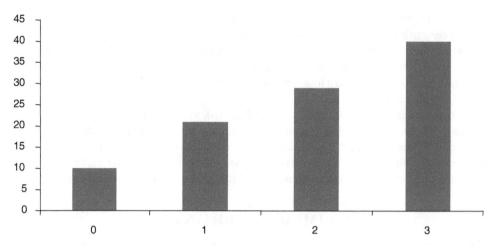

Figure 13.3 Percentage of CRT questions correctly answered
Source: SG Equity research.

CRT questions successfully answered. Only 40% of fund managers managed to get all three questions right. Effectively 60% didn't engage is sufficient self-regulation!

A recent study by Sweldens and colleagues (De Laughe *et al.*, 2008) studied the same game that is outlined above, but measured people on the basis of their degree of reliance upon their X-system.[3] If the depletion of resources is a problem, then those who rely on their X-system more should suffer poorer decision making when they have been forced to use up their store of self-regulatory ability. In order to achieve this, one group of players was subjected to a Stroop test. The Stroop test will be familiar to fans of Brain Training games – although they may not know its name. It presents the names of colours, and players have to name the colour in which the name of the colour is written, rather than the name of the colour. Thus the word RED may appear in blue ink, and the correct response is blue. It thus takes concentration and willpower to complete the Stroop test.

Figure 13.4 shows the overall percentage of time which people choose to invest depending upon their cognitive processing style and whether or not they had to complete the Stroop test. In the control condition (i.e. without the Stroop test), both those who relied on X- and C-system processing performed in the same fashion. They invested around 70% of the time (still distinctly suboptimally). The results were very different when self-regulation was depleted. Those with a very strong reliance on their C-system continued to do well, investing 78% of the time. However, those who relied heavily on their X-system suffered particularly badly. They invested only 49% of the time!

Given that this kind of behaviour might encompass up to 60% of fund managers, it isn't surprising that many professional investors don't feel inclined to accept the bargains being offered by Mr Market at the moment.

---

[3] They used a self-report approach. So people were measured on the basis of how much they agreed or disagreed with eight statements such as 'I tend to use my heart as a guide for my actions', 'I like to reply on my intuitive impressions', 'I don't have very good sense of intuition', etc. rather than a more clinical approach such as the CRT.

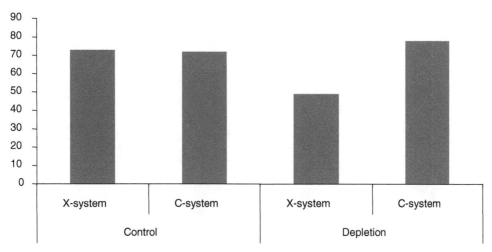

Figure 13.4   Percentage of time invested by processing style and test condition
Source: De Langhe *et al.* (2008).

THE BLANK SLATE

Investors should consider trying to adopt the Buddhist approach to time. That is to say, the past is gone and can't be changed, the future is unknown, and so we must focus on the present. The decision to invest or not should be a function of the current situation (from my perspective the degree of value on offer) not governed by our prior experiences (or indeed our future hopes). However, this blank slate is mentally very hard to achieve. Our brains seem to be wired to focus on the short term and to fear loss in an extreme fashion. These mental hurdles are barriers to sensible investment decision making in a bear market.

14

The Behavioural Stumbling Blocks
to Value Investing*

The fact that value outperforms over the long term is not new news. Yet despite this, there are relatively few 'true' value managers. This chapter seeks to explore the behavioural stumbling blocks that conspire to prevent us doing what we know to be right. Loss aversion, present bias, herding, availability and overconfidence are just a few of the hurdles that must be overcome to exploit value opportunities.

- Psychologists argue that knowledge and behaviour are not one and the same thing. That is to say, we sometimes do what we know to be wrong. For instance, the knowledge that safe sex can reduce the risk of HIV/AIDS doesn't always translate into the use of a condom. The same is true in other fields; simply knowing that value outperforms over the long term isn't enough to persuade everyone to be a value investor.

- Numerous other behavioural stumbling blocks help to explain why value investing is likely to remain a minority sport. Everyone is after the holy grail of investing, a strategy that never loses money! But it doesn't exist. Investing is probabilistic, so losses will occur. However, given our tendency to be loss averse (we dislike losses, more than we like gains) strategies that sometimes see short-term losses will be shunned.

- Long time horizons are integral to value investing. However, they are not natural to humans. Our brains appear to be designed to favour the short term. When faced with the possibility of a short-term gain, we get carried away and forget about the long term. So perhaps Keynes was correct when he wrote: 'Investment based on genuine long-term expectation is so difficult to-day as to be scarcely practicable.'

- Neuroscientists have found that social pain is felt in exactly the same parts of the brain as real physical pain. Value investing often involves going against the crowd, and hence involves social pain. So value investors are the financial equivalent of masochists.

- The stories associated with value stocks are generally going to be poor. There will be myriad reasons why any given stock is currently out of favour. It is exceptionally difficult to resist these stories, and instead focus on whether the bad news story is already in the price.

- As is ever the case, overconfidence also rears its ugly head. It is difficult to admit to ourselves (let alone to anyone else) that actually a simple rule can easily outperform us. We all like to think that we can pick stocks, or call asset classes, better than a rule or a model, but the evidence is not supportive of this misplaced, self-aggrandizing view.

- One final word of warning: we all set out with good intentions. However, psychologists have found that we massively overweight our current intentions in the prediction of our future behaviour. Thus, as much as we might say, 'OK, now I'm going to be a good value investor', the likelihood of us actually doing so is far, far less than we would like to believe.

KNOWLEDGE ≠ BEHAVIOUR

Knowing something to be true isn't always enough to promote changes in behaviour. So simply because we can show that value outperforms over the long term, it isn't easy to actually persuade everyone to adopt a value strategy.[1]

A recent paper by Dinkelman *et al.* (2006) makes the difference between knowledge and behaviour all too clear. They examined the difference between knowledge of HIV/AIDS and its prevention, and actual sexual behaviour (Figure 14.1). For example, 91% of men said they knew that the use of a condom could help to prevent the spread of HIV/AIDS, yet only 70% of them used a condom. Among women the situation was even worse: 92% reported that they knew condoms were useful in preventing HIV/AIDS transmission, but only 63% used them!

If knowledge can't change behaviour in these tragic circumstances, why on earth would we expect it to do so in the trivial world of investing?

LOSS AVERSION

Everyone is after the holy grail of investing: a strategy that works all the time. It doesn't exist, so you might as well stop looking, or, even worse, pretending that you have one. The nature of markets is highly probabilistic; uncertainty is central to the act of investing. So nothing is likely to work continuously.

Figure 14.2 shows the percentage of time that value returns are positive on an annual basis (and the percentage of time that they exceed the broad market return). On an annual basis you could reasonably expect value strategies to generate positive absolute returns around 70% of the time (based on MSCI value 1975–2006).

In 3 years out of every 10, you would see a negative return, and this negative return certainly dissuades many from following such an approach. We all dislike losses much more than we enjoy gains – a phenomenon known as loss aversion.

In many studies, people have been found to dislike losses at least twice as much as they enjoy gains. Consider the following bet: On the toss of a fair coin, if you lose you must

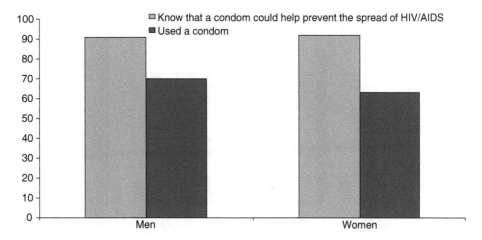

Figure 14.1   Percentage of respondents
Source: Dinkelman *et al.* (2006). DrKW Macro research.

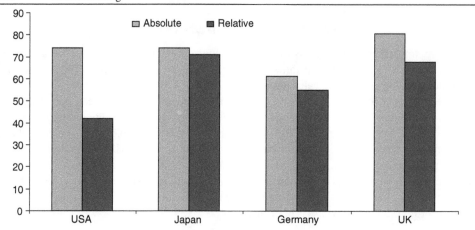

Figure 14.2 Percentage of time value strategies generate positive returns (absolute and relative)
Source: DrKW Macro research.

pay me £100. What is the minimum you need to win in order to make this bet acceptable to you?

In our survey of over 450 fund managers we found that the average response was £190! So professional fund managers are just as loss averse as the rest of us (see Figure 14.3).

Joel Greenblatt, in his wonderful *Little Book that Beats the Market* details the role that loss aversion plays in deterring investors from following his 'magic formula'. He notes,

> Imagine diligently watching those stocks each day as they do worse than the market average over the course of many months or even years ... The magic formula portfolio fared poorly relative to the market average in 5 out of every 12 months tested. For full-year period ... failed to beat the market average once every four years.

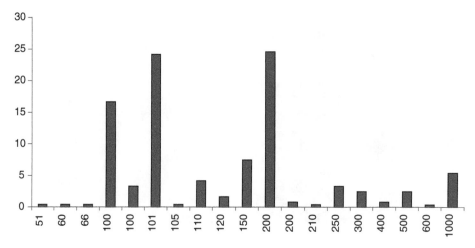

Figure 14.3 Fund managers are just as loss averse as everyone else (frequency %)
Source: DrKW Macro research.

So loss aversion certainly plays a pivotal role in dissuading people from becoming value investors.

DELAYED GRATIFICATION AND HARD-WIRING FOR THE SHORT TERM

Not only can value strategies go wrong but they can take time to work. When a value opportunity is exploited there are two ways for it to pay off. For instance, if I buy a significantly undervalued stock, it is possible that everyone else might realize that this is indeed a cheap stock and the price might correct. However, it is also possible that the stock remains undervalued and generates its higher long-run return by continuing to pay a high dividend yield. Both paths are possible, but when a value position is implemented, it is impossible to know *ex-ante* which mechanism will deliver the returns.

This means that value investors must have long time horizons. In our study of value investors we found they had an average holding period of 5 years, whereas the average holding period for a stock on the New York Stock Exchange is only 11 months (see Figures 14.4 and 14.5).

However, long time horizons don't come naturally to us humans. When we are faced with the possibility of a reward, our brains release dopamine. Dopamine makes people feel good about themselves, confident and stimulated. The majority of dopamine receptors are located in areas of the brain that are generally associated with the X-system (our fast and dirty mental system). The possibility of monetary reward seems to trigger the release of dopamine in the same way as enjoying food, or taking pleasure-inducing drugs (see Knutson and Peterson, 2005).

McClure *et al.* (2004) have recently investigated the neural systems that underlie decisions surrounding delayed gratification. Much research has suggested that people tend to behave impatiently today but plan to act patiently in the future. For instance, when offered a choice between £10 today and £11 tomorrow, many people choose the immediate option. However, if you asked people today to choose between £10 in a year, and £11 in a year and a day, many of those who went for the immediate option in the first case now go for the second option.

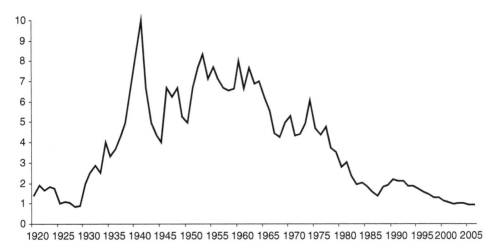

Figure 14.4 Average holding period for a stock on the NYSE (years)
Source: DrKW Macro research.

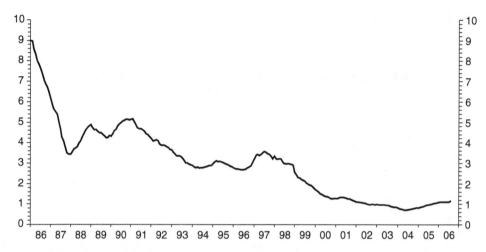

Figure 14.5   Average holding period for a stock on the LSE (years)
Source: DrKW Macro research.

In order to see what happens in the brain when faced with such choices, McClure *et al.* measured the brain activity of participants as they made a series of intertemporal choices between early and delayed monetary rewards. Some of the choice pairs included an immediate option; others were choices between two delayed options.

They found that when the choice involved an immediate gain, the ventral stratum (part of the basal ganglia), the medial orbitofrontal cortex, and the medial prefrontal cortex were all disproportionally used. All these elements are associated with the X-system. McClure *et al.* point out that these areas are also riddled by the mid-brain dopamine system. They note, 'These structures have consistently been implicated in impulsive behaviour.'

When the choice involved two delayed rewards, the prefrontal and parietal cortex were engaged (correlates of the C-system). The more difficult the choice, the more these areas seemed to be used. It is very hard for us to override the X-system. Frequently, the X-system reacts before the C-system has even had a chance to consider the problem. All too often, it looks as if we are likely to end up being hard-wired for the short term. So perhaps Keynes was right when he wrote, 'Investment based on genuine long-term expectation is so difficult to-day as to be scarcely practicable'. Patience really is a virtue.

In investment, loss aversion and time horizon are not independent issues. The more frequently you check a portfolio, the more likely it is that you will witness a loss. It is perfectly possible for a skilled fund manager to display three years of back-to-back declines. Figure 14.6 uses a constructed universe where all the fund managers have 3% alpha and a 6% tracking error. I then let the make-believe managers run money for 50 years. The chart illustrates the frequency of years of back-to-back underperformance. Around 70% of the make-believe fund managers displayed 3 or more years of underperformance!

A study by Goyal and Wahal (2005) shows why we need to explain the risks of investing to the end client far better than we currently do (Figure 14.7). It should be required reading by all pension plans and trustees. They review some 4000-plus decisions regarding the hiring and firing of investment manager by pension plan sponsors and trustees between 1993 and 2003. The results they uncover show the classic hallmarks of returns-chasing behaviour. The funds

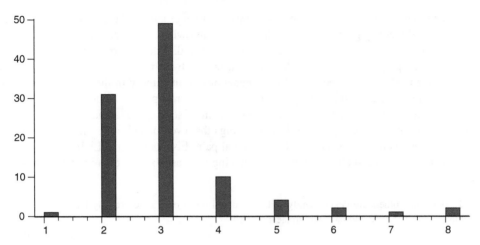

Figure 14.6 Frequency of cumulative years of underperformance
Source: DrKW Macro research.

the sponsors tend to hire have an average outperformance of nearly 14% in the 3 years before hiring, but they have statistically insignificant returns after the hiring. In contrast, those fired for performance reasons tend to have underperformed by around 6% in the 3 years leading up to the dismissal. However, in the 3 years after the firing, they tend to outperform by nearly 5%. A powerful lesson in the need to extend time horizons.

SOCIAL PAIN AND THE HERDING HABIT

In the past, we have mentioned that there is strong evidence from neuroscience to suggest that real pain and social pain are felt in exactly the same places in the brain. Eisenberger

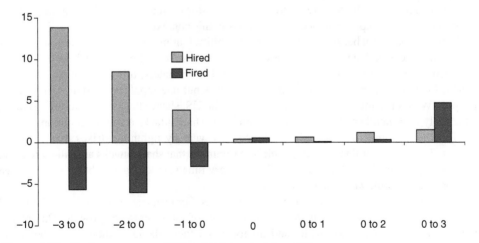

Figure 14.7 Performance around hiring and firing decisions (%)
Source: Goyal and Wahal (2005). DrKW Macro research.

and Lieberman (2004) asked participants to play a computer game. Players thought they were playing in a three-way game with two other players, throwing a ball back and forth.

In fact, the two other players were computer controlled. After a period of three-way play, the two other 'players' began to exclude the participant by throwing the ball back and forth between themselves. This social exclusion generates brain activity in the anterior cingulate cortex and the insula. Both of which are also activated by real physical pain.

Contrarian strategies are the investment equivalent of seeking out social pain. In order to implement such a strategy, you will buy the things that everyone else is selling, and sell the stocks that everyone else is buying. This is social pain. Eisenberger and Lieberman's results suggest that following such a strategy is like having your arm broken on a regular basis – not fun!

> To buy when others are despondently selling and sell when others are greedily buying requires the greatest fortitude and pays the greatest reward
>
> Sir John Templeton

> It is the long-term investor, he who most promotes the public interest, who will in practice come in for the most criticism ... For it is in the essence of his behaviour that he should be eccentric, unconventional and rash in the eyes of average opinion.
>
> John Maynard Keynes

> Worldly wisdom teaches that it is better for reputation to fail conventionally than to succeed unconventionally.
>
> John Maynard Keynes

POOR STORIES

When a value screen is performed (or any other screen for that matter), a list of stocks is generated. Upon production of this list, the first thing everyone does is look down the list and start to analyse the elements. For instance, 'I can't buy that stock, it's a basket case'. The preconceived stories associated with stocks begin to interfere. Just as glamour stocks have seductive stories of incredible future growth, so value stocks have myriad reasons for their cheapness. All of which conspire to prevent the investor from actually following the screen's suggestions. So perhaps ignorance really is bliss in this context.

Stories are powerful because they trigger availability. Our minds are not limitless supercomputers; they are bounded by cognitive resource constraints. Very often people think of memory as functioning like a picture postcard or a photo. Unfortunately, this isn't the way memory works. Memory is a process, into which the truth is but one input. For instance, if you ask people, 'Which is a more likely cause of death in the US, shark attacks or lightning strikes?', a bizarrely large number of people seem to think that shark attacks are more common, despite the fact that 30 times more people are killed each year by lightning strikes than by shark attacks. The reason for this error in people's reasoning is that shark attacks are salient (easy to recall – largely thanks to Jaws) and available (every time someone gets nibbled off the coast of Florida or Hawaii, we all hear about it).

The same thing happens when we hear other stories. For instance, when an IPO is launched you can bet it will have a great story attached, full of the promise of growth. This makes the 'growth' salient and available, and all too often these thoughts then crowd out other considerations such as the valuation – just as the vivid shark attack crowds out the more likely lightning strike.

The reverse happens with value stocks. The stocks will generally appear to be cheap, but investors will be able to find any number of arguments as to why they are likely to stay cheap. So the story will crowd out the fact of cheapness.

OVERCONFIDENCE

One of the key reasons that people don't follow quant models is their amazing overconfidence in their own abilities. The same is true when it comes to value investing. Rather than follow a simple rule like, say, buying the bottom 20% of the MSCI universe ranked by PE, investors often prefer to rely on their stock selection skills (however dubious these may be).

Both the illusion of control and the illusion of knowledge conspire to generate this over-confidence. The illusion of knowledge fosters the idea that because we know more, we must be able to make superior decisions. Intuitively, it is easy to see why having more information should enable you to make better decisions. However, much evidence has been collected to show flaws in this idea. The empirical reality appears to be that more information isn't the same as better information. All too often investors suffer a signal extraction problem, that is to say they struggle to extract the meaningful elements among the deluge of noise.

The illusion of control also plays a part. We are experts in magical thinking – that is, believing we can influence things that we clearly can't. An article by Pronin *et al.* (2006) explores several aspects of this behaviour. In one of their experiments, they told people they were investigating voodoo. Participants were paired (one of each pair actually worked for the experimenter and was either a pleasant person or a real pain in the neck). The stooge was always selected to be the 'victim', while the real participant was selected to stick pins into a voodoo doll ('witch doctor').

However, before they were asked to do this, they spent a little time with their partner in the experiment (who, remember, is either pleasant or exceedingly irritating). Then the 'witch doctor' was told to go into a room and generate 'vivid and concrete thoughts about the victim but not to say them aloud'. Then they were allowed to stick pins into a voodoo doll. After this, the experimenter asked the 'victim' if he had suffered any pains. Because he was a confederate of the experimenter he said 'yes, I have a bit of a headache'. The participant playing the witch doctor was then asked to complete a questionnaire including a question on the degree of culpability they felt for the 'victim's' pain. Amazingly, when dealing with the annoying 'victim', the 'witch doctors' felt much more responsible than they did with the normal 'victim', presumably because they had done more visualization of being angry at this person.

Several follow-up experiments were also conducted. One involved watching someone who was blindfolded throw a basketball. Participants were asked to either imagine the player making the shot, or imagine the player doing something else, like stretching. Those primed to think about the player making the shot thought they were much more responsible for the success or failure than those given the alternative scenario.

Finally, at a real basketball match, attendees were asked either to state how important a potential player was and why, or simply asked to describe the physical appearance of the player. After the match they were then asked to rate how responsible they felt for their team's performance. Once again, those primed to describe the players' importance felt much more responsible than those simply asked to describe the players (Figure 14.8).

In all three cases, those primed to think about the issues displayed significantly more 'magical thinking' than the controls. Investors are certainly likely to have thought about the

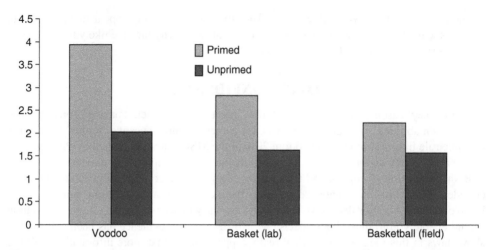

Figure 14.8   Degree of responsibility (1 = not responsible at all, 7 = totally responsible)
Source: Pronin *et al.* (2006). DrKW Macro research.

stocks they are selecting, and as such will feel 'responsible' for the outcomes even if they can't possibly influence them.

FUN

The final stumbling block which I want to cover here is, simply, fun. As Keynes opined, 'The game of professional investment is intolerably boring and over-exacting to anyone who is entirely exempt from the gambling instinct; while he who has it must pay this propensity the appropriate toll.'

Following simple rules and procedures isn't exactly great fun. Whereas filling your day by meeting companies and talking with sell-side analysts may be (although, personally, if this is your definition of fun, I suspect you need more help than I can offer you).

As Paul Samuelson said, 'Investing should be dull. It shouldn't be exciting. Investing should be more like watching paint dry or watching grass grow. If you want excitement, take $800 and go to Las Vegas.'

NO, HONESTLY I WILL BE GOOD

Let me end with one final word of warning: we all start out with the best of intentions but, as the saying goes, the road to hell is paved with good intentions. A recent paper by Koehler and Poon (2006) demonstrates the point perfectly. They asked participants to complete a questionnaire about giving blood at an upcoming donation clinic. People were asked to rate how likely they were to give blood, and also rate on a scale of 1 (strongly disagree) to 9 (strong agree) a series of statements concerning their attitudes on the subject, including a final question which read, 'Right now, as I think about it, I strongly intend to donate blood at the July 14–22 blood donation clinic.' This was used to gauge participants' current intention strength.

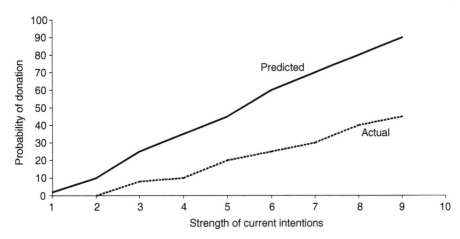

Figure 14.9   Predicted and actual probability of blood donation
Source: Koehler and Poon (2006). DrKW Macro research.

Figure 14.9 shows the predicted probability of blood donation and actual outcome of blood donation by the strength of current intentions. In general, people were massively too optimistic about their blood donation. On average, they were around 30 percentage points too optimistic. The predicted probability of blood donation rose much faster across the strength of current intentions, than the actual outcome. This implies that current intentions have an overly strong effect on prediction of behaviour, but not on behaviour itself.

So as easy as it might be to say, 'From now on I'm going to be a value investor', the likelihood of it actually occurring is highly remote.

Part III
The Philosophy of Value Investing

15

The Tao of Investing: The Ten Tenets of My Investment Creed*

Many times over the years I have been asked how I would approach investing. This chapter attempts to codify my beliefs (and provide some evidence for them). However, before embarking upon a journey into my investment creed, it is worthwhile asking a question that doesn't get asked often enough – What is the aim of investing? The answer to this question drives everything that follows. I feel that Sir John Templeton put it best when he said, 'For all long-term investors, there is only one objective – maximum total returns after taxes.' Nothing else matters. Then the question becomes: How should we invest to deliver this objective?

- **Tenet I: Value, value, value**. Value investing is the only safety first approach I have come across. By putting the margin of safety at the heart of the process, the value approach minimizes the risk of overpaying for the hope of growth.
- **Tenet II: Be contrarian.** Sir John Templeton observed that 'It is impossible to produce superior performance unless you do something different from the majority'.
- **Tenet III: Be patient**. Patience is integral to a value approach on many levels, from waiting for the fat pitch, to dealing with the value managers' curse of being too early.
- **Tenet IV: Be unconstrained.** While pigeon-holing and labelling are fashionable, I am far from convinced that they aid investment. Surely I should be free to exploit value opportunities wherever they may occur.
- **Tenet V: Don't forecast.** We have to find a better way of investing than relying upon our seriously flawed ability to soothsay.
- **Tenet VI: Cycles matter.** As Howard Marks puts it, we can't predict but we can prepare. An awareness of the economic, credit and sentiment cycles can help with investment.
- **Tenet VII: History matters.** The four most dangerous words in investing are 'This time is different'. A knowledge of history and context can help to avoid repeating the blunders of the past.
- **Tenet VIII: Be sceptical.** One of my heroes said 'Blind faith in anything will get you killed'. Learning to question what you are told and developing critical thinking skills are vital to long-term success and survival.
- **Tenet IX: Be top-down and bottom-up.** One of the key lessons from the last year is that both top-down and bottom-up viewpoints matter. Neither has a monopoly on insight.
- **Tenet X: Treat your clients as you would treat yourself.** Surely the ultimate test of any investment is: would I be willing to make this investment with my own money?

*This article appeared in Mind Matters on 24 February 2008. Copyright © 2008 by The Société Générale Group. All rights reserved. The material discussed was accurate at the time of publication.

Over the years, I have been asked many times how I would approach investment. Until today I have always shied away from answering directly. However, I feel it is time to codify my investment beliefs. This chapter represents my attempt to set out my own personal investment creed. However, before we embark upon this journey into the murky world of my beliefs, we need to frame the question. Essentially this amounts to asking: What is the aim of investing?

THE AIM OF INVESTING

This has always struck me as a question that could do with being asked a great deal more often than it actually is. From my perspective, Sir John Templeton put it best: 'For all long-term investors, there is only one objective – maximum total returns after taxes' Or, as Keynes put it: 'The ideal policy ... is where it is earning a respectable rate of interest on its funds, while securing at the same time that its risk of really serious depreciation in capital value is at a minimum.'

These definitions pretty much say it all. Of course, in today's world of fund supermarkets and the dominance of the relative performance derby, such simple concepts as total real return don't often feature in investment mandates (apart from hedge funds, of course). But surely, ultimately this is what any fund should strive to achieve.

Viewing the world in these terms also prevents us from falling into the modern finance obsession of alpha and beta. As I have written before (see Chapter 2), I reject CAPM on both empirical and theoretical grounds. Once CAPM is thrown out then concepts such as alpha and beta become meaningless, and one can focus on return generation in its own right rather than the distraction of decomposition.

Having set out our investment objective, it is time to turn to the philosophy of how this might be achieved. Below you will find my 10 tenets of investment. These represent my beliefs (and in some cases some evidence) on the way in which an investment operation should be run.

TENET I: VALUE, VALUE, VALUE

At the very heart of the approach I follow is the belief that the price I pay for an investment determines the likely return. No asset is so good as to be immune from the possibility of overvaluation, and few assets are so bad as to be exempt from the possibility of undervaluation. Thus an asset can be an investment at one price but not at another.

The separation between value and price is key, thus this approach inherently rejects market efficiency (in which price and value are equal). As Warren Buffett said, 'Price is what you pay, value is what you get'. However, the aim is obviously not to buy at fair value, because that will simply generate an average return.

Rather, investments should be purchased with a margin of safety. Any estimate of intrinsic value will only prove to be correct via the intervention of luck. Hence, buying only when a large discount to that estimate is available offers protection against being wrong. As Ben Graham said, the margin of safety is 'available for absorbing the effect of miscalculations or worse than average luck'.

Value investing is the only form of 'safety first' investing I have come across. It places risk management at the very heart of the approach. Of course, when I talk of risk management I am not talking of the modern pseudoscience so beloved by quants, but rather the 'permanent loss of capital'. Value investors implicitly try to mitigate 'value risk' (the risk of paying too much

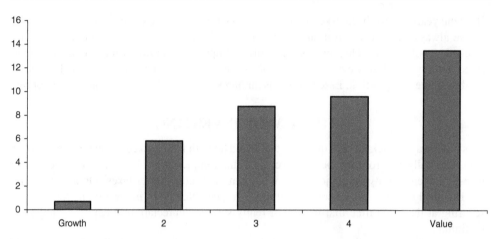

Figure 15.1   Global unconstrained value investing works! (1985–2008, % p.a.)
Source: SG Global Strategy research.

for something), and spend their time trying to figure out the degree of business and balance sheet risk they are faced with (as discussed in Chapter 11).

I would also suggest that value is an absolute concept, not a relative one. Arguing that a stock is attractive just because it is cheaper than its peers seems to be a route to disaster to me. The ratio of price to intrinsic value is the only measure that should matter.

This isn't the place for a full-scale review of the empirics that show the advantage offered by following a value approach. But to provide some limited evidence, Figures 15.1–15.3 show the role of value in three different contexts. Figure 15.1 shows the performance of an unconstrained global value approach to stock selection. It clearly shows the advantage a value perspective brings to an investor.

Nor, however, should asset allocators ignore value. Figure 15.2 shows the advantages of deploying capital when overall market valuations are cheap. It shows the real 10-year returns

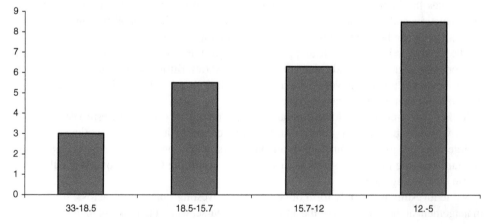

Figure 15.2   Real returns over the subsequent decade by purchase G&D P/E (% p.a.) (1871–2008)
Source: SG Global Strategy research.

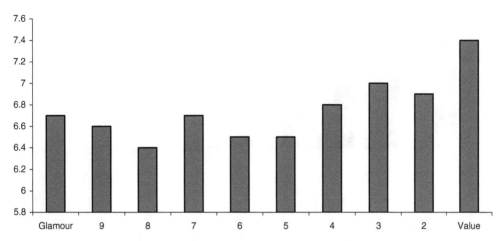

Figure 15.3 Average annualised 3-year bond returns, ranked by P/B decile (1990–2007)
Source: Brandes Institute.

based around the purchase point defined in terms of Graham and Dodd P/Es (current price over 10-year moving average earnings). Clearly value has a role to play in asset allocation as well as in stock selection.

Fixed-income investors would also be foolish to ignore value. My friends at the Brandes Institute performed an intriguing study last year on the performance of glamour and value bonds (defined as bonds from companies with high and low price to book ratios, respectively). They find that the bonds of value companies do considerably better than the bonds of glamour companies! So yet again the power of value shines through (Figure 15.3).

TENET II: BE CONTRARIAN

As Keynes opined, 'The central principle of investment is to go contrary to the general opinion, on the grounds that if everyone agreed about its merit, the investment is inevitably too dear and therefore unattractive.' Or, as Sir John Templeton observed, 'It is impossible to produce superior performance unless you do something different from the majority.'

Following a value-oriented approach will almost certainly lead you to a contrarian stance, because you are generally buying the unloved assets and selling the market's darlings.

Rather than worry over the latest survey of opinion, I prefer to infer the consensus from asset prices. The reason for this preference is essentially misanthropy. Just as House, the eponymous anti-hero of the US TV drama, refuses to talk to patients because they lie, I am generally mistrustful of survey responses. To my mind all too often they represent where people like to be allocated, rather than actually where they are positioned.

The power of a contrarian approach has been demonstrated by the work of Dasgupta *et al.*, (2006). They show that the stocks institutional fund managers are busy buying are outperformed by the stocks they are busy selling! They examined US fund managers' filings from 1983 to 2004. Each quarter, stocks are assigned to different portfolios conditional upon the persistence of institutional net trades (that is the number of consecutive quarters for which a net buy or a net sell is recorded). A persistence measure of −5 includes all stocks that have

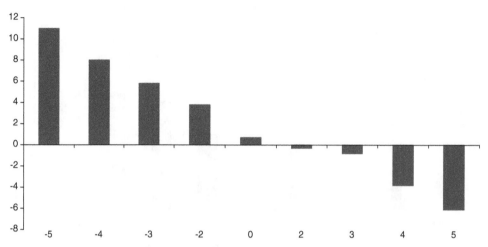

Figure 15.4   Abnormal returns over two years by buying persistence category (%)
Source: Dasgupta *et al.* (2006).

been sold for at least five quarters, and a persistence measure of 0 shows stocks that have been bought or sold in the current period.

Figure 15.4 shows the market-adjusted future returns for each persistence portfolio on a two-year time horizon. Even a cursory glance reveals the negative relationship between returns and institutional buying and selling. Over a two-year time horizon there is a 17% return difference – the stocks that the institutions sold most outperforming the market by around 11%, and the stocks they purchased most underperforming by 6%!

Dasgupta *et al.* also noted several characteristics of the stocks that fund managers seem to buy with high persistence. Such stocks tend to be liquid, growth (low book to market) stocks with high momentum. Conversely, those that inhabit the selling portfolio are generally less liquid, value stocks with poor past returns.

One final aspect of Dasgupta *et al.*'s work is noteworthy. They estimated a measure of how likely each manager is to herd (or conform, if you prefer). They called this measure the sheep index. They concluded: 'We find that about three-quarters of institutions display conformist patterns when faced with high-persistence stocks . . . our measure of conformism is pervasive . . . with the majority of managers displaying a positive sheep value.' As Ben Graham said, it requires 'considerable will power to keep from following the crowd'.

TENET III: BE PATIENT

Patience is integral to the value approach on many levels. As Ben Graham wrote, 'Undervaluations caused by neglect or prejudice may persist for an inconveniently long time, and the same applies to inflated prices caused by over-enthusiasm or artificial stimulants.'

Whenever a position is put on, one can never be sure whether it will work or not. Buying cheap stocks helps to generate long-run returns, but tells us nothing about the short-term prospects. Cheap stocks can always get cheaper, and expensive stocks can always get more expensive (in the short term).

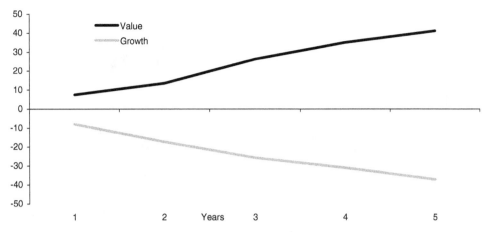

Figure 15.5 Patience is a virtue: cumulative excess returns over various holding periods
Source: SG Global Strategy research.

Thus patience is required. At the stock level, a value situation can lead to one of three possible outcomes:

1. A stock may rerate as the market corrects the underpricing.
2. The stock may stay depressed, but potentially generate a return through higher dividend payments.
3. The stock may never recover (aka value traps).

So patience is a prerequisite for value managers as long as we are dealing with the first two types of stocks, and a key problem when it comes to the third type of stock. Figure 15.5 shows the need for patience when it comes to global value investing.

The value strategy tends to outperform the market by around 7% in the first year. If you hold for another 12 months, an additional 6% is added to the return. However, holding for longer periods really creates opportunity. In the third year an amazing 12% outperformance of the market is recorded, followed by another 8% in the fourth year.

This receives practical support when one examines the average holding period of long-term successful value managers; their average holding period is around five years. A marked contrast to the churn and burn of the average mutual fund (Figure 15.6).

A long time horizon makes sense from the perspective of the drivers of returns as well. For instance, on a one-year view, 60% of your total return comes through changes in valuation (effectively random fluctuations in prices about which I know nothing). However, as we extend the time horizon, so the things I, as a fundamental investor, am meant to understand start to matter much more. For instance, over a 5 year horizon, some 80% of the total real return is generated through the price I pay and the growth in the underlying business.

However, it appears as if patient long-term investors are a vanishing species. As Keynes noted, 'Compared with their predecessors, modern investors concentrate too much on annual, quarterly, or even monthly valuations of what they hold, and on capital appreciation. ... And too little on immediate yield. ... And intrinsic worth.'

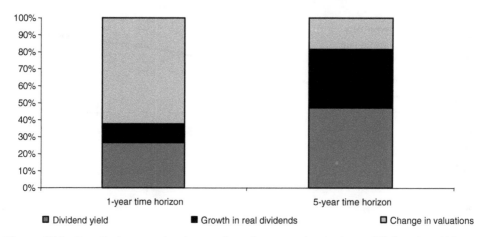

Figure 15.6 Contribution to total real return depends on your time horizon – US data since 1871
Source: SG Global Strategy research.

As Figure 15.7 shows, the average investor appears to have a chronic case of attention deficit hyperactivity disorder. The average holding period for a stock on the NYSE is six months! Under this time horizon, the only thing that any one cares about is: what is going to happen next quarter?

As Keynes opined, 'The spectacle of modern investment markets has sometimes moved me towards the conclusion that to make the purchase of an investment permanent and indissoluble, like marriage, except by reason of death or other grave cause, might be a useful remedy for our contemporary evils. For this would force the investor to direct his mind to the long-term prospects and to those only.'

Of course, the obsession with the short-term creates an opportunity. If everyone else is dashing around pricing assets on the basis of the next three months, then they are likely to

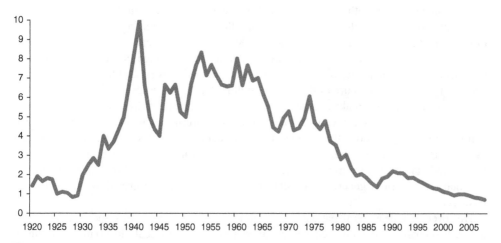

Figure 15.7 Average holding period for a stock on the NYSE (years)
Source: SG Global Strategy research.

mis-price assets for the longer term. So an opportunity for time arbitrage arises for the investor with a longer horizon. Sadly, as Keynes observed, 'investment based on genuine long-term expectation is so difficult today as to be scarcely practicable'.

This is not to say that the value approach leads one to be totally immune from the market. In the event of a value trap, patience can lead to disaster. To guard against this possibility, a lot of time should be spent on reviewing positions that move against you. If a position goes 'bad' then a review should be triggered. The aim of the review should be to start from a blank sheet of paper and consider what should be done now.

If nothing fundamental has changed (i.e. this is just a case of price volatility being an order of magnitude higher than fundamental volatility) then the opportunity arises for an increase in the position (assuming limits haven't been hit). If something fundamental and material has altered then the position can be cut.

Accepting the integral role of patience also means that leverage will be avoided. Leverage limits the staying power of an investor and thus must be shunned. As Keynes observed, 'An investor who proposes to ignore near-term market fluctuations needs greater resources for safety and must not operate on so large a scale, if at all, with borrowed money.'

Patience is also required because the curse of the value manager is to be too early – both in terms of the buy (known affectionately as premature accumulation) and sell decisions. Unfortunately, in the short term being early is indistinguishable from being wrong.

We followers of value tend to get out of positions when they start to look expensive, rather than when they look ridiculously overvalued. My own work is a litany of premature problem spotting. For instance, calling Thailand the next Mexico in 1995, arguing that the equity market was enjoying one last hurrah in 1997 (before losing my head in the mania of the tech bubble), pointing out the bubble characteristics of both the US housing market and commodities in 2005, and calling the mining sector a bubble in 2006.

If I was clairvoyant, I would be fully invested until the day before the crash and never buy until the bottom. However, since I don't possess a crystal ball (and I haven't met anyone else who does), I can see no alternative but to continue to act in a patient, cautious fashion. This means that positions need to be built slowly over time.

Patience is also required when the bottom-up search for value fails to uncover anything of merit. I have suggested that most investors suffer an action bias (see Chapter 17) – effectively a propensity to 'do' something. I have long found succour in the words of Winnie-the-Pooh, 'Never underestimate the value of doing nothing.' If I can't find something to invest in then I am best off doing nothing at all.

Warren Buffett often talks of the importance of waiting for the 'fat pitch'. 'I call investing the greatest business in the world,' he says, 'because you never have to swing. You stand at the plate, the pitcher throws you General Motors at 47! U.S. Steel at 39! and nobody calls a strike on you. There's no penalty except opportunity lost. All day you wait for the pitch you like; then when the fielders are asleep, you step up and hit it.'

However, most institutional investors behave 'like Babe Ruth at bat with 50,000 fans and the club owner yelling, "Swing, you bum!" and some guy is trying to pitch him an intentional walk. They know if they don't take a swing at the next pitch, the guy will say, "Turn in your uniform".'

Buffett often refers to *The Science of Hitting*, a book written by Red Sox legend Ted Williams. In it, Williams describes part of the secret to his phenomenal .344 career batting average. The theory behind Williams' extraordinary success was really quite simple (as many of the best ideas generally are).

He split the strike zone into 77 cells, each of which made up the size of a baseball, and rather than swing at anything that made its way into the strike zone, he would swing only at balls within his best cells, the sweet spot – the ones he knew he could hit. If balls didn't enter his best cell, he simply waited for the next one – even if it meant striking out now and then.

Thus, just as Williams wouldn't swing at everything, investors should wait for the fat pitch. Thus when the bottom-up search for opportunities fails, investors would be well advised to hold cash. As the Sage of Omaha has said, 'Holding cash is uncomfortable, but not as uncomfortable as doing something stupid.'

TENET IV: BE UNCONSTRAINED

One of the evils of modern-day finance is an obsession with pigeon-holing managers. This has always struck me as slightly daft. If I have a good manager why wouldn't I want him to invest where he thought the opportunity lay?

For instance, in my work over the last five months or so I have been trying to construct a portfolio of assets based around three themes: cash as a hedge against deflation (and to act as a feeder to deploy capital into my other two categories), deep value opportunities in both fixed income and equity space and, finally, sources of cheap insurance such as TIPS, gold and dividend swaps.

Of course today, most managers are forced to be specialist, leaving the 'asset allocation' decisions to the end client (a group who generally have an even more tenuous grasp on how to invest than the average fund managers). These constraints prevent investors from exploiting the full range of the opportunity set they are confronted by. A portfolio such as the one I have outlined would be unthinkable to many investors, or would require a large number of specialist managers.

Similarly, there may be times, like last year, when my analysis tells me the best place to be is net short. Early last year, my screens were throwing up the highest number of short ideas I have ever seen. Simultaneously, the long side was pretty much bereft of potential opportunities. This was a clear signal that the advantage was on the short side. Yet many managers found themselves constrained to be fully invested!

Artificially constraining a manager seems to be like hiring Robert Plant but telling him he can only sing lullabies. As long as I find investments within my 'circle of competence', to borrow Buffett's phraseology, why shouldn't I be free to exploit them?

TENET V: DON'T FORECAST

I have tried to make this a list of 'dos' rather than a list of 'don'ts' but I have to include one giant DON'T. The folly of forecasting is one of my pet hobby-horses. I simply can't understand why so many investors spend so much time engaged in an activity that has so little value, and so little chance of success.

For instance, let's say you invest according to the following process: forecast the economy, forecast the path of interest rates, forecast the sectors that will do well within that environment, and finally forecast the stocks that will do well within that sector.

Now let's assume you are pretty good at this and you are right on each forecast 70% of the time (massively above the rates actually seen). However, if you require all four forecasts to be correct, then you have just a 24% chance of actually getting it right! (This assumes that each of the forecasts is an independent event.) Now think about the number of forecasts an average analyst model contains. Sales, costs, taxes, etc. – no wonder these guys are never right.

In addition, even if by some miracle of divine intervention your forecast turns out to be correct, you can only make money from it, if (and only if) it is different form the consensus. This adds a whole new dimension of complexity to the problem.

Organizations like Starmine take great pride in revealing who the most accurate analyst is each year. However, if you cast your eye down the list of winners, sadly there is very little persistence. Effectively this suggests that a 'lucky fool' won the competition with an outlier forecast. It should also be noted that each year someone has to be the most accurate analyst! It doesn't mean they were actually right, potentially they were just less wrong than their brethren.

The evidence on the folly of forecasting is overwhelming and would fill many notes in its own right. However, let's just skate through a few charts which show just how appalling forecasting really is. Let's start at the top, the economists. These guys haven't got a clue. Frankly the three blind mice have more credibility than any macro-forecaster at seeing what is coming. Figure 15.8 shows that they constantly fail to predict recessions (until we are firmly in one), and even then they do so only under duress.

The analysts are no better. Their forecasting record is simply dreadful on both short- and long-term issues. My colleague Rui Antunes has examined the accuracy of analysts. Rather than doing the analysis at the aggregate level (as I have done in the past) Rui, ever the pedant, has investigated the scale of the error at the individual stock level.

Figure 15.9 shows the average scale of the analysts' forecast errors over time. In the USA, the average 24-month forecast error is 93%, and the average 12-month forecast error is 47% over the period 2001–2006. The data for Europe is no less disconcerting. The average 24-month forecast error is 95%, and the average 12-month forecast error is 43%. To put it mildly, analysts don't have a clue about future earnings.

Analysts' performance in divining the longer-term future is sadly no better than their performance in the short term. Figure 15.10 shows the 5-year forward growth rates from analysts, and the actual out-turns. Quintile 5 are all the stocks the analysts expect to grow fast, and quintile 1 are the stocks the analysts expect to grow slowly.

Even a cursory glance at the chart reveals that the outcomes show no statistical difference across quintiles. That is to say, analysts have absolutely no idea about forecasting long-term growth.

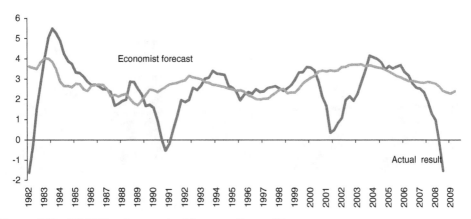

Figure 15.8 US GDP and economists' forecasts (4q ma, %)
Source: SG Global Strategy research.

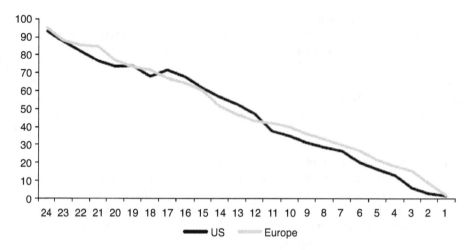

Figure 15.9 Forecast error over time: US and European markets 2001–2006, %
Source: SG Global Strategy.

My final rant on the folly of forecasting concerns target prices. Why do analysts persist in trying to forecast prices? As Ben Graham said, 'Forecasting security prices is not properly a part of security analysis.'

Figure 15.11 shows the embarrassing track record that analysts have managed to rack up with respect to target prices. For each year, I have taken the price of the security at the start of the year, and assumed that the analysts' target price is a view of where the price should be in 12 months' time. On average the analysts expect stocks to be 25% higher each year!

I have then contrasted this implied analyst view with the actual returns achieved across the same universe. As you can see, the results are not favourable to the worth of target prices. In four out of the nine years, analysts have not even managed to get the direction of change in prices correct! The absolute scale of the average forecast error is 25%.

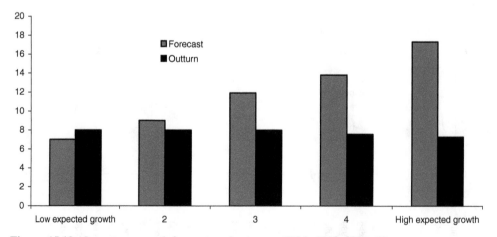

Figure 15.10 Long-term growth forecasts and outcomes (USA, 1982–2008, %)
Source: SG Global Strategy.

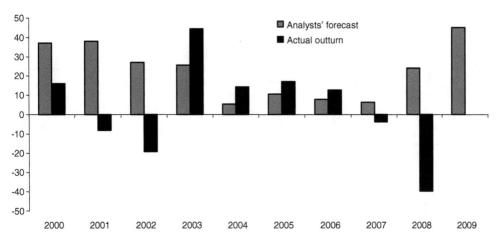

Figure 15.11   Analyst expected returns (via target prices) and actual returns (USA, %)
Source: SG Global Strategy.

The bottom line from this whistle-stop tour of the failure of forecasting is that it would be sheer madness to base an investment process around our seriously flawed ability to divine the future. We would all be better off if we took Keynes. suggested response when asked about the future, 'We simply do not know.'

TENET VI: CYCLES MATTER

The sixth tenet that I would like to suggest is that cycles matter – even for long-term investors. As Howard Marks of Oaktree Capital puts it, while we may not be able to predict, we can prepare. All sorts of cycles exist, economic, credit, and sentiment, to name but three.

It is often said that markets are driven by fear and greed. However, they generally only appear one at a time. The market's mood swings from irrational exuberance, to the depths of despair. Mr Market really is a manic depressive.

As Howard Marks wrote recently:

> In my opinion, there are two key concepts that investors must master: value and cycles. For each asset you're considering, you must have a strongly held view of its intrinsic value. When its price is below that value, it's generally a buy. When its price is higher, it's a sell. In a nutshell, that's value investing.
>
> But values aren't fixed; they move in response to changes in the economic environment. Thus, cyclical considerations influence an asset's current value. Value depends on earnings, for example, and earnings are shaped by the economic cycle and the price being charged for liquidity.
>
> Further, security prices are greatly affected by investor behaviour; thus we can be aided in investing safely by understanding where we stand in terms of the market cycle. What's going on in terms of investor psychology, and how does it tell us to act in the short run? We want to buy when prices seem attractive. But if investors are giddy and optimism is rampant, we have to consider whether a better buying opportunity mightn't come along later.

One of our proxies for where we stand is shown in Figure 15.12. It attempts in a simplistic fashion to measure where we stand in the oscillations between the zenith of euphoria and the nadir of despair. I certainly can't predict where it is going, but I can prepare for the swings,

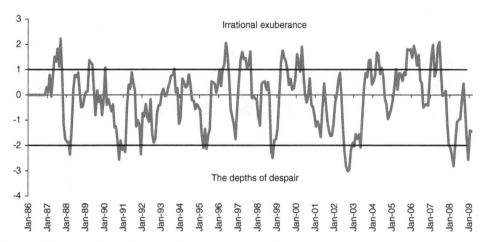

Figure 15.12   Our fear and greed index
Source: SG Global Strategy.

and try to take advantage of the opportunity set that is created by these swings. It gives rise to a sliding scale of capital commitment driven by a desire to lean against the wind.

In part this is obviously strongly related to tenet II on being contrarian. As Sir John Templeton said, 'To buy when others are despondently selling and to sell when others are avidly buying requires the greatest fortitude and pays the greatest rewards.'

As Seth Klarman notes in *Margin of Safety*,

> There are many explanations for volatility in business value. The 'credit cycle', the periodic tightening and relaxation of the availability of credit, is a major factor, for example, because it influences the cost and terms upon which money can be borrowed. This in turn affects the multiples that buyers are willing to pay for businesses. Simply put, buyers will willingly pay higher multiples if they receive low-rate non-recourse financing than they will in an unleveraged transaction.

Remembering that cycles occur is of vital importance, for it helps to remind one to sell as things become dear, and buy as they become cheap. But it also reinforces the need for slow position building, as we never know if we are at the top or the bottom of a cycle until after it has passed.

TENET VII: HISTORY MATTERS

Sir John Templeton also observed that 'This time is different' were the four most dangerous words in investing. Or as J.K. Galbraith said, the markets are characterized by

> Extreme brevity of the financial memory. In consequence, financial disaster is quickly forgotten. In further consequence, when the same or closely similar circumstances occur again, sometimes in a few years, they are hailed by a new, often youthful, and always supremely self-confident generation as a brilliantly innovative discovery in the financial and larger economic world. There can be few fields of human endeavour in which history counts for so little as in the world of finance.

Perhaps my favourite quotation on the lack of historical appreciation in finance comes from Jeremy Grantham who, when asked 'Do you think we will learn anything from this turmoil?' responded,

> We will learn an enormous amount in the very short term, quite a bit in the medium term and absolutely nothing in the long term. That would be the historical precedent.

Our industry often appears to be devoid of any appreciation of what has happened in the past. I often think that we would all be well served if, instead of studying the esoteric and complex maths of Black and Scholes and Itô's Lemma, those working in finance were required to study the history of what has gone before.

Strangely enough, the CFA ensures that its charter holders are conversant in the mechanics of DCF, and can recite the joys of VaR, but notably absent is a chapter (let alone a module) on the lessons offered by financial history. As Ben Graham argued, 'Prudence suggests that he [the investor] have an adequate idea of stock market history, in terms particularly of the major fluctuations... With this background he may be in a position to form some worthwhile judgement of the attractiveness or dangers... of the market.'

Nowhere is an appreciation of history more important than in understanding bubbles. As I have written before, we have long been proponents of the Kindleberger/Minsky framework for analysing bubbles (see Chapters 38 and 39 of *Behavioural Investing* for all the details). Essentially this model breaks a bubble's rise and fall into five phases, as shown below:

**Displacement → Credit creation → Euphoria →
Critical stage/Financial distress → Revulsion**

- **Displacement: The birth of a boom**
  Displacement is generally an exogenous shock that triggers the creation of profit opportunities in some sectors, while closing down profit availability in other sectors. As long as the opportunities created are greater than those that get shut down, investment and production will pick up to exploit these new opportunities. Investment in both financial and physical assets is likely to occur. Effectively we are witnessing the birth of a boom.

- **Credit creation: The nurturing of a bubble**
  Just as fire can't grow without oxygen, so a boom needs liquidity to feed on. Minsky argued that monetary expansion and credit creation are largely endogenous to the system. That is to say, not only can money be created by existing banks but also by the formation of new banks, the development of new credit instruments and the expansion of personal credit outside the banking system.

- **Euphoria**
  Everyone starts to buy into the new era. Prices are seen as only capable of ever going up. Traditional valuation standards are abandoned, and new measures are introduced to justify the current price. A wave of overoptimism and overconfidence is unleashed, leading people to overestimate the gains, underestimate the risks and generally think they can control the situation.

- **Critical stage/Financial distress**
  The critical stage is often characterized by insiders cashing out, and is rapidly followed by financial distress, in which the excess leverage that has been built up during the boom becomes a major problem. Fraud also often emerges during this stage of the bubble's life.

- **Revulsion**

  This is the final stage of a bubble's life cycle. Investors are so scarred by the events in which they participated that they can no longer bring themselves to participate in the market at all. This results in bargain basement asset prices.

As Table 15.1 shows, the key features of bubbles are unnervingly similar. While the specific details of each bubble are unique, the overall patterns are essentially the same. Surely learning to spot these signs would be a worthwhile pursuit.

TENET VIII: BE SCEPTICAL

In trying to write down the list of tenets that form the approach I follow, it was sometimes hard to work out where one tenet began and another ended. Being sceptical was one of those that seemed to be covered by other tenets, but I felt it was worthy of examination in its own right. One of my non-finance heros (Bruce Springsteen) once remarked that 'Blind faith in anything will get you killed'. I share this view on the dangers of lack of critical thinking.

Over the years, I have had the privilege of knowing some of the best investors (judged by both their decisions and their results). One of the hallmarks they share is a healthy degree of scepticism. Indeed, I would go as far as to say that they have a very different default when it comes to investing relative to the vast majority of fund managers. Their default option is non-ownership. They need to be convinced of the merits of an investment. This provides an inbuilt scepticism to their approach. They aren't willing to simply take things at face value. Their desire to understand the potential downside risks ensures that they focus on what could go wrong, rather than dreaming of what could go right.

Most fund managers (especially those engaged in the relative performance derby) are more concerned with tracking error than scepticism. Their default is: Why shouldn't I own this investment? This short-circuits the sceptical inquiries that mark out those top investors.

Scepticism is also vital for those of us whose work regularly takes them in the dark side (aka the short side). As mentioned in Tenet IV, I have no problem with being net short if that is where the opportunities lie. Indeed, I think short selling should be encouraged, not outlawed. As I have written many times before, the short sellers I know are among the most fundamentally oriented investors I have ever met. They take their analysis very seriously (as they should, since their downside is effectively unlimited). There can be no substitute for independent thinking, solid research and a healthy degree of scepticism.

TENET IX: BE TOP-DOWN AND BOTTOM-UP

I started my career in finance as an economist (not something I admit in public very often; in fact I started out as an econometrician, which is possibly even worse). However, one of the few things I learned from my years in the wilderness was that top-down and bottom-up are largely inseparable (much like value and growth – they aren't mutually exclusive; as Buffett said, they are joined at the hip).

In his book on value investing, Marty Whitman says 'Graham and Dodd view macrofactors . . . as crucial to the analysis of a corporate security. Value investors, however, believe that macrofactors are irrelevant.' If this is the case then I am very proud to say I am a Graham and Dodd fundamentalist.

Table 15.1 The pattern of historical bubbles

Event	South See Bubble (1710–1720)	First British railway boom (1845)	US 1873 railway boom	1920s US equity bubble
Displacement	Profit from conversion of government debt, supposed monopoly on trade with Spanish Americas	End of depression, new means of transport	End of the Civil War, settlement of the war	Decade of fast growth, end of WWI, rapid expansion of mass production
Smart money response	Insiders buy up debt in advance of conversion	Build a railroad	Construction of government subsidized railroads	Expansion of supply of new shares, creation of new closed end funds
Substaining the bubble	Development of the coffee house network for speculation	?	Additional railroad charters	Regional exchanges, growth of margin accounts and broker loans
Authoritative blessing	Government approval, royal involvement	Government approval of each railroad	Henry Varnum Poor and Charles Frances Adams	Blessing from Coolridge, Hoover, Mellon and Irving Fisher
Swindle/Fraud	Ponzi scheme	George Hudson paying dividends out of capital (Ponzi scheme)	?	Russel Snyder and Samuel Insull buying binge and debt mountain
Political reaction	Ex-post facto punishing of the directors, restrictions of the use of corporate form	Reform of accounting standards, rules passed so that dividends must be paid out of earnings not capital	?	Glass-Steagall Act, creation of the SEC, the holding company act.

(Continued)

Table 15.1 (*Continued*)

Event	1960s conglomerate mergers boom	1980s Japanese land and equity bubbles	TMT bubbles	Credit/Risk bubble
Displacement	Two decades of rising stock markets, the joy of growth investing	Financial liberalization, monetary easing	Widespread acceptance of the internet, strong growth and monetary easing	Low rates, rising house prices, Great Moderation
Smart money response	Emergence of professional conglomerates	Zaitech	Aggressive growth funds, stock options and IPO boom	Any and all kinds of leverage
Sustaining the bubble	Stock swaps to create apparent earnings growth	Cross share holders, latent asset value, PKO in '87	Pro forma earnings, new valuation measures, buybacks	New derivative structures – CDOs, CDOs squared, new mortgage products, buybacks
Authoritative blessing	McGeorge Bundy	Nomura calls for 80,000 by 1995	Greenspan	Greenspan, Bernanke, Bush
Swindle/Fraud	National Student Marketing Corp.	Recruit Cosmo, Bubble lady	Enron, WorldCom, Tyco etc	Mark to model/myth, Madoff, Stanford
Political reaction	Reform of accounting practice and the Williams Act	?	Sarbanes Oxley	??

Source: SG Global Strategy research.

While stock selection is best approached from the bottom-up, ignoring the top-down can be extraordinarily expensive. The last year has been a perfect example of why understanding the top-down can benefit and inform the bottom-up. The last 12 months have been unusual for value investors as two clear camps emerged from their normally more homogeneous whole.

A schism over financials has split value investors into two diametrically opposed groups. The optimistic/bottom-up view was typified by Richard Pzena. In his Q1 2008 quarterly report he wrote:

> A new fear has permeated conventional investment thinking: the massive leveraging-up of the recent past has gone too far and its unwinding will permanently hobble the global financial system. This view sees Bear Stearns as just one casualty in a gathering wave that has already claimed many US subprime mortgage originators along with several non-US financial institutions and will cause countless others to fail. And it sees the earnings power of those that survive as being permanently impaired.
>
> The obvious question then is, which scenario is more logical: the extreme outlook described above, given the long period of easy credit extended to unqualified individuals? Or the scenario of a typical credit cycle that will work its way out as other post-excess crises have, and without impairing the long-term ROEs of the survivors? We believe the latter.

The alternative view (pessimistic, top-down informed) is well summed up by Steven Romick of First Pacific Advisors in a recent interview in Value Investor Insight:

> VII: Has your negative general view on the prospects for financial services stocks changed at all?
>
> SR: We believe in reversion to the mean, so it can make a lot of sense to invest in a distressed sector when you find good businesses whose public shares trade inexpensively relative to their earnings in a more normal environment. But that strategy lately has helped to lead many excellent investors to put capital to work too early in financials. Our basic feeling is that margins and returns on capital generated by financial institutions in the decade through 2006 were unrealistically high. 'Normal' profitability and valuation multiples are not going to be what they were during that time, given more regulatory oversight, less leverage (and thus capital to lend), higher funding costs, stricter underwriting standards, less demand and less esoteric and excessively profitable products.

Essentially, the difference between these two camps comes down to an appreciation of the importance of the bursting of the credit bubble. Those who understood the impact of the bursting of such a bubble didn't go near financials (and are generally still not prepared to engage in knife-catching in this sector). Those who focused more (and in some cases exclusively) on the bottom-up just saw cheapness.

It often pays to remember the wise words of Jean-Marie Eveillard, 'Sometimes, what matters is not so much how low the odds are that circumstances would turn quite negative, what matters more is what the consequences would be if that happens.'

As mentioned above, while we can't predict we can prepare. The credit bubble wasn't a black swan, although we might not have been able to forecast when its demise would occur, we could at least prepare for its passing on by avoiding credit bubble-related stocks such as financials and housebuilders, for instance.

The bottom-up can also inform the top-down. As Ben Graham pointed out, 'True bargain issues have repeatedly become scarce in bull markets . . . Perhaps one could even have determined whether the market level was getting too high or too low by counting the number of issues selling below working capital value. When such opportunities have virtually disappeared, past experience indicates that investors should have taken themselves out of the stock market and plunged up to their necks in US Treasury bills.'

Another example of the complementary nature of top-down and bottom-up viewpoints is offered by Seth Klarman. In his insightful book, *Margin of Safety*, Klarman points out that the inflationary environment can have dramatic consequences for value investors:

> Trends in inflation or deflation also cause business values to fluctuate. That said, value investing can work very well in an inflationary environment. If for fifty cents you buy a dollar of value in the form of an asset, such as natural resource properties or real estate, which increases in value with inflation, a fifty-cent investment today can result in the realization of value appreciably greater than one dollar. In an inflationary environment, however, investors may become somewhat careless. As long as assets are rising in value, it would appear attractive to relax one's standards and purchase $1 of assets, not for 50 cents, but for 70 or 80 cents (or perhaps even $1.10). Such laxity could prove costly, however, in the event that inflation comes to be anticipated by most investors, who respond by bidding up security prices. A subsequent slowdown in the rate of inflation could cause a price decline.
>
> In a deflationary environment assets tend to decline in value. Buying a dollar's worth of assets for fifty cents may not be a bargain if the asset value is dropping. Historically investors have found attractive opportunities in companies with substantial 'hidden assets', such as an overfunded pension fund, real estate carried on the balance sheet below market value, or a profitable finance subsidiary that could be sold at a significant gain. Amidst a broad-based decline in business and asset values, however, some hidden assets become less valuable and in some cases may become hidden liabilities. A decline in the stock market will reduce the value of pension fund assets; previously overfunded plans may become underfunded. Real estate carried on companies' balance sheets at historical cost may no longer be undervalued. Overlooked subsidiaries that were once hidden jewels may lose their lustre.
>
> The possibility of sustained decreases in business value is a dagger at the heart of value investing (and is not a barrel of laughs for other investment approaches either). Value investors place great faith in the principle of assessing value and then buying at a discount. If value is subject to considerable erosion, then how large a discount is sufficient?
>
> Should investors worry about the possibility that business value may decline? Absolutely. Should they do anything about it? There are three responses that might be effective. First, since investors cannot predict when values will rise or fall, valuation should always be performed conservatively, giving considerable weight to worst-case liquidation value as well as to other methods. Second, investors fearing deflation could demand a greater than usual discount between price and underlying value in order to make new investments or to hold current positions. This means that normally selective investors would probably let even more pitches than usual go by.
>
> Finally, the prospect of asset deflation places a heightened importance on the timeframe of investments and on the presence of a catalyst for the realisation of underlying value. In a deflationary environment, if you cannot tell whether or when you will realize underlying value, you may not want to get involved at all. If underlying value is realized in the near-term directly for the benefit of shareholders, however, the longer-term forces that could cause value to diminish become moot.

Thus neither top-down nor bottom-up has a monopoly on insight. Both perspectives have something to offer the open-minded investor.

TENET X: TREAT YOUR CLIENTS LIKE YOU WOULD YOURSELF

The final tenet of my creed takes us almost a full circle back to the aim of investing (which for those with both pachyderm-like memories and the extraordinary stamina required to make it thus far through this chapter, will recall was where we started).

One of the most useful questions I think a fund manager can ask is: Would I do this with my own money? All too often those charged with the stewardship of other people's money seem to think that this gives them licence to behave in an odd fashion (true of both fund managers and the corporate executives charged with running companies).

John Bogle put it well when he said our industry has ceased to be a profession and has become a business. This is a lamentable state of affairs. When marketing men run investment firms the result will be the wrong fund at just the wrong time. Witness the surge in tech funds in the late 1990s, or the rise of commodity funds in more recent years. I have long argued that we need a version of the hippocratic oath in finance with an overt promise to 'first, do no harm'.

Paul Wilmott and Emanuel Derman recently proposed the following as the 'Modelers' Hippocratic Oath':

> I will remember that I didn't make the world, and it doesn't satisfy my equations.
>
> Though I will use models boldly to estimate value, I will not be overly impressed by mathematics.
>
> I will never sacrifice reality for elegance without explaining why I have done so.
>
> Nor will I give the people who use my model false comfort about its accuracy. Instead, I will make explicit its assumptions and oversights.
>
> I understand that my work may have enormous effects on society and the economy, many of them beyond my comprehension.

Instead of trying to maximize assets under management, many of the best investors have chosen to deliberately limit the size of their funds, so as not to reduce their ability to deliver returns. Of course, this is anathema to the fund supermarkets, but it strikes me as the only way to sensibly approach investing. As Jean-Marie Eveillard said, 'I would rather lose half my clients than lose half my client's money.'

Incentives can be aligned without too much difficulty. For instance, buy-side analysts should be paid on a (say) three-year view of overall performance of the fund at which they work. This prevents them gaming the system and insisting on having positions in the portfolio. I would also suggest that analysts should be generalists rather than specialists. This allows them flexibility to assess different opportunities in different areas, but ensures that a consistent framework is applied. However, here I am straying towards process rather than philosophy, which is the subject of this thesis.

Similarly, I am always happiest investing when I know the manager has a sizeable stake in the fund alongside my own, simply because this helps to ensure that he asks himself the question with which I started this section on a regular basis.

Managers who follow the kind of creed I have outlined above will also need to select their clients with care. Having clients who truly understand the way you invest is vital, after all there is little point in trying to follow a patient strategy if your capital is pulled at just the wrong moment. Using precommitment devices such as lock-ins makes sense in this context – see Chapter 12.

CONCLUSION

This is perhaps one of the most personal chapters I have ever written. It exposes my beliefs about the way in which investment should be approached. I have tried to avoid a discussion of process – not because I believe it to be unimportant (in fact nothing could be further from the truth, see the next chapter), but rather because I wanted to explore the philosophical beliefs that lie at the very core of the approach I follow.

Exposing one's beliefs can be a risky move, but just as sunlight is the best disinfectant, so I think exposing beliefs to critique is a useful exercise. Open and honest debate can often produce superior results. It is in this spirit that I have tried to explain the way I approach investing. It certainly isn't the only way we could approach the problem, but it is the way that makes the most sense to me.

The Ten Tenets of Investing

Tenet I: Value, value, value
Tenet II: Be contrarian
Tenet III: Be patient
Tenet IV: Be unconstrained
Tenet V: Don't forecast
Tenet VI: Cycles matter
Tenet VII: History matters
Tenet VIII: Be sceptical
Tenet IX: Be top-down and bottom-up
Tenet X: Treat your clients as you would treat yourself

16

Process not Outcomes: Gambling, Sport and Investment!*

> **Watching the Olympics and listening to several of the successful athletes, one of the inane questions from the interviewers often seemed to be, 'What was going through your mind before the event? Were you thinking of the gold?' The response time and again was the competitor was focused on the process, not the outcome. So it should be in investing as well. We have no control over outcomes, but we can control the process. Of course, outcomes matter, but by focusing our attention on process we maximize our chances of good outcomes.**

- Paul DePodesta of the San Diego Padres and Moneyball fame relates the following story on playing blackjack.

  > On one particular hand the player was dealt 17 with his first two cards. The dealer was set to deal the next set of cards and passed right over the player until he stopped her, saying: 'Dealer, I want a hit!' She paused, almost feeling sorry for him, and said, 'Sir, are you sure?' He said yes, and the dealer dealt the card. Sure enough, it was a four. The place went crazy, high fives all around, everybody hootin' and hollerin', and you know what the dealer said? The dealer looked at the player, and with total sincerity, said: 'Nice hit.' I thought, 'Nice hit? Maybe it was a nice hit for the casino, but it was a terrible hit for the player! The decision isn't justified just because it worked.'

- Psychologists have long documented a tendency known as outcome bias. That is the habit of judging a decision differently depending upon its outcome. For instance, if a doctor performs an operation and the patient survives then the decision is rated as significantly better than if the same operation results in the patient's death. Of course, the correctness of the doctor's decision should not be a function of the outcome, since clearly the doctor couldn't have known the outcome before the event.
- This emphasis on outcomes and not on process can be highly detrimental. Evidence suggests that holding people accountable for outcomes tends to (i) increase their preference for less ambiguity (even if the risk involved is equal), (ii) increase the collection and use of information, (iii) increase a preference for compromise options, and the selection of products with average features, and (iv) increase the degree of loss aversion. In investment terms, that translates as fund managers avoiding uncertainty, chasing noise, and herding with the consensus. Doesn't sound much like a recipe for good performance to me.

- The good news is that telling people to focus on the process (and telling them they will be evaluated on the basis of the process, rather than the outcome) leads to much better decision making. Most of the pitfalls mentioned above are mitigated when the decision process is the focal point. In investment, we have no control over the outcomes, the only thing we can control is the process. So it makes sense for us to concentrate on that.
- During periods of poor performance, the pressure always builds to change your process. However, a sound process can generate poor results, just as a bad process can generate good results. Perhaps we would be well served to remember the words of Sir John Templeton, 'The time to reflect on your investing methods is when you are most successful, not when you are making the most mistakes.'

Not so long along I came across the following post by Paul DePodesta on his blog from 10 June 2008. For those who have read Michael Lewis' *MoneyBall*, DePodesta will need no introduction. For those who haven't, a quick trip to that informational minefield that is Wikipedia should give you a flavour of the man (http://en.wikipedia.org/wiki/Paul_DePodesta).

Many years ago I was playing blackjack in Las Vegas on a Saturday night in a packed casino. I was sitting at third base, and the player who was at first base was playing horribly. He was definitely taking advantage of the free drinks, and it seemed as though every twenty minutes he was dipping into his pocket for more cash.

On one particular hand the player was dealt 17 with his first two cards. The dealer was set to deal the next set of cards and passed right over the player until he stopped her, saying: 'Dealer, I want a hit!' She paused, almost feeling sorry for him, and said, 'Sir, are you sure?' He said yes, and the dealer dealt the card. Sure enough, it was a four.

The place went crazy, high fives all around, everybody hootin' and hollerin', and you know what the dealer said? The dealer looked at the player, and with total sincerity, said: 'Nice hit.'

I thought, 'Nice hit? Maybe it was a nice hit for the casino, but it was a terrible hit for the player! The decision isn't justified just because it worked.'

Well, I spent the rest of that weekend wandering around the casino, largely because I had lost all of my money playing blackjack, thinking about all of these different games and how they work. The fact of the matter is that all casino games have a winning process – the odds are stacked in the favour of the house. That doesn't mean they win every single hand or every roll of the dice, but they do win more often than not. Don't misunderstand me – the casino is absolutely concerned about outcomes. However, their approach to securing a good outcome is a laser like focus on process . . . right down to the ruthless pit boss.

We can view baseball through the same lens. Baseball is certainly an outcome-driven business, as we get charged with a W or an L 162 times a year (or 163 times every once in a while). Furthermore, we know we cannot possibly win every single time. In fact, winning just 60% of the time is a great season, a percentage that far exceeds house odds in most games. Like a casino, it appears as though baseball is all about outcomes, but just think about all of the processes that are in play during the course of just one game or even just one at-bat.

In having this discussion years ago with Michael Mauboussin, who wrote *More Than You Know* (a great book), he showed me a very simple matrix by Russo and Schoemaker in *Winning Decisions* that explains this concept:

	Good Outcome	Bad Outcome
Good Process	**Deserved Success**	**Bad Break**
Bad Process	**Dumb Luck**	**Poetic Justice**

We all want to be in the upper left box – deserved success resulting from a good process. This is generally where the casino lives. I'd like to think that this is where the Oakland A's and San Diego Padres have been during the regular seasons. The box in the upper right, however, is the tough reality we all face in industries that are dominated by uncertainty. A good process can lead to a bad outcome in the real world. In fact, it happens all the time. This is what happened to the casino when a player hit on 17 and won. I'd like to think this is what happened to the A's and Padres during the post-seasons.

As tough as a good process/bad outcome combination is, nothing compares to the bottom left: bad process/good outcome. This is the wolf in sheep's clothing that allows for one-time success but almost always cripples any chance of sustained success – the player hitting on 17 and getting a four. Here's the rub: it's incredibly difficult to look in the mirror after a victory, any victory, and admit that you were lucky. If you fail to make that admission, however, the bad process will continue and the good outcome that occurred once will elude you in the future. Quite frankly, this is one of the things that makes Billy Beane [General manager of the Oakland A's] as good as he is. He is quick to notice good luck embedded in a good outcome, and he refuses to pat himself on the back for it.

At the Padres, we want to win every game we play at every level and we want to be right on every single player decision we make. We know it's not going to happen, because there is too much uncertainty . . . too much we cannot control. That said, we can control the process.

Championship teams will occasionally have a bad process and a good outcome. Championship organizations, however, reside exclusively in the upper half of the matrix. Some years it may be on the right-hand side, most years should be on the left. The upper left is where the Atlanta Braves lived for 14 years – possibly the most under-appreciated accomplishment by a professional sports organization in our lifetimes. In short, we want to be a Championship organization that results in many Championship teams.

I'll touch on our draft in greater detail in the next day or so, but I will say that we are proud of our process and it was carried out with discipline. Will it lead to a good outcome? We don't know for sure, but we have confidence in the group of picks that were made. I do know, however, that our process gets better every single year, and we expect it to be better again next year.

To me the similarities with investment are blindly obvious. We are an industry that is obsessed with outcomes over which we have no direct control. However, we can and do control the process by which we invest. This is what we should focus upon. The management of return is impossible, the management of risk is illusory, but process is the one thing that we can exert an influence over.

THE PSYCHOLOGY OF PROCESS

The need to focus on process rather than outcomes is critical in investing. Outcomes are highly unstable in our world because they involve an integral of time. Effectively, it is perfectly possible to be 'right' over a five-year view and 'wrong' on a six-month view, and vice versa.

Outcome Bias

People often judge a past decision by its ultimate outcome instead of based on the quality of the decision at the time it was made, given what was known at that time. This is outcome bias. For instance, the UK Parliament has decreed that if you kill someone while using a mobile phone in a car then you should receive a different sentence from someone who is caught using a mobile phone, but who didn't kill anyone.

Baron and Hershy (1988) have documented outcome bias in a wide range of experiments. For example, subjects are asked to rate the soundness of the physician's decision process (not outcome) in the following case:

A 55-year-old man had a heart condition. He had to stop working because of chest pain. He enjoyed his work and did not want to stop. His pain also interfered with other things, such as travel and recreation. A type of bypass operation would relieve his pain and increase his life expectancy from age 65 to age 70. However, 8% of the people who have this operation die from the operation itself. His physician decided to go ahead with the operation. The operation

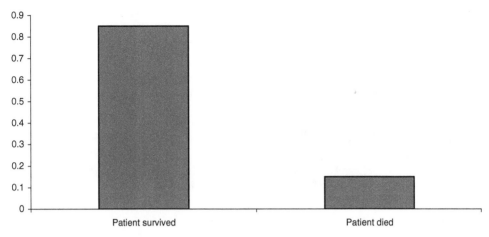

Figure 16.1   Average rating of the soundness of the decision
Source: Baron and Hershy (1988). SG Equity research.

succeeded. Evaluate the physician's decision to go ahead with the operation, on the following scale:

    3 – clearly correct, and the opposite decision would be inexcusable;
    2 – correct, all things considered;
    1 – correct, but the opposite would be reasonable too;
    0 – the decision and its opposite are equally good;
  −1 – incorrect, but not unreasonable;
  −2 – incorrect, all things considered;
  −3 – incorrect and inexcusable.

Subjects were also presented with the same task except that, in this alternative setting, the operation was unsuccessful and the patient died. Now, the correctness of the physician's decision should not be a function of the outcome, since clearly the doctor couldn't have known the outcome before the event. However, as Figure 16.1 shows, the doctor's decision rating was massively impacted by the outcome.

A further example provided by Baron and Hershy concerns a gamble. Consider the following:

> A 25-year-old man is unmarried and has a steady job. He receives a letter inviting him to visit Quiet Pond Cottages, where he has been considering buying some property. As a prize for visiting the property, he is given a choice between:
>
> Option 1: $200
> Option 2: An 80% chance of wining $300 and a 20% chance of winning nothing.
>
> He must mail in his decision in advance, and he will be told the outcome of Option 2 whether he chooses it or not.

If the subjects are acting rationally then the man should accept the gamble, as it has a higher expected outcome. Of course, the outcome once again should have no impact upon rating the

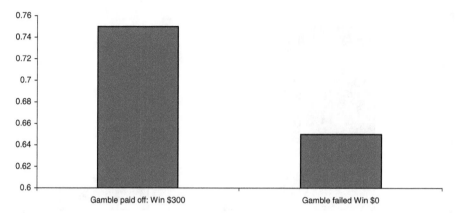

Figure 16.2   Average rating of the decision
Source: Baron and Hershy (1988). SG Equity research.

man's decision process. However, as Figure 16.2 shows, when the gamble paid off it was rated as a better decision than when it didn't!

This obsession with outcomes and the impact of outcome bias are clearly visible in our world.

Outcome Accountability

In addition, psychological evidence shows that focusing on outcomes can create all sorts of unwanted actions. For instance, in a world in which short-term performance is everything, fund managers may end up buying stocks they find easy to justify to their clients, rather than those that represent the best opportunity.

In their meta-study on accountability, Lerner and Tetlock (1999) show that holding people accountable for outcomes tends to:

(1) increase ambiguity aversion (increased preference for alternatives with less ambiguity despite equal risk);
(2) increase the collection and use of all information (both useful and useless);
(3) increase the preference for compromise options, and increase the selection of products with average features on all measures over a product with mixed features (i.e. average on four traits, preferred to good on two and bad on two);
(4) increase the degree of loss aversion.

None of these features is likely to serve investors well. Together they suggest that when every decision is measured on outcomes, fund managers are likely to avoid uncertainty, chase noise, and herd with the consensus. Sounds like a very good description of much of our industry to me.

Process Accountability

However, if we switch the focus from outcomes to process then things begin to change for the better. Simonson and Straw (1992) provide the classic evidence of a focus on process leading to better decisions than a focus on outcomes.

They asked participants to consider an American brewery that was planning to distribute its non-alcoholic and light beer (as repulsive as those ideas are to me) into Europe. The data they were given showed that both products had done roughly equally well in their test period. Subjects were asked to decide which of the two products should receive an extra $3m in funding. The instructions made it clear that the decision should be made on the basis of the potential benefit of the additional funding to the product and the company.

Subjects wrote down their decisions and a brief explanation of their decision. They were then given the following statement:

> Your recommendation to allocate the additional $3m to the (which you choose, either the light/non-alcoholic) beer was adopted by the president of the company and implemented. As you will note on the next page, the results have been rather disappointing.

The data indicated that sales and profits of the product that the subject had selected started OK, and then went down, and finally settled in a low constant pattern of sales. The sales and profits of the alternative product were also shown. They also went up initially, then down, but ended up settling at a higher level than the product chosen by the subjects.

Participants were then told that the company had decided to make an additional $10m available in funding. However, this time the money could be split between the two beers. The subjects were asked to allocate the $10m between the two beers.

In addition the subjects were told one of the following: (1) The information they had received was enough for a business school student to make a good decision (known as the base line). (2) If they made particularly good or bad choices their performance would be shared with other students and instructors. They were also told that their performance would be based on the outcome of the decision they took. (This was labelled outcome accountability). (3) Subjects were informed that their evaluation would be based on their effective use of decision strategies rather than the outcomes of those strategies. This group were informed that if they used particularly good or bad decision processes these would be shared with other students and instructors. (This was labelled process accountability.)

As Figure 16.3 shows, there was a marked difference in the allocations of these groups. The group who were focused on the outcome of their decision decided to allocate an average

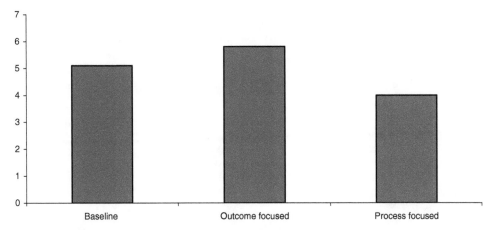

Figure 16.3 $m amount allocated to the first round beer choice
Source: Simonson and Straw (1992). SG Equity research.

of $5.8m to the beer they had originally selected. This is a classic example of the sunk cost fallacy. This is a tendency to allow past unrecoverable expenses to inform current decisions.

By comparison, the baseline subjects split the money roughly evenly, giving their previous choice $5.1m. However, the group told to focus upon the process of decision making rather than the outcome did much better. They only allocated $4m to the beer that they had originally chosen, giving the majority of the money to the more popular beer.

CONCLUSIONS

During periods of underperformance the pressure always builds to change your process. However, a sound process is capable of generating poor results, just as a bad process can generate good results. Perhaps we would all do well to remember the late great Sir John Templeton's words, 'The time to reflect on your investing methods is when you are most successful, not when you are making the most mistakes,' or indeed Ben Graham's exultation, 'The value approach is inherently sound ... devote yourself to that principle. Stick to it, and don't be led astray.'

17

Beware of Action Man[*]

What do goalkeepers facing a penalty and investors have in common? The answer is that both are prone to action. They feel the need to do something. However, inaction is also a decision. There are times when holding cash is perfectly acceptable, but this remains an anathema to many fund mangers. Perhaps they would be well served to remember Samuelson's advice that 'Investing should be dull. It shouldn't be exciting. Investing should be more like watching paint dry or watching grass grow.'

- Imagine you are goalkeeper facing a penalty kick. You have no idea which way the penalty taker will choose to direct the kick. You effectively make your decision simultaneously with the kicker. Should you dive left, right, or stay where you are in the centre of the goal?
- Most professional goalkeepers tend to dive either left or right. Indeed diving in one or other direction is the preferred action in a staggering 94% of cases. However, this is not the optimal solution. If you look at the percentage of penalties saved then it becomes clear that the optimal strategy (assuming no change in the behaviour of the kickers) is to stay in the centre of the goal! Goalkeepers display a distinct action bias.
- Evidence from experimental markets suggests that investors also display an action bias. For instance, an artificial market where fundamental value is easy to calculate and the resale of a share is prohibited, should display no trades above fundamental value. However, time and time again, such experiments reveal massive trading above fundamental value. This makes absolutely no sense. Since resale of the shares is outlawed, people can't be transacting in the hope of being able to exploit a greater fool. They are trading out of boredom – the action bias lives!
- Warren Buffett has talked in the past of investment being like a wonderful game of baseball, where there is no umpire calling balls or strikes. Essentially the investor can simply stand at the plate, and let as many pitches go past as he chooses, waiting for the fat pitch to turn up in his sweet spot. However, as Seth Klarman notes, 'Most institutional investors . . . feel compelled . . . to swing at almost every pitch and forgo batting selectivity for frequency.'
- The late great Bob Kirby once suggested that we should run 'Coffee Can Portfolios' in which investors would have to put stocks, and then not touch them – an idea he described as being passively active. However, Kirby noted that this approach was unlikely to be widely adopted as 'it might radically change the structure of our industry and might substantially diminish the number of souls able to sustain opulent life-styles through the money management profession'. Sounds like a good idea to me!

---

[*]This article appeared in Mind Matters on 7 January 2008. Copyright © 2008 by The Société Générale Group. All rights reserved. The material discussed was accurate at the time of publication.

For those who may not know, Action Man was a kid's figurine of a soldier, popular when I was growing up many moons ago. He was the embodiment of macho values, although the impact upon me of coming home from school one day to find that my sister had kidnapped my Action Man and forced him to play happy families with her Cindy doll will have to wait for another time! But my childhood issues aside, would you want an action man running your portfolio?

GOALKEEPERS AS ACTION MEN

Although not normally the stars of the team when it comes to action, it transpires that when it comes to penalty kicks top goalkeepers are action men. A recent study by Bar-Eli *et al.* (2007) reveals some fascinating patterns when it comes to trying to save penalties. In soccer (a sport I know essentially nothing about), when a penalty is awarded, the ball is placed 11 metres from the goal, and it is a simple contest between the goalkeeper and the kicker. The goalkeeper may not move from his line until the kick has occurred.

Given that in the average football match 2.5 goals are scored, a penalty (which has a 80% chance of resulting in a goal) can dramatically influence the result of the game. So unlike many psychological experiments the stakes are significant.

The authors examined penalty kicks from top leagues and championships world wide, and 311 such kicks were found. A panel of three independent judges was used to analyse the direction of the kick and the direction of movement by the goalkeeper. To avoid confusion, all directions (left or right) are relayed from the goalkeeper's perspective.

Table 17.1 shows the percentages of kick and dive combinations unveiled by Bar-Eli *et al.* in their data. Very roughly speaking, the kicks are equally distributed with around one third of the kicks aimed at the left, centre and right of the goal mouth. However, the keepers display a distinct action bias, they either dive left or right (94% of the time), hardly ever choosing to remain in the middle of their goal.

However, in order to assess 'optimal' behaviour we need to know the success rate from the combinations of kicks and jumps. This is revealed in Table 17.2. The best strategy is clearly when the goalkeeper stays in the centre of the goal. He saves some 60% of the kicks aimed at the centre, far higher than his saving rate when he dives either left or right. However, far from following this optimal strategy, goalkeepers stay in the centre just 6.3% of the time! The action bias displayed by the keepers is clearly a suboptimal behavioural pattern.[1]

Table 17.1   Joint distribution of dives and kicks

Dive direction		Left	Centre	Right	Total
Kick direction	Left	18.9%	0.3%	12.9%	32.2%
	Centre	14.3%	3.5%	10.8%	28.7%
	Right	16.1%	2.4%	20.6%	39.2%
	Total	49.3%	6.3%	44.4%	100.0%

Source: Bar-Eli *et al.* (2005).

---

[1] It is of course only optimal for the goalkeeper to stay in the centre of his goal given the current distribution of kicks. If goalkeepers all started staying in the middle of their goals, then the kickers would start shooting left and right exclusively, altering the distribution.

Table 17.2 Chances of stopping a penalty kick

Dive direction		Left	Centre	Right	Total
Kick direction	Left	29.6%	0.0%	0.0%	17.4%
	Centre	9.8%	60.0%	3.2%	13.4%
	Right	0.0%	0.0%	25.4%	13.4%
	Total	14.2%	33.3%	12.5%	100.0%

Source: Bar-Eli *et al.* (2005).

The reason for this action bias seems to be that it is regarded as the norm. A goalkeeper at least feels like he is making an effort when he dives left or right, whereas standing in the centre and watching a goal scored to the left or the right of him would feel much worse. Bar-Eli *et al.* confirm this by a questionnaire for top goalkeepers, which reveals this exact sentiment.

INVESTORS AND ACTION BIAS

In order to introduce you to the evidence on an action bias among investors I must first introduce the field of laboratory experiments in economics, specifically experimental asset markets.

These are great contraptions for investigating how people behave in a financial market context – without any complicating factors. These markets are very simple – consisting of just one asset and cash. The asset is a share that pays out a dividend once per period. The dividend paid depends upon the state of the world (four possible states). Each state is equally weighted (i.e. there is a 25% probability of each state occurring in any given period).

Table 17.3 shows the payouts and the probabilities. From these it is easy to calculate the expected value (simply the payoffs multiplied by their probabilities then multiplied by the number of time periods remaining).

Figure 17.1 shows the fundamental value of such an asset. It clearly decreases over time by the amount of the expected dividend paid out in each period. Now you might think that this was a simple asset to trade. However, the evidence suggests otherwise.

Figure 17.2 shows a typical result from one of these asset markets. The asset starts off significantly undervalued, and then rises massively above fair value, before crashing back to fundamental value in the final periods. This is nothing more than a simple bubble forming and bursting. Okay, so what has this got to do with action bias? Well, Figure 17.2 comes from a

Table 17.3 Probability and payoffs in experimental asset market

Probability	Payoff
0.25	57.5
0.25	37.5
0.25	27.5
0.25	17.5

Source: Lei *et al.* (2001).

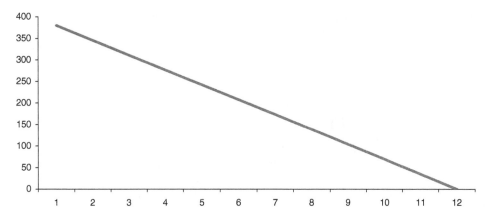

Figure 17.1   Fundamental value of stock in the experimental market
Source: Lei *et al.* (2001).

particularly interesting version of the experimental asset market run by Lei, Noussair and Plott (2001).

In this particular version of the game, once you had bought shares you were prohibited from reselling them. This rules out the possibility of a greater fool theory driving the bubble. That is to say, because you can't resell the shares, there is no point in buying them above fair value in the hope you can sell them on to someone else for even more gain. In effect participants were simply trading out of boredom! So it appears that investors also have a bias to action.

BUFFETT ON THE FAT PITCH

The madness of this bias to action lies in direct contrast to Warren Buffett's advice to wait for the fat pitch. He likes to compare investing with baseball, except in investing there is no umpire calling balls and strikes. So the investor can stand at the plate and simply watch pitches

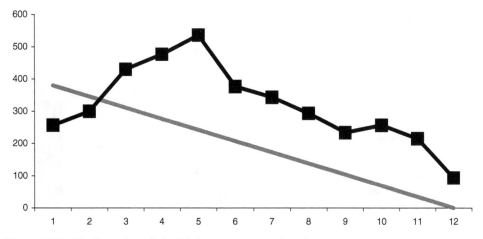

Figure 17.2   The formation of a bubble in an experimental market
Source: Lei *et al.* (2001).

go by him without ever being forced into a swing at a pitch. However, as Seth Klarman notes in his *Margin of Safety*, 'Most institutional investors . . . feel compelled to be fully invested at all times. They act as if an umpire were calling balls and strikes – mostly strikes – thereby forcing them to swing at almost every pitch and forego batting selectivity for frequency.'

BIAS TO ACTION PARTICULARLY PRONOUNCED AFTER POOR PERFORMANCE

One final aspect of the bias to action is especially noteworthy – it tends to intensify after a loss (a period of poor performance in our world). Zeelenberg *et al.* (2002) illustrate the way in which an inaction bias switches to an action bias by using a loss frame.

Zeelenberg *et al.* ask people to consider something like the following:

> Steenland and Straathof are both coaches of soccer teams. Steenland is the coach of Blue-Black, and Straathof is the coach of E.D.O. Both coaches lost the prior game with a score of 4–0. This Sunday Steenland decides to do something: he fields three new players. Straathof decides not to change his team. This time both teams lose with a score line of 3–0. Who feels more regret, coach Steenland or coach Straathof?

Participants saw this statement in one of three forms. Some saw it as presented above (i.e. framed in terms of a prior loss), others were simply given the second half of the above (i.e. no prior information), and the final group saw a version in which both coaches had won the previous week but lost this week.

Figure 17.3 shows the percentage of respondents specifying which coach would experience more regret. If the teams had won last week, then 90% of the respondents thought the coach making changes would feel more regret when the team lost this week (this is the well-known inaction or omission bias). However, look what happens when the situation is presented as the teams losing both weeks (as written above). Now the coach not taking any action was thought to be feeling more regret by nearly 70% of respondents – thus when dealing with losses the urge to reach for an action bias is exceptionally high.

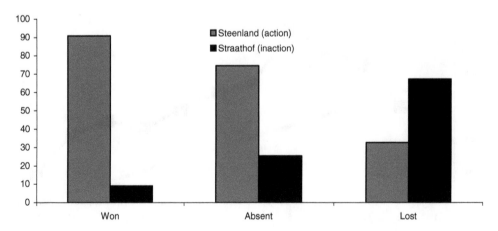

Figure 17.3   Percentage of respondents saying the coach would feel more regret
Source: Zeelenberg *et al.* (2002).

CONCLUSIONS

The psychological and experimental evidence seems to strongly suggest that investors are prone to an action bias. After all, they are engaged in 'active' management, but perhaps they would do well to remember that inaction is also a decision. As Paul Samuelson once opined, 'Investing should be dull. It shouldn't be exciting. Investing should be more like watching paint dry or watching grass grow. If you want excitement, take $800 and go to Las Vegas, although it is not easy to get rich in Las Vegas, at Churchill Downs, or at the local Merrill Lynch office.'

The legendary Bob Kirby once wrote of 'the Coffee Can Portfolio' (Kirby, 1984) in which investors would have to put stocks and then not touch them – an idea he described as being passively active. As Kirby noted:

> I suspect the notion is not likely to be popular among investment managers, because, if widely adopted, it might radically change the structure of our industry and might substantially diminish the number of souls able to sustain opulent life-styles through the money management profession.
>
> The Coffee Can Portfolio concept harkens back to the Old West, when people put their valuable possessions in a coffee can and kept it under the mattress. That coffee can involved no transaction costs, administrative costs, or any other costs. The success of the program depended entirely on the wisdom and foresight used to select the objects to be placed in the coffee can to begin with . . .
>
> What kind of results would good money managers produce without all that activity? The answer lies in another question. Are we traders, or are we really investors? Most good money managers are probably investors deep down inside. But quotrons and news services, and computers that churn out daily investment results make them act like traders. They start with sound research that identifies attractive companies in promising industries on a longer-term horizon. Then, they trade those stocks two or three times a year based on month-to-month news developments and rumours of all shapes and sizes.

Perhaps Blaise Pascal put it best when he said, 'All men's miseries derive from not being able to sit in a quiet room alone.'

18

The Bullish Bias and the Need for Scepticism. Or, Am I Clinically Depressed?*

Human beings are an optimistic bunch. Some 74% of fund managers think they are above average at their jobs, 70% of analysts think they are better than their peers at forecasting earnings, and a mere 9% of recommendations are sells! In part, this bullish bias stems from a natural tendency to look on the bright side of life. In part, it stems from self-serving bias and motivated reasoning. Perhaps the best way of resisting this siren call of bullishness is to focus on being an empirical sceptic – check your beliefs against reality on a regular basis.

- At the end of Monty Python's, *The Life of Brian*, those hanging on crucifixes begin singing 'always look on the bright side of life'. It would appear that the vast majority of people subscribe to this particular view of the world. Everyone seems to think that good things are much more likely to happen to them than bad things.

- What are the sources of this bullish bias? In part they stem from nature. That is to say, people may well have been hard wired by evolution to be optimistic. After all, a stone-age pessimist probably won't have bothered getting up to hunt mastodon. When faced with bad news over illness, say, those of an optimistic nature deal with the news much better than those with a pessimistic disposition. In fact, the parts of the brain that seem to generate the bullish bias are associated with the evolutionary older X-system (the more emotional aspects of decision making) rather than the more logical C-system.

- This natural tendency to be optimistic is reinforced by self-serving bias and motivated reasoning. For instance, if we jump on the scales in the morning, and they give us a reading that we don't like, we tend to get off and have another go – just to make sure we weren't standing in an odd manner. However, if the scales have delivered a number under our expectations, we would have hopped off the scales into the shower, feeling very good about life. This is motivated reasoning. We are very good at accepting information that agrees with us and questioning any information that disagrees with us.

- The best way of trying to catch this motivated reasoning (which again seems to have its roots in the subconscious X-system) is to deploy empirical scepticism. That is to say, if you believe something to be true, then test those beliefs against wide-ranging empirical data. See just how likely it is that your firm can attain 40% p.a. EPS growth over the next 10 years.

*This article appeared in Mind Matters on 12 February 2008. Copyright © 2008 by The Société Générale Group. All rights reserved. The material discussed was accurate at the time of publication.

- One final noteworthy point, the evidence suggests that the clinically depressed are the one group of people who see the world the way it really is. They don't have any illusions over their abilities, hence their depression! So perhaps investors face an unenviable choice, either be depressed and see the world the way it really is, or be happy and deluded. Personally I guess the best solution may be to be clinically depressed at work, but happy and deluded when you go home!

Optimism seems ingrained in the human psyche. When I asked a sample of over 500 professional fund managers how many of them were above average at their jobs, an impressive 74% responded in the affirmative. Indeed many of them wrote comments such as 'I know everyone thinks they are, but I really am'!

This trait is not unique to our industry. When teaching I generally find that 80% of students believe they will finish in the top 50% of my class! A recent paper by Lench and Ditto (2008) explores our tendencies to reach optimistic conclusions.

In their first experiment Lench and Ditto give participants a series of future life events. Each one is assigned a probability based on empirical evidence gathered from sources that reflected the participants' general peer group (at least that is what the participants are told). They are then asked to rate on a scale of 1 (very unlikely) to 9 (very likely) how likely it is that they themselves will encounter such an event (Figure 18.1).

Half of the participants were given optimistic statements drawn from three possible ranges of likelihood (high, medium, low) such as 60% of people will never experience a bout of unemployment, or 40% of people will have a starting salary over $60,000, and 15% of people live past 90 years of age.

The other half received similar statements but negative rather than optimistic. So they were told that 60% of people will experience a bout of unemployment, 40% of people have a starting salary of under $30,000, and that 15% of people will die before they reach 40 years of age.

The optimistic bias showed up as positive events receiving a much higher rating on likelihood of occurring than the negative events, despite the fact that each set of events had comparable base rate statistics.

Lench and Ditto suggest that optimism may well be the natural human default. Many such systems in the human mind are effectively fast and furious short cuts to decision making (see Chapter 1 of *Behavioural Investing* for more on this). In order to tease out whether optimism might be such behaviour, Lench and Ditto set up an experiment in which they can vary the time pressure. X-system functions tend to come to the fore under time pressure, so if optimism is a default option for humans then we are likely to see it exacerbated when time constraints are high.

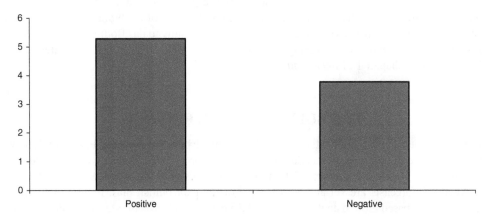

Figure 18.1   Average rating of likelihood of positive and negative events (1 = very unlikely, 9 = very likely)
Source: Lench and Ditto (2007).

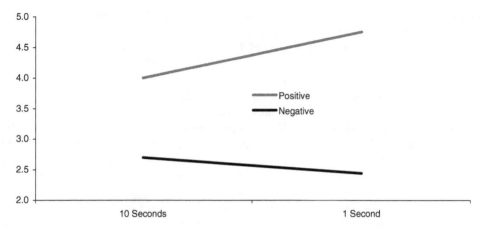

Figure 18.2   The impact of time constraint on number of good and bad events
Source: Lench and Ditto (2007).

This time, participants were placed in front of a computer screen and shown statements about future life events. They could press either a key labelled 'not me' or a key labelled 'me'. A base rate occurrence frequency was shown on the screen along with the event itself. The event either appeared for 1 second or 10 seconds. Six positive and six negative life events were used. Figure 18.2 reveals the results.

When allowed time to consider the life event, participants said that four of the six positive life events would happen to them, and only 2.7 of the negative life events would happen to them. When placed under time pressure, the number of positive life events rose to 4.75, while the number of negative life events fell to 2.4! This pattern is consistent with the idea that optimism is the default response.

Further evidence on the deep-seated nature of our optimism is found in recent work by Liz Phelps and colleagues (see Sharot *et al.*, 2007). They have been busy scanning people's brains while asking them to consider past and future good and bad events. When imaging positive future events (relative to negative ones) two key areas of the brain showed increased activation – the rostral anterior cingulate cortex and the amygdala. Both of these areas are associated with emotional processing, and are generally held to be neural correlates of the X-system (see Chapter 1 of *Behavioural Investing*).

THE BULLISH BIAS IN FINANCE

Evidence abounds that our industry is riddled with bullish bias. For instance, Figure 18.3 shows the percentage of stock recommendations accounted for by buys, holds and sells. Strangely enough some 91% of all recommendations are either buys or holds, a mere 9% are sells.

Analysts' forecasts are yet another example of rampant bullish bias. Figure 18.4 simply groups stocks based around analysts' views of 5-year forward growth rates. Quintile 1 has the lowest expected growth (around 6% p.a.), while quintile 5 has the highest expected growth rate (over 22% p.a.). The black bars represent actual out-turn after 5 years. Statistically there is no difference between the outturns for quintile 1 and quintile 5.

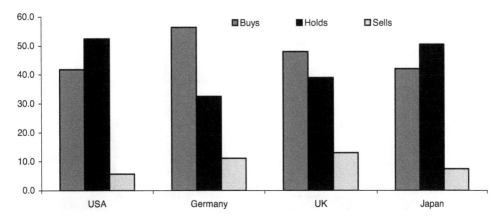

Figure 18.3   Percentage of recommendations across categories
Source: Bloomberg.

But note that the stocks the analysts were most bullish about suffered the biggest disappointment! The average long-term growth rate forecast is around 13% p.a., the average out-turn is around 8% p.a. – a forecast error of 500 bps!

Buy-side analysts don't appear to be any better in terms of forecasting. A recent paper by Groysberg *et al.* (2007) has explored the performance of the buy-side versus sell-side analysts. The results are fascinating to say the least.

A priori a good case can be made to suggest that buy-side analysts should be less biased than sell-side analysts. For instance, they have no conflict of interest issues with corporate finance work, they generally are less worried about corporate access as they can use their assets under management as an incentive for managements to meet with them, and their recommendations aren't publicly available for corporate scrutiny.

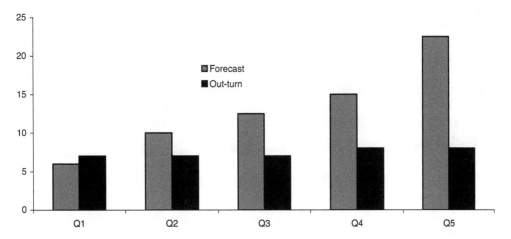

Figure 18.4   Long-term earnings growth forecasts and out-turns (% p.a.)
Source: SG Equity research.

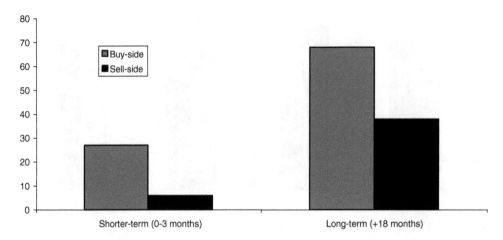

Figure 18.5   Mean absolute forecast error (%)
Source: Groysberg *et al.* (2007).

That said, buy-side analysts have their own incentive issues to deal with. In many conversations with hedge funds of late, the topic of how to deal with an analyst that has no positions in the portfolio has arisen. The fear of analysts trying to game portfolio managers to get their stocks into the portfolio is obviously non-negligible.

However, as an empirical sceptic the proof lies in the pudding. This is where the paper by Groysberg *et al.* comes into its own. They have managed to get hold of the data from one buy-side firm's analysts. Whenever a buy-side analyst made a forecast (had a view) this was matched against the data from the sell-side consensus. Of course, there is a small sample problem here; we are talking about just one firm. But on the basis that some evidence is better than no evidence, let's just accept Groysberg *et al.*'s statement that this was a large, well-respected research driven buy-side house, and examine their findings.

Groysberg *et al.* use the mean absolute forecast error as their measure of forecast accuracy. They examine the performance of buy- and sell-side analysts' earnings forecasts over the period 1997–2004.

Performance was tracked over two time horizons, the short term (0–3 months) and the long term (18 months and beyond). The results can be seen in Figure 18.5. Buy-side analysts were considerably less accurate than their sell-side brethren! At short horizons, the average buy-side analyst had a 27% forecast error against the sell-side analyst's 6% error. As we extend the time horizon, the performance becomes even worse. The sell-side had a mean absolute forecast error of 38% at the 18-month horizon and beyond, the buy-side had an astounding 68% mean forecast error!

THE SOURCES OF BULL

(I) Nature

Effectively the sources of the bullish bias can be split into those related to nature, and those related to nurture. So let's start with nature. Our brains have been designed by the process of evolution, unfortunately evolution tends to move at a glacial pace. So our minds are probably adapted to live on the African savannah of 150,000 years ago, certainly not the world in which we live today.

Many of the biases we have today presumably had some evolutionary advantage (although some may be spandrels, to borrow Stephen Jay Gould's expression for the by-products of evolution). What possible role could optimism have played in our evolution as a species?

Lionel Tiger argued in his book *Optimism: The Biology of Hope* (1979) that when early men left the forests and became hunters many of them suffered death and injury. Tiger suggests that humans tend to abandon tasks associated with negative consequences, so it was biologically adaptive for humans to develop a sense of optimism. After all, it takes a great deal of courage to take on a mastodon (a very large prehistoric elephant – like creature), and frankly not too many pessimists would even bother.

He also argues that when we are injured, our bodies release endorphins. Endorphins generally have two properties; they have an analgesic property (to reduce pain) and they produce feelings of euphoria. Tiger suggests that it was biologically adaptive for our ancestors to experience positive emotions instead of negative emotions when they were injured because it would reinforce their tendency to hunt in the future.

As with many evolutionary arguments there is an element of a Kipling-like 'just so' story:[1] However, it is likely that optimism did indeed bestow some advantage upon us. Indeed, Shelley Taylor and Jonathan Brown found that optimists seemed to cope far better (and survived much longer) when faced with dire news over illness (and indeed a wide range of other problems) – see Taylor and Brown, 1988. So optimism may well be a great life strategy. However, this doesn't make it a great market strategy, of course.

(II) Nurture – Self-serving Bias and Motivated Reasoning

Psychologists have often documented a 'self-serving bias' whereby people are prone to act in ways that are supportive of their own interests (see Chapter 51 of *Behavioural Investing* for more details).

A good example of this self-serving bias can be found in Moore *et al.* (2002). They experimented with 139 professional auditors. Participants were given five different auditing cases to examine. They concerned a variety of controversial aspects of accounting: for instance, one covered the recognition of intangibles, one on revenue recognition and one on capitalization of vs expensing of expenditures. The auditors were told that the cases were independent of each other. The auditors were randomly assigned to either work for the company or work for an outside investor considering investing in the company in question (Figure 18.6).

The auditors who were told they were working for the company were 31% more likely to accept the various dubious accounting moves than those who were told they worked for the outside investor! And this was in the post-Enron age!

This kind of motivated reasoning is sadly all too common. For instance, if we jump on the bathroom scales in the morning, and they give us a reading that we don't like, we tend to get off and have another go (just to make sure we weren't standing in an odd manner). However,

---

[1] For those unfamiliar with the great man's 'Just So' stories, they are creative tales of how many animals ended up as they have. For instance, the elephant in the stories ends up with a long trunk, because he disobeyed his mother, and drank from a river full of crocodiles, one of which grabbed his nose. As the elephant pulled back, his trunk was stretched, thus the shape we all know and love today.

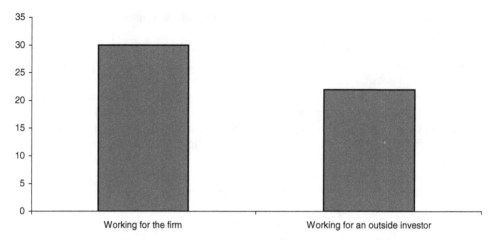

Figure 18.6 Percentage of auditors that allow various accounting measures to pass
Source: Moore *et al.* (2004).

if the scales have delivered a number under our expectations, we would have hopped off the scales into the shower, feeling very good about life.

Strangely enough, we see exactly the same sort of behaviour in other areas of life. Ditto and Lopez (1992) set up a clever experiment to examine just such behaviour. Participants were told that they would be tested for the presence of TAA enzyme. Some were told that the TAA enzyme was beneficial (i.e. 'people who are TAA positive are 10 times less likely to experience pancreatic disease than are people whose secretory fluids don't contain TAA'), others were told TAA was harmful ('10 times more likely to suffer pancreatic disease').

Half of the subjects in the experiment were asked to fill out a set of questions before they took the test, the other half were asked to fill out the questions after the test. In particular two questions were important. The first stated that several factors (such a lack of sleep) may impact the test, and participants were asked to list any such factors that they had experienced in the week before the test. The other question asked participants to rate the accuracy of the TAA enzyme test on a scale of 0 to 10 (with 10 being a perfect test).

Figures 18.7 and 18.8 show the results that Ditto and Lopez uncovered. In both questions there was little difference in the answers offered by those who were told having the TAA enzyme was healthy and those who were told it was unhealthy, provided they were asked before they were given the result. However, massive differences were observed once the results were given.

Those who were told the enzyme was healthy and answered the questions after they had received the test results, gave less life irregularities and thought the test was better than those who answered the questions before they knew the test result.

Similarly, those who were told the enzyme was unhealthy and answered the questions after the test results, provided considerably more life irregularities and thought the test was less reliable than those who answered before knowing the test result. Both groups behaved exactly as we do on the scales in the bathroom. Thus, we seem to be very good at accepting information that we want to hear while not only ignoring, but actively arguing against, information that we don't want to hear.

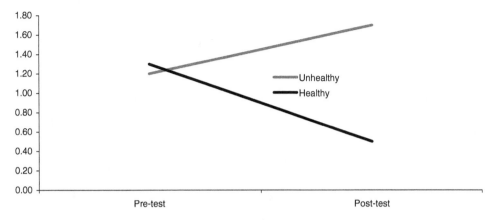

Figure 18.7 Number of test-affecting life irregularities cited
Source: Ditto and Lopez (1992).

Interestingly, Westen *et al.* (2005) found that such motivated reasoning is associated with parts of the brain that control emotion, rather than logic (the X-system, rather than the C-system). Committed Democrats and Republicans were shown statements from both Bush and Kerry and a neutral person. Then a contradictory piece of behaviour was shown, illustrating a gap between the rhetoric of the candidates and their actions. Participants were asked to rate how contradictory the words and deeds were (on a scale of 1 to 4). An exculpatory statement was then provided, giving some explanation as to why the mismatch between words and deeds occurred, and finally participants were asked to rate whether the mismatch now seemed so bad in the light of the exculpatory statement (Figure 18.9).

For instance, participants were told that the following statement was made by George Bush in 2000, 'First of all, Ken Lay is a supporter of mine. I love the man. I got to know Ken Lay

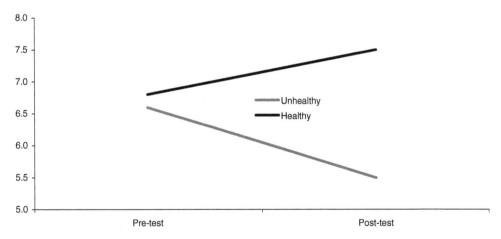

Figure 18.8 Perceived accuracy of TAA enzyme test
Source: Ditto and Lopez (1992).

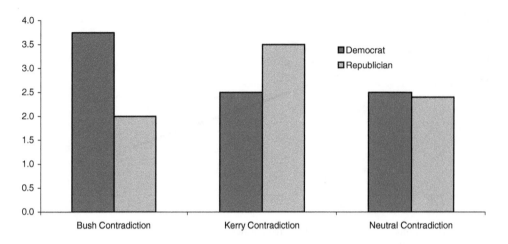

Figure 18.9 Behavioural ratings of the extent of the contradiction (scale 1 to 4, higher equals worse)
Source: Westen *et al.* (2005).

years ago, and he has given generously to my campaign. When I'm President, I plan to run the government like a CEO runs a company, Ken Lay and Enron are a model of how I'll do that.'

Then they were presented with a contradictory behavioural pattern, such as George Bush now avoids any mention of Ken Lay and is critical of Enron when asked. Finally, participants are given a exculpatory statement along the lines of 'people who know the President report that he feels betrayed by Ken Lay, and was genuinely shocked to find that Enron's leadership had been corrupt'.

Strangely enough, the Republicans thought that the Bush contradiction was far milder than the Democrats, and vice versa when considering the Kerry contradiction. Similar findings were reported for the question on whether the exculpatory statement mitigated the mismatched words and deeds.

Westen *et al.* found that the neural correlates of motivated reasoning were associated with parts of the brain known to be used in the processing of emotional activity rather than logical analysis. They note, 'Neural information processing related to motivated reasoning appears to be qualitatively different from reasoning in the absence of a strong emotional stake in the conclusions reached.'

Furthermore, Westen *et al.* found that after the emotional conflict of the contradiction has been resolved a burst of activity in one of the brain's pleasure centres can be observed (the ventral striatum). That is to say, the brain rewards itself once an emotionally consistent outcome has been reached. Westen *et al.* conclude, 'The combination of reduced negative affect ... and increased positive affect or reward ... once subjects had ample time to reach biased conclusions, suggests why motivated judgements may be so difficult to change (i.e. they are doubly reinforcing).'

Jeffrey Hales' has been exploring the tendency for investors to engage in motivated reasoning (Hales, 2007). In his experiment, Hales asks participants to forecast earnings for a real (but unnamed) firm on the NYSE. Each participant is given a recent history of the firm's earnings, news reports, a set of analyst's forecasts and comments. Each participant is given an incentive to provide an accurate forecast.

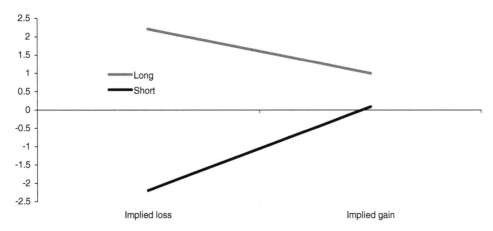

Figure 18.10 The impact of motivated reasoning on earnings forecasts (deviations from consensus)
Source: Hales (2006).

Directional preference (whether an investor benefits from a rising or falling stock) is randomized, with half the participants assigned a long position, and half a short position. The implications of the information given out are also manipulated. For half the participants the information implies that their investment position is likely to generate a positive return, for the others the outcome is likely to be a negative return.

The results show that investors' expectations of future earnings are influenced by what they would like to believe, even though they have an incentive to be accurate in their forecast. Figure 18.10 shows the results. When the consensus earnings number implies participants will have a profit on their investment position then, in general, their own forecasts remain pretty close to the consensus.

However, when a loss is implied by the consensus belief, then participants start generating forecasts that imply a profit for their position. So those holding a long end up with optimistic forecasts, and those with shorts start predicting a short fall!

As Hales puts it, 'Investors tend to agree unthinkingly with information that suggests they might make money on their investment, but disagree with information that suggests they might lose money.' Motivated reasoning at its best!

SCEPTICISM AS A DEFENCE

What can be done to offset this motivated reasoning? As ever, it isn't a case of waving a wand and watching a bias disappear. Given the evidence that both optimism and motivated reasoning stem from the subconscious X-system, we are often unaware that they have even occurred.

However, the evidence suggests that scepticism can be a useful tool in dealing with motivated reasoning. Within psychology there is a saying that if you can't debias then rebias. That simply means that if the X-system is operating at a subconscious level that we can't cognitively access, then the best we may be able to do is to turn that bias to our advantage.

Dawson *et al.* (2002) show that this strategy can be used in conjunction with motivated reasoning to improve decision making. They use a Wason selection task. Consider there are four playing cards laid out in front of you (E, 4, K, 7). Each card has a letter on one side, and a number on the other side (that much is true, you can take my word for it). However, you are asked to test the idea that if a card has an E, it should have a four on the other side. Which cards would you like to turn over to see if this proposition is true?

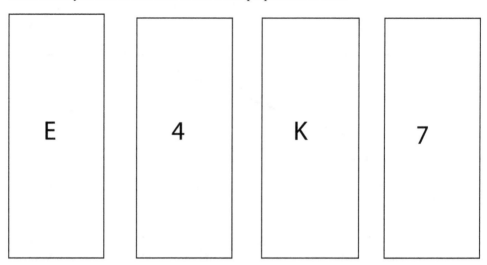

In the general population the correct answer is seen only around 10% of the time. In my sample of fund managers, only a mere 5% get this question right. It is the highest single failure rate out of any question that I ask!

Most people go for the E and 4. The correct answer is the E and 7. If you turn the E over and it doesn't have a 4 on the back, you have proved I was lying. If you turn the 7 over and it has an E on the back you have proved I was lying. Unfortunately, the 4 can't tell you anything. I said E had 4 on the reverse, not that 4 had E on the back. The habit of going for the 4 is known as confirmatory bias – a tendency to look for information that agrees with us, rather than looking for the information that would show we are wrong.

Dawson *et al.* use a variant of this test. They make participants take a test that measures their emotional responsiveness and volatility. They are then given the results, and read a passage on some new research which shows a link between performance on this test and early death. One group is told that early death is correlated with a low score; the other group is told that early death is related to a high score.

They are then given a sample from the research and asked to verify the earlier result. The sample they receive consists of four cards, just like the test above. In this case, the cards are labelled low score, high score, early death and late death.

Interestingly, when faced with a threatening situation people tend to solve the problem much more easily. For instance, among those participants who had a low score and were told that a low score could lead to early death, 55% turned over the correct cards, whereas of those with a high score only 10% solved the problem. This finding is reversed when the high scores are told that such a score can lead to early death (Figure 18.11).

As Dawson *et al.* point out, solving this problem is akin to asking 'Must I believe this?', rather than the less onerous 'Can I believe this?' that is usually deployed. The burden of proof is much higher under the first question than under the second. As investors we need to learn to ask the former question rather than relying on the second.

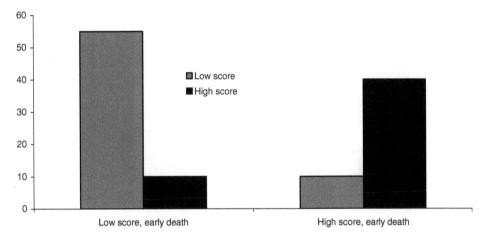

Figure 18.11   Percentage choosing the correct cards
Source: Dawson *et al.* (2002).

Indeed, when I studied some of the great value investors (see Chapter 23 of *Behavioural Investing*) I argued that they were expert at asking this 'Must' rather than 'Can' kind of question. I pointed out that because they generally run concentrated portfolios, the default stance for these investors was 'Why should I own this investment?' However, when fund managers are obsessed with tracking error and career risk, the default question changes to 'Why shouldn't I own this stock?'

A RATIONALE FOR EVIDENCE-BASED INVESTING

The best value investors seem to have scepticism as their default option. However, as I have written before, scepticism is rare. Our brains often seem wired to believe rather than question. **So we need to learn to confront our beliefs with empirical reality** (see Chapter 16 of *Behavioural Investing* which details this work).

This lays the foundation for what I have called Evidence-Based Investing. In medicine, there is a school of thought that suggests that we should use research to guide treatment. This movement goes by the name of Evidence-Based Medicine, and I think we need something similar in investing. Rather than simply asserting that something is true, I would like people to show me the evidence that this really is the case.

For instance, rather than simply telling me that stock can grow 40% p.a. over the next 10 years, show me the evidence from a large sample of firms, and examine the distribution of outcomes. Or if you believe that your stock can maintain its current ROIC, then have a look at the history and just see how likely it is that a company has been able to do so. Becoming an empirical sceptic (or should that be a sceptical empiricist?) seems to be the best way of trying to force yourself to carry out reality checks. Try to remember to live by the words of advice from Sherlock Holmes, **'It is a capital mistake to theorize before one has data. Insensibly one begins to twist facts to suit theories, instead of theories to suit facts.' And 'The temptation to form premature theories upon insufficient data is the bane of our profession.'**

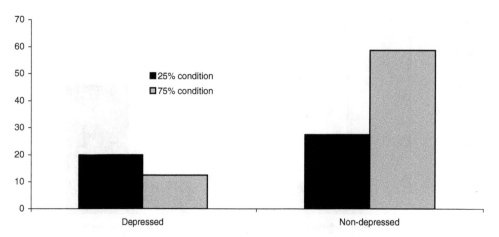

Figure 18.12 Illusion of control: % of time you have control over the light
Source: Alloy and Abramson (1979).

DEPRESSIVE REALISM

Perhaps one of the most intriguing findings from the study of optimism concerns its polar opposite – pessimism and depression. Many researchers have found that the only people who see the world the way it really is are the clinically depressed! They have no illusions over their own abilities. It is this realistic viewpoint that tends to lead them to depression.

Alloy and Abramson (1979) put participants in a room with a light and switch. Under one condition the light came on 25% of the time when the participants pressed the button, and 25% of the time when they didn't. In the second condition the light came on 75% of the time when the participants pressed the button and 75% of the time when they didn't.

Having taken part, participants were then asked how much of the time they were in control of the light. Figure 18.12 shows the results obtained. Those participants who scored highly on a pessimism test showed no illusion of control, unlike the others in the experiment.

Perhaps this leaves investors with an unenviable choice; either be depressed and see the world the way it is, or be happy and deluded. Personally, I guess the best solution may be to be clinically depressed at work, but happy and deluded when you go home (well, it works for me anyway!).

19

Keep it Simple, Stupid*

Too much time is spent trying to find out more and more about less and less, until we know everything about nothing. Rarely, if ever, do we stop and ask what we actually need to know!

- Our industry is obsessed with the minutia of detail. Analysts are often petrified of saying 'I don't know'. Something I personally have never had any issue with! It is a common misunderstanding that in order to make good decisions we need masses of information. However, nothing could be further from the truth.

- A new paper by Tsai *et al.* examines the confidence and accuracy of American football fans trying to predict the outcome of games. They found that people were just as accurate if they had six items of information as when they had 30! However, confidence (which exceeded accuracy at all levels of information) increased massively as the amount of information increased.

- This inability to process large amounts of information represents a cognitive constraint embedded within our brains. The simple truth is that our brains aren't supercomputers with limitless computational power. Rather than crashing mindlessly into our cognitive bounds, we should seek to exploit our natural endowment. So, rather than collecting endless amounts of information, we should spend more time working out what is actually important, and focusing upon that.

- When it comes to information overload, parallels exist between medicine and investing. For instance, in a certain hospital in Michigan, doctors were sending around 90% of all patients with severe chest pains to the cardiac care unit. However, they were admitting 90% of those who needed to be admitted, and 90% of those who didn't! They were doing no better than chance.

- The key reason for this seems to have been that the doctors were looking at the wrong information – effectively they were looking at a wide range of 'risk' factors such as age, gender, weight, smoking, etc. While these factors can define our probability of having a heart attack, they aren't good diagnostic tools to tell if you are actually having a heart attack.

- A complex set of statistical tables were introduced to help doctors to make better decisions. However, when these were removed, the doctors still made good decisions. They had learned to look at the correct information cues to make the best decision. Doctors using a very simple decision tree diagram delivered the best results. Similar devices could easily be deployed in the world of investing. As Warren Buffett says, 'investing is simple but not easy'.

*This article appeared in Mind Matters on 3 December 2007. Copyright © 2007 by The Société Générale Group. All rights reserved. The material discussed was accurate at the time of publication.

At the start of the year I did a two-hour Q&A session with a client on behavioural decision making. At the end of the session, my host walked me out and said, 'If you had to pick one word to describe your message which one would you choose?' My response was 'simplify'.

I have written before about the illusion of knowledge,[1] and when I present, I spend a reasonable amount of time talking about our obsession with knowing more and more about less and less, until we end up knowing nothing about everything. But rarely if ever do we stop and ask what do I need to know in order to actually take an investment decision.

In the past I have often used the work of Paul Slovic to illustrate that more information isn't necessarily better information. However, Slovic's work was published in 1973, and in the interests of replication and robustness I'm delighted to say that three researchers have recently shown exactly the same patterns that were uncovered by Slovic.

IS MORE BETTER?

Tsai, *et al.* (2008) show once again that, beyond a remarkably low level, more information translates into excessive confidence and static accuracy. They tested American football fans' ability to predict the outcome and point spread in 15 NCAA games. The information (selected by surveying non-participating football fans) was presented in a random order over five rounds. Each round revealed six items of information (called cues).

The information provided deliberately excluded team names as these were too leading. Instead they covered a wide range of statistics on football such as own fumbles, turnover margin, and yards gained.

Participants were 30 college and graduate students at the University of Chicago. On average, participants spent about one hour to complete the experiment in exchange for a fixed payment of $15. In addition, a reward of $50 was promised to the participant with the best performance. In order to take part in the study, participants had to pass a test demonstrating that they were highly knowledgeable about college football.

To see if more information was better information from a benchmark point of view, a stepwise logit regression was run on games not used in the actual test. While this sounds incredibly complex, all it really means is that new information was made available to the computer model in each round. This replicates the conditions faced by the experiment's human participants.

The results are shown in Figure 19.1. With just the first set of information (six cues) the model was around 56% accurate. As information was gradually added, the predictive accuracy rose up to 71% by the time all the available information was presented.

So, from a statistical modelling point of view, more information was indeed better information. However, when dealing with humans rather than computers a very different result was uncovered. The average performance of the participants is shown in Figure 19.2. Accuracy pretty much flatlines at around 62% regardless of the amount of information that was being provided. This performance is higher than the model on the earlier rounds, although not statistically so, but lower in the later rounds.

However, confidence tends to soar as more information is added. So, it starts off at 69% with 6 cues, and rises to nearly 80% by the time participants have 30 cues. So, just as with

---

[1] *See* Chapters 2 and 11 of *Behavioural Investing* (Wiley, 2007).

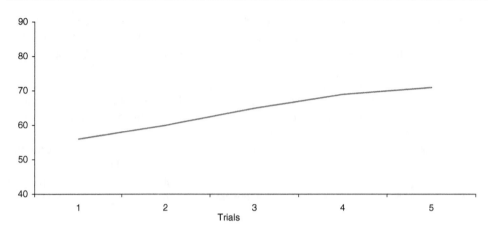

Figure 19.1 Accuracy of prediction from the computer model (%)
Source: Tsai *et al.* (2007).

Slovic's original study, confidence but not accuracy increases with the amount of information available.

This finding reflects the cognitive constraints suffered by the human mind. As George Miller found in 1956, the average human working memory (the brain's scratch pad, if you like) can handle seven bits of information (plus or minus 2).

Long before George Miller had discovered this cognitive bound, none other than Sir Arthur Conan Doyle had written the following words uttered by the ever insightful Sherlock Holmes:

> I consider that a man's brain originally is like a little empty attic, and you have to stock it with such furniture as you choose. A fool takes in all the lumber of every sort that he comes across, so

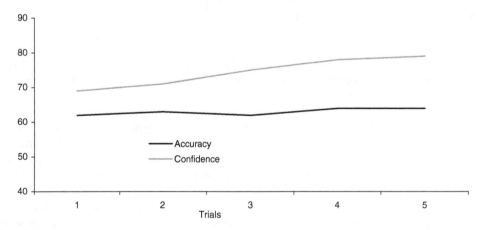

Figure 19.2 Accuracy and confidence of predictions from participants
Source: Tsai *et al.* (2007).

that the knowledge which might be useful to him gets crowded out, or at best is jumbled up with a lot of other things, so that he has a difficulty laying his hands upon it. But the skilful workman is very careful indeed as to what he takes into his brain-attic. He will have nothing but the tools which may help him in doing his work, but of these he has a large assortment, and all in the most perfect order. It is a mistake to think that the little room has elastic walls and can distend to any extent. Depend upon it, there comes a time when for every addition of knowledge you forget something you knew before. It is of the highest importance, therefore, not to have useless facts elbowing out the useful ones.

A Study in Scarlet

The simple truth is that we aren't supercomputers with unlimited power. Rather than trying to push the cognitive bounds of our brains, we should seek to best exploit our natural endowment. So, rather than collecting all the available information, we should spend more time working out what is actually important and focus on that.

KISS: KEEP IT SIMPLE, STUPID

Yet more evidence of our limited mental capacity is provided by a recent study by Dijksterhuis *et al.* (2006). In their study participants were asked to choose between four different cars. They faced one of two conditions: they were either given just four attributes per car (low load) or 12 attributes per car (high load). In both cases, one of the cars was noticeably 'better' than the others, with some 75% of its attributes being positive. Two cars had 50% of the attributes positive, and one car had only 25% of the attributes positive.

Figure 19.3 shows the percentage of participants choosing the 'best' car under each of the information conditions. Under the low level of information condition nearly 60% of subjects chose the best car. However, when faced with information overload, only around 20% of subjects chose the best car!

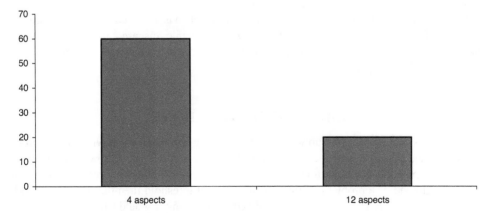

Figure 19.3 Percentage of participants choosing the 'best' car
Source: Dijksterhuis *et al.* (2007).

LESSONS FROM HEART ATTACKS

The original work in this field was done by Lee Green (Green and Yates, 1995). The problem arose in a hospital in Michigan. Physicians at this particular hospital tended to send around 90% of all patients with severe chest pains to the cardiac care unit. The unit was becoming seriously overcrowded, care standards were dropping and costs were rising.

The decision to send so many patients to ICU reflected concerns among doctors over the costs of a false negative (i.e. not admitting someone who should have been admitted). Fine, you might say, rather that than the alternative. However, this ignores the risks inherent in entering ICU. Around 20 000 Americans die every year from a hospital transmitted illness. The risks of contracting such a disease are markedly higher in ICU than in a conventional ward.

The most damning problem for the Michigan hospital doctors was that they sent around 90% of those who needed to be admitted and around 90% of those who didn't need to be admitted to ICU. They did no better than chance!

WHY?

Such a performance begs the question of why doctors found it so difficult to separate out those who needed specialist care from those who didn't. Green and Yates sought to explore exactly this issue.

The bottom line from their research was that doctors were looking at the wrong things. They tended to overweight 'risk factors' such as a family history of premature coronary artery disease, age, male gender, smoking, diabetes mellitus, increased serum cholesterol, and hypertension.

However, while these factors help to assess the overall likelihood of someone having cardiac ischemia, they have little diagnostic power. They aren't effective information cues, or as Green and Yates label them, they are pseudodiagnostic items. That is to say, 'they are additional information related to the diagnosis under consideration that influences decision makers' probability judgements but that are not of objective value in making the distinction between that diagnosis and other possibilities'.

Much better diagnostic cues are available. Research has revealed that the nature and location of patients' symptoms, their history of ischemic disease, and certain specific electrocardiographic findings are by far the most powerful predictors of acute ischemia, infarction, and mortality.

CAN ANYTHING BE DONE?

Green and his colleagues came up with the idea of using laminated cards with various probabilities marked against diagnostic information. The doctors could then follow these tables and multiply the probabilities according to the symptoms and test findings in order to estimate the overall likelihood of a problem. If this was above a set threshold then the patient was to be admitted to cardiac ICU, otherwise a normal bed with a monitor would suffice.

After this aid to decision was introduced, there was a marked improvement in the decision making of the doctors. They still caught a high proportion of problem cases, but they cut down dramatically on sending patients to ICU who didn't need to go.

Of course, this might indicate that the tool had worked. But, being good and conscientious scientists, Green *et al.* decided they had better check to ensure that this was the case. This was done by giving the doctors the decision tool in some weeks, and not giving them in other weeks. Obviously, if the tool is the source of the improved performance one would expect some deterioration in performance in the weeks when access to the aid was prohibited.

The results from this experiment showed something surprising. Decision making seemed to have improved regardless of the use of the tool! What could account for this surprising finding? Was it possible that doctors had memorized the probabilities from the cards, and were using them even when the cards weren't available?

This seemed unlikely as the various combinations and permutations listed on the card were not easy to recall. A quick test showed something else was afoot. In fact, the doctors had managed to assimilate the correct cues. That is to say, by showing them the correct items to use for diagnosis, the doctors emphasis switched from pseudodiagnostic information to truly informative elements. They started looking at the right things!

SIMPLICITY IS KEY

Based on this experience Green and Mehr (1997) designed a very easy-to-use decision aid, a series of yes/no questions (several orders of magnitude easier than the probability based measures originally built). The structure of the aid is shown in Figure 19.4.

If the patient displays a particular electrocardiogram anomaly (the ST change) then he is admitted to ICU straight away. If not, then a second cue is considered: whether the patient is suffering chest pains. If he is then again he is admitted to ICU, and so forth.

This makes the critical elements of the decision transparent and salient to the doctor. It also works exceptionally well in practice. Figure 19.5 shows the accuracy of the measures we have discussed here. The axis represent the two dimensions of our problem, the proportion of heart attack patients who are correctly diagnosed and sent to the ICU (vertical axis) and the proportion of non-heart attack patients who are also sent to ICU (horizontal axis).

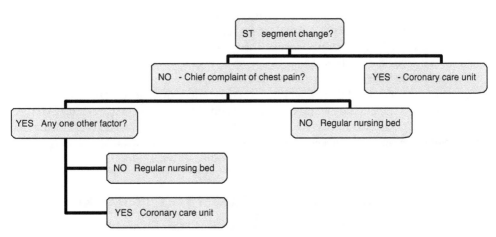

Figure 19.4 Admission decision for suspected MI
Source: Green and Mehr (1997).

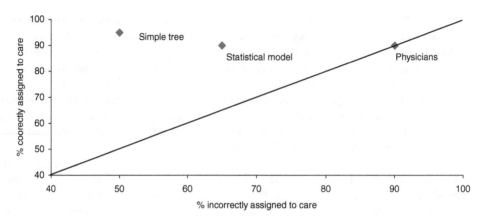

Figure 19.5   Performance of various groups in MI diagnosis
Source: Gigerenzer (2007).

The 45% line represents pure chance. Points above the diagonal represent a performance better than chance, while below the diagonal represents a worse than luck outcome.

The doctors originally did slightly worse than chance (as discussed above). The complex probability model can be set for various trade-offs, but I've selected the optimum trade-off to ensure that the highest proportion of those with heart attacks are correctly diagnosed. It is a marked improvement on the doctors' solo efforts; it characterizes more heart attack patients correctly, and vastly reduces the number of needless ICU admissions.

However, the simple decision tree does even better. It offers an even higher correct diagnosis and even greater reduction in needless admissions! So, fast and frugal decision making pays off in this domain.

EXPERTS FOCUS ON THE KEY INFORMATION

It is also noteworthy that Reyna and Lloyd (2006) explored heart attack diagnosis among various levels of experts. They found that the higher the level of expertise, the less information they needed to make accurate decisions. The experts essentially focused simply on what mattered most, and didn't allow themselves to be distracted by extraneous information.

Figure 19.6 highlights the correlations across knowledge groups between the myocardial infarction (heart attack) (MI) risk and the coronary artery disease (CAD) probability. The medical students decisions on admission were heavily influenced by both CAD and MI risks. In fact this pattern held until one got to the level of cardiologists. The highest skilled group, the cardiology experts only looked at the MI risks. Again this finding highlights the power of thinking about what matters rather than obsessing with ever more information.

FROM THE EMERGENCY ROOM TO THE MARKETS

Back to investment. Could something similar be designed for investors? Richard Thaler (one of the founding fathers of the field of behavioural finance) has recently referred to this kind of work as choice architecture. The essential aim is to help people to make good decisions

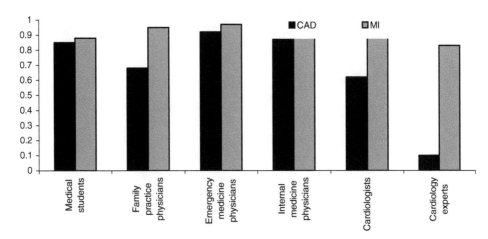

Figure 19.6 Correlations between MI risk and CAD probability with admission probability
Source: Reyna and Lloyd (2006).

by using rebiasing rather than debiasing. I have regularly urged investors to think about the factors that really matter for investment, one could easily imagine a fast and frugal decision making tree like the one shown in Figure 19.7 to help to keep investors focused on what really matters.

Investors may be well advised to remember the sage words of Warren Buffet 'Investing is simple but not easy'!

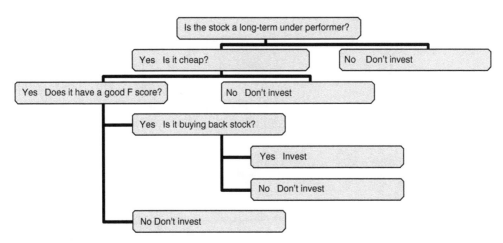

Figure 19.7 A simple contrarian decision tree
Source: SG Equity research.

20

Confused Contrarians and Dark Days for Deep Value*

These are dark days for deep value. Our basket of Graham-like stocks in Europe is down 24% so far this year, a performance matched by the stock picks of many of the best long-term value investors. In a world dominated by investors with chronic ADHD, in which the vast majority of investors end up chasing their own tails, taking a long-term view will almost certainly generate periods of underperformance. Investors should keep the faith: value isn't dead. One lesson from the TMT bust is that value will return to glory when investors lose their faith in the cyclicals pretending to be growth. Watch mining and the EM related plays.

- Our recent client meetings have confirmed a pattern that our deep value screens have been picking up: times are truly torrid for those following a sensible approach to investment. This view is echoed by the poor performance of purchases from some of the very best long-term value managers, down some 19% so far this year. Of course, they also often hold significant cash levels, and tend to view price declines as opportunities to buy more of their favourite stocks (assuming nothing fundamental has changed).

- Unfortunately, in a world in which investors seem to have developed a chronic case of attention deficit hyperactivity disorder (ADHD), short-term underperformance is punished severely. However, underperformance may well be the by-product of a sensible invest-ment strategy. The Brandes Institute has shown that the very best long-term (10-year) fund managers suffer marked periods of underperformance. In their worst single year, the best managers lagged their benchmark by nearly 20% on average. Even on a three-year view nearly 40% of the best managers were listed in the bottom decile in terms of performance.

- The good news is that there is light at the end of the tunnel for those who keep the faith. If value continues to perform as badly as it has the first half of the year, this will be one of the worst performances for value (relative to glamour) ever – even worse than the manic years of the TMT bubble! However, for those with patience this pain is more than compensated. Following periods of very poor value performance, value tends to re-bound strongly – delivering somewhere around 17% p.a. over glamour (for an average of 7 years).

- The experience of the TMT bust may hold some lessons as to when to expect deep value to return to grace. It wasn't until investors had totally lost faith in the cyclicals masquerading as growth that value started to return to grace. This time it is the mining and emerging

---

market related plays that are cyclicals pretending to be growth. Their time in the spotlight may be drawing to the end. As Sir John Templeton remarked, 'Bull markets are born on pessimism, grow on scepticism, mature on optimism and die on euphoria.' Lakshmi Mittal's recent ludicrous comment that 'I can say with considerable certainty that the volatile years of boom and bust are now relegated to the past' sounds pretty euphoric to me.

My recent marketing trips have only served to confirm that there are a number of very confused contrarians out there, and that deep value is having a truly torrid time. This comes as no surprise, given the way my own portfolio of deep value stocks has been performing.

The way I classify deep value opportunities is by using a screen designed by Ben Graham just before his death in the late 1970s. The list (supplemented by three of Rea's own requirements) was published by Rea in a *Journal of Portfolio Management* article in 1977, in order to qualify as a deep value opportunity the following criteria must be met:

1. a trailing earnings yield greater than twice the AAA bond yield;
2. a P/E ratio of less than 40% of the peak P/E ratio based on 5-year moving average earnings;
3. a dividend yield at least equal to two-thirds of the AAA bond yield;
4. a price of less than two-thirds of tangible book value;
5. a price of less than two-thirds of net current assets;
6. total debt less than two-thirds of tangible book value;
7. a current ratio greater than 2;
8. total debt less than (or equal to) twice net current assets;
9. compound earnings growth of at least 7% over 10 years;
10. two or fewer annual earnings declines of 5% or more in the last 10 years.

At the heart of Graham's approach is the concept of an appropriate margin of safety. That is to say, investors should always seek to purchase securities with a large discount between intrinsic value and market price. Indeed, Graham's own best-loved criterion was a price less than two-thirds of net current assets (number 5 above).

In today's world such 'net-nets' have become increasingly scarce. At the moment I can find two globally (in large cap space) – Taylor Wimpey and Barratt Developments, both UK house builders, showing perhaps that investors are pricing in the end of that industry! Indeed taking Taylor Wimpey, Barratt Developments and Persimmon together, analysts expect a 60% plus decline in earnings both this year and next year, and a minus 17% long-term growth rate! Surely this must be too pessimistic?

If he couldn't find 'net-nets' then Graham suggested that criteria 1, 3 and 6 were particularly important. Criteria 1 and 3 are effective valuation constraints, criterion 6 ensures that there is likely to be some equity value even in the event of liquidation. Currently, I can find zero stocks in the USA, 15 stocks in Europe and 20 stocks in Japan that manage to pass these deep value restrictions (in the large cap universe).

DARK DAYS FOR DEEP VALUE

As Tables 20.1 and 20.2 show, these baskets of stocks have delivered very poor absolute returns so far this year, with the European list down 24%, and the Japanese list down 15%. Of course, in relative terms these returns are much in line with the overall market. However, I am not a huge fan of relative performance as long-term readers of my articles will be aware.

DEEP VALUE WORKS OVER THE LONG TERM

This is the worst performance that such a screen has generated over the sample of the backtest (and indeed over its real-time existence). The good news is that over the long term deep value works (Figure 20.1). In fact, over the best part of the last two decades you would have almost doubled the market return in Europe by buying stocks that passed criteria 1, 3 and 6.

Table 20.1   European stocks passing criteria (1), (3) and (6)

Company name	Earnings yield	Dividend yield	1-month total return	3-month total return	6-month total return	YTD total return
Bellway PLC	11.7	3.5	7.4	−26.5	−38.4	−37.1
Boliden AB	16.5	4.9	−33.0	−42.4	−30.6	−53.2
Deutsche Lufthansa AG	13.9	6.9	4.7	−7.6	3.0	−8.3
ENI S.p.A.	10.9	5.2	−6.8	−7.2	3.6	−9.1
Home Retail Group PLC	13.1	5.7	3.9	0.7	−13.2	−26.2
Iberia Lineas Aereas de Espana S.A.	11.5	5.7	2.3	−29.3	−23.2	−40.4
Outokumpu Oyj	16.6	5.7	−32.0	−45.9	−18.0	−21.6
Parmalat S.p.A.	14.4	6.0	−3.3	−22.3	−24.2	−32.7
Persimmon PLC	17.2	6.4	−1.8	−44.3	−55.7	−54.3
Rautaruukki Oyj	11.2	6.7	−24.1	−27.1	−11.8	−19.4
Repsol YPF S.A.	10.7	4.1	−12.8	−16.1	4.1	−8.3
Royal Dutch Shell Class A	12.6	3.6	−7.9	−4.8	−4.3	−17.6
Tomkins PLC	11.5	7.7	−16.1	−27.0	−19.9	−19.9
Total S.A.	10.3	3.6	−7.5	−5.8	−1.1	−13.0
Vallourec S.A.	10.2	3.8	−13.8	7.2	38.6	0.7
Average			**−9.4/b**	**−19.9**	**−12.7**	**−24.0**

Source: SG Equity research.

Table 20.2   Japanese stocks passing criteria (1), (3) and (6)

Company name	Earnings yield	Dividend yield	1-month total return	3-month total return	6-month total return	YTD total return
Amada Co. Ltd.	9.7	2.9	−8.8	−3.3	−7.9	−17.2
Asahi Kasei Corp.	9.6	2.5	−4.7	−6.1	−15.7	−25.1
Astellas Pharma Inc.	9.1	2.8	−0.4	8.4	0.7	−6.2
Hoya Corp.	8.1	2.8	−9.1	−22.1	−32.7	−34.6
Itochu Techno-Solutions Corp.	7.7	2.7	2.5	6.1	15.4	−2.4
Kaneka Corp.	8.8	2.6	−1.4	−0.7	−11.4	−21.6
Makita Corp.	10.2	3.1	−1.7	12.3	−0.3	−13.8
Mitsubishi Gas Chemical Co. Inc.	12.3	2.3	−10.1	3.8	−25.5	−34.4
Mitsubishi Rayon Co. Ltd	7.5	3.4	10.0	6.0	−17.5	−34.3
Nisshin Steel Co. Ltd	10.3	2.3	−8.0	−11.6	−3.7	−13.2
NTT DoCoMo Inc.	7.5	3.2	5.0	3.7	−1.1	−11.2
Onward Holdings Co. Ltd	7.5	2.9	3.7	0.0	15.1	6.5
Sankyo Co. Ltd. (6417)	7.9	2.5	−8.7	7.5	28.4	28.9
Sekisui Chemical Co. Ltd	7.7	2.5	−2.5	1.3	3.9	−4.4
Shinko Electric Industries Co. Ltd	7.5	2.4	3.9	−2.6	−17.7	−35.8
Showa Shell Sekiyu K.K.	9.4	2.9	3.4	8.1	24.5	−3.6
Sumco Corp.	12.7	2.4	4.0	−5.7	−9.2	−22.4
Takeda Pharmaceutical Co. Ltd	8.4	3.4	−2.3	−3.4	−14.8	−15.9
TDK Corp.	9.4	2.2	−2.5	−4.6	−1.9	−20.0
Average			**−1.4**	**−0.1**	**−3.8**	**−14.8**

Source: SG Equity research.

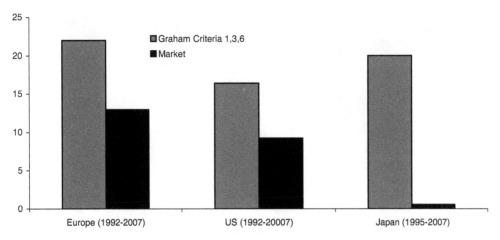

Figure 20.1   Deep value does work over the long haul (% returns p.a.)
Source: SG Equity research.

The returns in the USA and Japan are equally impressive. In both markets in some years I failed to find any stocks that passed all three criteria. In such years I assumed a zero return for that year – had I assumed a cash return then the overall returns would have been even higher!

VALUE OUT OF VOGUE

Nor is it only *my* screens that are having a tough time. According to the website Gurufocus, many of the top long-term performing value managers have been suffering a significant loss on the stocks that they have been buying over the last 12 months. Across the managers listed in Table 20.3, the average stock they have purchased in the last year is down 19% so far this year. (Of course, many of these managers have also been holding significant cash positions.)

Of course, some of the managers may not be too worried by this – after all they are long-term investors who tend to view price declines as an opportunity to buy more (assuming that nothing fundamental has changed).

Table 20.3   Performance of stocks bought in the last 12 months by…
(simple average %)

Bruce Berkowitz	−9	Mohnish Pabrai	−38
Charles Brandes	−29	Richard Pzena	−21
David Dreman	−19	Robert Rogriguex	−33
Dodge and Cox	−16	Ruane Cunniff	−16
Glenn Greenberg	−10	Seth Klarman	−9
Jean-Marie Eveillard	−7	Tom Gayner	−18
Martin Whitman	−35	Tweedy Browne	−13
Michael Price	−14	**Average**	**−19**

Source: Gurufocus.

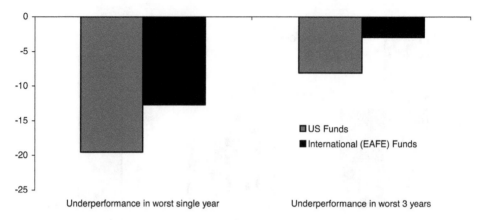

Figure 20.2   Top performing fund managers performance against benchmark in... (%)
Source: Brandes, Institute, SG Equity research.

SHORT-TERM UNDERPERFORMANCE IS A BY-PRODUCT OF A SENSIBLE INVESTMENT PROCESS

Short-term underperformance is often the by-product of a sensible investment process. For instance, if everyone else is dashing around trying to guess next quarter's earnings numbers, and you are exploiting a long-time frame, then you may well find yourself staring at the wrong end of a bout of underperformance.

Indeed, the Brandes Institute[1] has shown that the very best fund managers regularly suffer marked periods of poor performance. Examining some 591 US managers, and 147 EAFE managers they selected those with the best performance over a 10-year period. The best-performing US managers had outperformed the S&P 500 by an average of 2.5% p.a. over the decade, the best-performing EAFE beat the MSCI EAFE index by 4.6% p.a. over the decade.

Despite these impressive long-term outperformances, these groups were far from immune to the burden of short-term underperformance. In their worst year, the US managers lagged the index by 20 percentage points, the EAFE managers by 13 percentage points (Figure 20.2).

Alternatively, one might wonder how these long-term stars did relative to their competitors. Figures 20.3 and 20.4 show the percentage of the best long-term performing fund managers occurring bottom half of the performance decile. So, when performance is measured quarterly, almost every fund manager had appeared in the bottom decile. On a one-year basis, 75% of the best-performing fund managers had been in last place. **Even on a three-year horizon, between 20 and 30% of the best long-term managers were in the bottom decile!**

As one US-based fund manager said last week, 'What you are telling me is that to help my clients in the long-term, I should really suck now.'

---

[1] Death, Taxed and Short-Term Underperformance (February and July 2007), available from www.brandes.com/institute/BiResearch/.

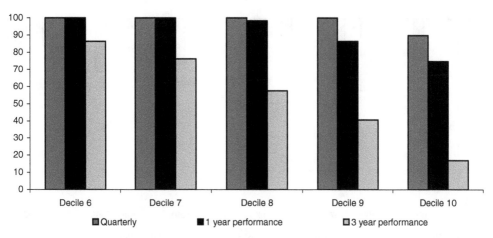

Figure 20.3 Percentage of long-term best investors appearing in lower performance deciles – USA
Source: Brandes Institute, SG Equity research.

IS THERE LIGHT AT THE END OF THE TUNNEL FOR VALUE?

The good news is that value isn't dead. Figure 20.5 shows the periods since 1960 when a simple value approach (buying high cash flow to price) has significantly underperformed glamour (low cash flow to price) for two years in the USA. Interestingly, the current experience is actually worse than the dot com years!

The good news is that value tends to bounce back after these two-year periods. Figure 20.6 shows the value outperformance from the end of the glamour surge to the beginning of the next glamour surge. Following a period of marked glamour action, value outperforms by nearly 17% p.a. (for an average of 7 years).

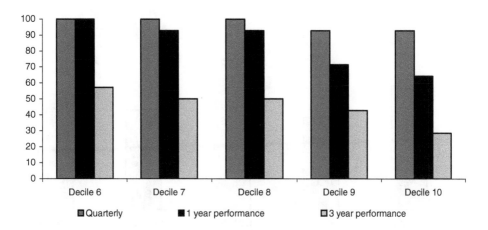

Figure 20.4 Percentage of long-term best investors appearing in lower performance deciles – EAFE
Source: Brandes Institute, SG Equity research.

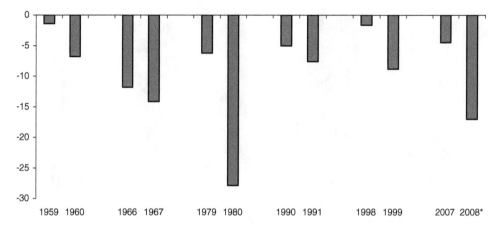

Figure 20.5 Percentage loss per year (value minus glamour) USA 1960–2008
Source: SG Equity research, *YTD.

Is there a likely catalyst for value returning to grace? The experience during the TMT bubble may offer some guidelines. As Figure 20.7 shows, it wasn't until investors had finally given up hope on TMT stocks that value returned to vogue.

This suggests that value won't be back in fashion until the last cyclical risk domino has fallen. To us, that means the mining stocks and the commodity/emerging market-related plays. Only when investors lose faith in these cyclicals turned structural growth stories are we likely to see a return to good old-fashioned value. The good news is: that day may be approaching (see Figure 20.8).

As the late great Sir John Templeton noted, 'Bull markets are born on pessimism, grow on septicism, mature on optimism and die on euphoria.' Lakshmi Mittal (of ArcelorMittal) recently pronounced, 'I can say with considerable certainty that the volatile years of boom and bust are now relegated to the past. We have succeeded in transforming ourselves into a profitable and sustainable industry.' Sure sounds euphoric to me!

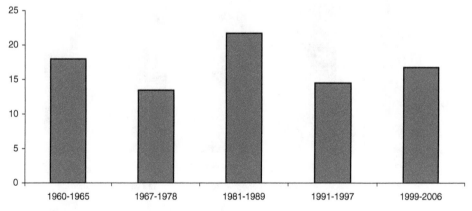

Figure 20.6 USA value minus glamour (% p.a.)
Source: SG Equity research.

Figure 20.7   TMT and value stocks (Jan 93 = 100)
Source: SG Equity research.

A bear market/recession environment may provide a timely opportunity to stock up on unloved, neglected deep value stocks. Of course, as Sir John also opined, 'To buy when others are despondently selling and to sell when others are greedily buying requires the greatest fortitude and pays the greatest rewards.'

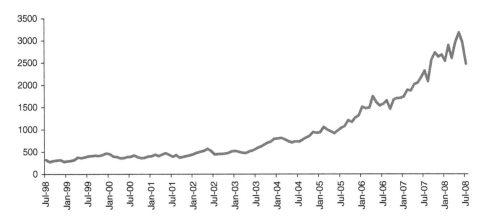

Figure 20.8   World mining sector price index
Source: SG Equity research.

Part IV
The Empirical Evidence

21

Going Global: Value Investing without Boundaries*

In a recent meeting I was asked if I had ever seen any work on value investing at the global level. I decided to investigate and see if my prior belief that value works across national boundaries was substantiated by the data. The good news is that it was. Allowing investors to seek out bargains wherever they are located and regardless of the industry in which they are operating makes sense both theoretically and empirically. In a world which seems to want to label and tightly box fund managers, such an approach will be unconventional. However, as Sir John Templeton said, 'It is impossible to produce superior performance unless you do something different from the majority.'

- As regular readers of *Mind Matters* will know, I favour an unconstrained approach to investing. This preference reflects both a belief that one should be allowed to exploit the opportunities whenever and wherever they arise. And also a belief that risk isn't measured by numbers such as the standard deviation, which renders most 'risk management' futile and means that tracking error has no meaning.

- However, I also regularly extol the benefits of confronting beliefs with empirical evidence. Thus it behoves me to show that my beliefs aren't at odds with reality. So does an unconstrained value-oriented approach work? I am relieved to say yes. For instance, looking at the individual performance across a group of major developed markets, value tends to outperform glamour by around 9% p.a. However, when an unconstrained approach across the developed markets is deployed, the return rises to 12% p.a. (and this is delivered with markedly less volatility than in the individual countries).

- Adding in emerging markets improves the prospects even further. The cheapest 20% of all stocks (measured across five valuation criteria), regardless of industry or geographic location, generated an average return of 18% between 1985 and 2007. That is a 15% premium over the most expensive stocks, and a 7% outperformance against the index.

- Of course, patience is key. Value investing requires a long time horizon. After all we never know when price and intrinsic value will be reconciled. The excess return gains to patience are impressive. While global value may have beaten the market by 7% p.a. with a one-year holding period, with a five-year holding period this turns into a 40% outperformance!

- So far we have been dealing with a simple strategy of buying the cheapest 20% of the market. However, this can translate into a very large number of stocks. For instance, in 2007

---

the cheapest 20% of the market covered some 1,800 stocks. However, if we were to run a concentrated portfolio, then unconstrained global value investing still works. Buying the 30 cheapest stocks results in an average return of nearly 25% p.a. Of course, the volatility of returns is higher, but volatility doesn't equal risk.

- The global value portfolio can also be used to help top-down investors by showing them the sources of value from a bottom-up perspective. Currently, Japan, South Korea and Taiwan are the sources of many value opportunities.

I was sitting in a meeting recently when one of the participants asked, 'Does value investing work at the global level?' This got me pondering. I've seen and done a lot of work on regional value strategies, but I've not seen much on the global scale.

Of course, several exceptionally good value investors such as Sir John Templeton and Jean-Marie Eveillard have shown that, in practice, value investing can be done on a global basis. As Sir John put it, 'It seems to be common sense that if you are going to search for these unusually good bargains, you wouldn't just search in Canada. If you search just in Canada, you will find some, or if you search just in the United States, you will find some. But why not search everywhere? That's what we've been doing for forty years; we search anywhere in the world' (speaking in 1979).

Certainly in theory, widening the opportunity set can do little to hurt a value strategy. But international value investing can also create issues, such as varying accounting standards. Certainly in the days before Enron *et al.* one of the most common refrains heard from US-based investors was concerns over the quality of the accounting.

From my perspective as an empirical sceptic, the key question is: What does the evidence show? Does value investing on an unconstrained global basis work? I am less than enamoured with limiting my opportunity set by imposing constraints such as 'not having more than X% in a certain sectors', or 'Y% in country Z'. So my interest lies in assessing unconstrained value strategies. In order to assess these questions I have used a universe of all developed and emerging markets over the time period 1985 onwards. To avoid confusing the results with any small cap effect, I set a minimum market capitalization of US $250m. I have also measured all returns in dollar terms.

Rather than contenting myself with just one definition of cheapness, I have used a combination of five – P/E, P/B, price/cash flow, price/sales and EBIT/EV. Each of these measures is ranked across the universe. These ranks are then totalled for each stock, and this combined score is ranked to give our value factor. In the first instance, value is defined as the cheapest 20% of the universe on this multi-value factor.

THE EUROPEAN EVIDENCE

Figure 21.1 shows the value outperformance relative to glamour in a number of large European countries. I've also plotted the value premium to an unconstrained approach across all the countries within Europe. This provides our first hint that expanding our boundaries can help to improve performance. In the individual countries covered value outperforms glamour by an average of around 8% p.a. At the European level, value outperforms glamour by just over 10% p.a.

Now, I am not a fan of measuring risk with reference to the standard deviation. I prefer Ben Graham's definition of risk as a permanent loss of capital. However, putting aside my personal preference, not only does the return increase, but the volatility of those returns also drops. Across the individual countries the average standard deviation of returns for a (long-only) value strategy is nearly 25% (Figure 21.2). For Europe as a whole this drops to 18% p.a.!

DEVELOPED MARKETS EVIDENCE

A similar pattern is uncovered if we extend the analysis to all the developed markets. Across six major developed markets (our European countries plus the USA and Japan), value outperforms

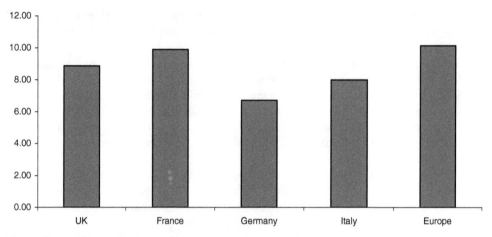

Figure 21.1 Long value/short glamour strategies annual performance (1985–2007, % p.a.)
Source: SG Equity research.

glamour by an average of around 9% p.a. However, across the developed markets, value
outperforms glamour by over 12% p.a. (Figure 21.3).

Once again this return enhancement was delivered with lower volatility of returns. The
average standard deviation of the long-only value strategies across the individual countries
was almost 25% p.a. However, the long-only value strategy across the developed markets
witnessed a standard deviation of just under 16% p.a. (Figure 21.4)

BRINGING IN THE EMERGING MARKETS

What happens if we bring in emerging markets? First, it is worth checking that value investing
works in the context of emerging markets. As Figure 21.5 shows, value works in emerging

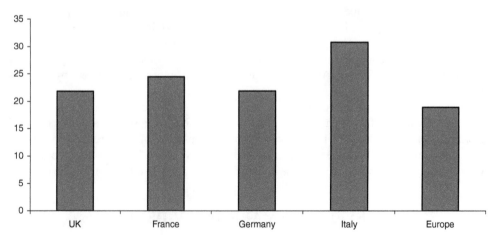

Figure 21.2 Standard deviation of returns (1985–2007, % p.a.)
Source: SG Equity research.

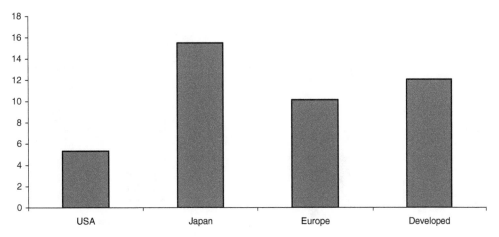

Figure 21.3   Value strategies in the developed markets (1985–2007, % return p.a.)
Source: SG Equity research.

markets just as it does in developed markets. The cheapest stocks outperform the most expensive stocks by over 18% p.a. and they beat the market by around 11% p.a.

However, the standard deviation of those long-only returns is much higher in emerging markets at over 40%. Of course, this just reflects the greater volatility of emerging markets relative to developed markets in general (with standard deviations of 32% vs 16% respectively).

When we combine the emerging and developed markets into a single universe, we find that value continues to work. Figure 21.6 shows the returns across the quintiles of value. The cheapest 20% of all stocks, regardless of industry or geographical location, generates an average return of 18%; the most expensive stocks generate a return of under 3% p.a. on average. Thus value outperforms glamour at the global level by 15%. This is an average 7% p.a. outperformance versus the equal weighted universe.

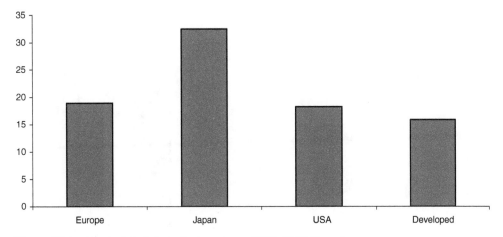

Figure 21.4   Standard deviation of value returns (1985–2007, % p.a.)
Source: SG Equity research.

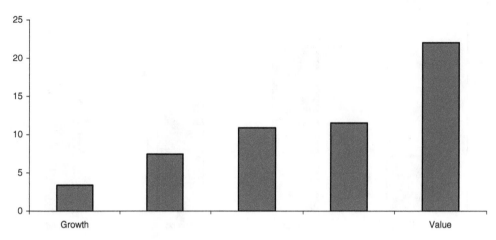

Figure 21.5   Emerging markets: value works (1985–2007, % p.a)
Source: SG Equity research.

The standard deviation of the long-only performance is around 19% p.a, which is much lower than the value strategy in the emerging markets alone, but not really much higher than that seen in the developed markets.

PATIENCE IS STILL A VIRTUE

As I have said before, patience is a key virtue for a value investor (see Chapters 30 and 31 of *Behavioural Investing*). As Ben Graham said, 'Undervaluations caused by neglect or prejudice may persist for an inconveniently long time.' Whenever a value position is established one can never be sure which potential return pathway will be taken. Effectively, any value position falls into one of three categories.

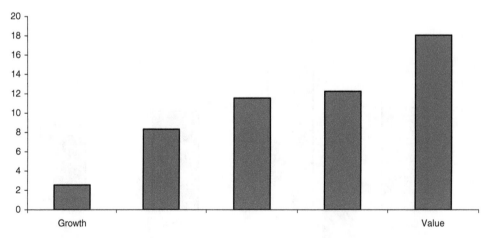

Figure 21.6   Global unconstrained value investing works! (1985–2007, % p.a.)
Source: SG Equity research.

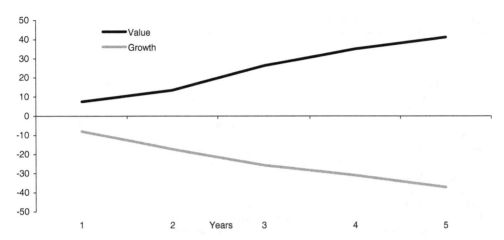

Figure 21.7 Patience is a virtue: cumulative excess returns over various holding periods
Source: SG Equity research.

1. Those that enjoy a re-rating as the market more generally recognizes that a mis-pricing has occurred.
2. Those that generate a higher return via dividend yield, but are not immediately re-rated.
3. Those that simply don't recover: the value traps.

So patience is a prerequisite for value managers as long as we are dealing with the first two types of stock, and a key problem when it comes to the third type of stock. Figure 21.7 shows the need for patience when dealing with global value investing.

The value strategy tends to outperform the market by around 7% in the first year. If you hold for another 12 months, an additional 6% is added to the return. However, holding for longer periods really creates opportunity. In the third year an amazing 12% outperformance of the market is recorded, followed by another 8% in the fourth year.

This receives practical support when one examines the average holding period of long-term successful value managers; their average holding period is around 5 years – a marked contrast to the churn and burn of the average mutual fund.

CONCENTRATED PORTFOLIO

Much of the above will make sense to most value investors. However, one thing will stand out as odd. The strategy outlined above effectively goes long the cheapest 20% of the market, and that can involve a large number of stocks. For instance, there were 1,800 stocks in the cheapest quintile at the end of 2007. What would happen if we ran a concentrated portfolio of, say, the cheapest 30 stocks (Table 21.1) in the entire universe?

The answer is that the strategy continues to do very well. Simply picking the 30 cheapest stocks regardless of their locale or activity and equal weighting them generates a return of nearly 25% p.a. This represents an outperformance of nearly 15% over the universe.

The annual time series of both the absolute and relative to market returns are shown in Figures 21.8–21.10. The absolute performance echoes a point I have been making recently on the poor performance of value strategies of late. In the historical context, this is on a par with the experience of 1998 and 1990.

Table 21.1   The 30 cheapest stocks globally

Company	Mkt Cap ($m)	Sector	Country	Rank
Solomon Mutual Savings Bank	294.2	Finance	South Korea	1
Primorskoye Morskoye Parakhodstvo A.O.	332.3	Transportation	Russia	2
Nacional Telefonos de Venezuela C.A.	903.1	Communications	Venezuela	3
Northwest Airlines Corp.	3,383.6	Transportation	United States	4
Qiao Xing Universal Telephone Inc.	255.3	Electronic Technology	China	5
Champion Technology Holdings Ltd	358.9	Technology Services	Hong Kong	6
Air Canada (Cl B)	1,209.7	Transportation	Canada	7
BRIT Insurance Holdings PLC	1,424.1	Finance	United Kingdom	8
Allco Equity Partners Ltd	365.7	Miscellaneous	Australia	9
Jereissati Participacoes S/A	477.9	Commercial Services	Brazil	10
Electricidad de Caracas C.A. S.A.C.A.	368.0	Utilities	Venezuela	11
Macquarie DDR Trust	991.1	Finance	Australia	12
Custodia Holding AG	1,008.2	Finance	Germany	13
Nafco Co. Ltd	417.1	Retail Trade	Japan	14
British Airways PLC	5,365.2	Transportation	United Kingdom	15
Bashneft	806.3	Energy Minerals	Russia	16
Invista Real Estate Inv. Management Hold. PLC	283.6	Finance	United Kingdom	17
Pacific Textiles Holdings Ltd	285.4	Process Industries	Hong Kong	18
Sumitomo Pipe & Tube Co. Ltd	253.8	Producer Manufacturing	Japan	19
US Airways Group Inc.	1,351.3	Transportation	United States	20
Norstar Founders Group Ltd	375.3	Consumer Durables	Hong Kong	21
Toenec Corp.	451.2	Industrial Services	Japan	22
Taihei Kogyo Co. Ltd	273.5	Industrial Services	Japan	23
Delta Air Lines Inc.	4,351.2	Transportation	United States	24
Sanei-International Co. Ltd	372.9	Consumer Non-durables	Japan	25
Koenig & Bauer AG	461.6	Producer Manufacturing	Germany	26
Vaudoise Versicherungen Holding	456.9	Finance	Switzerland	27
Turk Hava Yollari A.O.	1,285.3	Transportation	Turkey	28
Zeleziarne Podbrezova a.s.	258.9	Producer Manufacturing	Slovakia	29
Cemex Venezuela S.A.C.A	715.9	Non-energy Minerals	Venezuela	30

Source: SG Equity research.

In relative performance space (not my favourite way of looking at things by a long margin), the strategy is holding good so far this year, returning about the same as the average stock. The benefits of including the emerging markets in the universe can be clearly seen when looking at such years as 1999 (see Figure 21.9). While value in general was having a truly terrible time, the cheapest 30 stocks were doing exceptionally well. The vast majority of those stocks were Brazilian.

The returns of the concentrated portfolio are considerably more volatile than its big brother. This is only to be expected given the nature of the portfolio. It should, of course, be noted once again that price volatility is not the same thing as risk for value investors. Indeed, looking at the number of years of outright negative returns, the concentrated portfolio suffers such an occurrence only three times in the backtest period. This compares with six such occasions in the overall market – hardly evidence of excessive risk bearing to my mind!

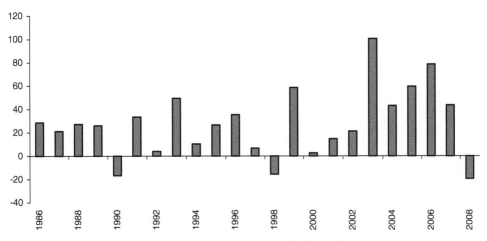

Figure 21.8   Absolute returns from cheapest 30 stocks – globally, %
Source: SG Equity research.

As noted in the previous section, patience goes hand-in-hand with the value approach. Figure 21.10 shows that this is just as true when we are running concentrated portfolios as when we run the full value portfolio. The returns take time to generate.

CURRENT PORTFOLIO STANCES

Therefore, unconstrained global value investing works. We can also use the value portfolio (this time using the full 1,800 stock version) to see if bottom-up analysis can reveal anything interesting from a top-down perspective. Figures 21.11 and 21.12 show the implicit country

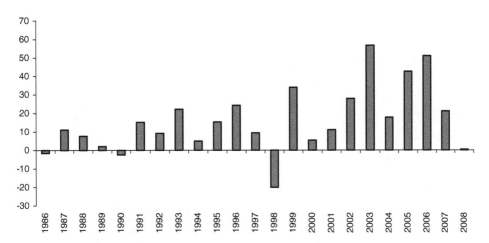

Figure 21.9   Relative returns from the cheapest 30 stocks against global equally weighted benchmark, %
Source: SG Equity research.

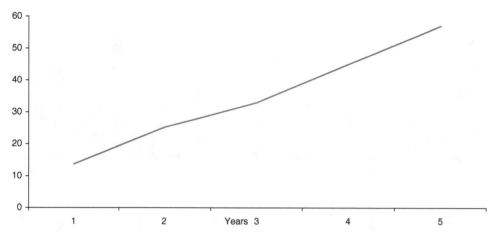

Figure 21.10 Cumulative excess returns over various holding periods (%)
Source: SG Equity research.

and sector bets nested within the value portfolio. In order to make the charts legible I've only plotted those positions that represent a 100 bp deviation from the equal weighted universe.

In terms of country positions, the single most striking feature is obviously the enormous underweight in China – suggesting very few value opportunities. The biggest overweights are Japan (at nearly 300 bp) and South Korea (at 200 bp). Taiwan and Thailand also feature in the lists of overweights.

In terms of the sector positions, the high overweight in financials won't come as any surprise (although I laid out the case that the financials are a potential value trap in Chapter 28). Combining the country and sector positions would argue that some of the Japanese financials look good value (a point we have made before). The non-energy minerals are generally Asian-based cement and steel producers. In the underweight category technology is heavily represented, as are the consumer non-durables and consumer services.

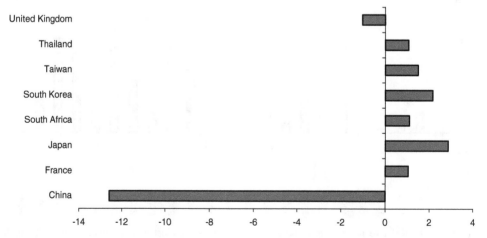

Figure 21.11 Country stances implied in the value portfolio (percentage points from benchmark)
Source: SG Equity research.

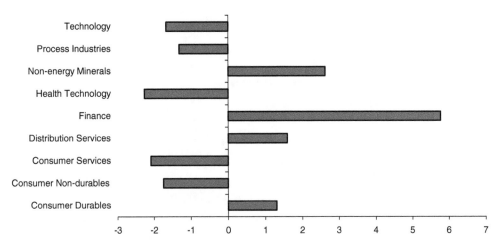

Figure 21.12   Industry stances implied in the value portfolio (percentage points from benchmark)
Source: SG Equity research.

CONCLUSIONS

The bottom line is that unconstrained global value investing works. Allowing investors to seek out bargains wherever they are located, and regardless of the industry in which they are operating makes sense both theoretically and empirically (see Table 21.1). In a world that seems to want to define fund managers into specific boxes this approach will be unconventional. However, as Sir John Templeton said, 'It is impossible to produce superior performance unless you do something different from the majority.'

22

Graham's Net-Nets: Outdated or Outstanding?*

One of Ben Graham's favoured valuation signals was a stock selling at a price below net current assets (that is selling for less than its 'net working capital, after deducting all prior obligations'). Graham's methods are often dismissed as anachronistic. However, rather than dismissing Graham's approach as outdated, our evidence shows that buying net-nets is still a viable and profitable strategy. Buying a basket of global net-nets would have generated a return of over 35% p.a. on average from 1985 to 2007. Right now, Japanese small caps are providing half of all the net-nets we can find.

- Warren Buffett once described Ben Graham's approach as 'cigar butt investing'. The basic idea was that the stocks which Graham liked were akin to cigar butts found on the street, still smouldering, from which it was possible to snatch one or two last puffs. This appeals to the cheapskate in me.
- It is well known that simple strategies based on cheapness (as measured by variables such as P/E, or P/B) tend to generate outperformance over the long term. However, as I have noted before, Ben Graham often preferred valuations based upon the balance sheet. In particular, he liked stocks trading at less than two-thirds of their net current assets.
- Testing such a deep value approach reveals that it would have been a highly profitable strategy. Over the period 1985–2007, buying a global basket of net-nets would have generated a return of over 35% p.a. versus an equally weighted universe return of 17% p.a.
- One doesn't really expect to find masses of stocks trading below two-thirds of net current assets. The net-nets portfolio contains a median universe of 65 stocks per year. Admittedly there is a hardly surprising small cap bias to the portfolio. The median market cap of a net-net is US$21m.
- Currently I can find somewhere around 175 net-nets globally. Interestingly, over half of these are in Japan. This clearly suggests that Japanese small caps are one of the best sources of bottom-up value ideas available.
- Running a net-net portfolio may well require nerves beyond those of most mortals. If we define total business failure as stocks that drop more than 90% in a year, then the net-nets portfolio sees about 5% of its constituents witnessing such an event. In the broad market only around 2% of stocks suffer such an outcome.

---

*This article appeared in Mind Matters on 30 September 2008. Copyright © 2008 by The Société Générale Group. All rights reserved. The material discussed was accurate at the time of publication.

- However, if one can avoid 'narrow-framing' and loss aversion, the overall portfolio suffered only three down years in our sample, compared to six for the overall market. As Graham himself opined, 'Our experience with this type of investment selection – on a diversified basis – was uniformly good . . . It can be affirmed without hesitation that it constitutes a safe and profitable method for determining and taking advantage of undervalued situations.' We couldn't have put it better!

On a spectrum of value investors that ranges from Ben Graham to Buffett and beyond to Bill Miller, I am firmly a Grahamite. Buffett once described Graham's approach as 'cigar butt investing'. The basic idea was that Graham liked stocks that were akin to cigar butts found on the street, still smouldering, and from which it was possible to snatch one or two last puffs. This appeals to the cheapskate in me (although I am glad to say I haven't had to resort to roaming the streets searching for cigar butts just yet . . . although in our industry it is probably only a matter of time before I end up on a park bench ranting at strangers about the evils of modern-day investing!).

It has long been known that strategies based on cheapness (as measured by variables such as P/E, P/B or dividend yield) tend to generate outperformance. However, Ben Graham often preferred valuations based upon the balance sheet (asset values).

In particular, Graham favoured net-nets. That is:

> The type of bargain issue that can be most readily identified is a common stock that sells for less than the company's net working assets alone, after deducting all prior obligations. This would mean that that the buyer would pay nothing at all for the fixed assets – buildings, machinery, etc., or any goodwill items that might exist. Very few companies turn out to have an *ultimate* value less than the working capital alone, although scattered instances may be found. The surprising thing, rather, is that there have been so many enterprises obtainable which have been valued in the market on this bargain basis.
>
> It is clear that these issues were selling at a price well below the value of the enterprise as a private business. No proprietor or majority holder would think of selling what he owned at so ridiculously low a figure . . . In various ways practically all these bargain issues turned out to be profitable and the average annual return proved much more remunerative than most other investments.

When Graham refers to net working capital, he means a company's current assets minus its total liabilities. Of course, Graham wasn't contented with just buying firms trading on prices less than net current asset value. He required an even greater margin of safety. He would exhort buying stocks with prices of less than two-thirds of net current asset value (further increasing his margin of safety). This is the definition we operationalize below. However, before we review our evidence, let's turn to Graham's own results.

In the *Intelligent Investor*, he provides a table (see Table 22.1) to illustrate the power of the net-net approach. The table shows the returns achieved by buying one share of each of the 85 companies that passed the net-net screen on 31 December 1957, and then holding them for two years.

Table 22.1 Profit experience of undervalued firms, 1957–1959

Location of market	Number of companies	Aggregate net current assets per share ($)	Aggregate price Dec 1957 ($)	Aggregate price Dec 1959 ($)
New York SE	35	748	419	838
American SE	25	495	289	492
MidWest SE	6	163	87	141
Over the Counter	20	425	288	433
Total	85	1831	1083	1904

Source: Intelligent Investor.

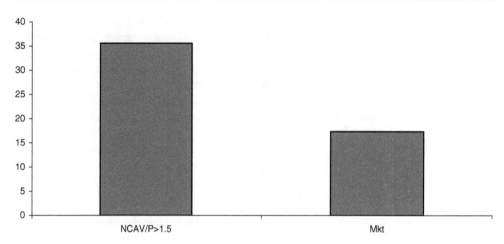

Figure 22.1 Global net-nets: performance average % p.a. (1985–2007)
Source: SG Equity research.

Graham notes, 'The gain from the entire "portfolio" in that period was 75%, against 50% for the Standard and Poor's 425 industrials. What is more remarkable is that none of the issues showed significant losses, seven held about even, and 78 showed appreciable gains.'

In 1986, Henry Oppenheimer published a paper in the *Financial Analysts Journal* examining the returns on buying stocks at or below 66% of their net current asset value during the period 1970–1983. The holding period was one year. Over its life, the portfolio contained a minimum of 18 stocks and a maximum of 89 stocks. The mean return from the strategy was 29% p.a. against a market return of 11.5% p.a.

GOING GLOBAL

I decided to test the performance of buying net-nets on a global basis. I used a sample of developed markets over the period 1985 onwards (all returns were in dollar terms). As shown in Figure 22.1, the returns to a deep value net-net strategy are impressive to say the least. An equally weighted basket of net-nets generated an average return above 35% p.a. versus a market return of 17% p.a.

Not only does a net-net strategy work at the global level, but it also works within regions (albeit to varying degrees). For instance, net-nets outperformed the market by 18%, 15%, and 6% in the USA, Japan and Europe, respectively.

THE CURRENT NET-NETS

Of course, one wouldn't really expect to find masses of stocks trading at below two-thirds net current assets. However, we end up with a median number of 65 stocks (mean 134 stocks) in the portfolio each year. Figure 22.3 shows the number of stocks appearing in the basket each year. It is instructive to note the firm bottom-up signal of value that emerged in 2003 – with

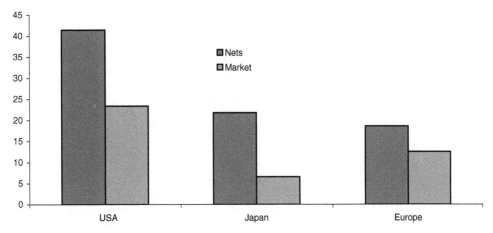

Figure 22.2 Regional performance of net-nets % p.a. (1985–2007)
Source: SG Equity research.

over 600 stocks at prices less than two-thirds net current asset value (if only we had listened to our models!!!). However, despite the market's decline this year, there are still only 176 firms trading as net-nets.

Of course, net-nets are usually a small cap strategy. Indeed, the median market cap of the current constituents is a mere US$21m (average US$124m).

Also of interest is the geographical distribution of the current constituents. As is shown in Figure 22.4, by far and away the biggest source of net-nets at the moment is Japan, followed by the USA and then the UK. This clearly suggests that Japan is the best source of bottom-up value currently available.

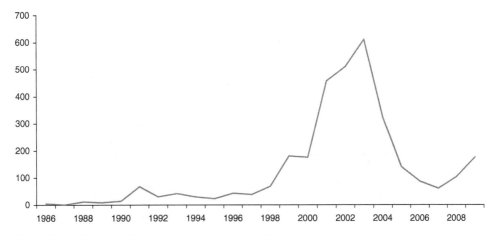

Figure 22.3 Number of stocks trading as net-nets – global
Source: SG Equity research.

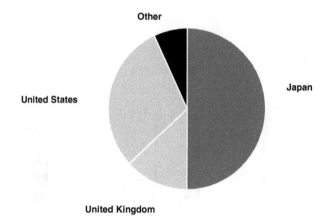

Figure 22.4   Geographical source of net-nets: current breakdown
Source: SG Equity research.

PERMANENT LOSS OF CAPITAL

Of course, Graham was also concerned with the dangers of permanent loss of capital. How does the net-nets strategy hold up under this light? On a micro basis, not so well. If we define a permanent loss of capital as a decline of 90% or more in a single year, then we see 5% of the net-nets selections suffering such a fate, compared with 2% in the broader market (Figure 22.5).

This relatively poor performance may hint at an explanation as to why investors shy away from net-nets. If investors look at the performance of the individual stocks in their portfolio rather than the portfolio itself (known as 'narrow-framing'), then they will see big losses more often than if they follow a broad market strategy. We know that people are generally loss averse, so they tend to feel losses far more than gains. This asymmetric response coupled

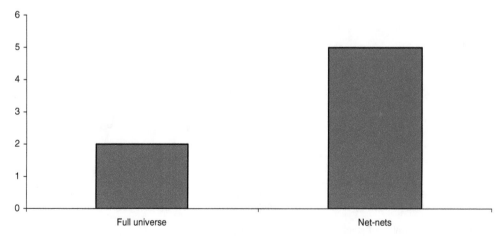

Figure 22.5   Percentage of the universe suffering a 'permanent loss of capital'
Source: SG Equity research.

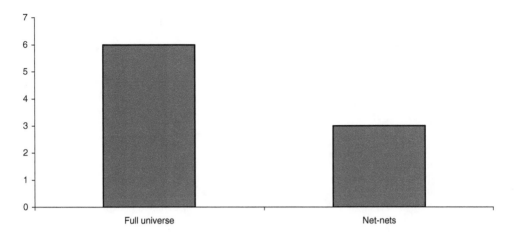

Figure 22.6 Number of years of negative returns
Source: SG Equity research.

with narrow framing means that investors in the net-nets strategy need to overcome several behavioural biases.

If one were to frame more broadly and look at the portfolio performance overall, the picture is much brighter. The net-net strategy only generated losses in three years in the entire sample we backtested. In contrast, the overall market witnessed some six years of negative returns (Figure 22.6).

CONCLUSION

Despite the widespread perception of Graham's preferred strategy as outdated, we find that for those prepared to deal with a degree of illiquidity it still offers outstanding opportunities.

As Graham himself opined, 'Our experience with this type of investment selection – on a diversified basis – was uniformly good … It can be affirmed without hesitation that it constitutes a safe and profitable method for determining and taking advantage of undervalued situations.' As is so often the case when following in Graham's footsteps, we couldn't have put it better!

Part V

The 'Dark Side' of Value Investing: Short Selling

23

Grimm's Fairy Tales of Investing[*]

Stories are great before bed, but are disastrous as a stock selection technique. Defining story stocks can be tricky, but stocks with a high price to sales are a good candidate. After all, if something is expensive against its own revenues you had better believe its story as that is all you have. However, such stocks are doomed to underperform massively, and thus should be avoided like the plague!

- Of the plethora of valuation measures that are available, price to sales is one that makes little sense to me. It has always struck me that those who use price to sales are drifting up the income statement in a desperate effort to find something that makes a stock look cheap. But a measure that ignores any concept of profitability has always seemed very dangerous to me.
- I'm not alone (for once). In April 2002, Scott McNealy, CEO of Sun Microsystems, lambasted the absurdity of investors who were willing to buy his stock at $64 – which was 10 times sales. He ridiculed the implicit assumptions that investors were backing, such as his having no employees to pay, and no taxes to pay. He concluded, 'Do you realize how ridiculous those basic assumptions are? You don't need any transparency. You don't need any footnotes. What were you thinking?'
- Despite these frank words, investors appear to continue to regularly fall for story stocks. For instance, in the USA the highest decile ranked by price to sales has a median price to sales ratio of over 10×! There are still plenty of story stocks lurking out there.
- However, story stocks seemed to be doomed to underperform. Hsieh and Walkling show that high price to sales stocks underperform stocks with similar market cap and price to book by nearly 25% over four years! Because these stocks are matched by price to book, this is more than just another example of the failure of growth stocks. Story stocks are even more dangerous to an investor's wealth!
- Bird and Casavecchia find similar evidence for Europe. Story stocks underperform low price to sales stocks by a massive 35% over three years. They also underperform the market by around 11% over three years. So the poor performance of story stocks seems to be common across markets.
- Story stocks also appear to be favourites of the churn and burn crowd. According to Hsieh and Walkling, the average story stock is held for just four months. This compares with the average holding period of 11 months across all the stocks on the NYSE.

---

[*]This article appeared in Global Equity Strategy on 4 April 2007. Copyright © 2007 by Dresdner Kleinwort, a Brand of Commerzbank AG. All rights reserved. The material discussed was accurate at the time of publication.

- Stories are compelling. They appeal to our intuitive X-system rather than the logical C-system. But perhaps investors would be well advised to follow Odysseus' example of putting beeswax in his crew's ears, and tying himself to the mast in order to avoid the disastrous, but oh so desirable, call of the Siren song.

Of the plethora of valuation measures that can be used, one I have tended to shy away from is price to sales. This measure has always struck me as a rather desperate attempt by those who use it to crawl up the income statement in an effort to end up with a nice low multiple.[1]

The sheer ridiculousness of the measure is revealed by *reductio ad absurdo*. Imagine I set up a business selling £20 notes for £19, strangely enough I will never make any money, my volume may well be enormous, but it will always be profitless. But I won't care as long as the market values me on price to sales.

But don't take my word for it. This is Scott McNealy, CEO of Sun Microsystems ($5.68)

> But two years ago we were selling at 10 times revenues when we were at $64. At 10 times revenues, to give you a 10-year payback, I have to pay you 100% of revenues for 10 straight years in dividends. That assumes I can get that by my shareholders. That assumes I have zero cost of goods sold, which is very hard for a computer company. That assumes zero expenses, which is really hard with 39,000 employees. That assumes I pay no taxes, which is very hard. And that assumes you pay no taxes on your dividends, which is kind of illegal. And that assumes with zero R&D for the next 10 years, I can maintain the current revenue run rate. Now, having done that, would any of you like to buy my stock at $64? Do you realize how ridiculous those basic assumptions are? You don't need any transparency. You don't need any footnotes. What were you thinking?
>
> Scott McNealy, *Business Week*, April 2002

A recent paper by Hsieh and Walkling (2006) explored the disastrous nature of high price to sale stocks. They call such beasts concept stocks, as you need to believe the concept in order to buy them, I prefer to call them story stocks.

The story attached to these stocks is always exciting. It offers the allure of growth. Simple stories are powerful motivators of behaviour. They appeal to the emotional X-system of the brain, rather than the logical C-system.

Indeed in his entertaining book, The *Seven Basic Plots*, Christopher Booker argues that one of the most common recurring story plots is rags to riches. As he notes, 'We see an ordinary, insignificant person, dismissed by everyone as of little account, who suddenly steps to the centre of the stage, revealed to be someone quite exceptional.' The investing equivalent of the rags to riches tale is a story stock. It is the same sort of mentality that drives people to buy lottery tickets despite their incredibly low probability of a high payoff.

Hsieh and Walkling define a concept stock as one with the price to sales ratio in the highest 10% of the universe. Figure 23.1 shows the median price to sales ratio for highest decile of US stocks (we've updated the Hsieh and Walkling data which ended in 1999). The true insanity of the dotcom bubble shines through as price to sales soared to nearly 48×! Also of note is the current reading of over 10× ... reread McNealy's quote above at this point! Over the full sample the average is average median price to sales is just under 9×. However, this is skewed by the bubble years. If we take the sample from 1967 to 1995, the average is only around 5.5×.

It is also worth pointing out that the average median price to sales ratio in the US market has been drifting up over time. Even a cursory glance at Figure 23.2 makes this immediately obviously. The current price to sales ratio is 1.8×, the full sample average is 0.9×, the 1967–1995 average is 0.6×.

---

[1] It is perfectly possible that investors might well anchor on the numeric value of more usual valuation measures such as the PE, and thus compare the low price to sales multiple favourably against this incorrect benchmark.

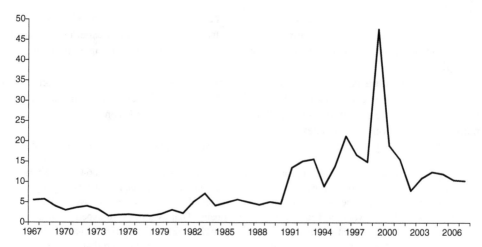

Figure 23.1 The median price to sales ratio of the highest decile (USA, x)
Source: Adapted from Hsieh and Walkling (2006). Dresdner Kleinwort Macro research.

It is tempting to believe that story stocks are the province of a few select industries. However, Hsieh and Walkling show that story stocks can crop up in a wide variety of industries. Oil and gas, metal and mining, chemicals, health services and even utilities have taken their turn in the spotlight. The new, new thing is always on the move. Investors are fickle beasts when it comes to the chasing the latest hot idea.

Story stocks with high price to sales ratios tend to be favourites of the churn and burn brigade. Figure 23.3 shows the average holding period over time. The average holding period for all stocks has declined massively (something we have noted many times before), but the holding period of story (or concept) stocks has shrunk even more! Between 1973 and 1981 the average stock was held for nearly 35 months, at the end of their sample this had fallen to just

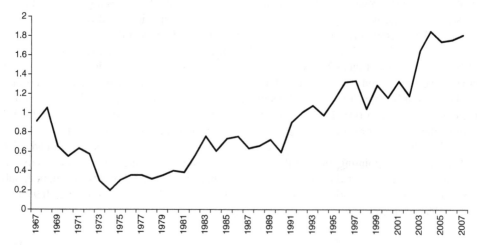

Figure 23.2 The median price to sales ratio of the US market (x)
Source: Adapted from Hsieh and Walkling (2006). Dresdner Kleinwort Macro research.

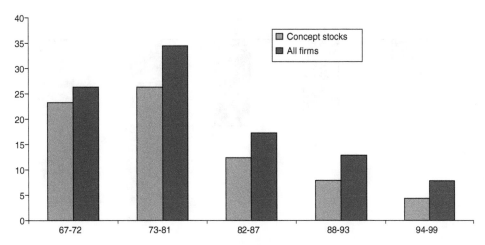

Figure 23.3   Average holding period (months)
Source: Adapted Hsieh and Walkling (2006). Dresdner Kleinwort Macro research.

8 months. Story stocks were held for an average 26 months between 1973 and 1981. However, by the end of Hsieh and Walkling's sample this had fallen to just 4 months.

Just in case you think all of this is purely a function of the internet bubble, Figure 23.4 shows the average holding period across a variety of international exchanges. The average NASDAQ stock is still only held for an average 4 months!

Hsieh and Walkling present evidence to show that high price to sales stocks significantly underperform other stocks. Ah, you may say, surely this is just another representation of the value premium. In order to try to account for this, Hsieh and Walkling match each story stock with another stock that is as close as possible in terms of size and price to book. Effectively both size and style are accounted for, so the performance of story stocks can be monitored semi-independently of other factors.

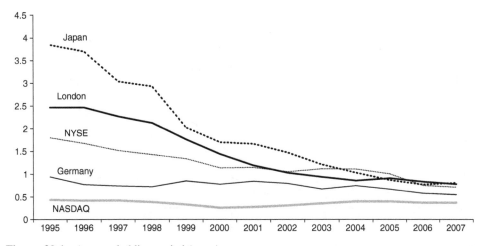

Figure 23.4   Average holding period (years)
Source: Dresdner Kleinwort Macro research.

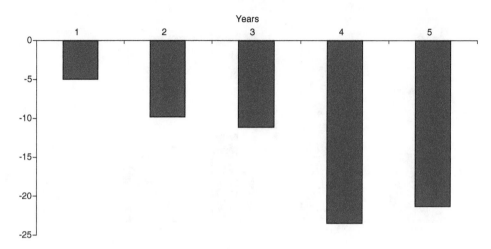

Figure 23.5 Story stocks underperform (% pa, vs. size and style matched) US, 1981–1999
Source: Adapted Hsieh and Walkling (2006). Dresdner Kleinwort Macro research.

As Figure 23.5 shows, story stocks have a torrid time even when style and size are accounted for. In the period post 1981, story stocks underperformed their matched counterparts by 5% in the first year, rising to a peak of 24% underperformance in the fourth year.

Nor is this evidence unique to the USA. Bird and Casavecchia (2007) show that within Europe a similar picture holds. They examine (country-adjusted) price to sales ratios within Europe. Figure 23.6 shows the performance of low price to sales, story stocks and the average firm. Much like the US data, story stocks massively underperform stocks with low price to sales (by over 35% over three years!) and they also underperform the market by nearly 12% over three years. So story stocks' poor performance seems to be common across markets.

The bottom line is that investors should avoid stocks with high price to sales. The stories attached to them are likely to be compelling, just as the Siren's song was to Odysseus.

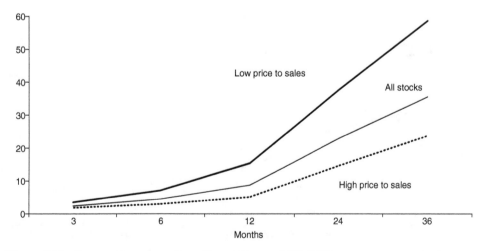

Figure 23.6 Story stocks underperform (% p.a.) Europe, 1989–2004
Source: Adapted from Bird and Casavecchia (2005). Dresdner Kleinwort Macro research.

Odysseus, of course, survived by having his crew tie him to the mast and ordering them to leave him there no matter how much he begged. The crew survived by plugging their ears with beeswax.

Perhaps investors should do the same thing when it comes to phone calls from brokers, and research notes proclaiming the next new thing. Rather than being seduced by stories, investors would be better off focusing on the facts, and perhaps pinning McNealy's wonderful quote by the side of their desks.

24

Joining the Dark Side: Pirates, Spies and Short Sellers[*]

What should you look for in a good short candidate? A superficially easy question, but one that most analysts don't seem to like to answer. A fact evidenced by a mere 10–15% of recommendations being sells! We examine three factors that seem to add up to a pretty good indication of a shorting opportunity. Essentially we look for expensive stocks, with deteriorating fundamentals and poor capital discipline. This 'unholy' trinity results in a basket that has historically declined around 6% p.a. Running the screen today reveals the highest ever number of stocks passing the shorting criteria. Perhaps it is time to join the dark side.

- Short sellers have been vilified almost since time immemorial. This has always struck me as strange, the equivalent of punishing the detective rather than the criminal. Perhaps this bizarre outcome has deterred many from exploring this path. However, my own bottom-up valuation work shows few bargains, we suspect that the opportunities may lie far more on the short side.

- What are the hallmarks of a good short candidate? We suggest an 'unholy' trinity of characteristics – a high-price-to sales ratio, deteriorating fundamentals (as measured by a low Piotroski F score) and poor capital discipline (as measured by high total asset growth). Each of these characteristics is a telling sign, but when combined together they become even more potent.

- Over the period 1985–2007 a portfolio of such European stocks rebalanced annually would have declined over 6% p.a. in absolute terms (the market was rising 13% p.a. over the period, to provide some context). The basket of stocks witnessed absolute negative returns in 10 out of 22 years. It underperformed the index in 18 of the 22 years. Similar findings also hold for the USA.

- The last few years have not been kind to this strategy. Three of the last five years have seen our short basket actually do better than the market! This attests to the extreme nature of the dash to trash that we have witnessed.

- Interestingly, we see a record number of stocks passing the criteria for membership of our short basket. In general over our sample the European basket holds around 20 stocks. Today

---

such a portfolio would have almost 100 members. In the USA, the basket holds an average of around 30 stocks; today 174 pass the short candidate criteria. Presumably this is the mirror image of my bottom-up valuation work which finds very few deep value opportunities to exploit. The opportunities are on the short, not the long, side currently. Perhaps it is time to join the dark side.

It never ceases to amaze me that whenever a major corporate declines, the short sellers are suddenly painted as financial equivalents of psychopaths. This is madness, rather than examining the exceptionally poor (and sometimes criminal) decisions that the corporate itself took, the short sellers are hauled over the coals.

As the *New York Times* recently reminded us, vilifying short sellers is nothing new.

> In the days when square-rigged galleons plied the spice route to the East, the Dutch outlawed a band of rebels that they feared might plunder their new-found riches.
>
> The troublemakers were neither Barbary pirates nor Spanish spies — they were certain traders on the stock exchange in Amsterdam. Their offence: shorting the shares of the Dutch East India Company, purportedly the first company in the world to issue stock.
>
> Short sellers, who sell assets like stocks in the hope that the price will fall, have been reviled ever since. England banned them for much of the 18th and 19th centuries. Napoleon deemed them enemies of the state. And Germany's last Kaiser enlisted them to attack American markets (or so some Americans feared).
>
> Jenny Anderson, *New York Times*, 30 April 2008

My own bottom-up valuation work finds little opportunity for investment at the moment. This suggests to me that the main opportunities may lie on the short side in the current market. So I guess I am joining the ranks of the dark side!

This remains anathema to analysts. As Figure 24.1 shows, the percentage of sell recommendations remains pathetically low. Indeed, recently my head of research introduced me to Figure 24.2, showing that SG had the highest percentage of sells among investment banks. (It makes a pleasant change to see SG at the top of a list on a positive note!)

All of this got me to thinking about how to identify potential short candidates. In keeping with Chapter 19 (on limited information), I want to focus on just a few key measures that stand out to me as sources of poor underperformance.

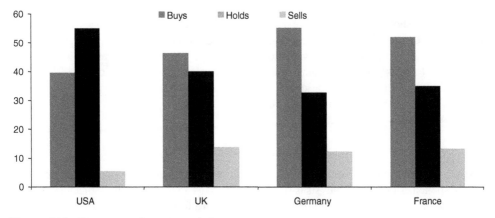

Figure 24.1   Percentage of recommendations.
Source: Bloomberg, SG Equity research.

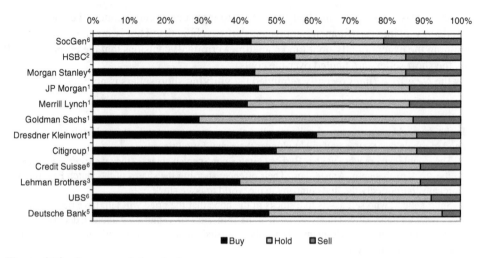

Figure 24.2   Recommendations by house.
Source: company report disclosures. [1]as of 31/12/07; [2]as of 15/02/08; [3]as of 29/02/08; [4]as of 03/03/08; [5]as of 11/03/08; [6]as of 18/03/08.

VALUATION

Most obviously (and unsurprisingly given my value bias) one of my primary sources of underperformance has to be high valuation. There are myriad methods of valuing a stock, of course. However, from the perspective of a short seller, one of the most useful is price-to-sales.

Focusing upon high price-to-sales stocks allows us to hone in on story stocks – those stocks that have lost all touch with reality. During periods of investor enthusiasm there is often a marked tendency to move up the income statement to try to keep valuation multiples 'low'. Indeed during the dotcom years, things were valued on measures such as average revenue per user, clicks and eyeballs!

So whenever I hear people using price-to-sales to justify a stock I can't help but think they are trying to hide something. However, as always I remain a proponent of Evidence Based Investing, so the proof is in the pudding. Does price-to-sales work as a strategy?

Figure 24.3 shows the performance of price-to-sales quintiles within Europe over the period 1985–2007. Unsurprisingly, the cheapest stocks outperform the most expensive stocks.

As a check on this particular valuation measure we regressed the returns from a long short price-to-sales portfolio against the value minus growth returns from MSCI Europe. A significant 'alpha' was found, so price-to-sales adds something extra above and beyond price-to-book (as per the discussion above).

FINANCIAL ANALYSIS

The second element of my short strategy is to examine the financial analysis of the company. My outspoken criticism of analysts is sometimes taken as a view that I think financial analysis is a waste of time. Nothing could be further from the truth. I am driven to despair by the fact that analysts spend so long wasting their time trying to do the impossible, such as forecast earnings, but I remain a fan of good solid fundamental-oriented research.

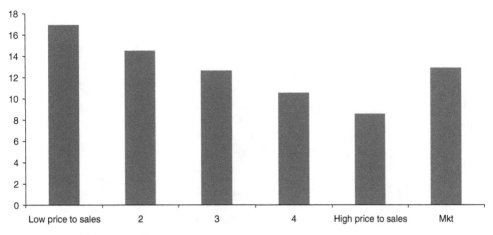

Figure 24.3 Price-to-sales quintiles (% p.a.).
Source: SG Global Strategy Research.

In the past I have advocated the use of the F score designed by Joseph Piotroski as a simple but highly effective method of quantifying a fundamental approach. In his original paper (Piotroski, 2000) he applied a fundamental analysis screen to help to tell good value from value traps. In a subsequent paper (Piotroski, 2004), he explored whether a simple financial screen could enhance performance across a variety of styles.

The screen Piotroski developed is a simple nine-input accounting-based scoring system. Table 24.1 shows the basic variables used in its calculation. Effectively, Piotroski uses indicators based on three areas of financial analysis in order to assess the likelihood of an improving fundamental backdrop.

Current operating profits and cash flow out-turns obviously provide information about the firm's ability to generate funds internally, and pay dividends. A positive earnings trend is also

Table 24.1 The Piotroski screen

Variable	Scoring
Profitability	
Return on assets	If ROA > 0 then score 1, otherwise 0
Change in return on assets	If change in ROA > 0, then score 1, otherwise 0
Cash flow from Operations	If CFO > 0 then score 1, otherwise 0
Accruals	If CFO > ROA, then score 1, otherwise 0
Leverage, Liquidity, and Sources of Funds	
Leverage	If change in long-term debt to total assets < 0 then score 1, otherwise 0
Liquidity	If the change in the current ratio > 0 then score 1, otherwise 0
Financing	If equity issuance is < 0 then score 1, otherwise 0
Operating Efficiency	
Margins	If change in gross margins > 0 then score 1, otherwise 0
Asset Turnover	If the change in asset turnover is > 0 then score 1, otherwise 0

Source: SG Global Strategy Research.

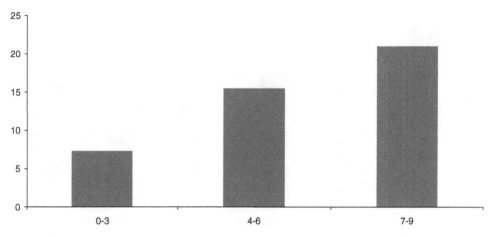

Figure 24.4 Performance of Piotroski screen in the USA (% p.a. 1972–2001).
Source: Piotroski (2004).

suggestive of an improvement in the fundamental performance of the firm. Earnings quality is also captured by looking at the relationship between cash flows and reported earnings.

The next three variables are designed to measure changes in the capital structure and general ability to meet debt-service obligations. If you like, these measures assess the likelihood of bankruptcy and bring the balance sheet into the overall score.

The last two elements of the overall F score are concerned with operating efficiency. The variables used will be familiar to fans of Du Pont analysis as they both come from traditional decomposition of ROA. Having assessed the measures as per Table 24.1, a firm's F score is simply the summation of the various individual components (thus it is bounded between 0 and 9).

Piotroski examines the performance of this score in the US market over the period 1972 to 2001. His main findings are shown in Figure 24.4 which maps out raw returns by the overall F score. The average raw (market-adjusted) return for firms with low F scores (0–3) is 7.3% p.a. (−5.5%). Firms with medium F scores (4–6) show raw (market-adjusted) returns of 15.5% p.a. (3%). Those firms with the highest F score (7–9) showed an average raw (market-adjusted) returns of 21% p.a. (7.8%). This certainly shows that fundamental analysis can be a source of alpha!

I find the European evidence to be similar (Figure 24.5). The average raw (market-adjusted) return for firms with low F scores (0–3) is 4.4% p.a. (−8%). Firms with medium F scores (4–6) show raw (market-adjusted) returns of 13.1% p.a. (0.5%). Those firms with the highest F score (7–9) showed an average raw (market-adjusted) return of 15% p.a. (2.5%).

Piotroski also explores how his measure performs in the context of value and growth stocks. As he notes:

> It is very difficult for investors to systematically identify meaningfully underpriced (overpriced) glamour firms (value firms), consistent with the gains to financial statement analysis-based strategies corresponding to the expected bias imbedded in each book-to-market portfolio. When FSCORE corresponds to the expected performance of these firms (i.e. strong performance for glamour and poor performance for value firms), each respective portfolio earns near the market return. Effectively, financial signals confirming the expectations that are likely already imbedded

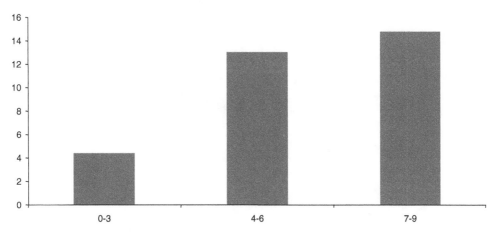

Figure 24.5 Performance of Piotroski screen in Europe (% p.a. 1985–2007).
Source: SG Global Strategy Research.

in price are assimilated into prices quickly, while contrarian signals are (generally) discounted until future confirmatory news is received. As a result, historical good news for glamour firms is unable to generate excess returns, while historical good news for value firms is a tradable opportunity, and vice-versa for trading opportunities conditional on bad news.

This finding is confirmed by our European data as Figure 24.6 shows. Value stocks with high F scores do particularly well (a raw return of over 20% p.a., some 4% better than the average value stock). However, growth stocks with low F scores do particularly poorly (a raw return of −0.7% p.a., some 9% worse than the average growth stock).

In the context of our combing for short candidates, this implies that we would be best to look at expensive stocks, so combining the first two components should give a reasonable

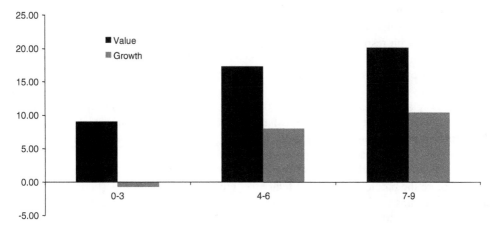

Figure 24.6 Performance of Piotroski screen in European value and growth universes (% p.a.)
Source: SG Global Strategy Research.

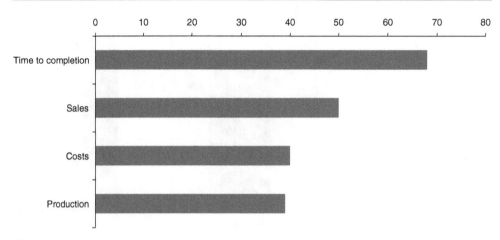

Figure 24.7 Percentage of managers saying their firm was too optimistic with regard to:
Source: McKinsey.

list of likely short candidates. However, I wish to examine one more important factor before producing a final list.

CAPITAL DISCIPLINE

The final element of my hunt for potential shorts is a lack of capital discipline. A survey conducted by McKinsey[1] (at last something useful from them!) revealed that corporates knew they weren't great at capital discipline. The survey of 'Corporate level executives' said '17 percent of the capital invested by their companies went toward underperforming investment that should be terminated and that 16 percent of their investments were a mistake to have financed in the first place'. Those working closer to the coal face (business unit heads and frontline managers) thought that even more projects should never have been approved (21% for each category!).

The survey also asked managers how accurate their forecasts were in various areas of corporate investment such as the time taken to complete the project, the impact on sales, costs, etc. The results are shown in Figure 24.7. Nearly 70% of the managers said they were too optimistic with respect to the time the project would take to complete (evidence of the well-known planning fallacy); 50% of the respondents said they were too optimistic about the impact the investment would have on sales; and over 40% were too optimistic about the costs involved!

The survey also revealed that nearly 40% of the respondents said that managers 'hide, restrict, or misrepresent information' when submitting capital investment proposals! The discouragement of dissent was also strongly noted, over 50% of those taking part said it was important to avoid contradicting superiors.

Given these kind of views, it isn't shocking to note the findings of Cooper *et al.* (2006). They explore the predictive power of total asset growth for stock returns (Figure 24.8). The advantage of using total assets is, of course, that it provides a comprehensive picture of overall investment/disinvestment.

---

[1] How Companies Spend Their Money: A McKinsey Global Survey, *McKinsey Quarterly*, June 2007

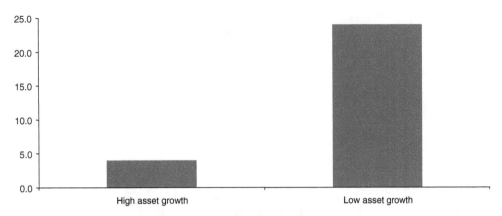

Figure 24.8 Asset growth performance (% p.a. USA 1968–2003).
Source: Cooper *et al.* (2006). SG Global Strategy Research .

In their US sample covering the period 1968–2003, Cooper *et al.* find that firms with low asset growth outperformed firms with high asset growth by an astounding 20% p.a. equally weighted. Even when controlling for market, size and style, low asset growth firms outperformed high asset growth firms by 13% p.a.

The European evidence is also compelling (Figure 24.9). Over the period 1985 to 2007, we find that low asset growth firms outperformed high asset growth firms by around 10% p.a. The bottom line is that capital discipline seems to be much neglected by firms and investors alike.

PUTTING IT ALL TOGETHER

So we have covered three potential sources of short ideas. What happens if we put them all together? The parameters I used to define my shorts were a price-to-sales > 1, an F score of 3 or less, and total asset growth in double digits.

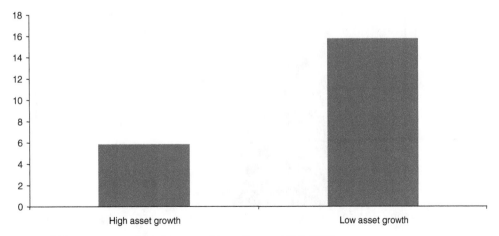

Figure 24.9 Asset growth performance (% p.a. Europe 1985–2007).
Source: SG Global Strategy Research.

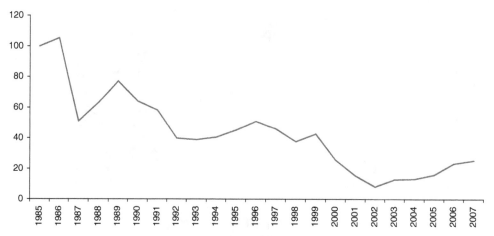

Figure 24.10   Absolute performance of our European short basket (1985 = 100).
Source: SG Global Strategy Research.

This proved to be a powerful combination. Between 1985 and 2007 a portfolio of such stocks rebalanced annually would have declined over 6% p.a. compared to a market that was rising at the rate of 13% p.a. in Europe (Figure 24.10)! Although I've not shown the result below, similar findings were also uncovered for the USA.

The basket of shorts generated a negative alpha in excess of 20% p.a. with a beta of 1.3. The basket witnessed absolute negative returns in 10 out of 23 years (45% of the time). Relative to the index it underperformed in 18 of the 23 years (81% of the time).

The average stock selected by the model falls 8% p.a. (median 9.6% decline). Some 60% of the screen picks witness absolute negative returns. Thus the model also tends to pick a few stocks that do exceptionally well on the long side – not good news for a short strategy. Hence,

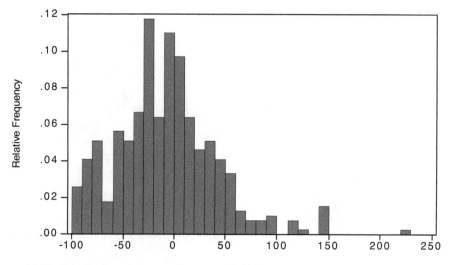

Figure 24.11   Distribution of returns – Europe 1985–2007.
Source: SG Global Strategy research.

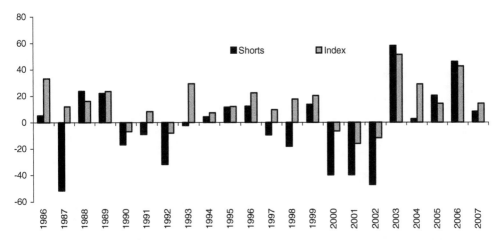

Figure 24.12 Annual returns of the European short basket and the index (% p.a.).
Source: SG Global Strategy research.

introducing the use of stop loss can improve the performance of our short basket significantly. For instance, putting a 20% stop loss in place raises the return from −6% p.a. to −13% p.a. (Figure 24.11).

I have often described much of the period since late 2002 as being characterized by the dash to trash. This can clearly be seen from Figure 24.12. 2003 saw the shorts outperforming the market by 6%! A feat repeated on a lesser scale in 2005 and 2006.

Despite the rocky road that this portfolio has suffered in recent years, I believe that it remains a sound method of looking for shorts, and if we are right that most of the opportunities are likely to be on the short side, then it could prove a useful tool in the future.

Two final charts echo one of the points I made at the outset of this chapter. They illustrate the number of stocks that the screen finds passing our criteria for being short candidates. In Europe (Figure 24.13), the average over our sample is around 20 stocks per year. Running the screen now reveals an all time high of almost 100 stocks passing the criteria.

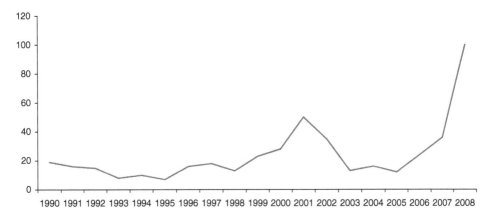

Figure 24.13 Number of stocks passing our short candidate criteria - Europe.
Source: SG Global Strategy Research.

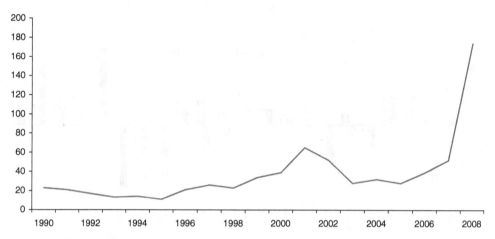

Figure 24.14 Number of stocks passing our short candidate screen - USA.
Source: SG Global Strategy Research.

In the USA (Figure 24.14), the average number of stocks in our short basket is around 30. Today, the screen finds no less than 174 stocks passing the criteria. This clearly demonstrates to me the lack of value I alluded to at the start of this chapter, and indeed suggests that the opportunities are now firmly on the short side.

25

Cooking the Books, or, More Sailing Under the Black Flag[*]

In good times, few focus on such 'mundane' issues as earnings quality and footnotes. However, this lack of attention to 'detail' tends to come back and bite investors during bad times. There are notable exceptions to this generalization. The short sellers tend to be among the most fundamentally driven investors. Indeed, far from being rumour mongers, most short sellers are closer to being the accounting police. To aid investors in assessing the likelihood of accounting shenanigans, I have designed the C-score. When combined with measures of overvaluation, this score is particularly useful at identifying short candidates.

- Contrary to the silly populist backlash which sees short sellers as rumour mongers and conspirators, they are actually among the most fundamentally driven of all the investors I interact with. Rather than being some malignant force within the markets, in my experience short sellers are closer to the accounting police (something the SEC once purported to do!).
- While companies often accuse short sellers of lying and conspiracy, it turns out that the accusers are often the guilty party. Owen Lamont from Chicago University has examined the battles between corporates and short sellers in the USA between 1977 and 2002. He found that ultimately it was the shorts that were right; the stocks underperformed the market by a cumulative 42% over three years after the start of the battle.
- Inspired by the shorts' focus on fundamentals, I have created a C (for cooking the books or cheating) score which seeks to capture how many of six common earnings manipulations a firm is engaging in. Of course, the C-score is only a first step in analysing whether a company is or isn't cooking its books.
- That said, the C-score does seem to have some power to separate out stocks which go on to underperform. Those stocks with high C-scores underperform the market by around 8% p.a. and 5% p.a. in the USA and Europe respectively (over the period 1993–2007).
- Of course, the C-score is likely to be more effective when it is used in tandem with some measure of valuation. After all, it is often the case that high-flying stocks will be more tempted to try to 'cheat' to maintain their status. This is borne out by the data. Stocks with a C-score of 5 and a price to sales ratio of greater than 2 tend to generate a negative absolute return of 4% (in both the USA and Europe). Around 50–60% of the stocks identified see negative returns.

After a 5-year bull run in earnings, investors are at risk of paying too little attention to earnings manipulation. In the good times, sadly few care about such mundane issues as earnings quality or footnotes (as foolish as that is). In the bad times, these characteristics tend to come back into widespread fashion.

However, in a world where most analysts are more concerned with forecasting quarterly earnings to two decimal places over the next five years, and writing up company press releases, their ability to actually analyse a company seems to be in danger of becoming a lost art.

The most fundamentally oriented analysts I have come across are without a doubt the short sellers. These guys, by and large, really take their analysis seriously (and so they should since their downside is effectively unlimited). So the continued backlash against short sellers as rumour mongers and conspirators simply leaves me shaking my head in bewilderment. I can only assume that those making these claims are either policy makers pandering to shorted companies, or shorted companies themselves. Rather than being some malignant force within the markets, in my experience short sellers are closer to accounting police.

COMPANIES LIE, SHORT SELLERS POLICE: THE EVIDENCE

This viewpoint was confirmed by a insightful study by Owen Lamont (2003) (then at Chicago University). He wrote a paper in 2003 examining the battles between short sellers and the companies they shorted. He examined such battles between 1977 and 2002 in the USA. He focused on situations where the company that was being shorted protested innocence by suggesting it was the subject of a bear raid, or a conspiracy, or alleged that the short sellers were lying. He also explored firms that requested investigation by the authorities into the shorts, urged the stock holders not to lend shares out, or even set up repurchase plans (presumably to create a short squeeze).

The results Lamont uncovered show the useful role played by short sellers. Figure 25.1 shows the average cumulative return to the shorted stock. In the 12 months after the battle started, the average stock underperformed the market by 24%. In the 3 years after the battle

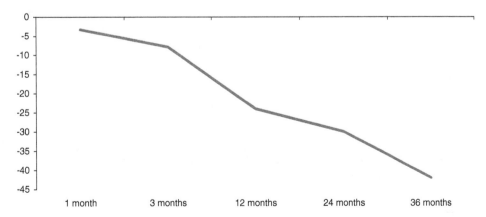

Figure 25.1 Cumulative market adjusted returns (%).
Source: Lamont (2003). SG Global Strategy Research.

commenced these stocks underperformed the market by 42% cumulatively! The shorts were right, it was often the companies that were lying and conspiring to defraud investors, not the reverse!

WHO IS COOKING THE BOOKS? THE C-SCORE

In the previous chapter we explored one method of screening for short candidates.[1] However, it occurred to me that a more accounting-based screen might also be useful in identifying potential shorts by looking at those who might well be cooking their books, or trying every last trick to ensure that they can beat the analysts' quarterly forecasts.

To this end I have created the C (for cooking the books or cheating) score to help measure the likelihood that a firm may be trying to pull the wool over investors' eyes. The score has six inputs, each designed to capture an element of common earnings manipulation:

1. A growing difference between net income and cash flow from operations. In general, managements have less flexibility in shaping cash flows than earnings. Earnings contain a large number of highly subjective estimates such as bad debts, pension returns, etc. A growing divergence between net income and cash flows may also indicate more aggressive capitalization of costs.
2. Days sales outstanding (DSO) is increasing. This, of course, signifies that accounts receivable are growing faster than sales. This measure is really aimed at picking up channel stuffing (sending inventory to customers).
3. Growing days sales of inventory (DSI). Growing inventory is likely to indicate slowing sales, never a good sign.
4. Increasing other current assets to revenues. Canny CFOs may know that investors often look at DSO and/or DSI, thus they may use this catch-all line item to help hide things they don't want investors to focus upon.
5. Declines in depreciation relative to gross property plant and equipment. To beat the quarterly earnings target, firms can easily alter the estimate of useful asset life.
6. High total asset growth. Some firms become serial acquirers and use their acquisitions to distort their earnings. High asset growth firms receive a flag in this score.

These elements are scored in a simple binary fashion, so if a company has increasing DSI it will receive a score of 1. These are then summed across the elements to give a final C-score bounded from 0 (no evidence of earnings manipulation) to 6 (all the flags are present).

DOES THE C-SCORE WORK?

The C-score is only a first step in analysing whether a company is or isn't cooking its books. However, it does seem to work relatively well. Figures 25.2–25.3 show the performance of stocks by C-score across Europe and the USA over the period 1993–2007 (portfolios are formed in June and held for one year).

---

[1] Just in case you are wondering about the alternative title for this chapter (More Sailing Under the Black Flag) this refers to the title of Chapter 24, 'Joining the Dark Side: Pirates, Spies and Short Sellers'.

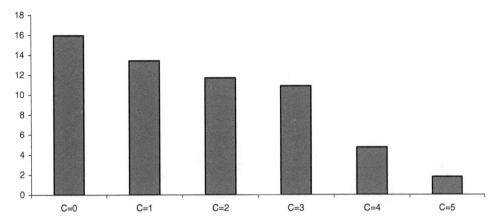

Figure 25.2 Performance across C-scores – USA (1993–2003) Mkt return 10% p.a.
Source: SG Global Strategy Research.

In the USA, stocks with high C-scores underperform the market by around 8% p.a., generating a return of a mere 1.8% p.a. In Europe, high C-score stocks underperform the market by around 5% p.a., although they still generate absolute returns of around 8% p.a.

Of course, the C-score is likely to be more effective when it is used in tandem with some measure of valuation. After all, it is often the case that high flying stocks (which are likely to be expensive) will be more tempted to alter their earnings to appear to maintain their high growth status, than value stocks. It is also likely that when these stocks get 'found out' the punishment will be considerably worse than that for a cheap stock.

This is borne out by the evidence. When we combine the C-score with a price to sales ratio greater than 2 the returns drop dramatically. In the USA this combination results in a negative absolute return of 4% p.a. (median stock return −6% p.a, and 54% of stocks seeing negative returns). In Europe, the combination of a high C-score and price to sales greater than 2 also generates a negative absolute return of 4% p.a. (median stock return −10% p.a. and 57% of stocks seeing negative absolute returns).

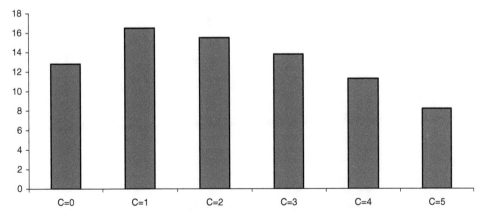

Figure 25.3 Performance across C-scores – Europe (1993–2003) Mkt return 13% p.a.
Source: SG Global Strategy Research.

26

Bad Business: Thoughts on Fundamental
Shorting and Value Traps*

In the previous chapters, I've argued that the perfect short candidate has four characteristics: overvaluation, deteriorating fundamentals, poor capital discipline and bad accounting. However, I have neglected the more classical 'fundamental' aspects of good short opportunities. I think these can be grouped into three elements: bad managers, bad companies and bad strategies. These are clearly not mutually exclusive categories. For those who can't or don't short, these elements should help to distinguish between value opportunities and value traps.

- In his excellent book, *Why Smart Executives Fail*, Sydney Finkelstein identifies seven traits that poor management tends to display. I've called these the 'seven habits of highly defective managers'. In essence, poor managers see themselves as dominating their field, identify exceptionally closely with the firm, appear extraordinarily decisive, won't tolerate dissent, love being the face of the company, refuse to recognize any problem as more than temporary, and never hesitate to return to their past triumphs in terms of strategy.
- Many common behavioural traits seem to underlie these failures. For instance, overconfidence, confirmatory bias, conformity and self-serving bias all align closely with the habits that Finkelstein outlines. Perhaps analysts would be well served to conduct a behavioural audit of the management they cover.
- Intriguingly, there is now a relatively substantial body of evidence that suggests that many managers share common traits with psychopaths (bar the homicidal and impulse control issues). In many ways bad managers are just successful psychopaths.
- Finkelstein also provides us with a checklist of questions to help to identify bad companies. Some elements are obvious, such as overly complicated and/or non-transparent accounting. Others that may prove useful include 'Is the management ignoring warnings?' and 'Is the new product just hype?'. These are aspects that most fundamental analysts see as within their purview, but seldom do I see them discuss such issues.
- Finally, we look at common 'strategy' failures from corporates. It is amazing how little we learn from history. The same mistakes seem to crop up time and again in terms of corporate failures. Paul Carroll and Chunka Mui identify seven common strategic errors in their entertaining book, *Billion Dollar Lessons*. These include the delusion of synergies, faulty financial engineering, deflated industry 'roll-ups' (failed serial acquirers), staying a misguided course, misjudged adjacencies and consolidation blues.

• Despite the rich history of corporate failures and flops, analysts seem intent on steering away from 'sell' recommendations. For instance, over the whole of 2008 less than 6% of recommendations were sells! This is all the more puzzling since the bad managers, bad business, bad strategy perspective is one that analysts should surely understand.

A TAXONOMY OF SHORTS

In the previous chapters, I have explored the quantitative aspects of good short candidates. I have argued that four traits make up the perfect short: overvaluation, deteriorating fundamentals, poor capital discipline and bad accounting.

Characterizing his portfolio of shorts, Greenlight Capital's David Einhorn describes them as

> Companies that have significant problems of various sorts: some have bad business practices or have played accounting tricks, others trade at very high multiples of earnings expectations that are unlikely to be achieved, while others have flawed business models and are unlikely to be long-term survivors.

Bruce Berkowitz approaches the same area from a slightly different perspective. He is a long-only fund manager. However, Berkowitz has come the closest I have found to guarding against confirmatory bias in the investment process. Instead of looking for the information that would support an investment, Berkowitz tries to 'kill the company'. As he says:

> We look at companies, count the cash, and then try to kill the company... We spend a lot of time thinking about what could go wrong with a company – whether it's a recession, stagflation, zooming interest rates or a dirty bomb going off. We try every which way to kill our best ideas. If we can't kill it, maybe we're on to something. If you go with companies that are prepared for difficult times, especially if they're linked to managers who are engineered for difficult times, then you almost want those times because they plant the seeds of greatness.

In a recent interview with the *Outstanding Investor's Digest*, Berkowitz gave a list of ways 'how companies can die and how they're killed'.

> Here are the ways you implode: you don't generate cash, you burn cash, you're over-leveraged, you play Russian Roulette, you have idiots for management, you have a bad board, you 'de-worsify', you buy your stock too high, you lie with GAAP accounting.

Jim Chanos, the undisputed king of short selling, outlined the four broad categories of short candidates he looks for in an interview with *Value Investor Insight* in 2005:

> The first and most lucrative are the booms that go bust. We've had our most success with debt-financed asset bubbles – as opposed to just plain asset bubbles – where there are ticking time bombs in terms of debt needing to be repaid, and where there are people ahead of the shareholders in the bankruptcy or workout process. The 'debt-financed' distinction is important. It kept us from shorting the Internet in the 90s – that was a valuation bubble more than anything else.

The second group of opportunities are those created by

> Technological obsolescence. Economists talk quite rightly about the benefits of 'creative destruction', where new technologies and innovations advance mankind and grow GDP. But such changes also render whole industries obsolete . . . what is playing out now is the transformation from analog to a digital world.[1]

---

[1] Jim suggests reading Clayton Christensen's *'The Innovator's Dilemma'* for a great book on this subject.

The third of Chanos' sources are those guilty of bad accounting.

> This can run the gamut from simple overstatement of earnings . . . to outright fraud. We're trying to find cases where the economic reality is significantly divorced from the accounting presentation of the business.

The final broad category . . .

> would be consumer fads. This is when investors . . . use recent experience to extrapolate ad infinitum into the future what is clearly a one-time growth ramp-up. People are consistently way too optimistic . . . Cabbage Patch kids in 1980s, NordicTrack in the early 1990s, Salton with the George Forman grills.

The overlap between these various descriptions is high. However, in the past I have devoted relatively little time to the flawed business models/bad managers category, so it is to this arena that I now turn.

BAD MANAGERS

Given our industry's love affair with meeting company management (something I, of course, remain deeply sceptical of), it is surprising that more hasn't been written on the nature of bad management.

One of my favourite books on corporate failures is Sydney Finkelstein's *Why Smart Executives Fail*. Instead of focusing on successes, as do most 'management' books, Finkelstein likes to explore corporate disasters.

When it comes to the traits of particularly bad managers, Finkelstein has identified a set to traits that are commonly found. I've called these traits the 'seven habits of highly defective managers'. Analysts might be well advised to see how many of these traits can be found among the corporate managers they love to meet.

Seven Habits of Highly Defective Managers

1. They see themselves and their companies as dominating their environments, not simply responding to developments in those environments.
2. They identify so completely with the company that there is no clear boundary between their personal interests and corporate interests.
3. They seem to have all the answers, often dazzling people with the speed and decisiveness with which they can deal with challenging issues.
4. They make sure that everyone is 100% behind them, ruthlessly eliminating anyone who might undermine their efforts.
5. They are consummate company spokespeople, often devoting the largest portion of their efforts to managing and developing the company's image.
6. They treat intimidating and difficult obstacles as temporary impediments to be removed or overcome.
7. They never hesitate to return to the strategies and tactics that made them and their companies successful in the first place.

BEHAVIOURAL FOUNDATIONS OF BAD MANAGEMENT

While pondering the traits of bad managers I began to wonder about the root causes of their poor decisions. This led me to try to outline the behavioural foundations of bad managements or, to put it another way: What are the biases that tend to lead managers down the wrong path?

I. Overoptimism and Overconfidence

Perhaps the most commonly encountered behavioural bias is overoptimism and overconfidence. I suspect that corporate managers generally display both in spades. The Duke University CFO survey is my favourite example of overoptimism. Each quarter Duke asks CFOs how optimistic they are on the outlook for the economy (0 = exceptionally pessimistic, 100 extraordinarily optimistic). They are also asked how optimistic they are on the outlook for their firm.

Figure 26.1 shows the most common delusions to be found among managers, good and bad. Managers are always much more optimistic on the outlook for their firm than they are on the outlook for the economy as a whole.

M&A is perhaps the best example of overconfidence on the part of corporate managers. According to the latest biannual KPMG survey of global M&A (15 October 2008), a truly staggering 93% of corporate managers think that their M&A adds value. This must surely be the most damning evidence of the overoptimism and overconfidence on the part of corporate managers that I have ever come across.

Figure 26.2 shows the contrast with an objective measure of M&A performance – it contrasts the percentage of firms who conducted M&A deals that managed to outperform industry peers in the stock market during the two years following the deal against managers' subjective belief regarding the percentage of deals that added value.

Strangely enough, the managers' beliefs are always massively above the objective measures. For instance, in the latest survey KPMG show that while 93% of managers think their M&A work added value, fewer than 30% of deals actually did.

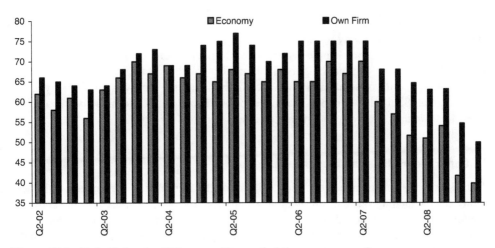

Figure 26.1 Duke University CFO survey: How optimistic are you on.... ?
Source: SG Global Strategy.

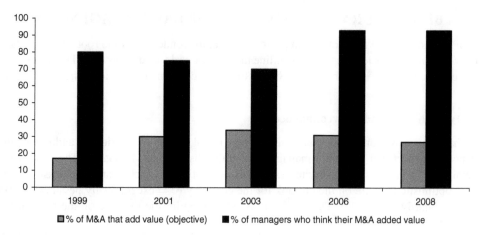

Figure 26.2   Objective or subjective: % of M&A deals that are successful
Source: KPMG, SG Global Strategy.

This figure also provides evidence of another behavioural trait that I often refer to: our very limited ability to learn from mistakes. You might have been forgiven for thinking that over the course of the last decade or so, managers might perhaps have come to realize that M&A should be treated with extreme caution. However, nothing could be further from the truth. In fact, corporate delusions with regard to the value of M&A only seem to have increased!

This shows that corporate managers just simply don't conduct any thorough post-deal performance analysis, or that, if they do, they simply ignore the outcome! A prototypical example of this failure to objectively measure the post-deal performance is provided by DaimlerChrysler. The merger failed on any operational definition. It destroyed value roughly equal to the total purchase price of Chrysler. Yet even after acknowledging these appalling consequences, the CEO Jurgen Schrempp continued to defend the merger as 'an absolutely perfect strategy'.

Unfortunately we, as a species, have a bad habit of confusing confidence with skill. For instance, if you go to the doctor and say 'Doctor, I have this dreadful rash', and he replies 'Don't worry, I know exactly what that is, take these tablets and you'll be fine in a week', the chances are you come away happy. In contrast, if the doctor were to reply 'Good god yes, that is horrible. I've never seen anything like it before. Do you think it might be contagious? Take these tablets, and if you're alive in a week come back and see me', you aren't likely to feel quite so great. Similarly, we expect managers to sound confident. Unfortunately, via a bizarre halo effect we then endow them with a high assessment of their skills.

II. Confirmatory Bias and Biased Assimilation

Just like the rest of us, managers tend to look for the information that agrees with them, rather than searching out the information which would show they were wrong (known as confirmatory bias, mentioned at the outset of this note). Not only do we tend to look for the information that agrees with us, we also tend to interpret neutral information in a fashion that supports us, and on hearing information that should lead us to change our minds, all too often it hardens our resolve – a process known as biased assimilation.

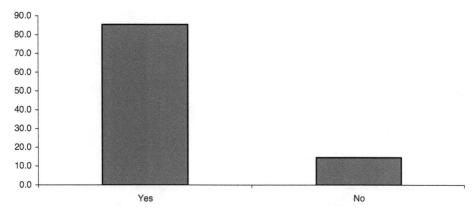

Figure 26.3   Would you invest the last 10% of the research funds? (% responding)
Source: Arkes and Blumer (1985). SG Global Strategy.

III. Conservatism

Managers often seem to suffer from a conservative bias – a habit of hanging onto their view for too long. This often appears to be driven by the perception of sunk costs. In their classic paper on the psychology of sunk costs, Arkes and Blumer (1985) show a number of experiments that illustrate the sunk cost fallacy. For instance, consider the following:

> As the president of an airline company, you have invested $10 million into a research project. The purpose was to build a plane that would not be detected by conventional radar, in other words a stealth plane. When the project is 90% completed, another firm begins marketing a plane that cannot be detected by radar. Also, it is apparent that their plane is much faster and far more economical than the plane your company is building. The question is: Should you invest the last 10% of the research funds to finish your plane? (Figure 26.3)

Now consider this:

> As the president of an aircraft maker, you have received a suggestion from one of your employees. The suggestion is to use the last $1 million of your research funds to develop a stealth plane. However, another firm has just begun marketing a stealth plane. Also, it is apparent that their plane is much faster and far more economical than the plane your company could build. The question is: Should you invest the last million dollars of your research funds to build the plane proposed by your employee? (Figure 26.4)

IV. Representativeness

Managers can fall into the trap of judging things by how they appear as opposed to how likely they actually are. An overreliance on simple stories is a hallmark of this kind of management thinking. The hope for synergies (discussed below) is often a great example of representativeness at work.

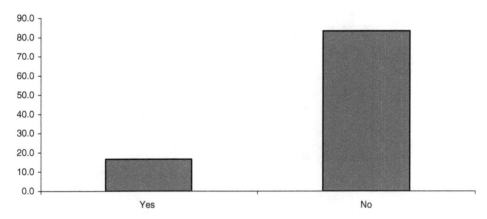

Figure 26.4   Would you invest the last million dollars of the research funds? (% responding)
Source: Arkes and Blumer (1985), SG Global Strategy.

V. Conformity and Groupthink

Dictatorial management styles are usually a disaster. Dissent is often a much underestimated tool for management. But it takes an unusual manager to deliberately cultivate dissent. It is far more common for managers to think they know best and surround themselves with people who are happy to reinforce their viewpoint.

Indeed, there is some powerful evidence to suggest that many managers share many of the same traits as psychopaths (bar the homicidal tendencies) – see Board and Fritzon (2005) and Babiak and Hare (2006). The Fast Company derived a quick and dirty test to see if your manager was a psychopath based on the work of the leading light in the field, Robert Hare. For each question, score two points for 'yes', one point for 'somewhat' or 'maybe', and zero points for 'no'.

1. *Is he glib and superficially charming?*
   Is he a likable personality and a terrific talker – entertaining, persuasive, but maybe a bit too smooth and slick? Can he pass himself off as a supposed expert in a business meeting even though he really doesn't know much about the topic? Is he a flatterer? Seductive, but insincere? Does he tell amusing but unlikely anecdotes celebrating his own past? Can he persuade his colleagues to support a certain position this week – and then argue with equal conviction and persuasiveness for the opposite position next week? If he's a CEO, can he appear on TV and somehow get away without answering the interviewer's direct questions or saying anything truly substantive?
   SCORE__

2. *Does he have a grandiose sense of self-worth?*
   Does he brag? Is he arrogant? Superior? Domineering? Does he feel he's above the rules that apply to 'little people'? Does he act as though everything revolves around him? Does he downplay his legal, financial, or personal problems, say they're just temporary, or blame them on others?
   SCORE__

3. *Is he a pathological liar?*
Has he reinvented his own past in a more positive light – for example, claiming that he rose from a tough, poor background even though he really grew up middle class? Does he lie habitually even though he can easily be found out? When he's exposed, does he still act unconcerned because he thinks he can weasel out of it? Does he enjoy lying? Is he proud of his knack for deceit? Is it hard to tell whether he knows he's a liar or whether he deceives himself and believes his own bull?
SCORE__

4. *Is he a con artist or master manipulator?*
Does he use his skill at lying to cheat or manipulate other people in his quest for money, power, status, and sex? Does he 'use' people brilliantly? Does he engage in dishonest schemes such as cooking the books?
SCORE__

5. *When he harms other people, does he feel a lack of remorse or guilt?*
Is he concerned about himself rather than the wreckage he inflicts on others or society at large? Does he say he feels bad but act as though he really doesn't? Even if he has been convicted of a white-collar crime, such as securities fraud, does he not accept blame for what he did, even after getting out of prison? Does he blame others for the trouble he causes?
SCORE__

6. *Does he have a shallow affect?*
Is he cold and detached, even when someone near him dies, suffers, or falls seriously ill – for example, does he visit the hospital or attend the funeral? Does he make brief, dramatic displays of emotion that are nothing more than putting on a theatrical mask and playacting for effect? Does he claim to be your friend but rarely or never ask about the details of your life or your emotional state? Is he one of those tough-guy executives who brag about how emotions are for whiners and losers?
SCORE__

7. *Is he callous and lacking in empathy?*
Does he not give a damn about the feelings or well-being of other people? Is he profoundly selfish? Does he cruelly mock others? Is he emotionally or verbally abusive toward employees, 'friends', and family members? Can he fire employees without concern for how they'll get by without the job? Can he profit from embezzlement or stock fraud without concern for the harm he's doing to shareholders or pensioners who need their savings to pay for their retirements?
SCORE__

8. *Does he fail to accept responsibility for his own actions?*
Does he always cook up some excuse? Does he blame others for what he's done? If he's under investigation or on trial for a corporate crime, like deceitful accounting or stock fraud, does he refuse to acknowledge wrongdoing even when the hard evidence is stacked against him?
SCORE__
Total____
If your boss scores: 1–4 | Be frustrated, 5–7 | Be cautious, 8–12 | Be afraid, 13–16 | Be very afraid.

VI. Self-serving bias

All too often, the separation between management and ownership (the agency problem) creates serious issues for investors. These are amplified by the fact that we all tend to suffer self-serving bias (a desire to put ourselves first). Witness the number of times that managers grant themselves options which clearly give them a different incentive scheme to shareholders. As Charlie Munger said, 'I think I've been in the top 5% of my age cohort all my life in understanding the power of incentives, and all my life I've underestimated it.'

It strikes me that rather than listening to the presentation that managements give, the canny analyst might be well served to watch their behaviour. If a plethora of these behavioural biases are present, then one should be worried about the quality of the management.

BAD COMPANIES

As well as listing out the seven habits of highly defective management, Finklestein provides a check list of questions to ask yourself to help to spot bad companies.

Unnecessary Complexity

1. Is the company's organizational structure convoluted or complex?
2. Is its strategy unnecessarily complex for an otherwise simple problem?
3. Is its accounting overly complicated, non-transparent, or non-standard?
4. Is it employing complicated or non-standard terminology?

Speeding Out of Control

5. Does the management team have enough experience to handle growth?
6. Are there small, yet, non-trivial, details or problems that seem to be getting overlooked by management?
7. Is management ignoring warnings now that could lead to problems later?
8. Is the company so successful or so dominant that it's no longer in touch with what it needs to do to remain on top?
9. Do the unplanned departures of senior executives signify deep problems?

The Distracted CEO

10. Do I have unanswered questions about the CEO's background and talent?
11. Is the CEO spending too much money to fulfill personal missions that don't necessarily benefit the company?
12. Are company leaders so consumed by money and greed that they're taking questionable or inappropriate actions?

Excessive Hype

13. Is it possible that the excitement around the company's new product is just hype?
14. Could the excitement around the company's M&A be hype?
15. Is the excitement around the company's prospects just unfulfilled hype?
16. Is the latest missed milestone part of a pattern that could signify deeper problems?

A Question of Character

17. Are the CEO and other senior executives so aggressive or overconfident that I don't really trust them?

This list provides a great checklist of running over companies. Just take banks as an example and see how many red flags you would have got from these 17 questions – at least 10 by my count.

BAD STRATEGIES

Having looked at bad managers and bad companies, it is now time to turn our attention to bad strategies. This, of course, raises the question of what is corporate strategy.

Michael Porter in his magnum opus, *Competitive Strategy*, identifies five forces that determine the strategy a firm should pursue – substitutes, suppliers, potential entrants, buyers and competitors. Sadly, the permutations and combinations of these factors are also endless, making its practical application a potential minefield.

Thankfully in their wonderful book, *Competition Demystified*, Bruce Greenwald and Judd Kahn have simplified the problem, and alight on the core factor that must be addressed when considering the fundamental dynamics of a company – barriers to entry. This is what Warren Buffett describes as economic moats. ('In business, I look for economic castles protected by unbreachable "moats".')

If there are no barriers to entry then ultimately the firm will simply end up earning 'normal profits', i.e. returns equal to the cost of capital. But even within this environment it may be possible to identify firms that are behaving in a poor fashion. In a world with no barriers to entry, the total emphasis must be on operational efficiency (the lowest cost producer). Hence finding a firm that (a) doesn't realize that it is in an industry without barriers to entry, or (b) isn't concentrating upon becoming the lowest cost producer, can create opportunities for shorting.

Greenwald and Kahn provide us with a simple three-stage process to follow when it comes to analysing competitive advantages:

(1) Identify the competitive landscape in which the firm operates. Which markets is it really in? Who are the competitors in each one?
(2) Test for the existence of competitive advantages in each market. Do incumbent firms maintain stable market shares? Are they exceptionally profitable over a substantial period?
(3) Identify the likely nature of any competitive advantage that may exist. Do the incumbents have proprietary technologies or captive customers? Are there economies of scale or regulatory hurdles from which they benefit?"

While this is an excellent framework for thinking about strategy as it puts the real key of barriers to entry at the heart of the approach, I fear it isn't often used. Instead a great deal of time and effort is wasted on 'strategy' with the great and the good all sitting around discussing their 'vision of the future'.

Some useful insight into the poor nature of strategic decisions comes from another excellent book on corporate failure, *Billion Dollar Lessons*. Authors Paul Carroll and Chunka Mui identify six broad categories[2] of 'strategic' errors that seem to be common routes to corporate disaster.

---

[2] They actually identify seven, but two are very similar, and I have chosen to combine them.

The Illusion of Synergy

A reliance on synergies in managers' thinking helps to explain why so many mergers and acquisitions fail. It is very easy to overestimate the available degree of synergies achievable, and if managers are overconfident and overoptimistic, this is only to be expected.

The evidence shows that synergies can be exceptionally difficult to realize. The 2006 KPMG survey shows that of the 30% of firms whose M&A added value, 61% met or exceeded their synergy targets. In contrast, for the 70% of deals that failed to add value, only 35% managed to achieve their expected synergies.

Yet despite this uncertainty over the achievement of synergies, some 43% of the expected synergy value was included in the purchase price. Perhaps even more astounding, the KPMG survey showed that only around 30% of firms had conducted a robust analysis of the expected synergies before the fact! Christofferson *et al.* (2004) investigated which synergies seemed to be easier to deliver from the managers' perspective. Expected revenue synergies appeared to be where managers were most likely to overestimate the available returns. Christofferson *et al.* found that nearly 70% of mergers failed to achieve the expected revenue synergies. Indeed, nearly one-quarter of mergers failed to achieve even 25% of the expected revenue synergies (Figure 26.5).

In contrast, managers seem to be much more able to deliver cost-cutting synergies – only 8% of mergers failed to deliver less than 50% of the expected cost-cutting synergies. Over 60% of mergers managed to deliver at least 90% of the expected cost-cutting synergies. However a quarter of mergers still managed to overestimate the scale of cost-cutting benefits by 25% (Figure 26.6).

Faulty Financial Engineering

Carroll and Mui (2008) use this to refer to legitimate, albeit aggressive, ways of using accounting or financing mechanisms. The aggressive approaches do sometimes lead to fraud because they are addictive. Once companies start, they can't stop. They have to keep increasing the aggressiveness until they cross the line into illegality (known as the moral slippery slope).

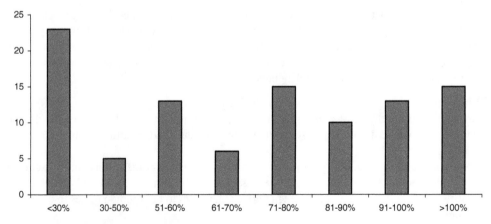

Figure 26.5   Percentage of expected revenues synergies achieved
Source: Chrstofferson *et al.* (2004) SG Global Strategy.

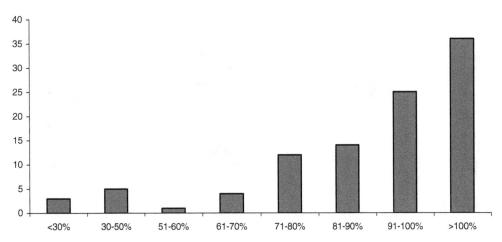

Figure 26.6   Percentage of expected cost synergies achieved
Source: Chrstofferson *et al.*, SG Global Strategy.

Deflated Industry 'Roll-ups'

As Carroll and Mui put it:

> Much to our surprise, we didn't just find tons of examples of companies that had run into problems while trying to 'roll up' an industry, buying dozens or even hundreds or thousands of local businesses and turning them into a regional or national behemoth. We found that many of these failed attempts ended in fraud. We also found it hard to uncover successful roll-ups! Companies that are sometimes cited as successes, such as Waste Management Incorporated and AutoNation Incorporated, went through horrific problems along the way and had to back off much of their initial roll-up strategies.

Staying the Misguided Course

This is nothing other than a manifestation of the conservatism bias address above. Carroll and Mui give the perfect example of Eastman Kodak. They point out that as long ago as 1981 Kodak was aware of the significant threat digital photography posed to the century-old film, paper and chemicals business. Yet although Kodak knew that the world would go digital, it thought it could use digital technology to 'enhance' its traditional business and kept investing heavily in that business. The result was neither fish nor fowl; it produced a digital camera that required film. Not a big seller! This is a prime example of Chanos' technological obsolesce.

Misjudged Adjacencies

This is the term that Carroll and Mui use for what Bruce Berkowitz describes as 'de-worsification' (as in 'diversification' – a term that originates with Peter Lynch as far as I can tell). While it may be tempting to move into other markets, all too often this strategy ends in tears. Carroll and Mui provide the example of a big cement company that went into bankruptcy proceedings after moving to a series of new markets, including lawn mowers. The

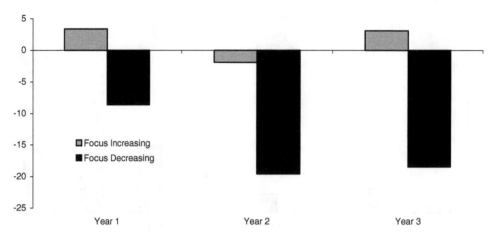

Figure 26.7 Performance of focus increasing/decreasing M&A (abnormal returns, %)
Source: Megginson *et al.* (2002). SG Global Strategy.

company's rationale was that its cement was used in homes, and homes love lawns, so it should start selling lawn mowers.

The consulting firm, Bain & Co. have shown that 75% of moves into so-called adjacent markets end in failure. The finance literature offers a cautionary tale for would-be diversifiers. A paper by Megginson *et al.* (2002) explores the performance of focus-decreasing and focus-increasing mergers. The results make unpleasant reading for those who argue that diversification is a good thing (Figure 26.7).

Using merger data covering 1977–1996, Megginson *et al.* find that mergers which increase focus deliver small but positive abnormal returns. In contrast, focus-decreasing mergers end up destroying a lot of value (with an abnormal return of nearly −20% over three years).

Consolidation Blues

The final group of common strategic errors that Carroll and Mui provide concerns mature or declining industries. Industries in this situation are faced with a diminishing pool of profits. This can trigger a consolidation wave in which one company tries to stave off the pressure by swallowing up the rest of the industry. Sadly, this can sometimes result in a race to the bottom. Carroll and Mui suggest the 'paging companies that were buying up other paging companies to consolidate that industry in the late 1990s, right before cell phones wiped out a vast chunk of that business' are a prime example of this viewpoint. In many ways this related the self-serving bias which I mentioned above. Corporate managers rarely wish to do themselves out of a job, so they tend to prefer being the consolidator rather than the consolidatee (despite the fact that this provides for the return of cash to the owners).

Part VI
Real-Time Value Investing

27

Overpaying for the Hope of Growth: The Case Against Emerging Markets*

Perhaps the most persistent 'mistake' I encounter among investors is the habit of overpaying for the hope of growth. Nowhere is this behaviour currently more evident than in the context of emerging markets. Emerging markets are trading on an incredible 40× cyclically adjusted earnings! Price action within the emerging markets looks to be following the pattern established by previous bubbles. A prima facie case for a bubble exists, yet investors simply don't want to hear any of the bad news. Instead they prefer to utter those four most dangerous words in investment . . . 'This time is different'. That has never yet ended well!

- Investors seem to be funnelling into any investment opportunity that offers them the hope of growth. Nowhere is this more evident than in the context of the emerging markets. I have a penchant for following the advice of Sir John Templeton, 'To buy when others are despondently selling and to sell when others are greedily buying.' So let me present a bear case on the emerging markets.
- Let us start with valuation. Emerging markets (EMs) are trading at a distinct premium to developed markets. For instance, EMs are on a trailing P/E of 22×, vs a 14 × multiple for the developed markets. Using our favoured valuation measure – the cyclically adjusted PE, emerging markets are trading on 40×! This is the same sort of valuation that developed markets reached during the dotcom madness.
- Indeed price action within the EMs is closely following the pattern that previous bubbles have established. In addition, those great return-chasing investors (the mutual fund buyers) have been pouring cash into EMs. This doesn't bode well for the return outlook!
- Of course, the bulls argue that decoupling means that 'This time is different'. However, analysts have been downgrading their numbers in EMs. We know that analysts generally lack the capability for independent thought, so this presumably reflects a real slowdown being seen by companies on the ground.
- Even if I suspend my disbelief in decoupling, there is an unfortunate empirical fact that investors seem happy to ignore. The data reveal a negative relationship between GDP growth and stock returns. The fastest-growing EMs have generally delivered the lowest stock returns, and the highest stock returns have been achieved by buying the slowest-growing EMs.

- The hope of growth is as seductive as the siren's song. However, for investors it is often as dangerous. Hope isn't an investment strategy. While the arguments that 'This time is different' are cacophonous, putting one's faith in this viewpoint has never yet been right!

THE SORRY TALE OF SIR ROGER

There appears to be a scarcity of critical thinking in our industry (and in life more generally for that matter). As an example of the latter consider the following strange story.

In her intriguing book *The Science of Sherlock Holmes*, E.J. Wagner recounts the true tale of Sir Roger Tichborne. In 1854, Sir Roger was reported as lost at sea. His mother refused to believe that her son, whom she had lovingly raised in France, was gone forever. She kept putting out inquiries, asking for any news on her son.

Twelve years after the loss of Sir Roger, it appeared that Lady Tichborne's prayers had been answered. She received a letter from Australia (from a lawyer) claiming to have found her son. The letter explained that having been shipwrecked, Sir Roger eventually made his way to Australia, where he became involved in a series of business ventures after having vowed to make a success of himself following his miraculous escape. Unfortunately, the businesses did not work as well as he had expected, and he had been too embarrassed to contact his mother.

However, he had recently seen her inquiries and was filled with remorse for the worry he had caused her over the years! The letter concluded with a request to send the money for the travel fare for Sir Roger, his wife and children.

Lady Tichborne was delighted to hear this news, and sent the relevant monies to allow for the family reunion. When Sir Roger arrived in England he was received by Lady Tichborne as her long lost son, and granted a stipend of £1,000 p.a.

However, not all the Tichborne family were quite as convinced that this new arrival was indeed the real Sir Roger. After all they reasoned, Sir Roger had been a lithe man of slim frame, the new arrival was obese in the extreme (to see photographs go to http://en.wikipedia.org/wiki/Tichborne_Claimant). While people can change their size, it is rare that tattoos disappear – Sir Roger had some, the new arrival had none. Nor is it easy to change one's eye colour. Sir Roger had blue eyes, the new arrival had brown eyes. He was also an inch taller than Sir Roger had been, didn't speak French (which Sir Roger did) and had a birth mark on his torso which Sir Roger didn't!

Somehow Lady Tichborne managed to ignore all this evidence. It was only after her death, that the family finally managed to show that the Australian import was an impostor. He ended up serving 10 years for imposture and perjury.

EMERGING MARKETS AS THE SIR ROGER OF INVESTMENT

Why I am recounting this tale of blindness to evidence? Well, it strikes me that investors may be doing something similar when it comes to commodities and emerging markets at the moment. So let me try to set forth a counter case against the bullishness that investors seem to be displaying on emerging markets.

Valuation

Let us start by examining the valuation of emerging markets. As Figures 27.1 and 27.2 show, regardless of whether we use P/E or P/B, emerging markets are trading at a premium valuation to their developed counterparties. On a 22× trailing P/E it is very hard to make any sort of valuation case for emerging markets as an asset class.

The situation becomes even worse if we use our preferred measure of valuation – the cyclically adjusted P/E. As Figure 27.3 shows, emerging markets are trading on nearly

Figure 27.1   Simple trailing P/E emerging vs developed
Source: SG Equity research.

40 × trend earnings! This is the same sort of valuation that developed markets reached during the dotcom madness.

A Bubble is Born

Not only can a case be made for extreme caution on valuation grounds, but the emerging markets are also showing classic bubble-like behaviour. For instance, in his latest commentary Jeremy Grantham of GMO points out that bubbles often announce themselves 'unequivocally, breaking well through the two-standard deviations [of detrended prices] (40-year events) that we deem to be a reasonable threshold for worrying about bubbles'.

Figure 27.2   P/B ratio emerging vs developed
Source: SG Equity research.

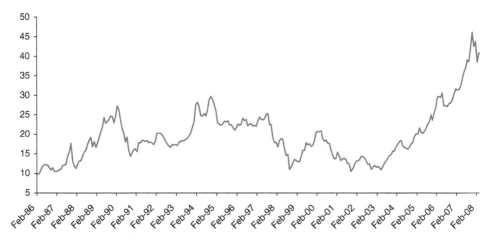

Figure 27.3   Cyclically adjusted P/E – emerging markets
Source: SG Equity research.

Using this kind of measure shows that there is a prima facie case for a bubble in emerging markets. Figure 27.4 shows the detrended prices (in US dollars) for emerging markets. They have clearly broken through the two standard deviation limit that GMO uses.

An alternative way of testing this idea is to see how the emerging markets' performance stacks up against our index of previous bubbles. To construct our bubble index we have examined the pattern contained within a variety of previous bubbles including the UK railroad stocks of the 1840s, the South Sea Bubble, Japan in the late 1980s, Gold in the 1980s, and the Tech bubble of 1999/2000 inter alia.

Figure 27.5 shows the primary pattern underlying past bubble experiences and the price action in the emerging markets. Again this would appear to strongly suggest that a bubble has indeed been underway in emerging markets.

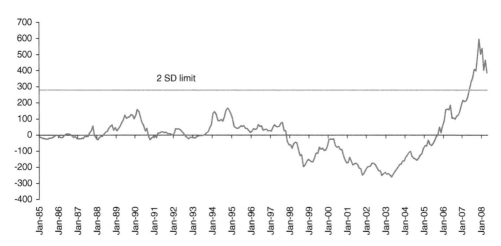

Figure 27.4   Detrended price on emerging markets – a bubble is born?
Source: SG Equity research.

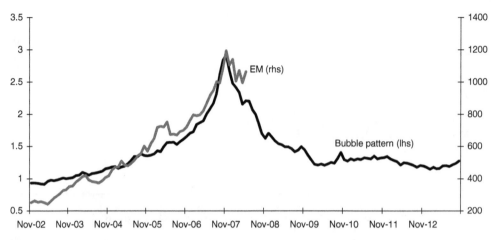

Figure 27.5 Emerging markets and our Bubble index
Source: SG Equity research.

The general enthusiasm for emerging markets is reflected in the popularity of such funds among Joe Sixpack. As Figure 27.6 shows, US mutual fund investors are pouring money into emerging market funds. Given their general timing abilities, this does not bode well for emerging market returns!

Decoupling and Deteriorating Fundamentals

Of course, all of this kind of analysis is ignored, because there is a simple 'compelling' story that emerging markets are decoupled from developed markets; that China *et al.* can grow fast enough to more than compensate for a slowdown in the developed world.

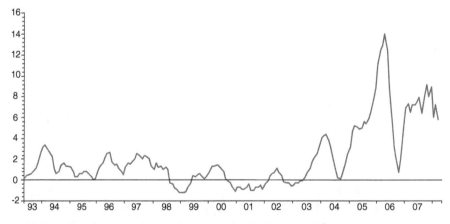

Figure 27.6 Inflows into emerging market mutual funds (6m sum, US$m)
Source: SG Equity research.

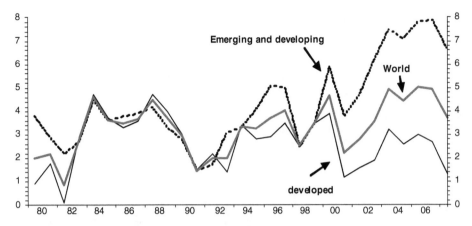

Figure 27.7   GDP growth in development and emerging markets
Source: SG Equity research.

Decoupling is unlikely to come to the rescue of the developed markets. We find it almost impossible to believe that emerging markets will be capable of withstanding a consumer-led recession in the developed markets.

As the chart (Figure 27.7) shows, the growth cycles of the emerging and developed markets are closely tied, to say the least. The very best that can be said of the economic decoupling story is that the Scottish verdict of case 'not' proven applies. Putting one's faith in decoupling seems foolhardy to us, as it represents a perfect example of what Sir John Templeton described as those four most dangerous words in investment, 'This time is different'!

In addition, analysts in emerging markets are downgrading their estimates (as shown in Figure 27.8). As we know, analysts are generally not capable of individual thought, so these downgrades are likely telling us what has already happened. That is to say, a slowdown in emerging markets is already under way!

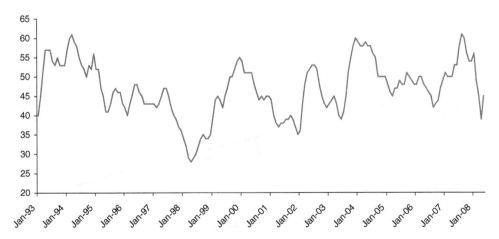

Figure 27.8   Analyst EPS optimism (upgrades as % of total, 3m ma, sa)
Source: SG Equity research.

Figure 27.9   36-Month rolling beta of Emerging markets against developed markets
Source: SG Equity research.

From a market perspective the concept of decoupling looks even more deluded than the economic case. Figure 27.9 shows the 36-month rolling beta for the emerging markets relative to the developed markets. They are still a high beta play. So decoupling on this measure can be debunked as a complete myth.

Overpaying for Growth

Even if we put aside our scepticism over decoupling, we find a problem with the idea that the 'growth' investors are chasing will generate returns. The decoupling story seems to rely upon a positive relationship between economic growth and stock returns.

However, looking at the data for the EM universe reveals a picture that is likely to be surprising to many investors. The relationship between real GDP growth rates and stock

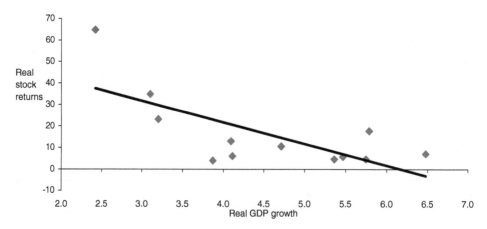

Figure 27.10   Emerging market real GDP vs real stock returns (1988–2007)
Source: SG Equity research.

returns is actually negative. The fastest-growing emerging markets have generally delivered the lowest stock returns, and the highest stock returns have generally been achieved by buying slow-growing emerging markets!

The most likely explanation for this 'odd' finding is just as at the stock level, investors overpay for the hope of growth. All too often we accept seemingly obvious statements as the truth. However, a little empirical scepticism reveals that those rotating into emerging markets for their 'growth potential' are likely to be severely disappointed (yet again).

Beware Dilution

One final word of warning for those wishing to invest in emerging markets concerns the risk of dilution (although in the developed markets investors seem to be cheering this on at the moment!). In the past we have shown that dilution is a problem for developed market investors (see Chapter 45 of *Behavioural Investing*).

The best way of measuring dilution is looking at the ratio of market capitalization to prices as suggested by Bernstein and Arnott (2003). In developed markets we found that this dilution effect is around 2–4% p.a. Figure 27.11 shows the index of dilution (ratio of market cap to prices) for the emerging markets universe. It is an order of magnitude worse than that seen in the developed markets, at around 13% p.a.!

So even if emerging markets do grow faster than developed markets, questions must be asked as to how much of this growth shareholders can capture. A reasonable amount of this growth will come from firms that aren't listed. As and when these firms list, the market as a whole will experience dilution (according to Speidell *et al.* (2005), this accounts for somewhere between one-third and one-half of the dilution we find). The rest comes from existing firms tapping investors for more and more cash. This level of dilution is non-negligible, and should be considered by investors when thinking about emerging markets.

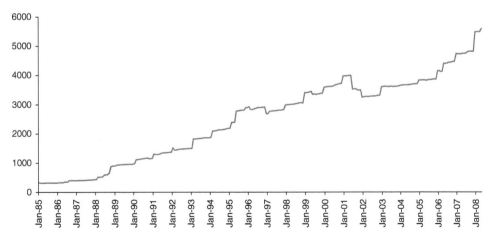

Figure 27.11   Dilution index (ratio of market cap to price) – emerging markets
Source: SG Equity research.

CONCLUSIONS

The price action and the cyclically adjusted valuation of the emerging markets provide a prima facie case of a bubble. As with most bubbles, a simple story seems to be luring investors much like a siren song. Sadly, it may well prove as dangerous! Perhaps the most persistent mistake I encounter is investors overpaying for the hope of growth. It always seems seductive to rotate to something proffering the hope of growth, but all too often we forget the lags that typify turning points. This is made all the more dangerous when the markets concerned are trading on massively elevated valuation multiples.

If (and when) the bubble in emerging markets bursts investors are unlikely to be particularly discriminating in their exit. As an asset class, the emerging markets look vulnerable to us. While the chorus of voices arguing that 'This time is different' are cacophonous, it may well be worth remembering that putting one's faith in such a view has never yet proved right.

28

Financials: Opportunity or Value Trap?*

Value investors are often a relatively homogeneous group. While each does its own research, they often tend to end up looking in the same places. This is a by-product of the tools and techniques they deploy in their quest for bargains. However, views on financials have created a schism in value land. One group thinks that financials are a clear opportunity. The other says that valuing financials in the wake of a bursting credit bubble is foolhardy. To us the margin of safety on the financials simply doesn't look big enough given the risks of a prolonged downturn.

- I have long argued that the long commodities/EM, short financials trade is the most over-crowded position in the market. I have no problem taking the opposite side of the popular long, and shorting the commodity and EM-related plays. However, the going long financials cause me more problems.
- One group of value investors, typified by Richard Pzena, argues that financials are exceptionally cheap. He argues that the current situation will not materially impair the future earnings power of the financials. As such the current situation is 'A typical credit cycle that will work its way out as other post-excess crises have, and without impairing the long-term ROEs of the survivors.' This appeals to the contrarian within me.
- However, on the other side, value investors like Steven Romick of FPA argue that 'Margins and returns on capital generated by financial institutions in the decade through 2006 were unrealistically high. "Normal" profitability and valuation multiples are not going to be what they were during that time.'
- At the end of the day the view on financials tends to hinge on your view of the impact of the bursting of the housing/credit bubble. My colleague Albert Edwards has argued (convincingly in my opinion for what it's worth) that a deep recession is a serious possibility. As the esteemed Jean-Marie Eveillard observed, 'Sometimes, what matters is not so much how low the odds are that circumstances would turn negative, what matters more is what the consequences would be if that happens.'
- With this in mind, we would suggest that investors seek a serious margin of safety when investing in financials. Looking back over the period since 1927, the price to book of US financials has averaged 1.38×, today they are trading on 1.32× – not much of a margin of safety there! At their lowest points, financials have traded in the range of 0.5–0.7× PB.

- On top of this, it should be remembered that book value can shrink as well. During the Great Depression (1929–1933) the book value of US financials halved! At the moment they are down around 6% from peak. Now I am not saying that this will be as bad as the great depression but it certainly gives pause for thought. Perhaps I am being too greedy by insisting upon bargain basement prices, but if value investing isn't about safety first then what is it about?

Rarely, if ever, have I come across a subject that divides value investors as much as their stance on financials over the last 6 to 12 months. In my experience I have often found that value investors, while plowing their own furrow, often tend to end up looking in the same places. This is a by-product of the tools and techniques they tend to deploy in their quest for bargains.

However, in the last year an enormous split has resulted in something close to internecine warfare. One group of value investors has been buying the financials all the way down; the other group has been shorting them aggressively.

Of course, by lumping all the financials together I am being unfair, but it gives a flavour of the deep divide within value land. The shorts have been 'right' so far this year. The average financial in the S&P 500 is down some 19%. Indeed the most shorted financials are down 35% YTD and the least shorted are down a mere 9% YTD, (Figure 28.1)

Of course, the various managements of these institutions continue to tell us that the crisis is over, and that they are well positioned and not to panic. However, these guys at best have absolutely no idea about what is going on, or at worst are just outright liars. For evidence see the recent collection of CEO comments,[1] or for the best of John Thain cast your eye over Figures 28.2 and 28.3 and then tell me again that company managements provide useful information!

The optimistic view of financials as an opportunity is typified by Richard Pzena. In his Q1 quarterly report he wrote:

A new fear has permeated conventional investment thinking: the massive leveraging-up of the recent past has gone too far and its unwinding will permanently hobble the global financial system. This view sees Bear Stearns as just one casualty in a gathering wave that has already claimed many US subprime mortgage originators along with several non-US financial institutions and will cause countless others to fail. And it sees the earnings power of those that survive is being permanently impaired.

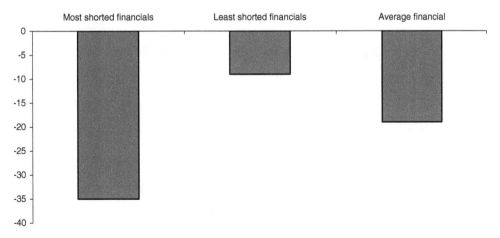

Figure 28.1   YTD performance of ... (%, USA)
Source: SG Equity research.

---

[1] http://www.portfolio.com/news-markets/top-5/2008/07/30/Regrettable-Comments-by-Bank-CEOs?page=1,

Merrill CEO Commentary: 2008

Date	Merrill CEO Comments
1/25	"I don't think that we are struggling...we are very well positioned to go forward into 2008."
4/3	"We have plenty of capital going forward and we don't need to come back into the equity market."
4/10	Merrill's cash reserve "is sufficient for the foreseeable future."
4/22	*Merrill Raises $9.5 bln in sale of debt and preferred*
5/7	"We have no present intention of raising any more capital."
7/18	"I don't think we want to do dumb things. We have been pretty balanced in terms of what we sold, and at what prices we sold them. We have not liquidated stuff at any prices we could get."
7/28	*Merrill to sell $8.5 bln in stock, unload CDOs at 22 cents on the dollar.*

Figure 28.2   Merrill CEO Commentary: 2008
Source: Merrill Lynch.

The obvious question then is: Which scenario is more logical: the extreme outlook described above, given the long period of easy credit extended to unqualified individuals? Or the scenario of a typical credit cycle that will work its way out as other post-excess crises have, and without impairing the long-term ROEs of the survivors? We believe the latter.

Indeed Pzena has even set up a new fund especially designed to take advantage of the opportunity he sees in financials, as well as having significant holdings of financials such as

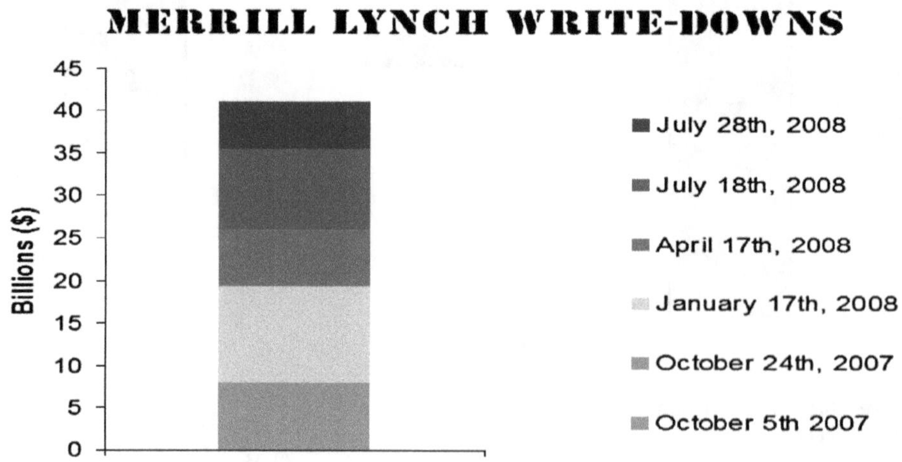

MERRILL LYNCH WRITE-DOWNS

Legend:
- July 28th, 2008
- July 18th, 2008
- April 17th, 2008
- January 17th, 2008
- October 24th, 2007
- October 5th 2007

Figure 28.3   Merrill Lynch write-downs
Source: Economicdata.

Freddie Mac, Fannie Mae (or fraudy and phoney as they have become known!) and Citigroup in his classic value fund.

The alternative view is well summed up by Steven Romick of First Pacific Advisors in a recent interview in *Value Investor Insight*:

> VII: Has your negative general view on the prospects for financial services stocks changed at all?
>
> SR: We believe in reversion to the mean, so it can make a lot of sense to invest in a distressed sector when you find good businesses whose public shares trade inexpensively relative to their earnings in a more normal environment. But that strategy lately has helped lead many excellent investors to put capital to work too early in financials. Our basic feeling is that margins and returns on capital generated by financial institutions in the decade through 2006 were unrealistically high. 'Normal' profitability and valuation multiples are not going to be what they were during that time, given more regulatory oversight, less leverage (and thus capital to lend), higher funding costs, stricter underwriting standards, less demand and less esoteric and excessively profitable products.

I have sympathies with both points of view. I have regularly argued that the long commodity, short financials is the most overcrowded trade out there, and as such financials appeal to the contrarian in me. Indeed I have no problem at all advocating a short commodities position.

However, I have also not found the financials to be trading at bargain basement prices and I have argued that the debubbling process is generally a long one – a matter of years not months.

At the end of the day the view on financials tends to hinge on your view of the impact of the bursting of the housing/credit bubble. If you share Albert Edward's view that it is likely to unleash a deep recession, then financials are not a good idea, strangely enough.

Support for this interpretation comes from the latest Federal Reserve senior loan officer. As Figures 28.4 and 28.5 show, both the demand for and supply of credit are evaporating. This effective shutdown of both sides of the market should be a serious concern for policy-makers, as it is one of the hallmarks of a liquidity trap.

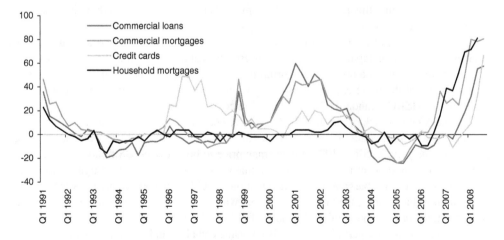

Figure 28.4 Supply side measures: Percentage reporting tightening conditions on. . .
Source: SG Equity research.

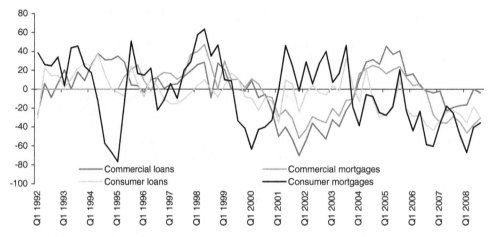

Figure 28.5   Demand side measures: Percentage reporting higher demand for...
Source: SG Equity research.

Note in particular how widespread the lack of demand for credit is, as well as the supply! This isn't just about the housing market. Obviously demand for mortgages (both commercial and residential) is lacking, but so is the demand for consumer and corporate credit.

However, I don't believe in taking investment positions based on forecasts, since forecasting is at best a fool's game. However, I am always mindful of the esteemed Jean-Marie Eveillard's words, 'Sometimes, what matters is not so much how low the odds are that circumstances would turn quite negative, what matters more is what the consequences would be if that happens.' Effectively, this is way of saying that it is expected value not probabilities that matter, a remote event with a huge negative payoff can cause you much heartache.

Thus, if one is going to invest in financials then a very large margin of safety is required. Do financials currently offer such protection? One of the ways I tend to view banks valuation is using the ratio of market capitalization to deposits (effectively an unlevered balance sheet). History teaches us that this ratio tends to bottom out between 3 and 4% (although banks will also trade on such measures before they go bust – witness Northern Rock).

Today, only a handful of banks trade at below 4% on this measure and all bar two are Japanese. The two non-Japanese exceptions are Bradford and Bingley and National City Corp. Of course, this suggests a potential opportunity of going long the cheap Japanese banks and shorting some of the more expensive banks (particularly those with a high emerging market exposure like HSBC, Standard Chartered and Banco Santander).

As a check on this lack of margin of safety I have been digging around and finally managed to come up with some data on price to book values from 1927 for the US financials. Figure 28.6 shows the picture. Since 1927, the average price to book on the US financials is around 1.38×. Today they stand at 1.32× – roughly in line with the average, but not bargain basement.

As the figure reveals, bargain basement valuations would mean somewhere between 0.5 and 0.75× book value. During the Great Depression, which was the last credit bust we witnessed in the west, the price to book of the financials fell from 2× to 0.5×.

Of course, this is only part of the story. Book value can also, and does, decline. Figure 28.7 shows that over the course of the Great Depression book value halved! So far in the present crisis, book value is down around 6%. Now I am not necessarily suggesting that the situation

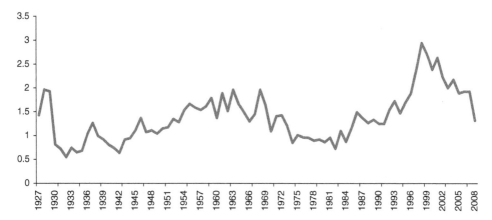

Figure 28.6   Price to book on US financials (x)
Source: SG Equity research.

is as bad as the Great Depression (I leave such outlandish proclamations to Albert), but it does give pause for thought.

The bottom line is that from my perspective the margin of safety simply isn't great enough given the risk involved. Perhaps I am being too greedy by insisting upon bargain basement valuations. However, to me this looks like a bursting bubble, not a normal credit cycle. And in those circumstances a exceptionally wide margin of safety should be required. As Seth Klarman wrote in his wonderful text, 'A margin of safety is achieved when securities are purchased at prices sufficiently below underlying value to allow for human error, bad luck or extreme volatility.' He also warns that 'The prospect of asset deflation places a heightened importance on the time frame of investments, and on the presence of a catalyst for the realization of underlying value. In a deflationary environment, if you cannot tell whether or when you will realize underlying value, you may not want to get involved at all.'

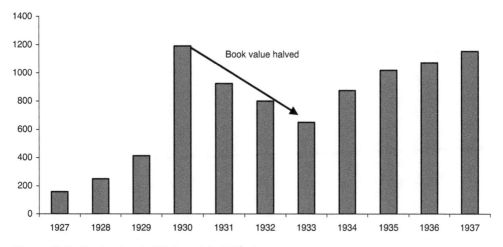

Figure 28.7   Book value for US financials (US$m).
Source: SG Equity Research.

29

Bonds: Speculation not Investment[*]

> It isn't often that Albert and I find ourselves on opposing sides of an investment debate. However, the current state of the government bond market has us divided. From my perspective as a long-term value-oriented investor, bonds simply don't offer any value. They already price in the US slipping into Japanese-style prolonged deflation. However, they offer no protection at all if (and it may be a big if) the Fed can succeed in reintroducing inflation (what Keynes described as the 'euthanasia of the rentier'). There may be a 'speculative' case for continuing to hold bonds, but there isn't an investment case.

- To my mind, in principle, government bond valuation is relatively simple. I see the value as the summation of three components: the real yield, expected inflation, and an inflation risk premium. The market tells us that the real yield for 10-year US government bonds is around 2%. Given that the nominal yield is also around 2% at the moment, the market is implying that inflation will be around 0% p.a. over the next 10 years.
- This suggests that the market believes that the USA will follow the Japanese path into slow grinding deflation. Unravelling the forward curve shows the market expecting 10y bonds to yield 3% in 10 years time! Surveys of long-term expectations show a different picture – they suggest that inflation will be around 2.5% p.a. over the next 10 years. This implies a radically different pricing of bonds. In a normal world, a 'fair value' for US government bonds would be around 4.5–4.75%.
- However, this isn't a normal world. The USA has become enormously over-leveraged. If deflation were to take hold, then debt deflation dynamics would be unleashed which would have truly horrible consequences for the economy. It is all too easy to see the bursting of the credit bubble causing a tsunami of deflation to sweep through the system.
- It took Japan seven years after its first encounter with deflation to instigate quantitative easing; the USA has started before deflation is actually here. Bernanke clearly believes that monetary policy is far from impotent at the zero bound. When talking to Japanese policy makers in 2000 he argued that measures such as money financed transfer (printing cash to pay for tax cuts), inflation targets and unconventional measures were all available even with interest rates at zero.
- What happens when an irresistible force hits an immovable object? I haven't a clue, and neither does any one else. However, the government bond market has clearly opted to believe in deflation. Thus if the Fed is successful then bonds offer no protection at all. The 'euthanasia of the rentier' will ensue.

[*]This article appeared in Mind Matters on 6 January 2009. Copyright © 2009 by The Société Générale Group. All rights reserved. The material discussed was accurate at the time of publication.

- Ben Graham said, 'An investment operation is one which, upon thorough analysis, promises safety of principal and a satisfactory return. Operations not meeting these requirements are speculative.' Bonds simply don't offer a satisfactory return (or indeed a safety of principal) at current yield levels. They, as Jim Grant put it, may well be 'return-free risk'. A speculative case of bond holding can still be made. In a myopic world, it may be possible to ride the news flow down. However, I am an investor not a speculator. So government bonds have no place in my portfolio.

It isn't often that Albert and I find ourselves on opposite sides of the debate. In fact in the last eight years I can't recall a single occurrence of such an event. Indeed I am not even sure that we have a truly deep divide at the moment; it may merely be a matter of time horizon and investment approach.

I tend to view the world through the lens of a long-term value-oriented absolute-return investor. Albert is often more willing to tolerate momentum-driven shorter term positions (believe it or not!). Perhaps it is these differences in approach that have led to us to adopt different positions on the merits of holding government bonds. In the interest of adding to the debate I will present the value-based bear-case here.

A LONG-TERM VIEW OF BONDS

Figure 29.1 shows the long-term history of US 10-year (or nearest equivalent) government debt. Over the very long-term the yield has averaged just over 4.5%. The figure makes it clear how anomalous the inflationary experience of the 1970s was. However, current yields are rapidly approaching all-time lows.

Of course, simply because yields are close to all-time lows isn't necessarily a sell signal. Witness the example of Japan. Figure 29.2 shows the long-term picture for Japanese 10-year government debt. I was working in Tokyo in 1995 and remembering thinking that as yields reached 3%, surely they couldn't go any lower. Of course, they went on to halve, and then halve again.

INTRINSIC VALUE FOR BONDS

How should one think about valuing bonds? I always have a simplistic view of the returns to a government bond holder. I generally view bonds as having three components: the real yield, expected inflation, and an inflation risk premium.

Figure 29.1 US 10-year government bond yields – a long-term perspective
Source: Homer, S. and Sylla, R. (2005).

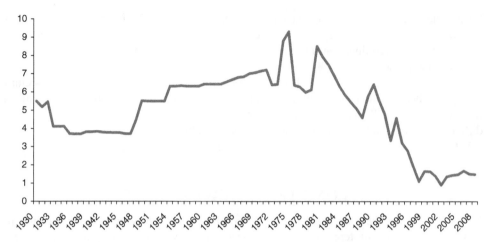

Figure 29.2 Japanese 10-year government bond yields – a long-term perspective
Source: Homer and Sylla (2005).

The real yield is generally said to be roughly equal to the long-term real growth rate (effectively creating an equilibrium condition between the marginal cost of capital and the marginal benefit of capital). Empirically this may be a dubious assumption as real yields and growth don't always enjoy a tight relationship, but it will do as a rough approximation. Of course, thanks to the use of index-linked (or inflation-protected) securities we have a live market in the real yield for many countries. In the USA, 10-year TIPs are yielding around 2%.

Expected inflation is the second component in our simple approach to bond valuation. This can be assessed in several ways. For instance, surveys such as the survey of professional forecasters (almost certainly an oxymoron) ask respondents to assess the expected inflation rate over the next 10 years. Figure 29.3 shows the expected inflation rate p.a. over the next

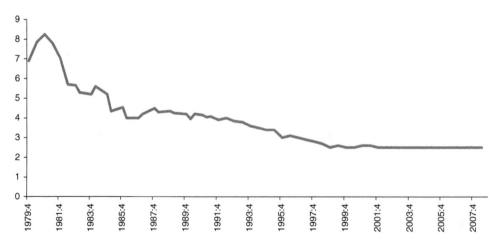

Figure 29.3 Survey of professional forecasters 10-year inflation expectation (% p.a.)
Source: SG Equity research.

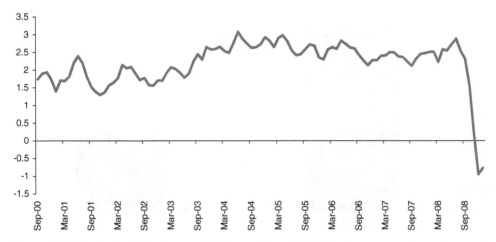

Figure 29.4   Implied inflation from nominal bonds minus TIPS (% p.a.)
Source: SG Equity research.

10 years according to this survey. At the risk of sounding like the Fed, inflation expectations remain surprisingly tightly anchored at 2.5% p.a.

In contrast, the market is pricing in a very different view (Figure 29.4). The gap between nominal bonds and TIPS gives a simple measure of implied inflation. With both groups of bonds yielding pretty much 2%, investors are implying zero inflation on a 10-year view!

Alternatively one can use inflation swaps to gain insight into the markets' pricing of future inflation (Figure 29.5). These instruments are now implying an inflation rate of just over 1.6% p.a. for the next 10-years. It is noteworthy just how recent the collapse in implied inflation has been!

The final component of our simple bond valuation approach is an inflation risk premium. Because inflation is obviously uncertain, a risk premium to compensate for the uncertainty is

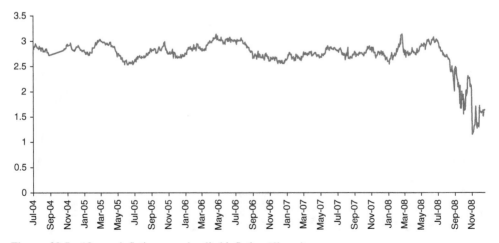

Figure 29.5   10-year inflation swap implied inflation (% p.a.)
Source: SG Equity research.

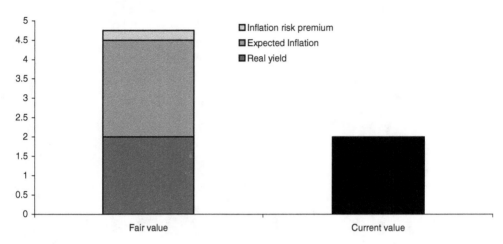

Figure 29.6   Rough fair-value bond benchmark vs actual yield
Source: SG Equity research.

required. Although hard to estimate, current academic work suggests a range of somewhere from 25 to 50 bps might be regarded as normal.

PUTTING IT ALL TOGETHER

Using this simple approach to a bond valuation yields Figure 29.6. A 'fair value' under 'normal' inflation rates would be somewhere around 4.75%. Today's yields at a fraction over 2% are woefully short of the estimated fair value under 'normal' conditions.

Even if we unravel the forward curve we find that the market thinks that 10-year bonds in 10 years' time will yield just 3% (Figure 29.7). The markets seem convinced that low yields are here to stay for a prolonged period.

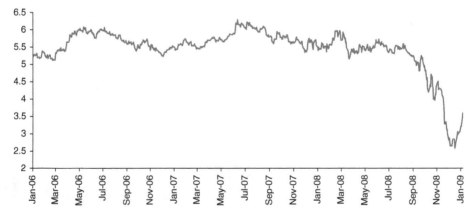

Figure 29.7   Forward 10-year bonds in 10 years' time
Source: SG Equity research.

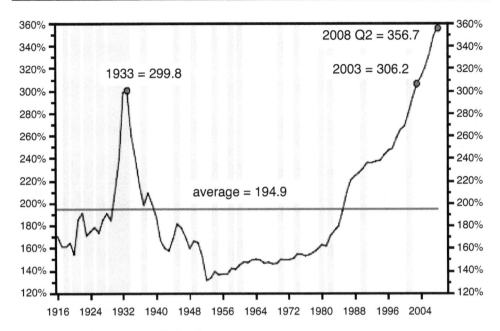

Figure 29.8 US total debt to GDP ratio
Source: Hoisington Investment Management.

INFLATION OR DEFLATION

As I have written many times before, I am torn on the issue of the inflation/deflation debate. History teaches us that bursting credit bubbles unleash massive deflationary impulses on an economy. With the US economy facing an enormous debt overhang, and the US consumer engaged in its first retrenchment in a quarter of a century, it is easy to see the dangers of debt deflation (Figure 29.8).

However, the Fed's reaction to the deflationary threat has been enormous. The quantitative and qualitative easing that the Fed has embarked upon is truly unprecedented. We are now in a brave new world of monetary experimentation (Figure 29.9).

Whether or not the Fed is successful in staving off inflation is certainly beyond my ken. Bernanke has made his game plan for avoiding deflation exceptionally clear. He will do whatever he can to prevent deflation occurring in the USA. In a speech given in 2000 to Japanese policy-makers Bernanke clearly acknowledged the greater threat that deflation posed in a highly leveraged economy, 'Zero inflation or mild deflation is potentially more dangerous in the modern environment than it was, say, in the classical gold standard era. The modern economy makes much heavier use of credit, especially longer-term credit, than the economies of the nineteenth century.'

Bernanke clearly believes that monetary policy is far from impotent at the zero interest-rate bound. In essence his argument is an arbitrage-based[1] one as follows:

---

[1] As Stephen Ross once said, to turn a parrot into a learned financial economist it needs to learn just one word: arbitrage. To my mind, economists are far too happy to rely on arbitrage assumptions to rule out solutions. Indeed, the second chapter of my first book, *Behavioural Finance*, is spent detailing failures of arbitrage (both causes and consequences thereof, including the ketchup markets!).

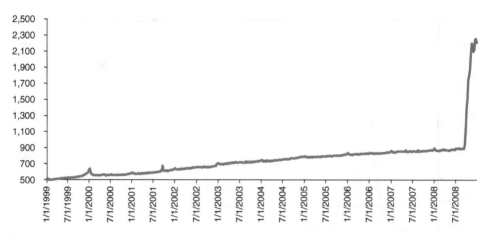

Figure 29.9   Fed's bastardization of the balance sheet (US$bn)
Source: SG Equity research.

Money, unlike other forms of government debt, pays zero interest and has infinite maturity. The monetary authorities can issue as much money as they like. Hence, if the price level were truly independent of money issuance, then the monetary authorities could use the money they create to acquire indefinite quantities of goods and assets. This is manifestly impossible in equilibrium. Therefore money issuance must ultimately raise the price level, even if nominal interest rates are bounded at zero.

In the speech he laid out a menu of policy options that are available to the monetary authorities at the zero bound. First, aggressive currency depreciation – this is obviously less of an option for the USA than it was for Japan, given the state of the rest of the world. Such a policy today would seem to be in danger of unleashing a 'beggar-thy-neighbour'/competitive devaluation response. Of course, this kind of policy is also more difficult when a great deal of overseas investors own your debt, and you don't want them to dump treasuries.

Second on Bernanke's list (although so far absent from the US response) is the introduction of an inflation target to help to mould the public's expectations about the central bank's desire for inflation. He mentions the range of 3–4%!

Third on the list was money-financed transfers. Essentially tax cuts financed by printing money. Obviously this requires coordination between the monetary and fiscal authorities, but this should be less of an issue in the USA than it was in Japan.

Finally, Bernanke argues that non-standard monetary policy should be deployed. Effectively, quantitative and qualitative easing. Bernanke has repeatedly mentioned the possibility of outright purchases of government bonds.

The Fed has followed this path once before – during World War II. As Sidney Homer and Richard Sylla write in their magnum opus *A History of Interest Rates* (gives you some idea what I did over Christmas!), 'Treasury war finance was based on a fixed schedule of yields. The Federal Reserve Banks bought whatever securities were required to maintain this schedule. Three-month Treasury bills were at 3/8%, one-year Certificates of Indebtedness were at 7/8%, short bonds were at 2%, longer bonds at $2^1/4$% and twenty-five to thirty-year bonds were at $2^1/2$%.'

Interestingly, Homer and Sylla note, 'When [World War II] ended, some people thought that the Treasury would not always be offering as much as $2^1/_2\%$. Perhaps rates as high as $2^1/_2\%$ would vanish forever. Therefore in 1945, after the war ended, purchases of the last issue of $2^1/_2\%$s approached \$20 billion. The Treasury indeed stopped issuing new bonds altogether.' This caused yields to drop to 1.93%! However, Homer and Sylla note that, 'This was the great crest of a 26-year bull bond market.'

One thing is clear. You don't want to be the last man holding bonds if the Fed goes down this route. This creates a beauty contest kind of game, where every bond investor is trying to second guess every other bond investor. Or as Warren Buffett put it (when comparing the stock market in 2000 with Cinderella at the ball, 'the giddy participants all plan to leave just seconds before midnight. There is a problem though: They are dancing in a room in which the clocks have no hands!'

Whichever combination of measures that Bernanke eventually opts to pursue his most telling comments come in the final lines of his speech to the Japanese policy-makers, 'Roosevelt's specific policy actions were, I think, less important than his willingness to be aggressive and to experiment – in short, to do whatever was necessary to get the country moving again.'

IS THE USA JAPAN?

While deflation is all but guaranteed in the short term, I am not as convinced that the USA will follow the Japanese route into a lost decade of deflation. As Keynes put it, 'The existing situation enters, in a sense disproportionately, into the formation of our long-term expectations; our usual practice being to take the existing situation and to project it into the future.'

My friend and erstwhile colleague, Peter Tasker (an expert of almost all things Japanese, having lived there since 1982) recently penned a note for my old shop on five key differences between the USA and Japan.

First and most obviously, the USA has had a much faster and clearer policy response than Japan ever enjoyed. For instance, the Bank of Japan (BoJ) didn't engage in any quantitative easing until 2001, some seven years after the Japanese economy first encountered deflation!

Secondly, Japan didn't really have any model to follow, the experience of the 1930s was a lifetime ago, and Japan's creeping deflation was a different beast from the rapid price-level declines that the USA experienced in the 1930s.

Thirdly, Japan was hindered by fiscal hawks who constantly sought to cut back on fiscal expenditure. The fiscal expenditure that did occur was not financed by the BoJ printing money, nor did it have any real use (remember the railways to nowhere?). A policy of fiscal restraint seems unlikely from the new US President. When combined with Bernanke this could be a potent combination for avoiding lasting deflation.

Fourthly, there are pronounced social and demographic differences between the USA and Japan. Japan's top-heavy ageing population made inflation a politically difficult solution. The USA has considerably more favourable demographics which may help to make a return of inflation a more politically viable strategy than in Japan.

Tasker's fifth key difference is not so promising for the USA (and is one that I mentioned above). When Japan was trapped in its deflationary spiral the rest of the world was doing pretty well on average. The USA faces a far tougher external environment in which to attempt reflation.

CONCLUSIONS

As far as I can see there is no investment case for government bonds yielding around 2%. As Ben Graham said, 'An investment operation is one which, upon thorough analysis, promises safety of principal and a satisfactory return. Operations not meeting these requirements are speculative.' Or, as Keynes opined, 'The term speculation [refers to] the activity of forecasting the psychology of the market, and the term enterprise [to the] activity of forecasting the prospective yields of assets over their whole life.'

To my mind a 2% nominal yield is not a satisfactory return. The markets are priced as if the USA is doomed to follow the Japanese example and enter a period of long, grinding deflation. While this may be the case, it is already reflected in prices, as such there is no value in government bonds. Even if yields were to collapse from 2% to 1%, investors would only make around 9% return.

If the alternative scenario comes to pass and the Fed successfully reintroduces inflation (leading to what Keynes so vividly described as the 'euthanasia of the rentier'[2]) then bonds look distinctly poor value, thus the risk is exceptionally high and skewed in one direction. As Jim Grant so elegantly put it, government bonds may well end up being 'return-free risk' (as opposed to their more normal nomenclature of risk-free return). If yields were to rise from 2% to 4.5% investors would stand to suffer a capital loss of nearly 20%.

Of course, there may be a speculative case for buying bonds. If the market is myopic (which it almost always is) then poor short-term economic data, and the arrival of outright deflation, could easily see yields dragged even lower. Thus riding the news flow may be a perfectly sensible but nonetheless 'speculative' approach. However, I am an investor not a speculator (as I have proved myself to be appalling at the latter), thus government bonds have no place in my portfolio.

---

[2] A rentier is one who lives off rent/income i.e. the bond holder.

30

Asset Fire Sales, Depression and Dividends*

> I have been trying to construct a portfolio around three basic ideas. Firstly, cash (as a deflation hedge), secondly deep value opportunities (in both fixed income and equity markets) and, finally, sources of cheap insurance (such as TIPS and gold). A new opportunity has arisen: dividend swaps. In Europe, the UK and Japan these appear to be priced for an environment worse than the Great Depression! Dividend swap prices imply a decline of over 60% peak to trough in dividends and then no recovery at all! They may also act as an inflation hedge. As a neophyte to this market, I fear I may be missing something, but it sure looks like an asset fire sale to me.

- A client recently suggested that I looked at dividend swaps from a deep value perspective. As I have often remarked, in the words of Winnie the Pooh, 'I am a bear of little brain and long words bother me', so it was with some trepidation that I embarked on some research into these assets.
- However, I was pleasantly surprised. Dividend swaps are relatively easy to understand (at least they appear to be – but I may have missed something!). Effectively this market allows investors to trade dividends separately from equities. As such they can also provide us with an insight into the market's view of the future path of dividends.
- The picture they paint isn't a pretty one. On current pricing, dividends are expected to decline peak to trough by over 60% in the UK, Europe and Japan. To put this in context, during the Great Depression, US dividends fell 55% peak to trough.
- Not only are dividends expected to collapse (not beyond the realms of possibility) but this market pricing implies that they will remain depressed almost forever. For instance, following an implied 66% decline in European dividends over the next three years, the market then expects them to grow by a mere 2% p.a. for the subsequent four years! This looks excessively pessimistic to me.
- In addition, dividend swaps may be of use as a cheap source of inflation insurance. As I have regularly stated I am seriously torn in the deflation/inflation debate. But if the Fed wins out and manages to reintroduce inflation, then earnings and dividends are likely to pick up (as a nominal series).

- All of which begs the question: Why are dividend swaps priced as they are? The only reason I can think of is that a combination of forced selling and oversupply has driven prices to excessively low levels. Whenever one sees forced selling or a supply–demand imbalance, the potential for a deep value position is created. I am at my happiest when I am buying from people who are selling regardless of value!

For most of last year, we were happy to sit on cash (or be short). However, towards the end of last year the market began to offer us some opportunities in two arenas. Firstly, deep value opportunities split between debt and equity. Our view was that each time the market presented deeply discounted value opportunities we would deploy cash into them, building up positions slowly.

Of course, if we had perfect foresight we would only buy at the bottom. Sadly we don't possess such a useful skill, so we are forced to deal with our limitations by adopting a slow but steady deployment of cash in the face of Mr Market's depressive phases. This remains our aim.

The second element of our strategy involved searching for assets that offer a cheap insurance policy to cover our ignorance. In particular, I have confessed to being torn in the debate over whether we are likely to experience deflation or inflation next. Thus I have attempted to seek out assets which offer potential returns in either scenario.

At the top of the list was US TIPS, with a sizeable real yield if the Fed wins the deflation battle, but a principal floor if it doesn't. Then came gold, of which I have always been slightly cautions as I have always been confused over a clear way of valuing it. However, in a world in which competitive devaluation and inflation are a risk, it made (and still makes) sense to me to hold gold as the one currency that cannot be devalued. Alternatively, if the world does go into deflation on a global scale, a financial Armageddon will ensue – so having a hard real asset could be a winner in this scenario as well.

DIVIDEND SWAPS: PRICED FOR WORSE THAN DEPRESSION!

A client recently suggested that I look at a third asset group that potentially fits both the deep value opportunity and the cheap insurance policy baskets – namely, dividend swaps. Now as I have said on many occasions my favourite (and potentially most apposite) quotation comes from Winnie the Pooh, 'I am a bear of little brain and long words bother me.' So it was with some trepidation that I began to explore the wonderful world of dividend swaps.

For those of you who understand these instruments, forgive me for teaching grandmothers to suck eggs. For those of you who don't, here is a five-line primer. Investment banks and the like end up being long dividends as a direct result of the structured products they create. Effectively, when you see products such as capital guaranteed bonds which offer exposure to the upside of equity markets, they are written in terms of capital gains, which results in the issuers being long the dividends. Institutions have taken to swapping these dividends in the same way as a plain vanilla rate swap.

This market allows investors to trade dividends independently of the market. This gives us the opportunity to explore the market's implied future dividend path. For markets outside the USA it isn't a pretty picture. As Figures 30.1 and 30.2 show, the Stoxx50, the FTSE100 and the Nikkei are all pricing in an environment worse than that experienced by the USA in the Great Depression.

For instance, European dividends are priced to decline by 40% in 2009, 38% in 2010 and a further 10% in 2011 – representing a total decline of 66% from peak to trough compared to a 55% decline in US dividends during the Great Depression!

Roughly speaking, the 2011 swap is pricing in a situation where only telecoms and utilities pay the same level of dividend they do today, while oil and gas stocks pay only 50% of their current dividend! All of this makes it look to us as if dividend swaps are another of those

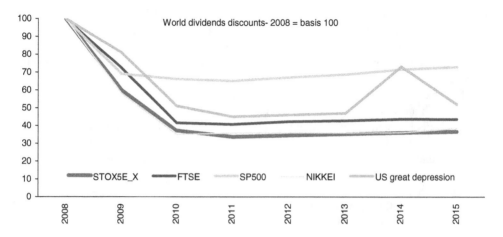

Figure 30.1   Dividend levels and implieds (2008=100)
Source: SG Global Strategy research.

assets that are pricing in revulsion (i.e. priced for depression) – much like corporate bond spreads.

Not only are dividends in Europe, the UK and Japan expected to collapse (not beyond the realms of possibility I agree), but they are also forecast to remain depressed almost forever! For instance, following the 66% decline over the next three years, European dividends are expected to grow by just 2.2% p.a. over the following four years!

A similar story can be found in the UK: a 60% decline peak to trough, then a mere 1.7% p.a. growth over the subsequent four years! Even in the Great Depression, once a floor was found, dividends grew by more than 4% p.a. (and that includes the sharp slump in dividends as the economy weakened once again in 1937 – if we take it up to end 1936, dividends grew at a rate of more than 17% p.a. for three years).

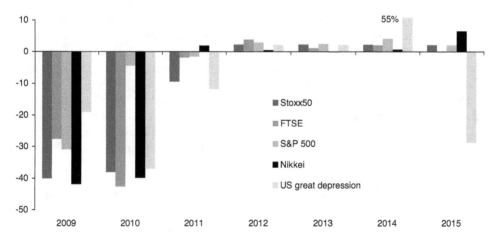

Figure 30.2   Year by year growth in dividends (implied)
Source: SG Global Strategy research.

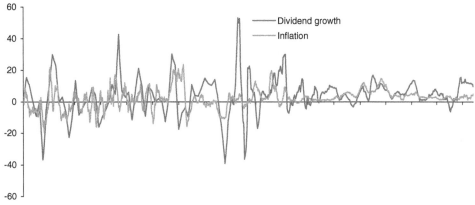

Figure 30.3   US dividend growth and inflation
Source: SG Global Strategy research.

DIVIDENDS AS AN INFLATION HEDGE

As I mentioned above, not only are dividend swaps priced for a situation worse than the great depression (making up a part of our deep value opportunities basket), but they are also potentially another form of cheap insurance against a return of inflation.

In theory, earnings and dividends are nominal concepts, and thus should generally keep pace with the inflation environment. If the Fed (and it may be a big if) is successful in engineering the return of inflation, then dividends should see a rise in nominal terms (Figure 30.3). As such, dividend swaps may prove to be another good source of cheap inflation insurance.

FORCED SELLERS AND OVERSUPPLY

All of this begs the question: Why are dividend swaps priced as they are? The only explanation I can come up with is that this is an asset fire sale, caused by a combination of forced sellers and oversupply. This, of course, is the very source of a good opportunity.

Whenever a forced seller can be found, an opportunity is potentially created. The forced seller, by its very nature, is selling regardless of value. As such, providing that I have a longer time horizon than the forced seller (which, as this is me we are talking about, is likely to be the case), then I can exploit their short-term need for liquidity, and in the process acquire an asset that is potentially very attractive.

Of course, I should conclude by reminding all that I am very much a novice in this area, I am sure there are much smarter people than me who deal with this kind of asset all day and every day. So maybe I am missing something really obvious. If so, I look forward to someone sending me an email pointing out my stupidity; if not, then it looks to me like dividend swaps are trading on prices that should be considered asset fire sales.

31

Cyclicals, Value Traps, Margins of Safety and Earnings Power[*]

Several clients have raised similar questions after my recent value screenings. They point out that some of the names I find are commodity related/industrial cyclicals made to look cheap by cyclically high earnings (something we ourselves have warned of many times this year). Ben Graham was aware of just this kind of problem, arguing that stocks should be evaluated on average earnings (based on 'five, seven or preferably ten years') rather than on current earnings. We have incorporated this into our deep value screen, and find nine S&P 500 stocks, and 31 European stocks that appear on our screen to be exceptionally cheap.

- My screens are throwing up stocks that are perhaps what we might call 'illusory value' – that is stocks which appear cheap simply because they have cyclically high earnings that are about to crater. To some extent I don't worry overly about such situations. The very essence of the risk management practice embodied within the margin of safety concept provides us with a cushion against the worst effects of earnings disappointment.

- For instance, on average over 1985–2007, those value stocks that have delivered the worst earnings growth have still generated a return around the level of the average stock. Their low price effectively provided some protection against poor outcomes. In contrast, the glamour stocks that deliver the worst earnings growth end up showing an average return of just 2% p.a.

- However, while the margin of safety is a useful protection it should be possible to improve returns by avoiding stocks which are likely to witness troubling earnings developments. Indeed, Ben Graham was mindful of the risks that value investors ran when it came to cyclicals. He urged that stocks should be valued against average earnings, not current earnings.

- We have tested Graham's suggestion by constructing PE's based on average earnings rather than just one-year earnings. The results show that this simple adjustment has significant merit. For instance, a simple PE strategy based on one-year trailing earnings has beaten the market by around 2–3% p.a. since 1985. However, a strategy using a 10-year Graham and Dodd PE shows a 5% p.a. outperformance on average.

- One of the other observations that our tests reveal is the indiscriminate nature of the market declines so far this year. All stocks are being sold to much the same extent. Unusually, value isn't offering any protection in this market.

- Graham argued that an investor should never pay more than 16× average earnings for any stock. We use this as an additional factor in our deep value screens to help to weed out those stocks whose apparent 'value' is really a function of cyclically high earnings. We have updated our value screens from last week. They show that a week is a long time in these markets! Last week just two stocks in the S&P 500 passed our deep value criteria, this week nine do (and all pass the new Graham and Dodd PE filter as well). In Europe, the number of stocks passing our criteria has soared from 34 to 52! Some 31 pass the new average earnings filter. Full lists can be found in Table 31.3.

A number of my recent value screens have featured stocks that are generally considered cyclicals (often with an industrial- or commodity-related bent). This has raised numerous eyebrows given our generally gloomy prognostications and our expressed caution on cyclicals and commodities in particular.

There are two reasons why such stocks might show up on our value screens. Firstly, they are nothing more than stocks at the peak of their profits cycle whose earnings are about to crater (effectively a form of value trap). Alternatively, they are companies (arguably like some of the integrated oils) that have not celebrated the rise of the underlying asset price.

To some extent we are protected against truly disastrous consequences stemming from the former situation by the margin of safety embedded within the process of buying cheap assets. This is the one form of risk management that makes sense! By buying stocks whose prices have already fallen we are reducing risk and increasing the likelihood of return.

Table 31.1 below shows how value offers us protection against negative outcomes. It shows the performance of stocks based on their valuation and assuming perfect foresight on the earnings front. This allows us to examine the performance across value stocks depending upon the earnings environment they end up facing.

By tracking across the first row of the table we can see how value stocks' returns change depending upon their earnings performance. Strangely enough the cheapest stocks that deliver the highest earnings growth generate the best returns. However, the protection of the margin of safety becomes clear as we move to the value stocks with the worst earnings growth – they still manage to generate pretty much a market level return.

In marked contrast, the glamour stocks (last line of the table) show the lack of protection inherent in buying stocks with high growth expectations embodied within their prices. The most expensive stocks that deliver the best earnings growth only manage to generate a return of around 8% p.a. on average (noticeably below the market return of 12% p.a.) However, this unimpressive performance pales into insignificance when compared to those high priced stocks that then go on to deliver the worst earnings growth, these stocks generate a return of 2% p.a. on average.

Just in case you were wondering, Figure 31.1 shows the percentage of value and glamour stocks appearing within each of the earnings quintiles. The market does a surprisingly good job at getting the general direction of growth right! A far higher percentage of glamour stocks end up in the highest growth quintile (44%) than corresponding value stocks (5%). However, given the mediocre returns such stocks achieve, it is clear that investors consistently overpay for growth.

Table 31.1 Returns split by earnings performance (Developed mkts 1985–2007) % p.a.

	Highest growth	2	3	4	Lowest growth
Value	19.8	21.6	17.7	15.9	11.9
2	20.6	18.0	13.7	11.0	10.9
3	17.8	14.0	11.6	9.87	8.10
4	15.7	10.5	8.55	6.67	6.12
Glamour	7.90	5.04	4.42	2.77	2.18

Source: SG Equity research.

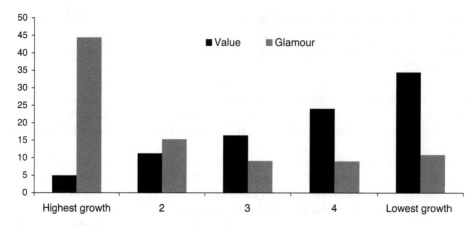

Figure 31.1 Distribution of stocks across earnings quintiles (%)
Source: SG Global Strategy research.

While the margin of safety may offer us some protection against the earnings out-turns, we obviously could try to enhance performance by avoiding those stocks that might just face the worst earnings outcomes.

This obviously raises the question of how we might go about trying to weed out the value traps that are about to witness an earnings implosion. As is ever the case, when trying to think about investment problems it usually pays to revisit the words of Ben Graham. He noted:

> The market level of common stocks is governed more by their current earnings than by their long-term average. This fact accounts in good part for the wide fluctuations in common-stock prices, which largely (though by no means invariably) parallel the changes in their earnings between good years and bad. Obviously the stock market is quite irrational in thus varying its valuation of a company proportionately with the temporary changes in its reported profits.
>
> A private business might easily earn twice as much in a boom year as in poor times, but its owner would never think of correspondingly marking up or down the value of his capital investment. This is one of the most important lines of cleavage between Wall Street practice and the canons of ordinary business. Because the speculative public is clearly wrong in its attitude on this point, it would seem that its errors should afford profitable opportunities to the more logically minded to buy common stocks at the low prices occasioned by temporarily reduced earnings and to sell them at inflated levels created by abnormal prosperity.
>
> Obviously it requires strength of character in order to think and to act in opposite fashion from the crowd and also patience to wait for opportunities that may be spaced years apart.

Rather than rely upon current earnings Graham had a simple yet powerful alternative – earnings power. As Graham opined:

> The concept of earning power has a definite and important place in investment theory. It combines a statement of actual earnings, shown over a period of years, with a reasonable expectation that these will be approximated in the future, unless extraordinary conditions supervene. The record must cover a number of years, first because a continued or repeated performance is always more impressive than a single occurrence and secondly because the average of a fairly long period will tend to absorb and equalize the distorting influences of the business cycle.

Graham suggested that earnings power (or average earnings) should cover a period of 'Not less than five years, preferably seven or ten years'. Of course, many object to the notion of simple moving averages of past earnings since they obviously ignore growth. However, as growth forecasts are notoriously unreliable this might not be such a bad idea. Graham argued that analysts should base 'The projection of future earnings and dividends ... (on) some past average as the best measure of the future'. Note that this statement is in terms of levels not growth rates!

THE EMPIRICAL EVIDENCE ON THE EARNINGS POWER APPROACH

Could such a deceptively simple idea improve the performance of a value strategy? To test this we used global developed market data since 1985. The answer we uncover is a resounding affirmative.

Figure 31.2 summarizes our findings. It shows the excess returns (i.e. after removing the market) as we vary the period over which we calculate the earnings. For a simple, one-year trailing PE, the cheapest stocks beat the market by around 2–3% p.a. In contrast, the most expensive stocks underperform the market by 8% p.a. Thus a long short strategy generates a return around 11% p.a.

When we use a 10-year moving average of earnings to calculate the E in our PE, the cheapest stocks outperform the market by over 5% p.a. on average. The return on the expensive stocks is an underperformance of around 7%. Thus the long short return rises to 13% p.a. on average.

Figure 31.3 shows the average annual performance across the deciles measured on 10-year earnings power. It is nearly monotonic. The chart reveals just what a bad investment stocks with a very high Graham and Dodd PE actually are. They essentially earn nothing! So you are paying for the pleasure of holding the stock.

One final observation before I move on to using the Graham and Dodd PE to improve our value screening. Figure 31.4 shows the performance of the long-only 10-year Graham and

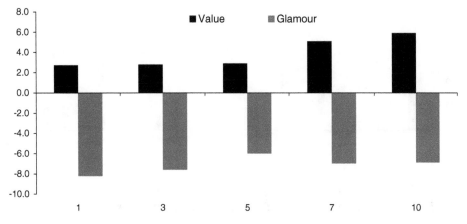

Figure 31.2 Excess returns % p.a. 1985–2008 as function of earnings horizon
Source: SG Global Strategy research.

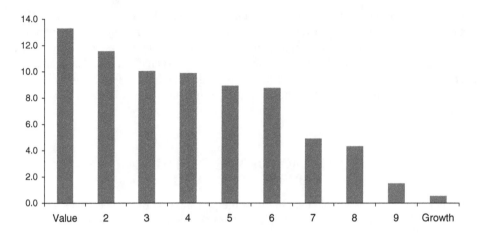

Figure 31.3 Graham and Dodd 10-year PE deciles (1985–2008, % p.a.)
Source: SG Global Strategy research.

Dodd PE strategy over our sample period. It clearly shows just how bad a time this has been for value investors.

A complementary perspective is given in Figure 31.5, which shows the year-to-date performance across deciles based on the 10-year Graham and Dodd PE. It highlights how indiscriminate the selling has been. Cheap stocks and expensive stocks (and everything in between) have been treated as equals.

USING GRAHAM AND DODD PEs IN OUR SCREENING

A simple cyclical adjustment seems to work well at improving the returns to basic value strategy, especially on the long side of the equation. As such it could be a useful tool in weeding

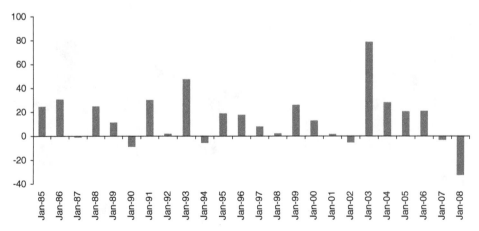

Figure 31.4 Time series profile of long-only Graham Dodd PE strategy, % return
Source: SG Global Strategy research.

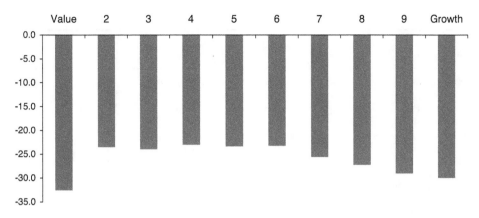

Figure 31.5 Year-to-date performance across 10-year PE deciles, %
Source: SG Global Strategy research.

out those cyclicals that crop up in value screens simply because their historic earnings are high.

Table 31.2 updates the European and US stocks that pass the Graham deep value screen. We have included an extra column which measures the Graham and Dodd PE. As Graham and Dodd noted:

> It is the essence of our viewpoint that some moderate upper limit must in every case be placed on the multiplier in order to stay within the bounds of conservative valuation. We would suggest that about sixteen times average earnings is as high a price as can be paid in an investment purchase of a common stock.
>
> Although this rule is of necessity arbitrary in its nature, it is not entirely so. Investment presupposes demonstrable value, and the typical common stock's value can be demonstrated only by means of an established, i.e., an average, earning power. But it is difficult to see how average earnings of less than 6% upon the market price could ever be considered as vindicating that price.

By overlaying our Graham and Dodd screen (based on an earnings yield of more than twice the AAA bond yield, a dividend yield of at least two-thirds of the AAA bond yield, and total

Table 31.2 S&P 500 stocks passing Graham and Dodd screen (criteria 1, 3 and 6)

Company name	Earnings yield (%)	Dividend yield (%)	G&D 10-year PE	Market cap. (m)
Ashland Inc.	12.0	4.4	4.7	2,988.1
Carnival Corp.	10.5	4.9	13.8	35,013.6
Chevron Corp.	15.2	3.9	13.8	195,100.2
ConocoPhillips	15.0	3.9	10.9	142,502.2
Dow Chemical Co.	12.3	6.7	11.4	37,069.3
Ingersoll-Rand Co. Ltd	12.3	3.6	10.1	15,350.7
Marathon Oil Corp.	22.2	3.6	10.1	43,210.6
Nucor Corp.	16.1	7.9	14.6	17,055.0
Tesoro Corp.	48.6	4.2	4.8	6,537.0

Source: SG Global Strategy research.

Table 31.3   DJ Stoxx 600 stocks passing criteria 1, 3, 6

Company name	Earnings yield (%)	Dividend yield (%)	G & D 10-year PE	Mkt cap (US$m)
Acerinox S.A.	12.3	3.6	11.7	6,367.8
Anglo American PLC	14.2	4.0	11.2	82,067.0
Antofagasta PLC	22.6	7.2	12.3	14,083.7
Bekaert S.A. N.V.	10.0	3.6	18.5	2,663.4
BHP Billiton PLC	14.3	3.8	18.3	212,730.6
Boliden AB	56.7	16.9	NA	3,437.4
BP PLC	14.4	6.0	10.9	230,903.4
Bulgari S.P.A.	10.2	6.5	15.4	4,179.8
Burberry Group PLC	10.1	3.9	NA	3,865.2
Carnival PLC	11.8	5.8	NA	34,394.8
Deutsche Lufthansa AG	23.1	11.5	11.9	12,160.4
ENI S.p.A.	19.8	9.4	8.1	133,727.6
Ericsson Sh B	15.2	5.6	15.4	37,334.5
Fortum Oyj	10.7	8.3	21.3	39,881.2
Galp Energia SGPS S/A	11.7	4.0	NA	22,262.6
GDF Suez S.A.	10.3	5.2	NA	57,362.9
Georg Fischer AG	23.2	10.0	8.7	2,472.2
Home Retail Group PLC	15.1	6.5	NA	4,513.2
Iberia Lineas Aereas de Espana S.A.	27.7	13.6	5.7	4,138.1
Kazakhmys PLC	45.3	6.1	NA	12,498.2
Kesa Electricals PLC	12.6	14.3	NA	2,511.4
Kesko Oyj	15.9	9.7	12.1	5,383.6
Konecranes Oyj	17.4	6.4	18.6	2,014.0
Koninklijke Philips Electronics N.V.	26.9	4.4	8.4	45,891.3
MAN AG	20.9	8.0	14.0	24,505.2
Neste Oil Oyj	19.0	8.4	NA	9,014.5
Nexans	16.2	4.4	NA	3,205.1
Nokia Corp.	15.9	4.5	14.3	148,896.8
Nokian Renkaat Oyj	10.4	3.8	25.3	4,342.9
Norddeutsche Affinerie AG	21.6	5.2	14.9	1,631.7
Norsk Hydro ASA	26.1	5.4	9.2	17,263.2
OMV AG	23.3	5.5	9.9	24,168.8
Orkla ASA	18.7	5.1	9.4	19,834.1
Outokumpu Oyj	44.1	15.0	5.7	5,576.6
Outotec Oyj	13.5	6.9	NA	2,305.4
Parmalat S.p.A.	28.0	11.6	NA	6,416.7
Persimmon PLC	37.4	13.9	4.7	4,809.1
Rautaruukki Oyj	28.0	16.9	8.4	6,004.3
Reed Elsevier N.V.	16.0	5.6	18.1	15,880.6
Repsol YPF S.A.	16.2	6.2	9.3	43,451.9
Royal Dutch Shell Class A	21.9	6.2	8.3	260,654.8
Salzgitter AG	31.7	6.0	7.5	8,409.9
Skanska AB	15.3	12.9	9.5	7,898.5
SKF AB	14.0	6.9	16.2	7,712.5
StatoilHydro ASA	12.5	7.7	12.5	99,064.4
Sulzer AG	10.9	3.7	26.6	4,935.2

(Continued)

Table 31.3 (*Continued*)

Company name	Earnings yield (%)	Dividend yield (%)	G & D 10-year PE	Mkt cap (US$m)
Tomkins PLC	15.7	10.6	7.1	3,151.8
Total S.A.	17.6	6.2	10.3	186,178.8
Umicore S.A.	32.5	4.1	12.9	5,959.9
Vallourec S.A.	18.3	6.8	19.2	14,205.2
Wacker Chemie AG	11.9	4.2	15.3	14,219.5
Wartsila Oyj	12.3	19.1	11.6	7,297.9

Source: SG Global Strategy research.

debt less than two-thirds of tangible book value) with a long-term PE limit 16× as suggested by Graham and Dodd, we can see which stocks in our selection are potentially vulnerable to an earnings collapse.

Tables 31.2 and 31.3 are updated to reflect market movements until the close of play on Friday 10 October. When we last ran this screen only two US stocks passed. Now nine pass, and they all have a Graham and Dodd PE of less than 16×. This increase in stocks passing is due to the collapse in prices of the US energy sector.

In Europe, the market move over the past week has increased the number of stocks passing our screen from 34 to 52! Of these 52, some 31 trade at Graham and Dodd PEs of less than 16×. They have been highlighted in the table.

32

The Road to Revulsion and the Creation of Value*

The inexorable march down the road to revulsion is throwing up some truly incredible investment opportunities. BAA-rated corporate bonds are now yielding the highest level since the 1930s – as Ben Graham said, corporate bonds 'should be bought on a depression basis'. Even in aggregate terms, equity markets are offering reasonable value. From a bottom-up perspective, great companies are available at bargain basement prices. Will I be early? Almost certainly yes. But as Jeremy Grantham noted recently, 'If stocks are attractive and you don't buy and they run away, you don't just look like an idiot, you are an idiot.'

- Unprecedented has become the most overused word in existence throughout this period. From our perspective the spike in market volatility is neither unprecedented nor unpredictable. Volatility spikes are not black swans, rather they occur when Mr Market goes from losing his head at the top to losing his nerve at the bottom. However, volatility has a degree of persistence. In the Great Depression volatility exploded and remained exceptionally high until well into the recovery!

- Perhaps the only solace to investors is that the road to revulsion ends in an investment nirvana – unambiguously cheap assets. The latest addition to the portfolio of deep value opportunities comes from fixed-income land. The yields on BAA-rated bonds are pricing an environment akin to the 1930. Senior secured debt is available for 50–70c on the dollar.

- Equity markets are also offering opportunities. Even at the market level, equities are looking attractive. The USA is trading on a Graham and Dodd PE of 15×, against an average of 18× since 1871. The UK is trading on 12× such a measure, against 16× since 1927. Could markets go lower? Of course. But from a long-term perspective they are attractive!

- While this may not be the 1930s, it is informative to see what happened to drag markets down to their all-time lows. Mapped onto today, the 1930s would require (reported) earnings to halve from current levels. Of course, equities are a claim on long-term cash flows, and as such very little of their value comes from the near term (less than 10% in a typical DCF), so if markets did follow the 1930s example, it would be a generational opportunity to buy.

- From a bottom-up perspective, the opportunities are even more compelling. In Europe and the UK nearly 1 in 10 stocks is passing our augmented Ben Graham screen. In Japan and Asia 1 in 5 stocks is passing the screen! Even 15 stocks within the S&P 500 are showing up as deep-value opportunities (full lists appear in Tables 32.2–32.6). Some have argued that

---

value stocks did particularly poorly during the Great Depression. The data show that they did no better or worse than other equities but did eventually rebound faster.

- Perhaps it is time to reintroduce the late, great Bob Kirby's idea of the coffee can portfolio – a basket of stocks that one would be happy to hide under the mattress and forget about. Of course, such an approach requires a long time horizon. Sadly, the institutional imperative to perform on all time horizons combined with the mad world of modern risk management hamper most investors' abilities to exploit the opportunities.

We seem to be marching inexorably down the road to revulsion (that final stage of a debubbing process) which terminates in a loathing of the assets in question and is characterized by unambiguously cheap asset prices (effectively my idea of heaven). My strategy for surviving this environment has been a barbell of deep value opportunities presented by Mr Market during his depressive phases, and cash. The aim is to slowly drip feed the cash into the deep value end of the barbell each time I can find some compelling opportunities. I recently supplemented this with some cheap inflation insurance (via TIPS and Gold). Given the gyrations we have observed I though it was worth while revisiting these elements.

VOLATILITY – NOT UNPRECEDENTED NOR UNPREDICTABLE

Unprecedented has become perhaps the most overused term in existence. However, the recent spike in volatility is neither unprecedented nor unpredictable. As Figure 32.1 shows, volatility has certainly been higher in the past. The volatility spikes are not black swan events, rather they are all too predictable – the result of exceedingly expensive equity markets receiving a reality check on their wildly optimistic assumptions. Effectively they occur when Mr Market goes from losing his head at the top to losing his nerve at the bottom.

It is also notable that volatility has a degree of persistence in the historical data – that is, high volatility often follows high volatility. In the period of the Great Depression volatility exploded and remained high until well into the recovery. Now not even my good friend and colleague, Albert Edwards expects our current woes to be as bad as the 1930s! He recently wrote 'Many dismiss comparisons with the Great Depression. I agree. The unfolding downturn won't be as bad', but he did go on to say that this is likely to be 'the next best (worst?) things' (see *Global Strategy Weekly*, 5 November 2008). Those looking for rapid declines in volatility may well be disappointed.

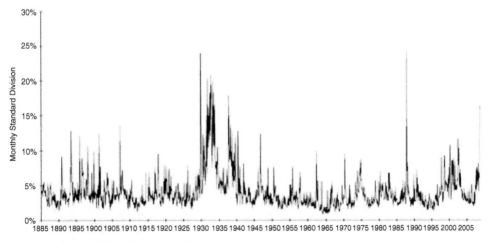

Figure 32.1 Volatility – here to stay?
Source: Schwert, SG Global Strategy research.

THE CREATION OF VALUE I: DEBT MARKETS

The good news from my perspective is that the higher volatility remains, and the lower the markets head, the greater the scale of the value opportunity that is created. A recent addition to the portfolio of deep value opportunities comes in the form of the corporate bond and distressed debt markets. Friends who are far more expert in this field than I, tell me that senior secured debt is available at 50–70c on the dollar. As this stands among the highest rated claims in the event of a bankruptcy there is a good chance you will get a full dollar back.

Corporate bonds look as if they are pricing in an environment akin to the 1930s. The spread between BAA and US treasuries is as high as it has been since the Great Depression. Currently it stands at over 550 bps, at the depths of the Depression it was just over 700 bps. This level of spread sits well with Ben Graham's advice that 'Bonds should be bought on a depression basis' (Figure 32.2).

The current spread suggests that the corporate bond market is pricing the highest default rate since the Great Depression – in line with Albert's view expressed above (Figure 32.3).

THE CREATION OF VALUE II: EQUITY MARKETS

The way I tend to look at valuations is to use cyclically adjusted valuation measures such as the Graham and Dodd PE (current price over a 10-year moving average of earnings). Figure 32.4 the long-term picture for the USA. The speed of adjustment is really quite breathtaking.

The S&P 500 is currently trading on 15.4× this measure. The average since 1881 is 18× including the bubble years, and 16× if we exclude the bubble. So US equities are now on the distinctly cheap side even in aggregate! I wasn't sure I would ever actually get to write those words!

As I have often stressed, valuations really don't matter for short-term returns. However, they are the primary determinant of long-term returns. Figure 32.5 shows the average 10-year real return achieved depending upon the starting Graham and Dodd PE. Today's market valuation

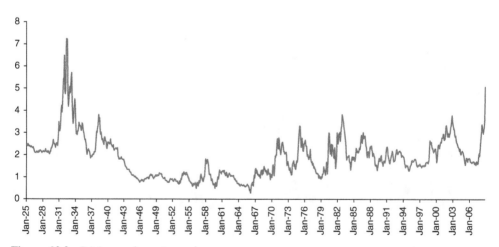

Figure 32.2   BAA spread over treasuries
Source: SG Global Strategy Research.

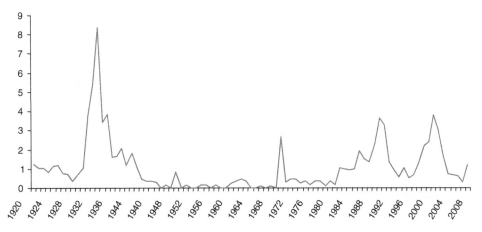

Figure 32.3   Default rate across all grades (%)
Source: Moody's.

puts us in the third column from the left – above-average returns, but not yet in the realm of the truly bargain basement.

Of course, this isn't to say that the market couldn't get cheaper. It is always worth remembering Isaac Newton's words, 'I can predict the motion of heavenly bodies but not the madness of crowds.' As Figure 32.5 shows, bargain basement valuations are still below the levels we see today. In general, revulsion is associated with around 10× on this measure, which, given 10-year average earnings of $52 per share, would give a S&P 500 level of around 500!

If one wanted to be truly depressing one could point out that the absolute minimum level of valuation that we have witnessed over the last 130 years is 5× on a Graham and Dodd measure (recorded at the lows of the market in the Great Depression). This would equate to an S&P 500 of 260! This isn't a forecast, and I am sure in today's world of professional investors almost constantly looking for opportunities, there is virtually no chance of an equity market at such ridiculous levels (but never say never!).

Figure 32.4   S&P 500 Graham and Dodd PE (X)
Source: SG Global Strategy research.

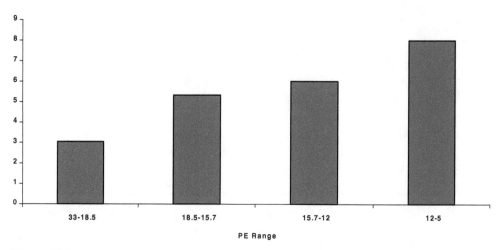

Figure 32.5   10-year real returns delivered depending upon starting Graham and Dodd PE
Source: SG Global Strategy research.

To give some flavour of just how bad things would have to be to drive markets to such appallingly low valuations, consider Figure 32.6. It shows the reported earnings per share for the S&P 500 since 1997. At the end of the data we have at present, I have mapped on the earnings path recorded during the 1930s.

Since the peak in 2007, reported earnings have effectively halved (driven by the write-offs in the financials). If this were the 1930s all over again, we would see a further halving of earnings from current levels! This is the kind of move that might catalyse myopic investors to create the ultimate panic.

Such a development would, of course, be irrational in the extreme (not that that rules it out!). Equities are a long duration asset, effectively being a claim on long-term future cash

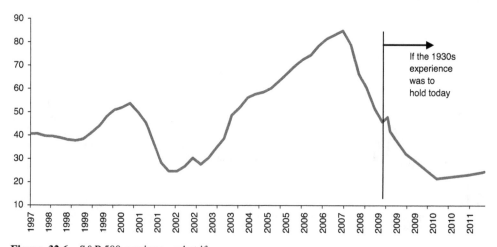

Figure 32.6   S&P 500 earnings – what if. . ..
Source: SG Global Strategy research.

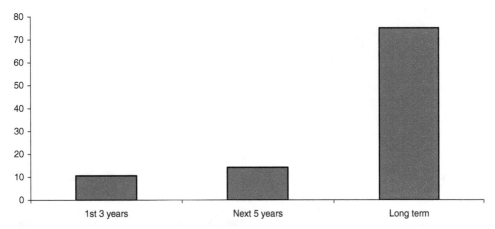

Figure 32.7 Contribution to value – S&P 500 DDM
Source: SG Global Strategy research.

flows. This point can be seen from any simple DCF[1] style calculation. I constructed a very simple DDM model for the S&P 500 in aggregate.

Figure 32.7 shows the proportion of value that is contributed in the first three years, the next five years, and the long-term. The first three years contribute a mere 10% to the total value. The next five years are slightly more important, representing some 15% of total value. However, the long-term provides far and away the greatest contribution to value, accounting for some 75% of the total value.

This simple exercise shows the relative unimportance of the next few years – even if they see earnings halve – to the long-term investor. Sadly, such a beast has become an increasingly rare commodity in the markets.

Figure 32.8 is one of my favourites; it shows the average holding period for a stock on the NYSE. It never ceases to amaze me just how short-term investors are. The **average** holding period is just seven months! Investors today make it look as if my 3-year-old nephew has a seriously long attention span. The market seems to have developed a chronic case of attention deficit hyperactivity disorder. The short term is the only thing that seems to matter to investors' today.

Of course, the USA isn't the only equity market in the world. Some of the other developed markets offer even better value than the US market. For instance, the UK market, when measured on a Graham and Dodd PE basis, is trading on 12× (and Europe is on a similar multiple). Thus they offer even greater valuation support, and potentially even more attractive long-term returns (Figure 32.9).

The view from the bottom up

While discussing market-level valuations can be fun, more insight is usually derived from looking at the situation from a bottom-up perspective. The simple reason being that, as Seth Klarman writes in his commentary on the new 6th edition of Graham and Dodd's *Security*

---

[1] It may seem odd for me to talk about DCF valuations given my recent attack on them (see Chapter 5). However, while I am a critic of their use (principally because of huge implementation issues), they do help to highlight the long-term nature of equity investment.

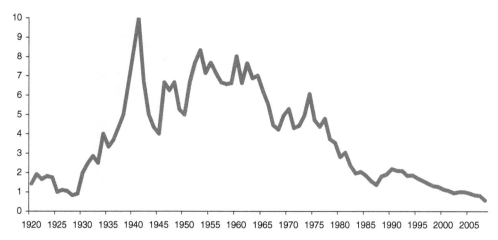

Figure 32.8 Average holding period for a stock on the NYSE
Source: SG Global Strategy research.

Analysis, value investors 'Don't need the entire market to be bargain priced, just 20 or 25 unrelated securities'.

As I have written many times before, the way I tend to assess bottom-up valuation is through a lens devised by Ben Graham shortly before his death. In order to qualify as a value opportunity the following criteria must be met:-

1. A trailing earnings yield greater than twice the AAA-bond yield.
2. A PE ratio of less than 40% of the peak PE ratio based on five-year moving average earnings.
3. A dividend yield at least equal to two-thirds of the AAA-bond yield.
4. A price of less than two-thirds of tangible book value.

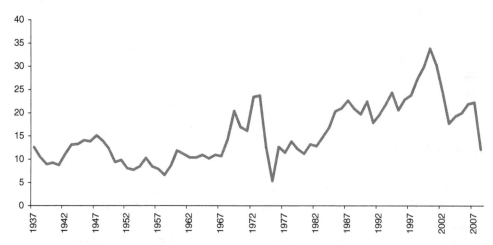

Figure 32.9 UK Graham and Dodd PE
Source: SG Global Strategy Research.

5. A price of less than two-thirds of net current assets.
6. Total debt less than two-thirds of tangible book value.
7. A current ratio greater than 2.
8. Total debt less than (or equal to) twice net current assets.
9. Compound earnings growth of at least 7% over 10 years.
10. Two or fewer annual earnings declines of 5% or more in the past 10 years.

Given the stringent range of these criteria it isn't surprising that we can't find any stocks that manage to pass all these tests in large-cap space. In terms of valuation, Graham's preferred measure was a price less than two-thirds of net current assets (the net-nets, that were explored in Chapter 22). However, on this basis we can't find many stocks in large-cap space that offer value.

If using net-nets failed, then Graham suggested the use of criteria 1, 3 and 6. These criteria collectively try to ensure that the stocks are cheap, returning cash to shareholders and not laden with debt (a very important factor given current market conditions).

As detailed in Chapter 31, I add one extra criteria to the list that Graham uses. I require that the Graham and Dodd PE is less than 16× – this is an attempt to weed out stocks whose value is illusory, being driven by cyclically high earnings.

Table 32.1 shows the percentage of stocks that are passing the various criteria across a selection of large markets. In the USA we can now find 15 stocks which pass criteria 1, 3 and 6 and have Graham and Dodd PEs of less than 16×. In Europe and the UK we can find nearly 1 in 10 stocks which pass these tests. In Japan and Asia this rises to 1 in 5! This is a value investor's version of heaven. (A full list of stocks passing the four criteria can be found at the end of this report – see Tables 32.2 and 32.3.)

I have one other observation before I leave this section. The nature of the sell-off this year has been exceptionally indiscriminate. This makes it very hard for a stock picker to add value. For instance, as Figure 32.10 shows, nearly 98% of stocks in the USA and Europe have delivered negative returns so far this year. Japan has faired slightly 'better' with only 92% of stocks showing a negative return! Even if you just look at stocks that have fallen by over 40%

Table 32.1 Percentage of stocks passing the Ben Graham criteria

Criteria	USA	Europe	UK	Japan	Asia
EY > (2*AAA)	48	53	53	78	63
PE < 40% of Peak PE	9	10	17	5	12
DY >= 2/3 of AAA	39	67	65	83	61
Price < 2/3 TBV	3	6	11	20	19
Price < 2/3 NCA	1	0	3	0	0
Total debt < 2/3 of TBV	38	39	43	69	73
Current ratio > 2	28	15	21	24	27
Total debt <= 2*NCA	20	17	25	36	27
CAGR >=7% over 10 years	69	67	49	68	78
2 or fewer earnings declines of -5%	5	8	15	6	11
Passing 1,3,6	4	14	12	47	33
1,3,6 and G&D PE <16	4	9	8	20	17

Source: Global Strategy research.

Table 32.2   S&P 500 stocks passing 1, 3, 6 and G&D PE <16×

Company name	EY> (2*AAA)	DY >= 2/3 of AAA	Graham and Dodd PE	Market cap. (US$)
Allegheny Technologies Inc.	47.6	3.7	8.7	8,777.1
Carnival Corp.	19.6	10.7	7.4	35,013.6
Chevron Corp.	13.6	3.9	15.4	195,100.2
ConocoPhillips	17.3	4.5	9.4	142,502.2
Cummins Inc.	20.8	3.4	14.1	12,877.1
Dow Chemical Co.	18.0	9.8	7.7	37,069.3
Gap Inc.	11.0	3.5	10.3	15,619.5
Illinois Tool Works Inc.	11.3	4.1	14.6	28,381.4
Ingersoll-Rand Co. Ltd	20.6	6.0	6.0	15,350.7
KLA-Tencor Corp.	15.9	3.8	10.6	9,216.1
Marathon Oil Corp.	29.0	4.9	7.7	43,210.6
Molex Inc.	10.6	3.5	12.2	5,024.5
Nucor Corp.	19.4	9.6	12.1	17,055.0
Tesoro Corp.	59.7	5.9	3.9	6,537.0
Valero Energy Corp.	54.9	4.1	4.6	37,582.3

Source: SG Global Strategy research.

so far this year, we find that all three markets have witnessed between 60 and 70% of stocks decline by such an amount. In a normal year around 30% of stocks show a negative return, and 20% or so fall by more than 10%. This shows the highly unusually nature of the events we have been observing.

Further evidence of the indiscriminate nature of selling can be found in Figure 32.11. It shows the year-to-date (YTD) performance of global deciles based around the Graham and Dodd PEs. Value stocks have suffered more than all others else – being down some 56% so far this year. In contrast, the most expensive stocks have fallen by 48%. This kind of selling is usually suggestive of the presence of a forced seller (perhaps the forced exit of some highly leveraged players). Whenever I see the presence of a forced seller I get excited. After all, this

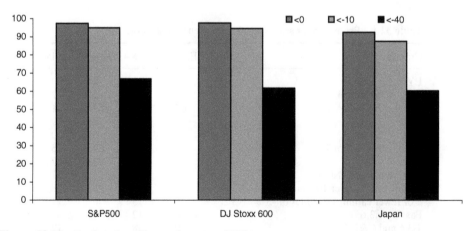

Figure 32.10   % of stocks with negative return YTD
Source: SG Global Strategy research.

Table 32.3   DJ Stoxx 600 stocks passing 1, 3, 6 and G&D PE <16×

Company name	EY> (2*AAA)	DY> = 2/3 of AAA	Graham and Dodd PE	Market cap. (US$)
Acerinox S.A.	12.4	3.6	11.6	6,367.8
Anglo American PLC	19.1	5.4	8.3	82,067.0
Antofagasta PLC	21.9	6.9	12.7	14,083.7
Bekaert S.A. N.V.	16.8	6.1	11.0	2,663.4
BHP Billiton PLC	18.2	4.9	14.5	212,730.6
BP PLC	11.7	4.9	13.4	230,903.4
Bulgari S.P.A.	10.5	6.7	15.0	4,179.8
Charter International PLC	36.4	5.3	7.3	2,619.6
Deutsche Lufthansa AG	27.8	13.8	9.9	12,160.4
ENI S.p.A.	16.4	7.8	9.9	133,727.6
Eramet S.A.	22.4	5.9	14.9	13,062.3
Georg Fischer AG	30.1	13.0	6.7	2,472.2
Iberia Lineas Aereas de Espana S.A.	20.1	9.9	7.8	4,138.1
Kesko Oyj	14.7	8.9	13.1	5,383.6
Konecranes Oyj	21.5	7.9	15.0	2,014.0
Koninklijke DSM N.V.	13.8	7.0	5.7	7,877.0
Koninklijke Philips Electronics N.V.	33.9	5.6	6.6	45,891.3
MAN AG	28.8	11.0	10.2	24,505.2
Modern Times Group MTG AB	16.1	4.0	15.2	4,669.9
Nokia Corp.	17.8	5.1	12.8	148,896.8
Nokian Renkaat Oyj	16.6	6.0	15.9	4,342.9
Norddeutsche Affinerie AG	24.9	6.0	12.9	1,631.7
Norsk Hydro ASA	33.6	7.0	7.1	17,263.2
OMV AG	30.2	7.1	7.6	24,168.8
Orkla ASA	22.7	6.2	7.7	19,834.1
Outokumpu Oyj	54.2	18.5	4.6	5,576.6
Persimmon PLC	61.0	22.7	2.9	4,809.1
Rautaruukki Oyj	33.4	20.2	7.1	6,004.3
Repsol YPF S.A.	19.2	7.4	7.8	43,451.9
Royal Dutch Shell Class A	20.4	5.8	8.9	260,654.8
Salzgitter AG	39.7	7.5	6.0	8,409.9
Skanska AB	17.2	14.5	8.4	7,898.5
SKF AB	16.6	8.3	13.7	7,712.5
StatoilHydro ASA	13.5	8.3	11.5	99,064.4
Swatch Group AG	15.3	3.5	11.7	16,151.1
Tomkins PLC	21.9	14.7	5.1	3,151.8
Total S.A.	15.6	5.5	11.6	186,178.8
Umicore S.A.	50.7	6.3	8.3	5,959.9
Vallourec S.A.	26.5	9.8	13.3	14,205.2
Wacker Chemie AG	13.2	4.7	13.8	14,219.5
Wartsila Oyj	15.5	24.0	9.3	7,297.9

Source: SG Global Strategy Research.

kind of seller is selling regardless of value, and hence creates an opportunity for those with a longer time horizon (back to that again).

One of the common misperceptions I encounter is that value suffered massively more than other styles or indeed the market overall during the Great Depression. According to the evidence shown in Figure 32.12, this is a myth.

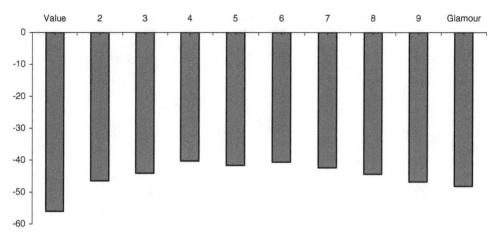

Figure 32.11 YTD performance of global Graham and Dodd PE deciles
Source: SG Global Strategy research.

The chart shows the p.a. decline from the 1929 peak to the trough in 1932. As becomes obvious from even a cursory glance at the chart, value did no better and no worse than the glamour stocks or indeed the market overall. While I am clearly not claiming that value was a great absolute return strategy during the Great Depression, we can at least kill the myth that value was worse than any other form of equity investment in the Depression. Thus the Depression was also a period of indiscriminate selling, much like the one we are witnessing today.

THE CREATION OF VALUE III: CHEAP INSURANCE

The final element of my strategy for surviving this environment is looking for sources of cheap insurance in the face of ignorance and uncertainty. As I mentioned, I am torn on the

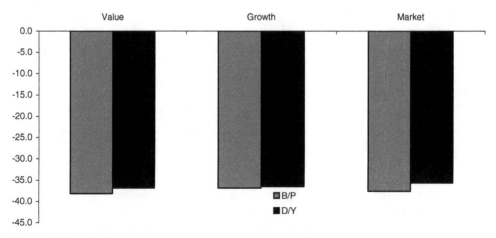

Figure 32.12 Absolute returns % p.a. 1929 – Bottom 1932
Source: SG Global Strategy research.

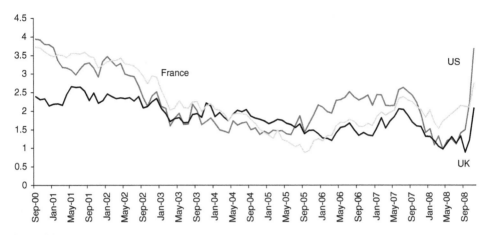

Figure 32.13   Real yields (%)
Source: SG Global Strategy research.

deflation/inflation debate at the moment. For a long time Albert and I have been warning of the dangers of a massive deflationary impulse unleashed by the first consumer retrenchment in a quarter of a century.

However, I am not sure that either of us had imagined that the Fed would be quite so willing to bastardize its balance sheet in such spectacular fashion, or in such a short time period. I am still not sure that the route they are using is necessarily massively inflationary, but that must certainly be the danger.

As such I've been looking for assets that would give me cheap sources of inflation protection. The most obvious of these is the index-linked bonds offered by governments. Such instruments have seen their yields rise dramatically of late – perhaps a flight to liquidity but again this presents an excellent opportunity for long-term patient investors. It is also noteworthy that the rise in real yields (Figure 32.13) hasn't just been a US phenomenon (although it is in the USA where the rise has been the greatest, and the yields are the highest).

CONCLUSIONS: THE RETURN OF THE COFFEE CAN PORTFOLIO

The road to revulsion is throwing up some exceptionally attractive opportunities for investors. In many ways, perhaps we are being offered the investment opportunity of a lifetime in areas such as the corporate bond markets.

In aggregate, equity markets are cheap, perhaps not at their ultimate bottom but cheap nonetheless. For those focused on long-term returns, equities are pretty attractive as an asset class. From a bottom-up perspective, the equity market is offering some excellent companies at truly bargain prices for those with the fortitude to shut their eyes, or at least switch off their

Table 32.4   FT All share stocks passing 1, 3, 6 and G&D <16×

Company name	EY> (2*AAA)	DY>= 2/3 of AAA	Graham and Dodd PE	Market cap. (US$)
AGA Rangemaster Group PLC	28.5	16.9	3.6	819.0
Anglo American PLC	19.1	5.4	8.3	82,067.0
Anglo Pacific Group PLC	27.9	7.1	13.6	375.1
Antofagasta PLC	21.9	6.9	12.7	14,083.7
BHP Billiton PLC	18.2	4.9	14.5	212,730.6
Bovis Homes Group PLC	24.0	11.6	5.0	1,479.2
BP PLC	11.7	4.9	13.4	230,903.4
Braemar Shipping Services PLC	19.6	9.2	11.5	184.0
Castings PLC	17.3	6.3	9.0	244.6
Charter International PLC	36.4	5.3	7.3	2,619.6
Computacenter PLC	23.7	10.3	3.3	597.9
Diploma PLC	10.5	6.7	12.1	310.8
Domino Printing Sciences PLC	12.5	6.1	12.9	758.7
Greggs PLC	11.2	4.6	14.0	990.7
Headlam Group PLC	19.5	12.2	10.7	718.0
Hornby PLC	15.2	8.0	11.0	141.1
JD Sports Fashion PLC	20.9	3.6	12.7	340.6
Kier Group PLC	17.1	4.8	9.1	699.9
Millennium & Copthorne Hotels PLC	29.0	7.2	7.0	2,400.7
Morgan Sindall PLC	20.1	8.2	10.1	889.2
Persimmon PLC	61.0	22.7	2.9	4,809.1
PZ Cussons PLC	10.9	4.6	14.3	1,634.2
Royal Dutch Shell PLC (CL B)	16.8	4.8	11.5	257,534.8
St Ives PLC	22.3	24.2	3.2	341.4
T. Clarke PLC	12.7	10.6	7.0	137.9
Ted Baker PLC	12.3	5.6	13.1	400.5
Tomkins PLC	21.9	14.7	5.1	3,151.8

Source: SG Global Strategy Research.

screens and buy. The institutional imperative to perform on every time horizon hampers this ability in a particularly frustrating way. Investors are looking at the short term, and ignoring the long-term opportunities they are being offered.

As I was completing this chapter, a friend[2] sent me a great speech by Jim Fullerton (former Chairman of Capital Group) written in 1974. It concluded with a quotation from Dean Witter speaking in May 1932 which I found apposite in the extreme. 'Some people say they want to wait for a clearer view of the future. But when the future is again clear, the present bargains will have vanished. In fact, does anyone think that today's prices will prevail once full confidence has been restored?'

Perhaps it is time we reintroduced the late, great Bob Kirby's idea of the coffee can portfolio – in which investors would have to put stocks and then not touch them – an idea he described as

---

[2] Thank you very much indeed Christian.

Table 32.5   MSCI Japan stocks passing 1, 3, 6, and G&D <16×

Company name	EY > (2*AAA)	DY >= 2/3 of AAA	Graham and Dodd PE	Market cap. (US$)
Advantest Corp.	8.4	4.6	10.3	4,629.3
Aisin Seiki Co. Ltd	25.5	4.7	9.2	10,490.6
Alps Electric Co. Ltd	6.1	5.0	8.3	1,761.7
Asahi Glass Co. Ltd	13.0	3.5	14.3	15,726.9
Bridgestone Corp.	10.4	1.6	15.2	13,869.0
Brother Industries Ltd	17.2	3.8	10.8	2,827.9
Canon Inc.	14.5	4.2	13.1	58,623.6
Citizen Holdings Co. Ltd	8.3	3.5	15.5	2,931.1
Dai Nippon Printing Co. Ltd	7.1	3.8	16.1	10,510.3
Daihatsu Motor Co. Ltd	10.6	2.2	16.4	5,111.3
Daiichi Sankyo Co. Ltd	7.8	4.0	16.3	21,216.0
Dainippon Sumitomo Pharma Co. Ltd	8.2	2.3	16.4	3,627.8
Denki Kagaku Kogyo K.K.	6.7	4.9	12.7	1,544.1
Denso Corp.	21.1	3.8	9.8	26,223.0
Fuji Media Holdings Inc.	5.1	2.7	16.0	3,392.3
FUJIFILM Holdings Corp.	9.6	1.6	14.7	17,842.4
Hitachi Chemical Co. Ltd	17.7	3.7	9.7	3,894.2
Hitachi High-Technologies Corp.	13.4	2.1	14.8	2,272.7
Hoya Corp.	15.0	5.2	12.5	10,149.2
Ibiden Co. Ltd	22.9	4.1	11.4	5,789.6
Ito En Ltd	5.7	2.7	15.5	1,539.6
Itochu Techno-Solutions Corp.	9.9	3.4	13.6	1,983.5
JSR Corp.	15.8	3.4	13.5	5,653.7
JTEKT Corp.	19.4	3.4	14.6	5,232.2
Kaneka Corp.	13.3	3.9	9.6	2,124.5
Kansai Paint Co. Ltd	11.5	2.7	15.4	1,725.3
Kyocera Corp.	12.5	2.7	11.1	15,886.5
Mabuchi Motor Co. Ltd	7.2	3.1	11.4	2,304.4
Makita Corp.	19.6	5.9	14.0	4,509.1
Mitsubishi Gas Chemical Co. Inc.	25.9	4.8	9.7	3,282.7
Mitsubishi Rayon Co. Ltd	10.9	5.0	11.5	1,829.5
Mitsumi Electric Co. Ltd	27.8	4.9	13.8	2,760.7
Murata Manufacturing Co. Ltd	11.4	3.3	12.4	10,883.0
NGK Spark Plug Co. Ltd	12.1	3.2	12.6	2,829.9
NHK Spring Co. Ltd	23.5	3.9	12.1	1,714.2
Nippon Electric Glass Co. Ltd	21.4	1.8	13.1	7,682.9
Nippon Steel Corp.	21.9	4.3	13.1	31,840.7
Nissan Chemical Industries Ltd	12.4	2.9	16.2	1,891.3
Nisshin Steel Co. Ltd	31.9	7.2	11.3	3,131.5
Nitto Denko Corp.	17.7	5.1	9.6	7,026.6
Nok Corp.	21.7	2.9	7.8	3,537.6
OKUMA Corp.	32.3	5.1	13.9	1,780.4
OMRON Corp.	14.5	3.1	14.7	4,542.4
Onward Holdings Co. Ltd	11.3	4.4	13.4	1,535.5
Ricoh Co. Ltd	16.8	3.8	8.5	11,832.8
Rohm Co. Ltd	6.9	3.2	9.1	6,774.3
Sekisui Chemical Co. Ltd	8.7	2.8	-185.0	3,174.6
Sharp Corp.	15.7	4.7	11.9	18,680.2
Shinko Electric Industries Co. Ltd	18.8	6.1	7.1	1,522.8
Showa Shell Sekiyu K.K.	16.6	5.1	12.6	4,175.2

(Continued)

Table 32.5   (*Continued*)

Company name	EY > (2*AAA)	DY >= 2/3 of AAA	Graham and Dodd PE	Market cap. (US$)
Sony Corp.	20.2	1.4	12.0	39,915.8
Stanley Electric Co. Ltd	14.6	2.7	15.3	4,363.0
Sumitomo Electric Industries Ltd	16.3	2.9	14.8	9,974.8
Sumitomo Metal Mining Co. Ltd	39.6	5.0	9.0	10,766.2
Suzuken Co. Ltd	11.5	2.5	13.3	3,776.1
Takeda Pharmaceutical Co. Ltd	9.4	3.8	16.2	42,142.9
TDK Corp.	20.1	4.7	9.3	7,610.7
THK Co. Ltd	15.6	4.0	10.0	2,212.6
Tokai Rika Co. Ltd	29.0	5.9	7.0	2,355.8
Tokyo Electron Ltd	24.3	5.1	12.9	10,865.0
Tokyo Steel Manufacturing Co. Ltd	8.6	2.6	12.2	2,018.3
Toppan Printing Co. Ltd	9.0	3.4	15.8	7,608.6
Toyoda Gosei Co. Ltd	20.7	4.0	11.3	4,858.7
Toyota Boshoku Corp.	32.0	5.1	9.4	5,588.2
Toyota Industries Corp.	14.0	3.3	16.0	11,052.3
Ushio Inc.	10.5	2.2	15.4	2,563.5
Yamaha Corp.	24.9	6.5	12.9	3,939.8
Yamaha Motor Co. Ltd	27.8	4.6	6.7	6,924.2
Yamato Kogyo Co. Ltd	26.1	2.5	9.9	2,898.3

Source: SG Global Strategy Research.

being passively active. As Kirby opined:

> I suspect the notion is not likely to be popular among investment managers, because, if widely adopted, it might radically change the structure of our industry and might substantially diminish the number of souls able to sustain opulent life-styles through the money management profession.
>
> The coffee can portfolio concept harkens back to the Old West, when people put their valuable possessions in a coffee can and kept it under the mattress. That coffee can involved no transactions costs, administrative costs, or any other costs. The success of the programme depended entirely on the wisdom and foresight used to select the objects to be placed in the coffee can to begin with ...
>
> What kind of results would good money managers produce without all that activity? The answer lies in another question. Are we traders, or are we really investors? Most good money managers are probably investors deep down inside. But quotrons and news services, and computers that churn out daily investment results make them act like traders. They start with sound research that identifies attractive companies in promising industries on a longer-term horizon. Then, they trade those stocks two or three times a year based on month-to-month news developments and rumours of all shapes and sizes.

This looks like a great time to start to fill up your coffee can.

As if all this wasn't enough, Mr Market is offering you the opportunity to protect yourself from the ravages of inflation in an exceptionally cheap way. With all of these opportunities available I have never been more bullish! Will I be early? Almost certainly yes, but if I can find assets with attractive returns and I have a long time horizon I would be mad to turn them down. As Jeremy Grantham said in his Q3 letter, 'If stocks are attractive and you don't buy and they run away, you don't just look like an idiot, you are an idiot.'

Table 32.6 MSCI Asia stocks passing 1, 3, 6 and G&D PE <16×

Company name	EY> (2*AAA)	DY>= 2/3 of AAA	Graham and Dodd PE	Market cap. (US$)
Acer Inc.	13.6	9.1	13.4	4,710.8
Advanced Semiconductor Engineering Inc.	22.7	17.1	10.6	5,248.9
Ambuja Cements Ltd	22.3	4.0	14.2	4,810.5
Aneka Tambang	59.8	23.9	8.5	4,524.6
Asia Cement Corp.	15.5	10.7	15.8	3,997.6
ASM Pacific Technology Ltd	16.3	14.0	11.2	2,872.5
ASUSTeK Computer Inc.	21.2	7.7	7.3	11,199.3
Bumi Resources	50.7	10.0	12.2	12,152.6
Cheung Kong (Holdings) Ltd	18.3	3.8	8.2	42,824.3
China Merchants Holdings (International) Co. Ltd	12.5	5.4	16.3	14,962.8
China Motor Corp.	15.6	4.7	2.7	1,043.6
China Shipping Development Co. Ltd	26.5	9.7	12.0	8,785.1
China Travel International Investment Hong Kong Ltd	12.1	6.5	11.3	3,753.5
Chinese Estates (Holdings) Ltd	72.1	7.2	4.7	4,176.7
CITIC Pacific Ltd	82.9	23.6	3.0	12,352.5
CNPC (Hong Kong) Ltd	12.2	5.2	11.4	3,099.9
Compal Electronics Inc.	22.5	15.2	6.6	4,179.4
Cosco Pacific Ltd	31.7	15.6	6.2	5,987.0
Daelim Industrial Co. Ltd	49.8	8.4	4.6	6,603.0
Denway Motors Ltd	18.9	7.0	9.0	4,829.9
Evergreen Marine Corp. (Taiwan) Ltd	21.9	10.6	10.2	2,769.5
Feng Hsin Iron & Steel Co. Ltd	16.0	10.8	11.5	961.5
Formosa Chemicals & Fibre Corp.	17.4	14.1	12.1	14,141.8
Formosa Plastics Corp.	16.4	13.1	13.9	16,071.8
Formosa Taffeta Co. Ltd	25.0	18.3	11.7	1,695.9
GAIL (India) Ltd	12.0	3.6	13.2	8,949.5
Globe Telecom Inc.	13.6	10.2	14.8	5,038.3
GS Engineering & Construction Corp.	17.5	3.7	11.8	8,255.2
Hang Lung Group Ltd	28.9	3.6	10.4	5,927.9
Hang Lung Properties Ltd	24.3	5.0	12.0	13,289.2
Hang Seng Bank Ltd	11.0	7.3	15.4	39,442.5
Henderson Land Development Co. Ltd	32.6	4.8	5.9	13,381.1
Hon Hai Precision Industry Co. Ltd	17.3	5.6	14.2	39,189.5
Hopewell Holdings Ltd	33.4	13.1	11.4	3,169.7
Hysan Development Co. Ltd	34.4	5.5	6.9	2,959.8
Hyundai Development Co.	20.2	3.9	12.2	7,311.5
Inventec Corp.	27.7	16.3	5.1	1,407.6
Jiangxi Copper Co. Ltd	37.0	7.9	8.3	7,418.5
Keppel Corp. Ltd	15.9	7.0	16.1	14,329.7
Kerry Properties Ltd	41.9	8.1	6.9	11,441.2
Kingboard Chemical Holdings Ltd	33.9	10.2	5.0	4,986.2
Korea Zinc Co. Ltd	47.3	4.0	7.0	2,444.9
Lite-On Technology Corp.	16.6	14.3	6.5	3,758.0
MiTAC International Corp.	39.3	14.1	5.0	1,408.2

(Continued)

Table 32.6   (*Continued*)

Company name	EY> (2*AAA)	DY>= 2/3 of AAA	Graham and Dodd PE	Market cap. (US$)
Nan Ya Plastics Corp.	19.4	16.8	11.1	20,219.6
Neptune Orient Lines Ltd	55.8	14.6	3.4	4,058.2
NWS Holdings Ltd	25.9	13.0	12.8	5,369.8
Oil & Natural Gas Corp. Ltd	14.3	4.9	13.2	52,286.1
Orient Overseas (International) Ltd	57.2	66.9	3.1	4,629.8
Pakistan State Oil Co. Ltd	30.6	8.8	8.7	1,049.9
POSCO	16.7	3.6	10.0	46,041.8
S-Oil Corp.	12.4	23.6	12.1	9,412.3
SembCorp Industries Ltd	14.6	7.4	13.4	7,194.7
Shanghai Industrial Holdings Ltd	15.0	6.1	9.8	4,670.1
Shun Tak Holdings Ltd	28.7	8.8	7.5	3,660.1
Singapore Airlines Ltd	16.7	9.9	9.0	13,410.8
Singapore Telecommunications Ltd	10.5	5.3	13.6	42,760.0
Sino Land Co. Ltd	29.9	7.4	7.7	9,697.5
SINOPEC Shanghai Petrochemical Co. Ltd	14.6	5.7	8.9	4,440.5
SK Telecom Co. Ltd	10.7	4.4	13.1	21,430.3
Steel Authority of India Ltd	31.4	6.3	11.5	19,008.6
Sun Hung Kai Properties Ltd	21.4	4.9	9.6	34,787.8
Swire Pacific Ltd	40.1	7.5	6.7	20,899.6
Synnex Technology International Corp.	11.1	6.9	14.4	2,707.9
Taiwan Semiconductor Manufacturing Co. Ltd	11.3	8.2	15.0	48,935.9
TECO Electric & Machinery Co. Ltd	17.7	12.1	11.6	940.8
Television Broadcasts Ltd	11.9	7.4	13.6	2,631.1
Tung Ho Steel Enterprise Corp.	22.0	14.5	12.8	1,559.7
U-Ming Marine Transport Corp.	29.1	23.5	10.1	2,344.5
United Microelectronics Corp.	14.7	10.6	5.3	7,773.9
UOL Group Ltd	52.1	8.2	6.5	2,502.2
Venture Corp. Ltd	25.8	13.6	6.1	2,441.2
Wharf (Holdings) Ltd	38.5	5.6	6.1	12,822.1
Yanzhou Coal Mining Co. Ltd	19.4	5.0	9.1	9,749.7
Yue Yuen Industrial (Holdings) Ltd	12.7	6.3	9.8	4,980.0
Yulon Motor Co. Ltd	16.8	4.7	4.6	1,405.7
Zhejiang Expressway Co. Ltd	16.6	9.2	13.3	6,949.8

Source: SG Global Strategy Research

33

Revulsion and Valuation*

We have long argued that the final stage of the de-bubbling process is revulsion. This phase is characterized by overwhelmingly cheap asset prices. Recent price moves in the UK and European stock markets have taken us to levels that have generally been associated with revulsion (i.e. 10×). Of course, cheap markets can always get cheaper, but for the long-term investor this may provide an excellent entry point. From a bottom-up viewpoint, the general cheapness of the market is confirmed. Of special note is the quality of stocks that are currently passing our deep value screens – names like Microsoft, BP, Novartis and Sony!

- The hallmark of revulsion is unambiguously cheap asset prices. The speed of the market's unravelling means that we are rapidly approaching the levels of valuation that are normally associated with revulsion. For instance, the UK and European markets are trading on 10× Graham and Dodd PEs (current price over 10-year moving average earnings).
- Of course, valuation isn't a binding constraint in the short term. Cheap stocks can always get cheaper, and more expensive stocks can always get more expensive. However, for long-term investors these are compelling valuations indeed.
- In the past I was often told that my favoured valuation measures were anachronistic, that they failed to capture growth, and were at best simplistic and at worst stupid. However, in recent weeks, investors have started to raise a different question. Rather than arguing that my use of 10-year average earnings ignores growth, they now argue that this measure has been inflated by good growth in recent years! Perhaps this switch in concern is the best sign of the times!
- Bottom-up valuations show a similar picture. Around 60–70% of stocks are trading on Graham and Dodd PEs of less than 16× ('the maximum price one should be willing to pay for an investment' according to Ben Graham).
- A more stringent approach favoured by Graham focused on stocks that pass three criteria – an earnings yield that is at least twice the AAA bond yield, a dividend yield that is at least two-thirds the AAA bond yield, and total debt that is less than two-thirds of tangible book value. I add an extra condition, which is that a stock must have a G&D PE of less than 16×. When running this test, I find fewer stocks passing the screen than passed in November last year, largely as a result of the dividend cuts. However, the quality of the names appearing is very high – stocks such as Microsoft, BP, Novartis, Sony and SK Telecom all appear. For those with a taste for the more adventurous, a truly deep value net-net screen reveals that Japanese small caps are just about the cheapest assets in the world.

- The slow deployment of cash into deep value opportunities remains my chosen path. The closer we move to revulsion, the more cash I will seek to deploy. The road to revulsion is unpleasant, but it ends in value investor nirvana.

I have long argued that the final stage of any de-bubbling process is revulsion. The key hallmark of revulsion is unambiguously cheap asset prices. Revulsion is also characterized by us being embarrassed to admit that we work in finance. On a personal note, we must surely be getting closer to revulsion on this basis. I was in the north of England a few weeks ago and took a cab. The driver asked me what I did for a living, and I had to wrack my brains for an answer that in those parts would be more socially acceptable than a banker – not easy since up there even paedophiles probably get a better press these days!

Indeed, the speed of the market's unravelling means that we are now rapidly approaching levels of valuation normally associated with revulsion. Figure 33.1 shows our perennial favourite among the valuation measures – the Graham and Dodd PE. This measures current price against a 10-year moving average of reported earnings.

We are currently trading on 13.6× this measure – the cheapest we have seen since 1986. The average since 1871 is 18×. So we are definitely on the cheap side of fair value. However, we are not yet at bargain basement levels. This tends to occur at around 10×. This represents an S&P 500 of around 500. In the depths of the great depression, we saw an all-time low in terms of valuation when you could have bought the S&P 500 for just 5× 10-year earnings.

As I have pointed out many times before, valuation isn't a binding constraint in the short term: cheap stocks can always get cheaper and expensive stocks can always get more expensive. However, it is the primary determinant of long-term returns.

To illustrate this point, Figure 33.2 shows the real returns achieved over the subsequent decade based around a purchase point defined in terms of the Graham and Dodd PE. We are currently in the third column from the left, which represents above-average (but not yet superb) returns that are likely to be achieved by a Rip Van Winkle investor who can buy and forget about them for the next 10 years.

One of the interesting comments that has appeared in my meetings with clients over recent weeks concerns the denominator in the Graham and Dodd PE. In the past, I have been told that my measure fails to capture growth, and that using a 10-year moving average of earnings is simplistic, even stupid. Such comments have disappeared over the last year. Instead they

Figure 33.1   US Graham and Dodd PE – S&P 500
Source: SG Global Strategy.

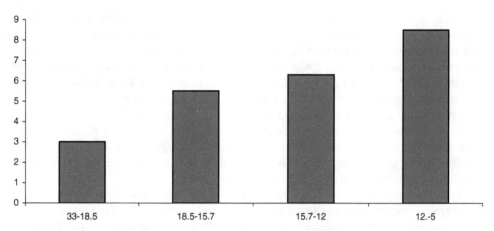

Figure 33.2 Real returns over the next decade by purchase G&D PE (% p.a.)
Source: SG Global Strategy.

have been replaced by investors suggesting that the 10-year moving average is too high! If ever there was a sign of the times, this must surely be it!

I would argue that the 10-year moving average is just fine. After all it contains the post-bubble destruction of earnings as well as the more recent boom (and bust). Figure 33.3 shows the 10-year moving average of reported earnings that is used as the denominator in the Graham and Dodd PE. I can find no discernible change in its growth over the most recent period. So I would submit that it is still a sensible method to use. Indeed those arguing that it is flawed are running the risk of committing the same mistake that I made in 2003, ignoring the models when you have built them to work!

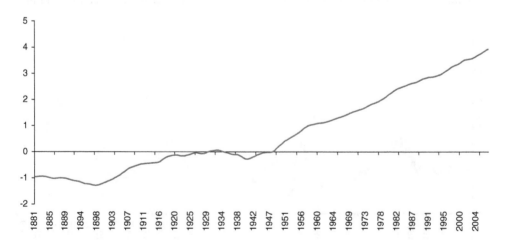

Figure 33.3 S&P 500 10-year moving average of reported earnings (log)
Source: SG Global Strategy.

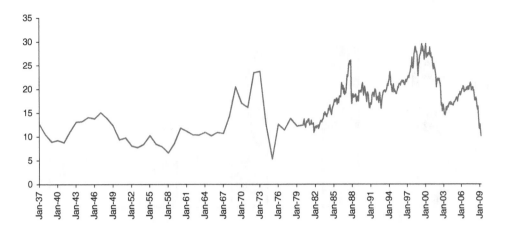

Figure 33.4   UK Graham and Dodd PE – the UK arrives in revulsion
Source: SG Global Strategy.

Of course, the USA isn't the only equity market in the world – and while the USA isn't yet in revulsion, the UK and Europe do appear to be there already. Figure 33.4 shows the Graham and Dodd PE for the UK; we are currently trading at 10× on this measure. This is the cheapest the UK market has been since the mid-1970s. Of course, in the mid-1970s the UK had a secondary banking crisis and had to go to the IMF and ask for a bailout (sounds kind of familiar doesn't it!).

The history for Europe is much shorter than that available in the USA or the UK. However, to give some idea of what the situation might have looked like, Figure 33.5 shows an artificial history pre-1982, calculated by applying the average discount on Europe post-1982 to the long-run US history. The data post the vertical black line is the real data for Europe.

Figure 33.5   European G&D PE with artificial histroy
Source: SG Global Strategy.

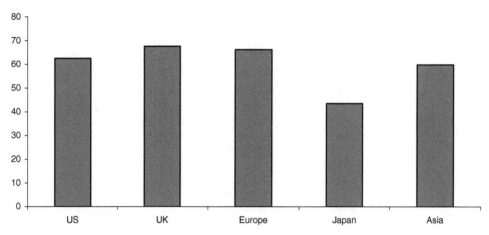

Figure 33.6 Percentage of stocks with G&D PEs < 16×
Source: SG Global Strategy.

Europe is currently trading on a G&D PE of 10×, the lowest valuation since 1982. Just like the UK, Europe has arrived in revulsion territory.

BOTTOM-UP PERSPECTIVE

As I have often said, top-down valuation can only get you so far. A bottom-up perspective can also add insights. There are, of course, myriad ways to think about bottom-up valuations, but as befits me I like a simple approach.

For instance, Figure 33.6 shows the percentage of stocks in each market that are currently trading on less than 16× Graham and Dodd PEs. Why 16×? Because that is the level that Graham described as 'the maximum one should be willing to pay for an investment'.

This generally confirms the top-down viewpoint. Most markets appear to have somewhere between 60–70% of stocks on Graham and Dodd PEs of less than 16×. So value investors should be in their element.

The problem of the disappearing dividends

A more stringent approach was recommended by Ben Graham shortly before his death. He argued that stocks should have an earnings yield at least twice the AAA bond yield, a dividend yield at least two-thirds the AAA bond yield, and total debt less than two-thirds of tangible book value. To this list I have added a constraint that it must have a G&D PE of less than 16×.

Table 33.1 shows the percentage of large cap stocks in each country/region passing these four criteria. Despite the fact that the markets are now below the levels seen in November 2008, the number of bottom-up opportunities is actually lower. The reason for this is all too obvious, dividends have been cut. So in past runs of the screen, stocks such as Pfizer and Nokia have appeared, and then proceeded to cut their dividend.

Table 33.1 Percentage of large cap stocks passing Graham criteria (ex Financials)

	Now	Nov-08
USA	2	4
Europe	6	9
UK	6	8
Asia	16	17
Japan	20	20

Source: SG Global Strategy

Quality and deep value

That said, the quality of the stocks that are passing the deep value screen is impressive. Normally when I run these screens I get a list of stocks I have never heard of (which doesn't stop me from buying them, of course). However, I am now seeing names that I actually know. For instance, Microsoft is appearing in the US screen, BP in the UK, Novartis in the European, Sony in Japanese, and SK Telecom in the Asian version (a full list of the stocks appears in Table 33.2 on the next page). This suggests that it is perfectly possible for investors to build diversified global portfolios of deep value stocks provided that they are prepared to shut their eyes for the next few years.

Small caps and net current assets

For those who are still worried about the use of earnings-based valuations, an alternative is to return to a balance sheet approach which Ben Graham would have approved.

In particular, Graham favoured net-nets. That is:

> The type of bargain issue that can be most readily identified is a common stock that sells for less than the company's net working assets alone, after deducting all prior obligations. This would mean that the buyer would pay nothing at all for the fixed assets – buildings, machinery, etc., or any goodwill items that might exist. Very few companies turn out to have an *ultimate* value less than the working capital alone, although scattered instances may be found. The surprising thing, rather, is that there have been so many enterprises obtainable which have been valued in the market on this bargain basis.
>
> It is clear that these issues were selling at a price well below the value of the enterprise as a private business. No proprietor or majority holder would think of selling what he owned at so ridiculously low a figure ... In various ways practically all these bargain issues turned out to be profitable and the average annual return proved much more remunerative than most other investments.

When Graham refers to net working capital, he means a company's current assets minus its total liabilities. Of course, Graham wasn't content with just buying firms trading on prices less than net current asset value. He required an even greater margin of safety. He would exhort the buying of stocks with prices of less than two-thirds of net current asset value (further increasing his margin of safety).

Table 33.2 Stocks passing the Graham criteria

Company name	EY> (2*AAA)	DY>2/3 of AAA	Mkt cap ($)	G&D PE	Country
Allegheny Technologies Inc.	31.9	4.0	1,916.9	8.6	United States
Analog Devices Inc.	9.7	4.2	5,428.5	16.0	United States
Carnival Corp.	16.0	8.8	16,403.5	8.3	United States
Cummins Inc.	20.6	3.0	4,188.5	11.8	United States
Illinois Tool Works Inc.	11.9	4.3	14,210.3	13.9	United States
Microsoft Corp.	11.8	3.0	143,582.6	14.7	United States
Robert Half International Inc.	11.2	3.0	2,326.4	14.9	United States
Rowan Cos. Inc.	34.2	3.6	1,368.5	7.2	United States
Texas Instruments Inc.	10.2	2.9	18,318.6	13.7	United States
Tiffany & Co.	13.9	3.8	2,344.0	11.0	United States
Acerinox S.A.	14.6	4.3	2,914.0	10.0	Spain
Bekaert S.A. N.V.	19.8	7.2	957.1	9.5	Belgium
BP PLC	15.1	8.0	117,959.7	10.4	United Kingdom
Charter International PLC	22.9	5.3	977.1	11.3	United Kingdom
Compagnie Financiere Richemont S.A.	14.1	3.9	15,845.1	10.7	Switzerland
Deutsche Lufthansa AG	30.4	15.1	5,040.3	9.1	Germany
ENI S.p.A.	17.3	9.3	79,816.0	7.6	Italy
Iberia Lineas Aereas de Espana S.A.	20.7	10.2	2,191.5	7.7	Spain
Kesko Oyj	11.5	6.2	2,082.1	11.3	Finland
Konecranes Oyj	22.6	7.2	956.7	14.3	Finland
Koninklijke Boskalis Westminster N.V.	17.6	8.8	1,640.2	13.9	Netherlands
MAN AG	27.6	6.6	5,967.4	9.1	Germany
Nexans	11.2	7.1	1,080.8	7.5	France
Nokian Renkaat Oyj	12.7	4.5	1,471.3	14.6	Finland
Novartis AG	9.8	5.0	82,096.0	12.9	Switzerland
OMV AG	24.2	5.3	7,826.3	7.2	Austria
Orkla ASA	21.3	5.8	5,927.6	8.3	Norway
Persimmon PLC	36.6	13.6	1,450.1	4.7	United Kingdom
Repsol YPF S.A.	22.4	8.6	18,744.9	6.9	Spain
Royal Dutch Shell Class A	18.9	7.3	133,757.1	7.0	Netherlands
Salzgitter AG	34.7	6.6	3,372.8	7.0	Germany
Skanska AB	12.0	8.5	2,883.6	9.1	Sweden
Societe BIC	9.7	3.7	2,376.0	15.3	France
StatoilHydro ASA	12.5	4.0	52,021.2	10.9	Norway
Sulzer AG	23.5	6.9	1,305.5	12.6	Switzerland
Swatch Group AG	15.1	3.5	6,372.8	12.3	Switzerland
Total S.A.	16.9	6.6	111,692.6	11.0	France
Vallourec S.A.	33.0	12.2	4,222.6	10.8	France
Wacker Chemie AG	17.7	6.2	3,116.5	10.5	Germany
AGA Rangemaster Group PLC	27.8	16.5	76.6	3.7	United Kingdom
Air Partner PLC	16.2	7.7	58.0	12.6	United Kingdom
Bovis Homes Group PLC	19.1	9.2	658.8	6.4	United Kingdom
BP PLC	15.1	8.0	117,959.7	10.4	United Kingdom
Braemar Shipping Services PLC	20.6	9.7	72.3	10.9	United Kingdom
Castings PLC	21.8	7.9	79.0	7.1	United Kingdom
Charter International PLC	22.9	5.3	977.1	11.3	United Kingdom
Computacenter PLC	17.6	7.6	282.6	4.8	United Kingdom
Diploma PLC	11.4	7.2	174.5	11.1	United Kingdom
Greggs PLC	10.0	4.1	537.7	16.0	United Kingdom

Table 33.2 *(Continued)*

Company name	EY> (2*AAA)	DY>2/3 of AAA	Mkt cap ($)	G&D PE	Country
Headlam Group PLC	18.2	11.3	238.7	11.6	United Kingdom
Hornby PLC	21.5	11.3	40.7	7.8	United Kingdom
Kier Group PLC	15.0	4.2	464.0	10.5	United Kingdom
Millennium & Copthorne Hotels PLC	11.6	3.4	792.7	7.6	United Kingdom
Persimmon PLC	36.6	13.6	1,450.1	4.7	United Kingdom
Renishaw PLC	15.9	8.5	314.8	9.1	United Kingdom
Royal Dutch Shell PLC (CL B)	17.5	6.8	127,661.0	8.8	United Kingdom
St Ives PLC	32.0	34.8	70.5	2.3	United Kingdom
T. Clarke PLC	11.6	9.7	72.4	7.6	United Kingdom
Ted Baker PLC	11.2	5.1	195.7	14.3	United Kingdom
Acer Inc.	12.0	8.0	3,495.2	15.2	Taiwan
Aneka Tambang	46.4	18.6	954.2	11.0	Indonesia
ASM Pacific Technology Ltd	11.7	9.0	1,122.7	10.6	Hong Kong
ASUSTeK Computer Inc.	21.4	7.8	4,048.4	7.5	Taiwan
Bumi Resources	51.3	10.1	1,245.6	12.4	Indonesia
Cheung Kong (Holdings) Ltd	19.4	4.0	19,062.2	7.8	Hong Kong
China Shipping Development Co. Ltd	22.8	8.3	1,314.0	15.5	China
China Travel International Investment Hong Kong Ltd	10.2	5.5	807.5	14.0	Hong Kong
Chinese Estates (Holdings) Ltd	41.1	4.1	2,346.1	8.4	Hong Kong
CITIC Pacific Ltd	63.4	18.1	3,811.6	4.1	Hong Kong
CNPC (Hong Kong) Ltd	10.6	4.5	1,511.1	13.4	Hong Kong
Compal Electronics Inc.	17.5	11.8	2,268.9	8.7	Taiwan
Cosco Corp. (Singapore) Ltd	19.0	9.9	1,040.2	14.2	Singapore
Cosco Pacific Ltd	26.7	13.2	1,649.4	7.7	Hong Kong
Denway Motors Ltd	13.3	4.9	2,258.1	13.7	Hong Kong
Evergreen Marine Corp. (Taiwan) Ltd	28.1	13.5	1,160.4	8.0	Taiwan
Feng Hsin Iron & Steel Co. Ltd	14.6	9.8	549.2	13.4	Taiwan
Formosa Chemicals & Fibre Corp.	25.6	20.8	5,550.9	8.4	Taiwan
Formosa Plastics Corp.	18.0	14.4	7,777.6	12.8	Taiwan
Formosa Taffeta Co. Ltd	28.1	20.5	775.5	10.6	Taiwan
GAIL (India) Ltd	11.1	3.4	3,308.1	14.3	India
Hang Lung Group Ltd	29.6	3.7	3,611.6	10.9	Hong Kong
Hang Lung Properties Ltd	22.0	4.6	8,003.8	14.1	Hong Kong
Hang Seng Bank Ltd	11.7	7.7	21,439.4	14.4	Hong Kong
Henderson Land Development Co. Ltd	30.0	4.4	7,249.8	6.6	Hong Kong
Hopewell Holdings Ltd	32.0	12.5	2,496.2	11.7	Hong Kong
Hysan Development Co. Ltd	33.2	5.3	1,594.3	7.0	Hong Kong
International Container Terminal Services Inc.	14.5	3.3	412.8	14.6	Philippines
Inventec Corp.	21.0	12.4	755.5	7.0	Taiwan
Jiangxi Copper Co. Ltd	25.0	5.3	1,086.6	13.5	China
Keppel Corp. Ltd	16.8	8.5	4,491.7	11.5	Singapore
Kerry Properties Ltd	36.4	7.0	2,715.3	8.7	Hong Kong
Kingboard Chemical Holdings Ltd	26.4	7.9	1,391.9	6.8	Hong Kong
Korea Electric Power Corp.	9.8	3.2	9,920.8	7.5	South Korea
Lite-On Technology Corp.	16.9	14.5	1,316.4	6.4	Taiwan
MiTAC International Corp.	31.3	11.2	560.2	6.5	Taiwan

(Continued)

Table 33.2   (*Continued*)

Company name	EY> (2*AAA)	DY>2/3 of AAA	Mkt cap ($)	G&D PE	Country
MTR Corp. Ltd	16.3	2.7	12,682.4	14.5	Hong Kong
Nan Ya Plastics Corp.	24.7	21.3	7,246.9	8.8	Taiwan
Oil & Natural Gas Corp. Ltd	14.3	4.9	28,444.9	13.4	India
Orient Overseas (International) Ltd	41.1	48.0	1,451.9	4.5	Hong Kong
POSCO	15.1	3.2	17,695.2	11.4	South Korea
PTT Exploration & Production PCL	15.2	5.8	8,153.8	15.2	Thailand
S-Oil Corp.	13.6	9.7	3,808.3	11.1	South Korea
SembCorp Industries Ltd	14.4	5.3	2,430.5	11.3	Singapore
Sesa Goa Ltd	44.5	5.1	1,223.9	10.2	India
Shanghai Industrial Holdings Ltd	11.0	4.4	2,472.8	13.4	Hong Kong
Singapore Airlines Ltd	16.9	10.1	7,774.6	8.9	Singapore
Singapore Press Holdings Ltd	10.6	10.6	2,794.0	10.4	Singapore
Singapore Telecommunications Ltd	9.9	5.0	25,277.6	14.7	Singapore
Sino Land Co. Ltd	27.3	6.8	3,778.6	8.8	Hong Kong
SINOPEC Shanghai Petrochemical Co. Ltd	13.5	5.3	799.1	10.2	China
SK Telecom Co. Ltd	12.5	5.2	9,808.8	11.3	South Korea
Steel Authority of India Ltd	26.0	5.2	6,040.2	14.5	India
Sun Hung Kai Properties Ltd	18.7	4.3	20,162.6	11.2	Hong Kong
Swire Pacific Ltd	36.4	6.8	9,348.0	7.4	Hong Kong
Taiwan Secom Co. Ltd	9.5	7.8	595.5	15.9	Taiwan
TECO Electric & Machinery Co. Ltd	15.7	10.8	521.6	13.5	Taiwan
Television Broadcasts Ltd	11.2	7.0	1,524.3	15.2	Hong Kong
Tung Ho Steel Enterprise Corp.	22.6	15.0	603.9	12.8	Taiwan
U-Ming Marine Transport Corp.	24.3	19.5	1,099.3	12.7	Taiwan
United Microelectronics Corp.	13.3	9.6	2,902.3	6.2	Taiwan
UOL Group Ltd	11.1	4.5	862.9	5.6	Singapore
Walsin Lihwa Corp.	9.9	5.8	493.9	6.1	Taiwan
Wharf (Holdings) Ltd	33.7	4.9	5,849.8	7.4	Hong Kong
Yanzhou Coal Mining Co. Ltd	15.8	4.1	1,389.6	11.8	China
Yue Yuen Industrial (Holdings) Ltd	14.8	6.0	3,086.1	10.6	Hong Kong
Yulon Motor Co. Ltd	14.9	4.2	653.5	5.3	Taiwan
Advantest Corp.	7.5	4.1	2,179.3	11.8	Japan
Aisin Seiki Co. Ltd	21.0	3.9	4,604.3	11.3	Japan
Ajinomoto Co. Inc.	6.5	2.5	4,811.6	16.3	Japan
Alps Electric Co. Ltd	9.4	7.7	506.9	5.4	Japan
Asahi Kasei Corp.	16.4	4.3	4,485.8	15.2	Japan
Brother Industries Ltd	15.9	3.6	1,865.4	12.0	Japan
Citizen Holdings Co. Ltd	11.0	4.7	1,343.9	12.2	Japan
Dai Nippon Printing Co. Ltd	8.4	4.5	5,966.8	13.6	Japan
Daihatsu Motor Co. Ltd	11.2	2.3	3,265.4	16.2	Japan
Daiichi Sankyo Co. Ltd	8.7	4.5	11,452.7	15.0	Japan
Dainippon Sumitomo Pharma Co. Ltd	8.6	2.4	3,304.6	15.7	Japan
Denki Kagaku Kogyo K.K.	9.0	6.6	821.7	9.4	Japan
Denso Corp.	16.4	2.9	16,856.5	12.7	Japan
Fuji Media Holdings Inc.	6.1	3.2	2,698.1	13.6	Japan
FUJIFILM Holdings Corp.	11.8	2.0	9,718.3	12.1	Japan
Hitachi Chemical Co. Ltd	15.1	3.2	2,088.0	11.9	Japan
Hitachi High-Technologies Corp.	17.0	2.6	1,701.9	11.9	Japan

Table 33.2   (*Continued*)

Company name	EY> (2*AAA)	DY>2/3 of AAA	Mkt cap ($)	G&D PE	Country
Ito En Ltd	6.7	3.1	1,157.6	13.3	Japan
Itochu Techno-Solutions Corp.	13.0	4.5	1,233.6	10.7	Japan
JTEKT Corp.	27.1	4.8	1,723.0	11.0	Japan
Kaneka Corp.	12.9	3.7	1,702.1	9.8	Japan
Konami Corp.	10.1	4.1	2,042.6	11.8	Japan
Kyocera Corp.	10.1	2.1	10,900.6	13.4	Japan
Mitsubishi Gas Chemical Co. Inc.	24.3	4.5	1,909.5	10.4	Japan
Mitsubishi Rayon Co. Ltd	13.9	6.4	1,096.5	9.5	Japan
Mitsumi Electric Co. Ltd	24.2	4.3	1,095.3	16.2	Japan
Murata Manufacturing Co. Ltd	9.5	2.7	8,214.8	14.8	Japan
NGK Spark Plug Co. Ltd	13.3	3.6	1,780.5	12.3	Japan
NHK Spring Co. Ltd	27.5	4.6	830.1	10.5	Japan
Nippon Steel Corp.	22.5	4.4	18,037.7	13.0	Japan
Nissan Chemical Industries Ltd	13.5	3.2	1,196.3	15.4	Japan
Nisshin Steel Co. Ltd	23.7	5.4	1,534.7	15.3	Japan
Nitto Denko Corp.	16.3	4.7	3,140.2	10.4	Japan
Nok Corp.	23.0	3.1	1,258.6	7.7	Japan
OMRON Corp.	16.3	3.5	2,548.2	13.3	Japan
Onward Holdings Co. Ltd	14.3	5.6	888.6	10.8	Japan
Panasonic Electric Works Co. Ltd	10.7	4.3	4,575.3	16.4	Japan
Ricoh Co. Ltd	13.9	3.1	8,318.2	10.5	Japan
Rohm Co. Ltd	6.1	2.8	5,705.2	9.9	Japan
Sharp Corp.	12.4	3.7	8,638.0	15.4	Japan
Shimamura Co. Ltd	11.2	2.3	1,884.8	16.3	Japan
Shinko Electric Industries Co. Ltd	9.7	3.1	1,247.5	14.6	Japan
Sony Corp.	21.2	1.4	17,011.7	11.6	Japan
Stanley Electric Co. Ltd	17.0	3.1	1,909.3	13.7	Japan
Sumitomo Electric Industries Ltd	15.5	2.7	6,222.9	15.8	Japan
Sumitomo Heavy Industries Ltd	28.4	4.0	1,617.4	14.3	Japan
Sumitomo Metal Mining Co. Ltd	26.0	3.3	5,846.1	14.1	Japan
Takeda Pharmaceutical Co. Ltd	10.9	4.4	33,021.6	13.9	Japan
TDK Corp.	17.8	4.2	4,302.4	10.3	Japan
THK Co. Ltd	12.6	3.3	1,545.2	12.9	Japan
Tokyo Steel Manufacturing Co. Ltd	7.2	2.2	1,531.8	14.9	Japan
Toppan Printing Co. Ltd	10.6	4.0	4,189.6	13.4	Japan
Toyoda Gosei Co. Ltd	19.0	3.7	1,771.4	12.9	Japan
Toyota Boshoku Corp.	22.5	3.6	1,817.7	13.3	Japan
Yamaha Corp.	25.6	6.7	1,534.1	12.5	Japan
Yamato Kogyo Co. Ltd	25.4	2.4	1,479.5	11.0	Japan
Yokogawa Electric Corp.	13.9	5.0	916.4	14.6	Japan

Source: SG Global Strategy

In today's market place, the vast majority of net-nets will tend to be small caps. Figure 33.7 shows the number of stocks that pass the net-net test over time. Currently I am finding the highest number of net-nets I have ever come across.

The geographical breakdown of the net-nets is revealing (Figure 33.8). Half of all the net-nets I can find are actually in Japan. This suggests that Japanese small caps may be one of the cheapest asset classes on earth!

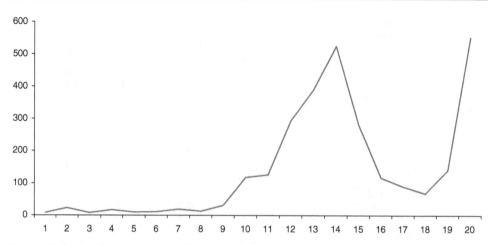

Figure 33.7   Number of stocks passing the net-net test over time
Source: SG Global Strategy.

CONCLUSIONS

The pursuit of value is one of the key tenets of my investment creed. From both a top-down and a bottom-up viewpoint I am being offered some truly incredible opportunities (especially outside of the USA). Top-down valuation shows that the UK and Europe are both at levels that could be considered reflective of revulsion.

From a bottom-up perspective, for those with long time horizons, buying a diversified deep value quality set of stocks hasn't been easier for years. For those with a thirst for adventure, Japanese small caps look exceptionally good value at the moment.

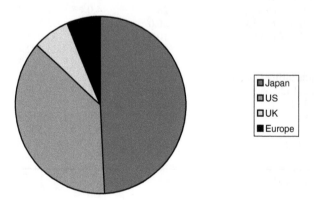

Figure 33.8   Geographical breakdown of the current net-nets
Source: SG Global Strategy.

34

Buy When it's Cheap – If Not Then, When?*

Is valuation alone enough of a reason to buy equities? To assess this I have looked at how a 'value' investor would have done by buying US equities when they traded on a 10× Graham and Dodd PE over history. The curse of value (selling too early in a boom, and buying too early in a bust) is demonstrated. Buying at 10× meant buying on average four months before the market bottomed, and suffering a subsequent 20% loss. However, one only had to wait for a year on average before the market returned to the level at which it was purchased. This strikes me as a small price to pay for admitting that I won't catch the exact bottom except by luck. So buy when it's cheap and be patient.

- Is valuation alone enough of a reason to buy equities? In the short term, valuation isn't a binding constraint. Cheap stocks can always get cheaper, and expensive stocks can always get more expensive. However, it is the primary determinant of long-term returns. Thus with the UK and European markets currently trading at revulsion level valuations of 10× Graham and Dodd PEs, there is a compelling investment case for a long-term investor.
- Even better news is that buying markets when they are cheap limits the downside for a patient investor. Historically, investors haven't *ever* lost money on a 10-year horizon when they purchased equities in the lowest quartile of valuations.
- However, as Keynes noted, long-term investment 'is so difficult today as to be scarcely practicable'. Today, the vast majority of investors seem to be obsessed with career risk. To gauge the scale of the career risk being faced, I examined how a hypothetical 'value' investor would have fared when buying the US market when it was cheap.
- I have often said that big bear markets result in G&D PEs of around 10×. So I had our hypothetical investor buy equities when the market reached that level. The results display the curse of the value manager (premature accumulation) – markets continued to decline by an average 20% after breaching the 10× level. However, this occurred fast: on average the buying occurred just four months before the market bottom. This seems to me to be a small price to pay for recognizing that I won't be able to call the bottom. In addition, you only had to wait 12 months before the market got back to the level at which you purchased.
- As a robustness check, we changed the benchmark from 10× to 13× (the upper bound for cheap markets). This exercise showed that similar patterns emerge. Investors bought too early (again witnessing an average 17% decline after they had bought), while the time to

---

market bottom was extended (unsurprisingly) to an average nine months. The time horizon for the market to recover to the purchase level was 17 months.

- We have to recognize that we simply won't catch the exact bottom, except via extreme good fortune. Valuation gives a good signal as to when to return to the markets. Buy when it's cheap – if not then, when?

I recently wrote that both the UK and European stock markets had finally reached levels of valuation characteristic of revulsion, and that such levels offered compelling opportunities for long-term investors. As usual I remain agnostic on the short-term outlook.

As I have stated many times before, cheap stocks can always get cheaper and expensive stocks can always get more expensive in the short term. However, valuations are the primary determinant of the long-term returns.

Figure 34.1 shows the probability of various real returns over a 10-year time horizon given the conditional valuation of the market. The *y* axis shows the level of real return, the *x* axis shows the probability of achieving that given level of return (or better).

Thus, when the market is in its cheapest quartile (based on Graham and Dodd PEs – a range of between 7 and 13×), there is a 52% probability of generating a 10% or higher return p.a. over the next decade. In contrast, there is only a 16% probability of generating a 10% or higher return p.a. if you buy the equity market when it is in the highest quartile in terms of valuation (a G&D PE range of 20–34×).

Figure 34.1 also highlights that buying the market when it is in the lowest valuation quartile offers significant downside protection for a long-term investor. Historically, investors have never lost money on a 10-year horizon when they have purchased in the lowest quartile of valuations. Sadly very few seem to care about the long-term anylonger. As Keynes opined, 'Investment based on genuine long-term expectation is so difficult today as to be scarcely practicable. He who attempts it must surely lead much more laborious days and run greater risks than he who tries to guess better than the crowd how the crowd will behave'.

The curse of the value investor is clear – we will be too early to sell in a boom, and too early to buy in a bust. But just how much career risk is likely to be entailed in buying when markets are cheap? In order to try to assess this I have looked back at what would have happened in the past if you had started to purchase equities at two different levels of valuation.

I have often said that big bear markets seem to end up with G&D PEs of around 10×. So I looked back over history to see what would happen if you bought US equities when they were trading on a G&D PE of 10×. Table 34.1 summarizes my findings. As per the curse of the value investor, the market is bought before it hits bottom – on average the market declined

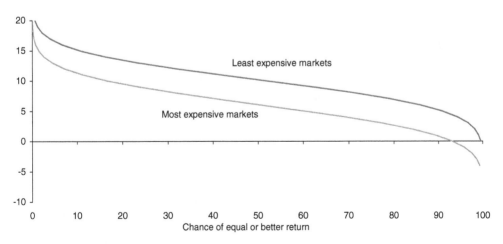

Figure 34.1 Probabilities of various real returns over 10 years (based on US data 1926–2008)
Source: SG Global Strategy.

Table 34.1   Buying at 10× G&D PE

Date of purchase	% decline from purchase to market trough	Months to market trough	Months before mkt return to purchase level
Sept. 1917	−16	3	18
Oct. 1931	−53	8	21
Mar. 1942	−4	1	3
Mar. 1982	−1	4	6
Average	**−19**	**4**	**12**

Source: SG Global Strategy.

a further 20% after we breached the 10× G&D PE. However, this drop was fast, occurring in an average four months! This doesn't seem overly premature to me. Of course, I would love to buy only at the very bottom, but I know that will never occur (except via the divine intervention of luck). In terms of just how patient an investor would have had to have been in order to see the market recover to the point at which they purchased, a mere year did the trick on average.

Of course, the astute reader will have noticed the small sample size of the above observations (just four). As an alternative I decided to see what would happen if you had purchased equities when they dropped to 13× (the upper limit for the cheapest quartile of market valuations). Once again the curse of the value manager appears, with the market continuing to decline an average 17% after the 13× limit is pierced (Table 34.2). Unsurprisingly, the time to the market trough tends to extend (an obvious function of using a higher PE) to an average nine months. I would argue that this is still not a disaster. How patient would one have to be? It took an average of 17 months for the market to return to the price level at which our hypothetical value investor bought.

Table 34.2   Buying at 13× G&D PE

Date of purchase	% decline from purchase to market trough	Months to market trough	Months before mkt return to purchase level
Apr. 1884	−16	10	20
Jan. 1907	−6	1	3
May 1913	−14	20	13
Jan. 1917	−29	11	28
Aug. 1931	−66	10	24
Nov. 1937	−12	5	50
Feb. 1941	−20	15	8
Feb. 1949	−5	5	23
Aug. 1974	−12	5	5
Jan. 1977	−5	6	6
May 1981	−17	13	17
Feb. 1984	−4	6	4
Average	**−17**	**9**	**17**

Source: SG Global Strategy.

As Seth Klarman has said,

While it is always tempting to try to time the market and wait for the bottom to be reached (as if it would be obvious when it arrived), such a strategy has proven over the years to be deeply flawed. Historically, little volume transacts at the bottom or on the way back up and competition from other buyers will be much greater when the markets settle down and the economy begins to recover. Moreover, the price recovery from a bottom can be very swift. Therefore, an investor should put money to work amidst the throes of a bear market, appreciating that things will likely get worse before they get better.

35

Roadmap to Inflation and Sources of Cheap Insurance[*]

As I have written previously, I am torn between deflation unleashed by a bursting credit bubble, and the inflationary pressures of the policy response. Irving Fisher was adamant that a debt-deflation spiral could be ended by inflation. Romer has argued 'devaluation followed by rapid monetary expansion' ended the depression. In the past, Bernanke provided a list of policy options which serve as signposts to the return of inflation (although his recent comments seem to be barking up the wrong tree). I've been trying to construct a set of cheap insurance policies which either pay out under both inflation or deflation, or provide inflation protection.

- Both Albert and I are relatively agnostic over the inflation/deflation debate. We can see merits in both sets of arguments. In face of this uncertainty, I decided to return to history and see what it has to say about the way out of a depression. Irving Fisher (infamous in finance for his erroneous predictions of a new era in 1929) studied the dynamics of debt-deflation. He argued that it was always possible to stop or prevent a depression simply by using inflation.
- Christina Romer (the head of the Council of Economic Advisers and expert on the 1930s) has argued that it was 'devaluation followed by rapid monetary expansion' that brought the great depression to an end. Her work provides empirical support for Fisher's views. In the past, Bernanke has set out a clear set of policy options which are available at the zero bound. However, his recent comments that 'recovery is not going to happen until the financial markets and the banks are stabilized' seem to fly in the face of the 1930s experience, where Romer notes, 'Strengthening the real economy improved the health of the financial system.'
- If the most politically acceptable way out of the current mess is inflation, then we need to think about ways of protecting ourselves from the financial implications of this eventuality. For some time, I have been suggesting a three-pronged strategy – cash as a hedge against deflation (and to deploy into opportunities), deep value opportunities (both fixed income and equity) and, finally, a set of cheap insurance policies.
- These cheap insurance policies either pay out regardless of the inflation/deflation outcome, or are hedges against the return of inflation. In the former category, we have US TIPS and Gold. TIPS imply only 1% p.a. inflation over the next 10 years, which seems low. In the event of deflation, I have my principal returned. Gold does well under a scenario of competitive devaluation (as the only hard currency left), and does well under deflation, as our financial system is likely to implode.

---

[*]This article appeared in Mind Matters on 19 March 2009. Copyright © 2009 by The Société Générale Group. All rights reserved. The material discussed was accurate at the time of publication.

- In the inflation protection category, we have dividend swaps, inflation swaps and selected European CDSs. The first two are cheap protection against the return of inflation (as indeed are the cheap equities in the deep value section of the portfolio). The third is a hedge against the break-up of the Eurozone brought on by the pressure of a fixed exchange rate in an economic slump (*à la* Gold Standard). If anyone were to contemplate leaving the Euro publicly, then the Spanish and Portuguese CDSs would explode.

As Albert and I regularly point out during meetings, we have never been more unsure on the inflation/deflation outlook. I have previously said I was torn between the deflationary impact of the bursting credit bubble, and the inflationary pressures of the policy response. When we read something by the deflationists we sit there nodding our heads in agreement, then we pick up something by the proponents of a return of inflation and we find ourselves agreeing with that as well. The respective sides seem deeply entrenched in their positions.

In contrast, we are trying to keep an open mind on the subject. Albert is biased towards a Japanese style outcome, and I am biased towards an inflationary outcome, but neither of us has any strong conviction.

FISHER AND THE DEBT-DEFLATION THEORY OF DEPRESSIONS

In the face of this uncertainty I decided to return to history and see what it has to say about the way out of a depression. My first point of call was Irving Fisher's 'The debt-deflation *Theory of Great Depressions*' published in 1933.[1] Fisher is probably most infamous to those in finance for his pronouncements of a new era of permanently high stock prices in 1929. But in the wake of his disastrous calls he turned to trying to understand the experience of the depression. Incidentally, he also invented the Rolodex.

In his debt-deflation theory, he posits 'two dominant factors' in driving depressions, 'Namely over-indebtedness to start with and deflation following soon after . . . . In short, the big bad actors are debt disturbances and price-level disturbances.' He continues,

> Deflation caused by the debt reacts on the debt. Each dollar of debt still unpaid becomes a bigger dollar, and if the over-indebtedness with which we started was great enough, the liquidation of debt cannot keep up with the fall of prices which it causes. In that case, the liquidation defeats itself. While it diminishes the number of dollars owed, it may not do so as fast as it increases the value of each dollar owed.

That is to say, debt-deflation spirals can easily become self-reinforcing.

The good news is that Fisher is also very clear on how to end a debt-deflation spiral:

> It is always economically possible to stop or prevent such a depression simply by reflating the price level up to the average level at which outstanding debts were contracted by existing debtors and assumed by existing creditors . . . I would emphasize . . . that great depressions are curable and preventable through reflation and stabilization.

The irony of Fisher's route out of deflation is that, probably only the Fed – after helping lead us into this mess[2] – can now get us out of it.

ROMER'S LESSONS FROM THE GREAT DEPRESSION

After reading Fisher's analysis of the 1930s, I came across a recent speech given by Christina Romer, who is now the head of the Council of Economic Advisers, and who made her name in

---

[1] Available from www.fraser.stlouisfed.org/docs/meltzer/fisdeb33.pdf. This is one of few articles published in Econometrica that I have ever read!

[2] See Bill Flecksenstein's excellent book *Greenspan's Bubbles* or John Taylor's insightful paper 'The Financial Crisis and the Policy Responses: An empirical analysis of what went wrong', available from www.stanford.edu?~johntayl/FCPR.pdf, or any of Albert Edwards' myriad of rants on Greenspan.

academic circles studying the events which ended the Great Depression. In the speech, Romer offers six lessons from the Great Depression for the current juncture.

Lesson 1: Small Fiscal Expansion has Only Small Effects

Romer wrote a paper in 1992 arguing that fiscal policy was not the key driver in the recovery from the Great Depression. Not because fiscal expansion is ineffectual per se, but rather because the fiscal stimulus that was conducted wasn't large. As Romer notes, 'When Roosevelt took office in 1933, real GDP was more than 30% below its normal trend level . . . The deficit rose by about one and a half percent of GDP in 1934.'

Lesson 2: Monetary Expansion can Help to Heal an Economy Even When Interest Rates are Near Zero

Romer notes that actually it was the Treasury rather than the Federal Reserve that drove the monetary expansion (a peculiarity of the system under the Gold Standard). In April 1933, Roosevelt suspended convertibility to gold on a temporary basis, and the dollar depreciated. When the USA returned to gold at the new higher price, gold flowed in, allowing the Treasury to issue gold certificates which were interchangeable with Federal Reserve notes. As Romer notes, 'The result was that the money supply, defined narrowly as currency and reserves, grew by nearly 17% per year between 1933 and 1936.' Romer argues that this 'Devaluation followed by rapid monetary expansion broke the deflationary spiral' – empirical evidence to support Fisher's hypothesis outlined above.

Lesson 3: Beware of Cutting Back on Stimulus too Soon

The monetary expansion seems to have produced remarkable results in terms of real growth: the US economy grew by 11% in 1934, 9% in 1935 and 13% in 1936 in real terms. This lulled the authorities into thinking that all was well with the system again. Hence, in 1937, the deficit was reduced by approximately 2.5% of GDP. Monetary policy was also tightened. As Romer notes, 'The Federal Reserve doubled the reserve requirement in three steps in 1936 and 1937.' She concludes, 'taking the wrong turn in 1937 effectively added two years to the depression.'

Lesson 4: Financial Recovery and Real Recovery Go Hand in Hand

Romer points out the inseparable nature of the real and financial recoveries. This meshes with our analysis that the banks aren't really the problem in a debt-deflation environment, rather they are a symptom of the problem. The current policy in the USA seems to be aimed at 'fixing the financial system', witness Bernanke's recent comments 'Recovery is not going to happen until the financial markets and the banks are stabilized'. This appears to be a misperception. As, Romer notes, 'Strengthening the real economy improved the health of the financial system. Bank profits moved from large and negative in 1933 to large and positive in 1935, and remained high through the end of the depression.'

Investors seem to be rather excited about banks posting profits at the moment. Frankly, if a bank didn't post a profit in this environment it should be shot out of kindness. The environment for profitability from banks has rarely been better, but that doesn't make them solvent. If you were starting a business today, then setting up a bank would be a very attractive option.

However, history – as represented by the balance sheet – cannot simply be ignored when it is inconvenient. As John Hussman noted,

> The excitement of investors last week about Citigroup posting an operating profit in the first two months of the year simply indicates that investors may not fully understand the term 'operating profit'. Citigroup could burst into flames while Vikram Pandit sells lemonade in the parking lot, and Citi would still post an operating profit. Operating profits exclude what happens on the balance sheet.

Lesson 5: Worldwide Expansionary Policy Shares the Burdens

Given the worldwide nature of the current slump, Romer makes an interesting point on the effectiveness of competitive devaluations, 'Going off the gold standard and increasing the domestic money supply was a key factor in generating recovery . . . across a wide range of countries in the 1930s . . . These actions worked to lower world [real] interest rates . . . rather than just to shift expansion from one country to another.'

This is something that Albert and I have been discussing of late. We have been pondering the possibility of competitive devaluation (obviously ultimately a zero sum game in terms of exchange rates) having enough of an impact on local monetary creation to increase inflationary expectations, thus helping countries to reflate. It appears as if Romer has sympathy with this view.

Lesson 6: The Great Depression did Eventually End

The final lesson that Romer offers may be of use to investors at the current juncture. She makes the point that the Great Depression did finally end. As Romer puts it

> Despite the devastating loss of wealth, chaos in our financial markets, and a loss of confidence so great that it nearly destroyed American's fundamental faith in capitalism, the economy came back. Indeed, the growth between 1933 and 1937 was the highest we have ever experienced outside of wartime. Had the U.S. not had the terrible policy-induced setback in 1937, we, like most other countries . . . would probably have been fully recovered before the outbreak of World War II:

This is a reminder that the current obsession with no scenario being too pessimistic is probably ill advised.

BERNANKE AND THE POLICY OPTIONS

The final source for signposts to watch comes from a speech given by Bernanke in 2000 to Japanese policy-makers. As I wrote in Chapter 32 in this speech Bernanke clearly acknowledged the greater threat that deflation poses in a highly leveraged economy, 'Zero inflation or mild deflation is potentially more dangerous in the modern environment than it was, say, in the classical gold standard era. The modern economy makes much heavier use of credit, especially longer-term credit, than the economies of the nineteenth century.'

Bernanke clearly believes that monetary policy is far from impotent at the zero interest rate bound. In essence his argument is an arbitrage based[3] one as follows:

> Money, unlike other forms of government debt, pays zero interest and has infinite maturity. The monetary authorities can issue as much money as they like. Hence, if the price level were truly independent of money issuance, then the monetary authorities could use the money they create to acquire indefinite quantities of goods and assets. This is manifestly impossible in equilibrium. Therefore money issuance must ultimately raise the price level, even if nominal interest rates are bounded at zero.

In the speech, he laid out a menu of policy options that are available to the monetary authorities at the zero bound. First, aggressive currency depreciation, as per Romer's analysis of the end of the Great Depression. Second on Bernanke's list is the introduction of an inflation target to help mould the public's expectations about the central bank's desire for inflation. He mentions the range of 3-4%!

Third on the list was money-financed transfers. Essentially tax cuts financed by printing money. Obviously this requires coordination between the monetary and fiscal authorities, but this should be less of an issue in the USA than it was in Japan. Finally, Bernanke argues that non-standard monetary policy should be deployed. Effectively, quantitative and qualitative easing. Bernanke has repeatedly mentioned the possibility of outright purchases of government bonds – as the UK is now doing.

This menu should provide us with a roadmap of policy options to watch for. If (and when) the deflationary pressure builds, we should expect to see more and more of these options wheeled out. Note that we aren't talking about trying to 'fix the system', to reflate the bubble (which would be the equivalent of giving crack cocaine to a heroin addict trying to deal with withdrawal). Rather, the suggestion from Fisher is that inflation erodes the real value of debt; it is the most painless way out of our current mess. Whether the authorities can create just a little inflation remains to be seen, as does their ability to actually create inflation in any way. Such imponderables are beyond my ken.

INVESTMENT IMPLICATIONS: CHEAP INSURANCE

Howard Marks recently suggested that today's investment decisions must focus on 'value, survivability and staying power'. These factors lie at the heart of the three-pronged approach that I have been suggesting since the end of October last year.

The first prong is cash. This is a legacy from the lack of opportunities that characterized markets in the last few years. But it is also a hedge against outright deflation. The second prong is deep value opportunities in both debt and equity markets. The third element is sources of cheap insurance. The idea behind this element of the portfolio is to prepare for a wide variety of outcomes by buying cheap insurance (which ideally, although not always, pays off in multiple states of the world). Of course, it should be noted that the purchase of cheap equities also contains an inflation hedge element.

---

[3] As Stephen Ross once said, to turn a parrot into a learned financial economist it needs to learn just one word: arbitrage. To my mind economists are far too happy to rely on arbitrage assumptions to rule out solutions. Indeed, the second chapter of my first book, *Behavioural Finance*, is spent detailing failures of arbitrage (both causes and consequences thereof, including the ketchup markets!).

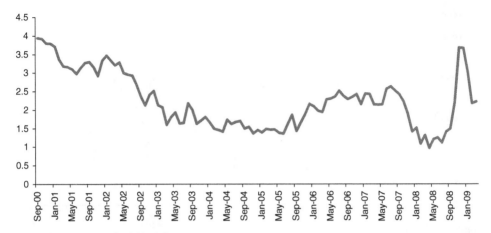

Figure 35.1   US TIPS yield (%)
Source: SG Global Strategy.

Inflation/deflation Insurance I: TIPS

The first and most obvious source of inflation/deflation protection when I first started thinking about this subject was US TIPS. These bonds have a deflation floor on the principal, so in the event of deflation I receive my cash back – representing a real rate of return equivalent to whatever the deflation rate is. In the event of inflation, I get whatever the yield is on the TIPS when I purchase them plus the inflation, of course (buying the new issue TIPS avoids the problem of accrued inflation).

When I started looking at TIPS, the yield was over 3.5% (Figure 35.1). This has dropped since then, resulting in the 10-year TIPS delivering a 9% return since the end of October. The 10-year TIP is currently yielding 2.1%, against the 10-year nominal bond yield of 3%. This implies that the market expects US inflation to be a mere 1% p.a. over the next decade – which strikes me as an exceptionally low rate.

Inflation/deflation Insurance II: Gold

The second inflation/deflation hedge I suggested in late October was gold. Now, gold concerns me for a variety of reasons, not least of which is that it has no intrinsic worth: I can't really value gold – beyond extraction cost.

However, it has some attractive features from an insurance point of view. Most obviously, in a world of competitive devaluations, gold is the one currency that can't be debased. Thus it provides a useful hedge against the return of this sort of beggar-thy-neighbour policy. In the event of significant prolonged deflation, what is left of our financial system is likely to collapse, thus holding a money substitute isn't such a bad idea against this cataclysmic outcome.

Of course, recently everyone has been talking about gold (not hugely surprising given that it is up some 30% since late October) – something that makes me nervous. However, gold is institutionally massively under-owned, so while it may have been moving up the list of attractive assets of individual investors (if the EFTs are anything to go by) and sensible hedge funds (such as Greenlight, Paulson, Third Point, Eton Park and Hayman), the mainstream institutional appetite for it has remained depressed (Figure 35.2).

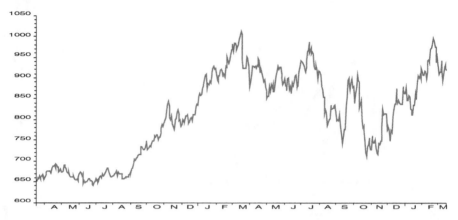

Figure 35.2   Gold ($)
Source: SG Global Strategy.

Inflation Insurance I: Dividend Swaps

As we noted in Chapter 30 the European and UK dividend swap markets are pricing in an outcome that implies greater dividend declines than witnessed in the USA during the Great Depression. The pricing then implies that essentially the dividends won't recover, pretty much forever. This strikes me as excessively pessimistic.

In addition, dividends have a relatively close relationship with inflation. Thus dividend swaps look like a deeply distressed asset fire sale, with the added advantage of offering inflation insurance if I buy the longer dated swaps (up around 7% from my original note in February). The most common rebuttal to my fondness for dividend swaps is counterparty risk. However, the European dividend swaps (Figure 35.3) have an exchange listed future, which obviously doesn't have any counterparty issues.

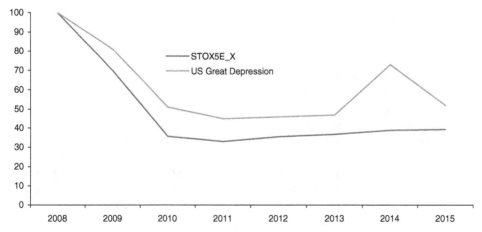

Figure 35.3   Dividend swaps (2008 = 100)
Source: SG Global Strategy.

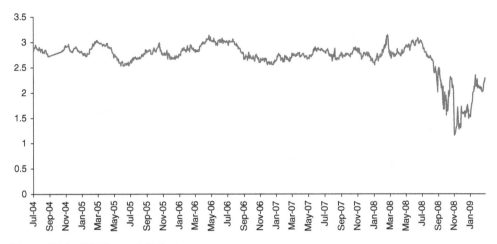

Figure 35.4 US 10-year inflation swap
Source: SG Global Strategy.

Inflation Insurance II: Inflation Swaps

The second of the pure inflation hedges comes via the inflation swap market. Figures 35.4 and 35.5 show the zero-coupon fixed rate necessary to build a swap against zero coupon CPI appreciation over 10 years. When I first looked at the US version in January the rate was mere 1.5%. Today it has risen, although not dramatically, to 2.3%.

However, the cheapest inflation swaps in the world seem to be Japanese swaps. They are available for −2.5%! Both the US and Japanese inflation swaps strike me as cheap ways of buying inflation insurance at the moment. Although counterparty risk is obviously a significant factor in these long-duration swap transactions.

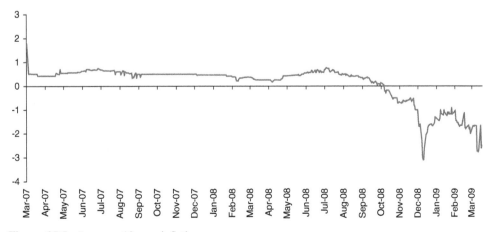

Figure 35.5 Japanese 10-year inflation swap
Source: SG Global Strategy.

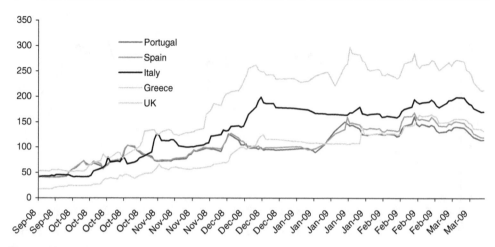

Figure 35.6 Five-year sovereign CDSs
Source: SG Global Strategy.

Eurozone Break-up Insurance: Spanish and Portuguese CDS

The final element of the insurance policy concerns the risk of a euro break-up. In a world of competitive devaluation, it isn't clear that the Eurozone will be able to stand the pressure. The one area of the world which has anything like the gold standard in place is the Eurozone. As Albert opines during our meetings with clients, this is less a function of economic realities and more a function of political expediency.

To protect against this risk (or even rising perceptions of this risk) the natural insurance is provided by the CDS market (Figure 35.6). If even one country was to publicly contemplate leaving the Eurozone then these CDS spreads would explode. I find it hard to believe that Portuguese and Spanish CDSs are below those of the UK – where we have the ability (and have used it) to print our own money.

36

Value Investors versus Hard-Core Bears: The Valuation Debate*

My recent bout of bullishness has revealed that our mailing list has two distinct constituencies. One group might be best described as value investors. The other group are probably best characterized as hard-core bears. The first group understand my desire to become more bullish as valuations drop. The second tend to argue that my valuation measures are overly generous. In particular, they are arguing that the 10-year earnings behind the Graham and Dodd PE are overstated. My examination of both the top-down and bottom-up viewpoints finds little support for this accusation.

- Go back a few years and I was regularly told that my Graham and Dodd PEs (G&D) were making the market look expensive because they used 10-year average earnings which didn't reflect high secular growth rates. I am now being told that my measures make the market look artificially cheap as the earnings for the last 10 years have been overstated. I suspect these swings tell us more about market psychology than about valuation.

- To test the hard-core bears case I decided to conduct a robustness check on the valuation measure that I favour. The simplest check is just to look at the earnings deviations from trend over the last 10 years. On our measure the average deviation from trend for the S&P 500 (with the trend estimated since 1950) is −1.4%. Effectively the last 10 years have seen both boom and bust, thus the G&D PE averages out the cyclical extremes just as it is meant to.

- A second simple method of checking the robustness of the G&D approach is to use longer moving averages for the calculation of earnings. The longer the moving average, the less weight the last 10 years will have, of course. Thus we constructed G&D PEs based on 20-year and 30-year moving averages of earnings. Comparing the current G&D PEs on these various measures to their long-run averages shows a tight range of outcomes. The most optimistic measure shows a 5% undervaluation, the most conservative shows 2% overvaluation. Effectively, they all show the US market to be around fair value.

- As a final check on the soundness of our valuation approach, I've had a look at normalized earnings from a bottom-up perspective. To do this, I took both the average and the median ROE over the last 10 years, and then multiplied them by current book value. Using the average ROE gives an EPS of around $50 for the S&P (exactly the same number as our top-down measures use); this uses a 1.2% ROE for financials! A median ROE approach gives a significantly higher number of $79 per share.

---

*This article appeared in Mind Matters on 28 April 2009. Copyright © 2009 by The Société Générale Group. All rights reserved. The material discussed was accurate at the time of publication.

- Of course, it is unlikely that the financials will earn the 19% ROE they have earned in the past. However, even if I halve this ROE going forward, and assume a further 25% contraction in book value, then I end up with an EPS of $67 for the S&P index. Even using the harsh assumption, that not only do we see this sort of decline in the financials, but that energy, materials, industrials, consumer discretionary, IT and telecoms all see a halving of their ROEs, then I still end up with $48 per share. I would argue that all these measures show that the G&D PE is a valid and robust measure of valuation.

My recent adventures into the land of bull, admittedly a strange place for a bear to end up, have revealed that Albert and I have two distinct constituencies on our mailing list. One group might be described as value investors. They can understand my desire to become bullish as valuations drop. The other group might be best characterized as hard-core bears. They have a much harder time with my valuation-inspired change of stance.

The latter group have been sending me emails saying that my valuation measures overstate the scale of normalized earnings and thus I am wrong to be bullish. This is a far cry from the years of meetings when I was regularly told in no uncertain terms that my Graham and Dodd valuation measures were far too harsh as they excluded growth. I have a sneaking suspicion that this itself may well tell us a fair amount about the current psychology of the market (Figure 36.1).

Inspired by this backlash I have been thinking up ways of testing to see if the Graham and Dodd PE measures that I prefer are unduly biased. The basic gist of the hard-core bears' arguments seems to be that earnings over the last 10 years have been enormously inflated by the use of leverage (especially in the realm of financials).

I have strong sympathies with this view. After all I have repeatedly used charts such as Figure 36.2 to show that earnings were at extraordinarily high cyclical extremes in 2007. However, if one looks over the last 10 years, the average deviation from trend is actually minus 1.4%. That is to say, the last 10 years have seen both boom and bust, thus the Graham and Dodd PE averages out the cyclical extremes, i.e. tech bust and current bust offsetting the exceptional highs of the credit bubble.

A TOP-DOWN CHECK ON ROBUSTNESS

When Graham and Dodd wrote *Security Analysis* in 1934 they were in a very similar situation. Indeed their rationale for using 'five, seven or preferably ten years' of earnings to calculate the PE was driven by a desire to avoid being swept up in the business cycle.

We can use similar logic to see if the valuation picture changes dramatically as we alter the length of the moving average we use to construct the Graham and Dodd PE. If the picture

Figure 36.1 Graham and Dodd PE for the S&P 500 – robust or rubbish?
Source: SG Global Strategy.

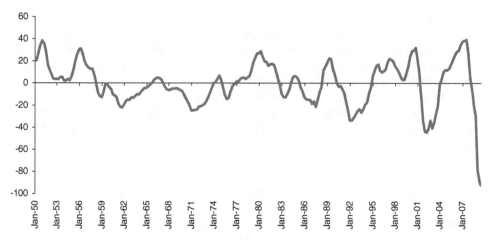

Figure 36.2 US S&P 500 earnings deviations from trend
Source: SG Global Strategy.

changes massively, then this is a good hint that our most recent 10-year period of earnings is particularly unusual. Figure 36.3 shows the G&D PE based upon our standard 10-year average earnings, but supplemented by two further measures based on 20-year average earnings and 30-year average earnings.

As even a cursory glance at the chart reveals, there is very little difference between the various measures (Table 36.1). This strongly suggests that average 10-year earnings are not significantly over-inflated, as the hard-core bears suggest.

NORMALIZED EARNINGS: A BOTTOM-UP VIEW

As is often the case I find that a bottom-up perspective can be exceedingly useful in clarifying issues, so I decided to investigate the topic of normalized earnings from this viewpoint. I

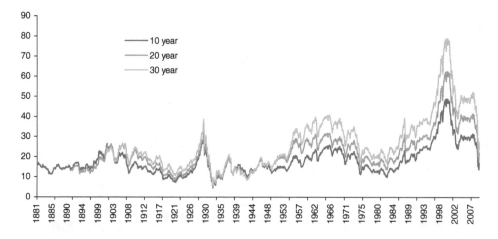

Figure 36.3 Various extended Graham and Dodd PEs for the S&P 500
Source: SG Global Strategy.

Table 36.1   Various Graham and Dodd PEs for the S&P 500

	Average	Current
10 year	18.0	17.0
20 year	22.0	22.1
30 year	27.0	27.6

Source: SG Global Strategy.

calculated both average and median ROEs for each company in the S&P 500 over the last 10 years. Table 36.2 shows the ROEs we found aggregated at sector level.

To convert these to earnings I multiplied them by the current book value. Table 36.3 shows the results of this exercise. Using the average ROE over the last 10 years (combined with current book value) reveals that bottom-up normalized earnings per share for the S&P 500 is around $50 (exactly the same number we get from using a 10-year average of market level EPS). It is noteworthy that the financials have a very low average ROE of just 1.2% (thanks to the recent implosion).

However, the average may not give us the best estimate of normality as it is easily skewed by a couple of extreme observations. Thus, I also used the median ROE over the last 10 years. Using this method reveals a higher bottom-up normalized earnings number of $79 per share.

Of course, this is based on the median ROE and current book value which may be poor assumptions, as the hard-core bears point out. It seems highly unlikely that financials will earn anything like the nearly 19% ROE they have earned over the past decade. In addition the use of current book values may overstate the case. As I have regularly pointed out, book values can also be very misleading. As Figure 36.4 shows, during the great depression the book value of financials effectively halved.

So far during this crisis, financials book values are down around 25%. To show the impact of the financials upon our normalized bottom earnings I shrunk their book values a further 25% from current levels, and halved their median ROE to just over 9%. This leads to a drop in our EPS figure from $79 to $67 (still well above the $50 we use in our top-down measure).

Table 36.2   Average and median ROEs over the last 10 years for S&P 500

	Median ROE	Average ROE
Energy	16.5	18.1
Materials	14.1	10.8
Industrials	24.7	28.2
Consumer discretionary	18.7	5.7
Consumer staples	30.4	188.7
Health care	18.7	19.9
Financials	18.2	1.2
IT	43.2	67.2
Telecos	22.4	−4.8
Utilities	11.9	12.0

Source: SG Global Strategy.

Table 36.3   Estimates of bottom-up normalized earnings

Sector	Using average EPS	Using Median EPS
Energy	11.9	13.1
Materials	1.2	1.7
Industrials	6.9	7.1
Consumer discretionary	10.4	4.6
Consumer staples	4.9	9.1
Health care	9.0	10.0
Financials	−10.2	18.6
IT	10.6	9.1
Telecos	2.2	2.6
Utilities	3.2	3.1
Market EPS	50.1	79.0

Source: SG Global Strategy.

Picking on the financials alone is unfair. So as a stress test (a much overused term of late) I decided (somewhat arbitrarily I admit) to halve the median ROEs of the energy, material, industrial, consumer discretionary, IT, and telecommunications sectors (although I left the current book value alone, unlike the financials). These sectors were chosen as they seemed to be particularly exposed to a deleveraging US consumer and a slowing economy in general.

Table 36.4 shows the impact of this scenario. The normalized bottom-up EPS comes out at $50 – coincidentally the same number that we use for the top-down measure.

CONCLUSIONS

Despite the worries expressed by the hard-core bears, I can find little evidence from either a top-down or bottom-up perspective that shows earnings over the last 10 years to be seriously inflated.

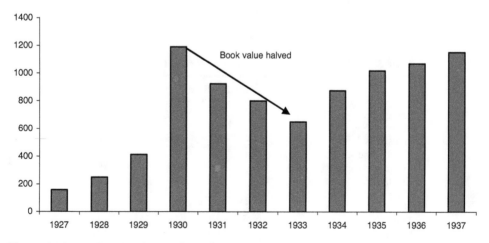

Figure 36.4   US financials: book value during the great depression
Source: SG Global Strategy.

Table 36.4 Our harsh scenario for bottom-up normalized EPS

Sector	EPS
Energy	6.6
Materials	0.8
Industrials	3.6
Consumer discretionary	2.3
Consumer staples	9.1
Health Care	10.0
Financials	7.0
IT	4.6
Telecos	1.3
Utilities	3.1
Market EPS	48.2

Source: SG Global Strategy.

One of the painful lessons I learned in 2003 was that it is a very bad idea to think you know more than your models do. I fear those who are arguing that measures like Graham and Dodd PEs are invalid may be in danger of falling into exactly this pitfall. I will continue to use this approach, and will allow it to dictate the degree of bullishness that I express.

References

Alloy, L.B. and Abramson, L.Y. (1979) Judgement of Contingency in depressed and non-depressed students: Sadder but Wiser? *Journal of Experimental Psychology*, 108(4), 441–485.

Anginer, D., Fisher, K.L. and Statman, M. (2007) Stocks of admired companies and despised ones. Available from www.ssrn.com.

Ariely, D. and Loewenstein, G. (2006) The heat of the moment: The effect of sexual arousal on sexual decision making, *Journal of Behavioral Decision Making*, 19, 87–98.

Ariely, D. and Wertenbroch, K. (2002) Procrastination, deadlines and performance: Self control by precommitment, *Psychological Science*, 13(3), 219–224.

Arkes, H.R. and Blumer, C. (1985) The Psychology of Sunk Costs, *Organizational Behavior and Human Decision Processes*, 35(1), 124–140.

Babiak, P. and Hare, R. (2006) *Snakes in Suits: When Psychopaths go to Work*. Collins.

Bar Eli, M., Azar, O.H., Ritov, I., Keidar-Levin, Y. and Schein, G. (2007) Action bias among elite soccer goalkeepers: The case of penalty kicks, *Journal of Economic Psychology*, 28(5), 606–621.

Baron, J. and Hershey, J.C. (1988) Outcome bias in decision evaluation, *Journal of Personality and Social Psychology*, 54, 569–579.

Baumeister, R.F. (2003) The psychology of irrationality: Why people make foolish, self-defeating choices. In Brocas, I. and Carrillo, J.D. (eds) *The Psychology of Economic Decisions, Volume 1: Rationality and Well-Being*. Oxford University Press.

Bernstein, W.J. and Arnott, R.D. (2003) Earnings Growth: The Two Percent Dilution, *Financial Analysts Journal*, 59(5), 47–55.

Bird, R.G. and Casavecchia, L. (2005) Value enhancement using momentum indicators: The European experience, *International Journal of Managerial Finance*, 3(3), 229–262.

Board, B.J. and Fritzon, K. (2005) Disordered personalities at work, *Psychology, Crime and Law*, 11(1), 17–32.

Bridgewater Daily Observations (2009) The performance of individual stocks during the Great Depression, 12 February.

Bulkley, G., Harris, D.F. and Herrerias, R. (2004) Stock returns following profit warnings: A test of models of behavioural finance.

Carroll, L. (1865) Alice's Adventures in Wonderland. Macmillan.

Carroll, P.B. and Mui, C. (2008) *Billion Dollar Lessons: What You Can Learn from the Most Inexcusable Business Failures of the Last 25 Years*. Portfolio.

Chan, L.K.C., Dimmock, S.G. and Lakonishok, J. (2006) Benchmarking money manager performance: Issues and evidence. NBER working paper 12461.

Chan, L.K.C., Karceski, J.J. and Lakonishok, J. (2003) The level and persistence of growth rates. *Journal of Finance*, 58(2), 643–684.

Christofferson, S.A., McNish, R.S. and Sias, D.L. (2004) Where mergers go wrong, McKinsey on Finance (Winter).

Clarke, R., de Silva, H. and Thorley, S. (2006) Minimum variance portfolios in the US equity market, *Portfolio Management*, Fall.

Cleese, J. and Chapman, G., Dead Parrot Sketch, Monty Python's Flying Circus.

Cohen, R.B., Polk, C.K. and Silli, B. (2009) Best Ideas (March 18, 2009).

Cooper, M.J. and Gubellini, S. (2007) The critical role of conditioning information in determining if value is really riskier than growth. Available from www.ssrn.com.

Cooper, M.J., Gulen, H. and Schill, M.J. (2006) What best explains the cross-section of stock returns? Exploring the asset growth effect. Available from www.ssrm.com.

Cusatis, P. and Woolridge, J.R. (2008) The accuracy of analysts' long-term earnings per share growth rate forecasts, Penn State University working paper.

Dasgupta, A., Prat, A. and Verardo, M. (2006) The Price of Conformism. EFA 2006 Zurich Meetings.

Dawson, E., Gilovich, T. and Regan, D.T. (2002) Motivated reasoning and performance on the Wason selection task, *Personality and Social Psychology Bulletin*, 28(10), 1379–1387.

De Langhe, B., Sweldens, S., Van Osselaer, S.M.J. and Tuk, M.A. (2008) The emotional information processing system is risk-averse: Ego-depletion and investment behaviour. Available from www.ssrn.com.

Dijksterhuis, A., Bos, M.W., Nordgren, L.F. and van Baaren, R.B. (2006) On making the right choice: The deliberation without attention effect, *Science*, 311(5763), 1005–1007.

Dinkelman, T., Levinsohn, J.A. and Majelantle, R.G. (2006) When knowledge is not enough: HIV/AIDS information and risky behaviour in Botswana. NBER working paper.

Ditto, P.H. and Lopez, D.F. (1992) Motivated Skepticism: Use of differential decision criteria for preferred and non-preferred conclusions, *Journal of Personality and Social Psychology*, 63, 568–584.

Einhorn, D. (2008) Private Profits and Socialized Risk, Speech at Grant's Spring Investment Conference.

Eisenberger, N.I. and Lieberman, M.D. (2004) Why rejection hurts: a common neural alarm system for physical and social pain, *Trends in Cognitive Sciences*, 8(7), 294–300.

Evans, J.ST.B.T., Barston, J.L. and Pollard, P. (1983) On the conflict between logic and belief in syllogistic reasoning, *Memory and Cognition*, 11(3), 295–306.

Fama, E.F. and French, K.R. (2000) Forecasting Profitability and Earnings, *The Journal of Business*, 73(2), 161–175.

Fama, E.F. and French, K.R. (2004) The capital asset pricing model: Theory and evidence. Available from www.ssrn.com.

Fama, E.F. and French, K.R. (2007) Migration, *Financial Analysts Journal*, 63(3), 48–58.

Fernandez, P. (2004) Are calculated betas worth for anything? Available from www.ssrn.com.

Forsythe, G. (2007) Don't overpay today for growth tomorrow, *Schwab Investing Insights*, March.

Garner, R., Gillingham, M.G. and White, C.S. (1989) Effects of 'seductive details' on macroprocessing and microprocessing in adults and children, *Cognition and Instruction*, 6, 41–57.

Goyal, A. and Wahal, S. (2005) The selection and termination of investment management firms by plan sponsors, *Journal of Finance*, 63(4), 1805–1847.

Graham, B. and Dodd, D.L. (1934) *Security Analysis*. McGraw-Hill.

Graham, B. and Dodd, D.L. (2008) *Security Analysis*, 6th edition. McGraw-Hill.

Grantham, J.R. (2006) Oh Brave New World I, October.

Green, L. and Mehr, D.R. (1997) What alters physicians' decisions to admit to the coronary care unit? *Journal of Family Practice*, 45(3), 209–210.

Green, L.A. and Yates, J.F. (1995) Influence of pseudodiagnostic information on the evaluation of ischemic heart disease, *Annual of Emergency Medicine*, 25, 451–457.

Greenwald, B. and Kahn, J. (2005) *Competition Demystified: A Radically Simplified Approach to Business Strategy*. Portfolio.

Greenwald, B.C.N., Kahn, J., Sonkin, P.D. and van Biema, M. (2004) *Value Investing: From Graham to Buffett and Beyond*. John Wiley & Sons, Inc.

Groysberg, B., Healy, P.M., Chapman, C.J., Shanthikumar, D.M. and Gui, Y. (2007) Do buy-side analysts out-perform the sell-side? HBS working paper. Available from www.ssrn.com.

Hales, J. (2007) Directional preferences, information processing, and investors' forecasts of earnings, *Journal of Accounting Research*, 45(3), 607–628.

Haughen, R.A. (1999) *The New Finance: The Case Against Efficient Markets, 2E*. Prentice Hall.

Hirshleifer, D. (2001) Investor psychology and asset pricing, *Journal of Finance*, 56(4), 1533–1597.

Homer, S. and Sylla, R.E. (1996) *A History of Interest Rates*. Rutgers University Press.

Hsieh, J. and Walkling, R.A. (2006) The history and performance of concept stocks, *Journal of Banking and Finance*, 30(9), 2433–2469.

Hsu, J.C. and Campollo, C. (2006) New frontiers in index investing: An examination of fundamental indexation. Available from www.researchaffiliates.com.

Huettel, S.A., Mack, P.B. and McCarthy, G. (2002) Perceiving patterns in random series: Dynamic processing of sequence in prefrontal cortex, *Nature neuroscience*, 5(5), 485–490.

Jacobs, B. (2009) Tumbling tower of Babel: Subprime securitization and the credit crisis, *Financial Analysts Journal*, 65(2), available from http://www.cfapubs.org/doi/pdf/10.2469/faj.v65.n2.6

Kirby, R. (1976) You need more than numbers to measure performance. In Ellis, C. and Vertin, J. (eds) *An Investor's Anthology: Original Ideas from the Industry's Greatest Minds*. John Wiley & Sons, Inc.

Kirby, R.G. (1984) The Coffee Can Portfolio, *The Journal of Portfolio Management*, 11(1).

Klarman, S.A. (1991) *Margin of Safety: Risk-Averse Value Investing Strategies for the Thoughtful Investor*. HarperCollins.

Knutson, B. and Peterson, R. (2005) Neurally reconstructing expected utility, *Games and Economic Behavior*, 52, 305–315.

Lamont, O. (2003) Go down fighting: Short sellers vs firms, available from http://www.haas.berkeley.edu/groups/finance/lamontpaper.pdf.

LaPorta, R. (1996) Expectations and the cross-section of stock returns, *Journal of Finance*, 51(5), 1715–1742.

Lei, V., Noussair, C. and Plott, C.R. (2001) Nonspeculative bubbles in experimental asset markets: Lack of common knowledge of rationality vs. actual irrationality, *Econometrica*, 69(4), 831–859.

Lench, H.C. and Ditto, P.H. (2008) Automatic optimism: Biased use of base rate information for positive and negative events. *Journal of Experimental Social Psychology*, 44, 631–639.

Lerner, J.S. and Tetlock, P.E. (1999) Accounting for the effects of accountability. *Psychological Bulletin*, 125(2), 255–275.

Lewellen, J. (2009) Institutional investors and the limits of arbitrage. Unpublished paper.

Loeb, G.M. (1996) *The Battle for Investment Survival*. John Wiley & Sons, Inc.

Markowitz, H. (2005) Market efficiency: A theoretical distinction and so what? *Financial Analysts Journal*, 61(5) 17–30.

McCabe, D.P. and Castel, A.D. (2008) Seeing is believing: The effect of brain images on judgements of scientific reasoning, *Cognition*, 107, 343–352.

McClure, S.M., Laibson, D.I., Loewenstein, G. and Cohen, J.D. (2004) Separate neural systems value immediate and delayed monetary targets, *Science*, 306, 503–507.

Miller, G.A. (1956) The magical number seven, plus or minus two: Some limits on our capacity for processing information, *Psychological Review*, 63(2), 81–97.

Minahan, J. (2009) Investment Belief Systems: A Consultant's Perspective. In Wagner, W.H. and Rieves, R.A. (eds) *Investment Management*. John Wiley & Sons, Inc.

Montier, J. (2002) *Behavioural Finance: Insights in Irrational Minds and Markets*. John Wiley & Sons Ltd.

Montier, J. (2007) *Behavioural Investing: A Practitioner's Guide to Applying Behavioural Finance*. John Wiley & Sons Ltd.

Moore, D.A. (2002) Auditor independence, conflict of interest and unconscious intrusion of bias. Unpublished paper.

Morgan, A., Nail, L.A. and Megginson, W.L. (2002) The determinants of positive long-term performance in strategic mergers: Corporate focus and cash. Available from www.ssrn.com.

Oppenheimer, H.R. (1986) Ben Graham's Net Current Asset Values: A Performance Update. *Financial Analysts Journal*, 42(6), 40–47.

Petkova, R. and Zhang, L. (2005) Is value riskier than growth? *Journal of Financial Economics*, 78, 187–202.

Piotroski, J.D. (2000) Value investing: The use of historical financial information to separate winners from losers, *Journal of Accounting Research*, 38, 1–41.

Piotroski, J.D. (2004) Further evidence on the relation between historical changes in financial conditions, future returns and the value/glamour effect. Unpublished working paper.

Plassmann, H., O'Doherty, J., Shiv, B. and Rangel, A. (2008) Marketing actions can modulate neural representations of experienced pleasantness, *The Proceedings of the National Academy of Sciences*.

Posen, A. (2009) A proven framework to end the US Banking CrisisTestimony before the SEC of US Congress.

Pronin, E., Wegner, D.M., McCarthy, K. and Rodriguez, S. (2006) Everyday magical powers: The role of apparent mental causation in the overestimation of personal influence, *Journal of Personality and Social Psychology*, 91(2), 218–231.

Reyna, V.F. and Lloyd, F. (2006) Physician decision making and cardiac risk: Effects of knowledge, risk perception, risk tolerance, and fuzzy processing, *Journal of Experimental Psychology: Applied*, 12, 179–195.

Romer, C. (1992) What ended the Great Depression?, *The Journal of Economic History*, 52(4), 757–784.

Schill, M. (2005) The thoughtful forecaster. Available from www.ssrn.com.

Scott, J., Stumpp, M. and Xu, P. (1999) Behavioral bias, valuation and active management, *Financial Analysts Journal*, 55(4), 49–57.

Sharot, T., Riccardi, A.M., Raio, C.M. and Phelps, E.A. (2007) Neural mechanisms mediating optimism bias, *Nature*, 450(7166), 102–105.

Shiv, B., Carmon, Z. and Ariely, D. (2005) Placebo effects of marketing actions: Consumers may get what they pay for, *Journal of Marketing Research*, 42, 383–393.

Shiv, B., Loewenstein, G., Bechara, A., Damasio, H. and Damasio, A. (2005) Investment Behavior and the negative side of emotion, *Psychological Science*, 16(June), 435–439.

Simonson, I. and Straw, B.M. (1992) De-escalation strategies: A comparison of techniques for reducing commitment to losing courses of action, *Journal of Applied Psychology*, 77, 419–426.

Slovic, P. (1973) Behavioural problems of adhering to a decision policy. Unpublished paper available from http://www.decisionresearch.org/people/slovic/.

Speidell, L., Stein, G., Owsley, K. and Kreuter, I. (2005) Dilution is a drag... The impact of financings in emerging markets, *The Journal of Investing*, 14(4).

Statman, M., Fisher, K.L. and Anginer, D. (2008) Affect in a behavioural asset pricing model. Available from www.ssrn.com.

Stickel, S.E. (2007) Analysts incentives and the financial characteristics of Wall Street darlings and dogs, *Journal of Investing*, 16(3).

Taylor, S.E. and Brown, J.D. (1988) Illusion and well-being: A social psychological perspective on mental health, *Psychological Bulletin*, 103(2), 193–210.

Taylor, S, and Butcher, M. (2007) Extra-legal defendant characteristics and mock juror ethnicity re-examined, *Proceedings of the BPS*.

Tsai, C.I., Kalyman, J. and Hastie, R. (2008) Effects of amount of information on judgment accuracy and confidence, *Organizational Behavior and Human Decision Processes*, 107, 97–105.

Vuolteenaho, T. (2006) Beta arbitrage as an alpha opportunity. Arrowstreet Capital white paper.

Waber, R.L., Shiv, B. and Ariely, D. (2008). Commercial Features of Placebo and Therapeutic Efficacy, *Journal of the American Medical Association*, 299(9), 1016–1017.

Westen, D., Blagov, P.S., Harenski, K., Kilts, C. and Hamann, S. (2005) An fMRI study of motivated reasoning: Partisan political reasoning in the U.S. Presidential Election. Unpublished paper.

Weisberg, D.S., Keil, F.C., Goodstein, J., Rawson, E. and Gray, J.R. (2008) The Seductive Allure of Neuroscience Explanations, *Journal of Cognitive Neuroscience*, 20(3), 470–477.

Wiggins, R.R. and Ruefli, T.W. (2005) Schumpeter's Ghost: Is hypercompetition making the best of times shorter? *Strategic Management Journal*, 26(10), 887–911.

Williams, J.B. (1997) *The Theory of Investment Value*. Fraser Publishing Co.

Zeelenberg, M., Van Den Bos, K., van Dijk, E. and Pieters, R. (2002) The inaction effect in the psychology of regret, *Journal of Personality and Social Psychology*, 82, 314–327.

Zweig, J. (2007) *Your Money and Your Brain: How the New Science of Neuroeconomics Can Help Make You Rich*. Simon & Schuster.

Index